The Child in the Family and the Community

SECOND EDITION

Janet Gonzalez-Mena
Napa Valley College

Merrill,
an imprint of Prentice Hall
Upper Saddle River, New Jersey   Columbus, Ohio

Library of Congress Cataloging-in-Publication Data

Gonzalez-Mena, Janet.
    The child in the family and the community/Janet Gonzalez-Mena.—2nd ed.
      p. cm.
    Includes bibliographical references and index.
    0-13-754706-4
    1. Socialization. 2. Child rearing. 3. Family.   I. Title.
  HQ783.059   1998
  649′.1—dc21   97-5316
                                                    CIP

Cover photo: SuperStock
Editor: Ann Castel Davis
Production Editor: Mary M. Irvin
Photo Coordinator: Anthony Magnacca
Design Coordinator: Karrie M. Converse
Text Designer: STELLARViSIONs
Cover Designer: Ken MacKay
Production Manager: Patricia A. Tonneman
Electronic Text Management: Marilyn Wilson Phelps, Matthew Williams, Tracey Ward, Karen Bretz
Director of Marketing: Kevin Flanagan
Marketing Manager: Suzanne Stanton
Advertising/Marketing Coordinator: Julie Shough

This book was set in Zapf Book by Prentice Hall and was printed and bound by R. R. Donnelley & Sons. The cover was printed by Phoenix Color Corp.

 © 1998 by Prentice-Hall, Inc.
Simon & Schuster/A Viacom Company
Upper Saddle River, New Jersey 07458

Earlier edition, © 1993, by Macmillan Publishing Company.

Photo credits: Rebecca N. Gilbert, pp. 4, 185, 274, 320; Doris Pfalmer, pp. 6, 44, 46, 58, 61, 80, 84, 117, 120, 123, 133, 154, 159, 174, 175, 184, 186, 195, 204, 214, 218, 237, 241, 262, 264, 306; Frank Gonzalez-Mena, pp. 9, 21, 28, 40, 57, 70, 74, 89, 104, 121, 128, 138, 144, 150, 156, 170, 182, 207, 212, 232, 245, 261, 286, 292, 305, 314; Laura Vitale, pp. 15, 31, 34, 35, 316, 326, 327; Jim Darter, pp. 45, 52, 84, 116, 163, 192, 223, 228, 250, 322.

Printed in the United States of America

10 9 8 7 6 5 4 3 2 1

ISBN: 0-13-754706-4

Prentice-Hall International (UK) Limited, *London*
Prentice-Hall of Australia Pty. Limited, *Sydney*
Prentice-Hall of Canada, Inc., *Toronto*
Prentice-Hall Hispanoamericana, S. A., *Mexico*
Prentice-Hall of India Private Limited, *New Delhi*
Prentice-Hall of Japan, Inc., *Tokyo*
Simon & Schuster Asia Pte. Ltd., *Singapore*
Editora Prentice-Hall do Brasil, Ltda., *Rio de Janeiro*

To Mo,
who always gave me such a lot to think about!

Preface

This is a personal book, written to the reader from the author about the socialization of young children. It focuses on childrearing, caring, and early education within a developmental context. The style is different from most textbooks because of its emphasis on real life experience, personal insight, and academic discipline. The theory lying behind the practical emphasis is explained in terms of specific concrete examples.

This text approaches learning by using a Piagetian theory of knowledge acquisition and construction, where learners attach new schema to existing ones. In other words, readers are encouraged to reach into their own experience to make sense of new information in terms of their existing knowledge.

Because whatever we read is always filtered through our own subjective experience, this text acknowledges that fact and capitalizes on it. The author lets her voice come through as she tells personal stories and shares insights. Students are asked regularly to look at the issues, information, and examples the text presents in terms of their own ideas, feelings, and experience. Examples given are designed to appeal to both traditional and nontraditional students by reflecting the demographics of the United States today.

Based on twenty-six years of experience teaching a course on socialization called "Child, Family, and Community," this text gives information that students need to work with and rear young children. It is written for early-childhood students who plan to be teachers, caregivers, childcare workers, family childcare providers, or parents. General education students will also benefit. Trainers in the field find the book valuable for use in inservice training for teachers and childcare workers; parent educators find it useful as well.

HOW THE SECOND EDITION IS DIFFERENT

This new edition focuses on up-to-the-minute issues, and gives an even broader coverage of topics. The reference lists are extensive and represent an expansive view of culture and gender issues, reflecting both recent and classic well-respected works in the field. This edition contains even more material on cultural perspectives, and racial, class, and gender issues, always emphasizing a multicultural/antibias approach for a pluralistic America.

New pedagogical features include a chapter opener that begins with *In this chapter you'll discover,* and another called Test Yourself. The Test Yourself section provides a list of instructional objectives that can easily be turned into quizzes or examinations by the teacher. Each chapter closes with a list of discussion questions, followed by a section called Personal Reflections. The latter section is designed to take discussions into the personal realm and can be useful in journal writing as well.

Perhaps the highest compliment paid to this text was a remark made by an African-American community college instructor. The occasion was a statewide discussion of rewriting the early-childhood course curriculum to infuse diversity into each class. The instructor announced that she wasn't going to touch her Child, Family, and Community class, because with "Janet's book as the text the course already met the diversity requirement."

SUMMARY OF CHAPTERS

Part 1, The Child: Socialization in a Developmental Context, examines the developmental context of socialization, providing information about the foundations of socialization and examining four major issues of the first five years.

The reader is led to examine brief overviews of three perspectives of child development theory, and then is introduced to the dynamic theory on which this book is based. An inclusive theory, it regards behavior as a result of the interplay of the biological organism (and his or her individual genetic makeup) with developmental stage theory, behaviorism, and social learning theory.

Chapter 1, Attachment, looks at Erik Erikson's stage of Trust versus Mistrust and examines how attachment relates to this stage. Building relationships and meeting needs are important themes of this first chapter, which looks at both childcare and parenting. The attachment of a prenatally drug-exposed baby is a sidelight of this chapter.

Chapter 2, Autonomy, explores the toddler behaviors that indicate the push toward becoming a separate independent individual—behaviors such as rebellion and negativity, exploration, self-help skills, and a sense of possession. Loss and separation and helping toddlers develop the skills needed to cope are also features of this chapter.

Teen parents—children raising children—is a sidelight of this chapter.

Chapter 3, Initiative, explores the development of a conscience by explaining the second two of Erik Erikson's conflicts, Autonomy versus Shame and Doubt and Initiative versus Guilt. Also featured are the role of imagination and fantasy; a look at shy children and aggressive children; and how to empower children.

Sidelights of this chapter include a look at a child with Attention Deficit Hyperactive Disorder (ADHD) and addressing the roots of violence by teaching problem-solving skills.

Chapter 4, Self-Esteem, discusses what self-esteem is and how to influence it. Dimensions of self-esteem are laid out and suggestions of how to promote self-esteem are given. The chapter also includes an examination of the relationship of cultural differences to self-esteem and how an antibias approach can promote self-esteem.

A sidelight of this chapter is a peek into a preschool staff meeting where teachers discuss the self-esteem of four-year-old Travis.

PART 2, The Family: Socialization for High Self-Esteem in Healthy Families, looks at the socialization of the child in a family context and is designed to present a view of the array of components essential for high self-esteem and mental health.

Chapter 5, Goals, Values, and Culture, starts with a look at cultural differences in goals and values and the relationship of those goals and values to childrearing. It explores contrasting cultural patterns and the cultural conflicts that sometimes occur. Another major theme of this chapter is teaching morals and values to children.

A sidelight of this chapter is a comparison of the values of independence and interdependence and how they show up in childrearing practices.

Chapter 6, Childcare: An Extension of the Family, looks at childcare as a childrearing environment that supplements the home. The state of childcare in America today is examined as well as the issues of affordability and availability. Quality is considered as well as what goes into making for quality childcare settings. The concept of the gap between school and home is discussed, and there is an exploration of parent-provider relations.

Sidelights of this chapter are the stories of Debbie, Walt, and Sean, who are looking for childcare for their children.

Chapter 7, Disciplining for High Self-Esteem, starts by defining the word *discipline.* It looks at seven ways to *prevent* the need for controlling children's behavior, then examines seven ways to respond to unacceptable behavior.

Sidelights of this chapter are the story of one mother who stopped using punishment and started using consequences to guide the behavior of her son; the story of a mother who has abused her child; and the story of what one town did to work toward preventing physical abuse of its children.

Chapter 8, Accepting Feelings, starts with the proposition that all feelings are positive and need to be accepted, and then discusses how we learn feelings, including cultural scripts. Ways to teach children to express and cope with feelings are explored.

Sidelights of this chapter show how Marcie, stepmother of Amy, learns to cope with her anger in healthy ways, and how Julie, another mother, learns to let go of responsibility for her child's feelings.

Chapter 9, Problem Solving, is about conflicting needs and what to do about them. What to do when the child has the problem is different from what to do when the parent has the problem or when both have problems. The chapter also explains the problem-solving process and gives a structure to follow. How problem solving relates to cognitive development is also explored.

When parents don't know about using problem-solving approaches, emotional abuse can occur. A sidelight of this chapter is the story of Brian, a stepfather who was emotionally abused as a child. Brian refuses to do the same to his stepchildren.

Chapter 10, Strokes and Affirmations: A Path to Self-Esteem, looks closely at promoting self-esteem in specific ways. The chapter advocates using strokes to change behavior and affirmations to create "self-fulfilling prophecies." Adult self-esteem relates to child self-esteem, so suggestions for how adults can work on their own self-esteem are included.

A sidelight of this chapter tells how Mary and her daughter Susan disagree over the need for stroking Susan's son, Jake. Another sidelight is the story of how Jennifer, a single parent, discovers that she is inadvertently sexist in the ways she strokes her children.

Chapter 11, Modeling and Teaching Sex Roles, starts with a quick history of the struggle for women's equality and goes on to look at sex equity and childrearing. The relationship of choice of toys to broadening or narrowing children's options is explored. Language issues and differential socialization are examined and guidelines for parents and teachers are laid out.

A sidelight of this chapter is a discussion about cultural differences in sex roles, and where traditional roles end and oppression begins.

Chapter 12, Stress and Success in Family Life, looks at what it takes to be a healthy family and examines the lives of six families who, in spite of many stresses, are struggling to be successful. This chapter touches on the issues of substance abuse, divorce, child custody, and poverty. It examines the influence of family structure and makeup and includes nuclear families, single parenting, stepfamilies and blended families, teen parents, and special needs children.

A sidelight of this chapter looks at what families do in early childhood that helps ensure later school success.

Part 3, The Community: Socialization in the Community Context, looks at the broader issues of socialization. The child, with developmental issues unfolding within the family, is now viewed in a community context. Part 3 includes society's goals and values from a "majority" and "minority" perspective and discusses the effects of racism, classism, and sexism on the socialization of children.

Chapter 13, Community Resources, looks at the way the community serves and supports families through social networks and institutions. The chapter shows how the six families of chapter 12 connect to the resources in their community.

A sidelight of the chapter is a description of various ways that families find and get connected to community resources.

Chapter 14, Socializing Agents, looks at a number of agents, including the family, schools, peer group, and the media. The chapter also examines factors in socialization such as inequity and diversity, classism, and racism.

Sidelights of the chapter include a look into what "ready to learn" really means and also recommendations regarding television and young children.

Chapter 15, Social Policy Issues, considers what the community can do to ensure that all children get an equal chance to develop high self-esteem and fulfill themselves in this society. This chapter examines social policy issues and addresses the question, Who is responsible for America's children? It ends with a discussion of child advocacy.

Sidelights of the chapter include culturally responsive care, recommendations for childcare, and statistics responding to the question, Does every child get an equal start?

ACKNOWLEDGMENTS

Joan Kliger for stimulating my reading and ongoing exploration of issues of culture, gender, and family; Nevin Saunders for reading and commenting on text, and for continual support and encouragement; Beverly Aguilar, Carole Kelly, Evie Trevethan, Jill Schrutz, Missy Danneberg, and all the others who so kindly read sections of the manuscript and gave me feedback; the number of community college teachers who, over the years, have given me ideas and input on teaching the course, "Child, Family, and Community"; Wanda Hass at Napa Valley College Library for providing a continuous flow of interlibrary loan books over the more than two-year period of finally putting this manuscript together; Barry Bussewitz for discussing important antibias issues with me; Mary Smithberger for her warmth and dedication to changing things for children and families; Pat Nourot for her input, for her fine work in the field, and for her friendship; Jim Greenman for input on specific cultural issues in early childhood programs; Tad Parker, for her constant warm support; Ron Rhyno, Antonia Lopez, Intisar Shareef, Shirley Adams, Shanta and Milan Herzog, Christane Temple, Joyce Gerring, Catherine MacDonald, Norma Quan Ong, Louis Torelli, Joyce Hahn, Virginia Dunstan, Marcus Lopez, Enid Elliot, Rick Kool, Felicia Shinnamon, Maggie Cole, Lorraine Segal, Barry Bussewitz, and Lauren Coodley for interesting cultural and equity discussions; Louise Derman-Sparks and the other leaders and participants of Early Childhood Educators Equity Network Santa Barbara retreat for an antibias perspective; Diane Carey, President of Napa Valley College, for her support of children and families; my teachers, Lilian Katz, Betty Jones, and Liz Prescott, who gave of their knowledge and encouraged me to think for myself; Magda Gerber, who opened my eyes to infancy; the parents, children, and teachers I've known in my twenty-five years of involvement in various early childhood programs, including The Community Education Center, Escuela Cuauhtemoc, Cañada College Child Care Center, Family Service Agency of San Mateo County, San Mateo, Solano, and Napa County's Head Starts, Suisun Valley Children's School, Redwood City Parent Co-op, and Napa Valley College Child and Family Center; and the people at Prentice Hall: Ann Davis, Carol Sykes, Mary Irvin, Pat Tonneman, Karrie Converse, and Anthony Magnacca. I also appreciate the insights and comments of the reviewers of my manuscript: Carol Gestwicki, Central Piedmont Community College; Phyllis Heath, Central Michigan University; Linda H. Richey, Tennessee Technological University; and Linda Stoner, San Joaquin Delta College. Last but not least, I thank my family: my sister, Margaret Hill, my mother, Mary Waldron, my cousin, Diane

Lang, my children, Bruce, Bret, Robin, Adam, and Tim, and especially my husband, Frank Gonzalez-Mena; and a special thanks to Frank's parents, Alicia Petersen de González Mena and Frank González-Frese, now deceased, who gave me firsthand experience of what it's like to live in a multicultural family.

Contents

PART 1

The Child: Socialization in a Developmental Context   1

CHAPTER 1

Attachment   5

CHAPTER **2**

Autonomy   29

CHAPTER **3**

Initiative   53

CHAPTER **4**

Self-Esteem   75

PART **2**

The Family: Socialization for High Self-Esteem in Healthy Families   97

CHAPTER **5**

Goals, Values, and Culture   105

CHAPTER **6**

Childcare: An Extension of the Family   129

CHAPTER **7**

Disciplining for High Self-Esteem   151

CHAPTER

Accepting Feelings   171

CHAPTER 9

Problem Solving   193

CHAPTER **10**

Strokes and Affirmations: A Path to Self-Esteem   213

CHAPTER **11**

Modeling and Teaching Sex Roles   233

CHAPTER **12**

Stress and Success in Family Life   251

PART **3**

The Community: Socialization in the Community Context 271

CHAPTER **15**

Social Policy Issues　　315

Index　　333

PART 1

THE CHILD: SOCIALIZATION IN A DEVELOPMENTAL CONTEXT

I ask my students to examine their own assumptions about child development by doing the following exercise. I indicate a line on the floor with an *X* at each end. I designate one end the "flower" and the other the "tree." Then I explain that I want each participant to decide where he or she stands.

I start at the flower end and explain how a child is like a flower. I paint a word picture of a seed planted in good soil and carefully nurtured as it grows. I explain that all the potential of the flower is already in the seed and that all that is necessary for it to be fulfilled is that its needs be met. One must water, feed, and protect the plant, but need not direct its growth, because it has in it the capacity to know its own direction. Given a nurturing environment, one can count on the plant's sense of self-direction to be the right one.

Then I ask the participants to consider the tree on the other end of the continuum. The tree also has potential contained in its seed, and it also must have its needs met to grow. However, in order to have a tall, straight, shade-giving tree, it is necessary to clip and prune. The tree will be very different if left to grow wild. One must direct its growth if it is to be the very best tree it can be. Left to chance, it may grow crooked or too bushy, or its many limbs may crowd each other and be unattractive. Therefore, besides the nurturing that must be done, one must also watch the direction of the growth—guiding and controlling it.

When I finish my speech, most students dutifully pick their spots on the continuum—a few going to stand at either end, and the bulk of the rest clustering around the middle—either dead center or off toward one end or the other. I then ask the students farthest out on either end to discuss with each other why they chose the position they did.

What ensues is a discussion about the basic nature of the child. The flower-end person paints a picture of a little being that is placed on earth to grow and develop according to some internal process that is preprogrammed into the package. Sometimes the student relates this process to a divine plan of some sort; at other times divinity is not included in the picture. No matter how it's stated, it becomes clear that within the organism is a benevolent driving force guiding it toward health and wholeness, supplying it with behaviors that meet its needs. The child (or the flower) who isn't stunted or warped by neglect, abuse, or other negative factors *unfolds* in the way he or she was designed to unfold. It's a natural process and a beautiful one. You can almost see a rosebud opening before your very eyes as this process is being described. It's awe inspiring. [1]

The person at the other end of the spectrum has a different view, and is usually cynical about the rosy picture painted at the opposite end. This person also sees a driving force from within, but one that puts temptations and obstacles in the way of positive growth. It too is a natural process—but one that needs constant monitoring and intervention if it is to result in a desirable end product. Children are not naturally born pure and good; they cannot be allowed to just unfold according to their human nature. The words vary with the person's philosophical stance or religious background, but what is clear is that the child's sense of direction is not always toward the good. Some people feel that the natural inclination of human nature is *never* toward the good. Others see progress through life as a crooked path; if the final destination is to be desirable, a good firm adult hand is needed to control the stroll through childhood. Some say that it's more natural to be bad than it is to be good. *Sin* is a word that comes up in this discussion. If the child is to turn out all right, it's vital that adults take a strong hand in guiding the direction of the development. [2]

The students in the middle make a case for how both ends are true, and that it's impossible to exclude either. Once in a while there's a student who refuses to stand on the continuum at all. That student says that the child has no basic nature and that there is no driving force. What determines the kind of adult that the child becomes is how the environment shapes him or her. This student subscribes to the principle that the person is the sum total of all of his or her behavior and that behavior is set by what happens, not by any built-in sort of unfolding mechanism, divine plan, invisible force, or natural motivation toward either good or bad. This person has the same idea of the importance, indeed the *necessity*, of controlling the behaviors the child exhibits, through careful attention to and manipulation of the rewards and punishments the child receives. This person usually stresses rewards over punishments because the positive approach is more effective and predictable than the negative one. [3]

All of these views are simplistic. In reality, development is more dynamic and involves a much more complex picture. Children grow and change through a complicated process comprised of many interacting elements, some that can be controlled and others that cannot. A *dynamic theory* is more in keeping with the information and experience on which this book is based. According to this view of growth and development, behavior is the result of the interplay of the biological organism (and his or her individual genetic makeup) with culture, developmental stage, environmental input, and the natural inclination to imitate or model after others.

We each carry within our selves a personal view of how growth and development works, whether or not we are aware of the existence of our own viewpoint. This personal view influences what we actually see when we are around children, how we interpret their behavior, and what we perceive their needs to be. Most of all, our viewpoint determines our own behavior and our approaches to socialization. Keep that fact in mind as you read this text. Your view of the basic nature of the child and how development comes about will influence what you learn from your reading. [4]

NOTES

1. Child development textbooks are written from an academic perspective that brings out the many complexities of the developmental process. Although not one is written purely from the "flower" view of the basic nature of the child, most show leanings in that direction. The very word *development* means to "unfold."

2. I've never seen a child development text written from this point of view; however, I've read parenting books that were. Also, many parents I've known have felt strongly that when children are left to grow as in the "flower" theory, they will turn out "spoiled" or "rotten" (their words—not mine).

3. This *behaviorist* view of the child goes along well with the "tree" end of the continuum; however, a basic difference is that behaviorism is scientific and quite detached from such concepts as "bad" and "good." Behaviors are more likely to be seen as acceptable or unacceptable rather than branded with moral judgments.

4. An interesting book for an academic exploration of child development theories is *Comparing Theories of Child Development* by R. Murray Thomas (Belmont, CA: Wadsworth Publishing Company, 1985).

ATTACHMENT

CHAPTER 1

In this chapter you'll discover:

> How "getting in sync" with a baby relates to attachment
> What helps babies develop trust
> How parents can become attached to their baby before it is born
> Whether "bonding" at birth is essential
> How to determine whether parents are attached to their baby
> How to determine whether babies are attached to their parents
> What factors affect attachment patterns
> How childcare affects attachment
> Whether all behaviors of good parents and good caregivers should be similar

TEST YOURSELF

Look for the answers to these questions as you read the chapter:

1. What does synchrony between a caregiver and baby mean? Can you describe a synchronous interaction?
2. What is attachment and why is it important?
3. What is Erik Erikson's first psychosocial crisis?
4. How does attachment occur? Is the process the same in every situation? In every culture?
5. What is the difference between bonding and attachment?
6. What are some signs of infant attachment?
7. What are some obstacles to bonding? To attachment?
8. What is "separation" and what does it have to do with attachment?
9. What are some variations in attachment patterns?
10. How does infant mortality rate affect attachment patterns and caregiver behaviors?
11. How does childcare affect attachment?
12. What qualities should caregivers and parents share? How are parents and caregivers different from each other?

The basis of socialization is attachment, and the basis of attachment is a synchronous relationship, which grows from a number of synchronous interactions. Here's what a synchronous interaction looks like:

Synchrony

A caregiver is bent over a three-month-old baby lying on her back. The caregiver is expressionless. The baby rounds her mouth and lets out a breathy sound while reaching out her arms. The caregiver responds by widening her eyes, rounding her own mouth, and imitating the sound. She reaches for the baby's hands and holds them in her own. The baby pulls her hands away, kicks her feet, and widens her own eyes in imitation of the caregiver. The caregiver smiles. The baby smiles back. The caregiver keeps smiling, makes clucking noises, and claps her hands. The baby turns away. "Oh, that was too much for you," responds the caregiver, quieting her activity. The baby looks back. The caregiver smiles. The baby smiles, then arches and reaches. "You want up?" the caregiver asks, reaching out her arms to the child.

These two are "in sync" with each other. The caregiver is sensitive to the baby's signals and reads the turning away as a need to tune out, not a personal rejection of her. The baby knows how to "light up" the caregiver's face. The caregiver knows how to "turn on" the baby. The two are good together. If they are not already attached, they are becoming attached.

Babies become attached when people in their lives are sensitive and responsive. That means that they pay attention to the baby's signals and read them accurately, responding readily and appropriately.

These two are "in sync" with each other.

BUILDING BASIC TRUST IN INFANCY THROUGH MEETING NEEDS

Imagine yourself a very young baby, lying asleep in a crib. You open your eyes—suddenly you're wide awake. You see nothing except a blur of light—there are no objects, no movement within your visual range. You feel a very uncomfortable sensation in your midsection. You squirm around. Changing position doesn't help. Suddenly you feel desperate. The sensation in your midsection takes over your whole body. You squeeze your eyes shut tight and open your mouth wide. Into your ears comes a piercing sound. You don't know that it's your own cry. You only know that something is terribly wrong and your whole being reacts to it. Your heart pounds, your face burns, and you scream in agony, then gasp for breath, only to start screaming again once you get your lungs full. You're like this for what seems an eternity, but is actually less than two minutes. You feel something touch you. You open your eyes and find something very distinctive and vaguely familiar in front of the blur of light that was all that was there before. The something moves in a way that makes you feel comfortable. As you pause for breath, you hear another sound—not the high agonized one of before, but a soft, soothing one. You feel a blanket of pleasure surround you, providing immeasurable relief, and, true to your most cherished hope, you find yourself lifted in the air out of the loneliness—the isolation—and snuggled into a pair of warm arms. You're basking in the glow of the feelings of this, when—wonder of wonders—something familiar touches your cheek. You jerk toward the something, manage to get your mouth around it, and begin sucking. A warm, sweet sensation floods your mouth and you're in heaven.

That's one scenario—here's another:

You wake up in heaven, surrounded by human warmth, touch, sound, and smells. You open your eyes drowsily, look at the familiar sight of your favorite human, close them again, and snuggle deeper into the comfort around you. But that comfort quickly dissolves as a midsection pain swells out over your whole body. You scream in agony, but only once. Immediately you find in your mouth something to suck on and suck you do, letting the warm sweetness take you back to heaven.

These two scenes illustrate how needs, attachment, and trust all come in a bundle in the beginning of life. The scenes are slightly different. In the first one, the infant wakes up alone and must signal the caregiver to meet hunger and comfort needs. In the second scene, the infant wakes up already in the arms of the caregiver, who may even anticipate the needs before the infant signals them.

You may prefer one scene over the other—you may actually feel critical of the nonpreferred one. However, both of these patterns of relating to the needs of the very young infant lead to healthy attachment of a type that serves the individual and the culture. It's important to remember that attachment patterns are related to parental values and goals. Parents rear their children to fit the world as they perceive it. (See chapter 5 for more on this subject.)

WHAT IS ATTACHMENT AND WHY IS IT IMPORTANT?

Attachment is a lasting emotional relationship that begins to develop in infancy and serves to tie the infant to one or more people in his or her life. It is a two-way process—adults (usually parents) attach to infants and infants attach to adults (parents). This two-way process results in a *significant relationship*.

Attachment is vital. It is a means of ensuring survival of the child and also of the species. It creates the caring (the feeling) that motivates the *action* of giving care. It ensures that nurturing and protection will be provided to the relatively helpless infant. But beyond physical survival, the first attachment(s) provide(s) the basis for all future relationships.

Developing a Sense of Trust

If the infant finds that when needs arise they are met with reasonable promptness, as in the two scenes above, he or she comes to see the world as a welcoming place. A sense of trust grows from fulfillment and satisfaction in the first year of life. Infants who are left screaming for long periods, gripped in the agony of hunger pangs, come to see the world as an unfriendly place. They find that they can't trust anyone to take care of them. If they give signals and no one responds, they see themselves as powerless and the world as cold and hostile. When these children grow out of infancy, they continue to view the world with distrust.

This early issue of developing trust versus mistrust was originally defined and described by Erik Erikson, who sees life as a series of what he calls psychosocial crises (see Figure 1-1).

Trust is a lifelong issue for all of us. However, children who develop a sense of distrust in infancy grapple with the issue more intensely than others. Some of these children are left with unresolved trust issues; others successfully deal with the problem if the situation changes and those around them become more responsive and meet their needs more promptly. [1] Children with unresolved trust issues often reach adulthood still seeking the early caregiver who left their needs unmet. Because

Infancy	Basic Trust	versus	Basic Mistrust
Toddlerhood	Autonomy	versus	Shame and Doubt
The Preschool Years	Initiative	versus	Guilt

FIGURE 1-1

Erikson's Psychosocial Crises of the Early Years

From Erik Erikson, "Eight Stages of Man," *Childhood and Society* (New York: W. W. Norton, 1963).

Attachment may begin prenatally, as parents begin to relate to their visions of the growing fetus.

it is never too late to resolve trust issues, some adults continually choose to connect to people who treat them much as their early caregiver(s) did. They put themselves back into their infant situation, to give themselves another chance to relive the situation and manage a different outcome. [2] The human being is very resilient!

Attachment is a powerful process—and it seems that even a little goes a long way. Look at studies of survivor types—children who manage to cope and live a productive life in spite of factors in their early years that work against that. The one thing that all these survivor children have in common is a person they could attach to sometime in their first year—even though it might not have been an ideal attachment or a long-lasting one. [3]

HOW ATTACHMENT OCCURS

In a model situation in European-American middle-class society, attachment begins prenatally, as two parents begin to relate to their visions of the growing fetus. This is a two-way process, as the fetus becomes familiar with the outside happenings that come into the womb. For instance, babies are born recognizing the sound of their mothers' voices.

Many parents cannot relate to the reality of a baby until it is actually born. They may feel more attached to the pregnancy than to the product—the growing fetus. However, parental attachment can begin at birth—or thereafter—even if there has been no prenatal attachment.

Back to the ideal. If all goes well during the birth, and if hospital procedures allow, the parents may spend an hour or so "bonding" with their baby right after birth. This get-acquainted period can be a great bonus to future attachment. Imagine a peaceful hour in which the new family member is alert and responsive and the parents are completely available and attentive. They're not distracted by any medical or health procedures; they're not feeling some kind of obligation to be elsewhere, doing something more important. They are fully present and receptive. They see the value of establishing this new relationship. Sometimes this is a love-at-first-sight experience, full of emotion and wonder. Tears may flow. When all goes well, the family "bonds," that is, establishes the beginning of an emotional tie to one another. Though not exactly the same as attachment, bonding is a means of facilitating the later process, which grows over a period of time. [4]

It is important to realize that wonderful though immediate bonding at birth may be, not all relationships grow from a love-at-first-sight beginning. And not all love-at-first-sight relationships last. Relationships take work; no instant cementing can take the place of the long period of sensitive interaction that eventually grows into a lasting attachment.

Let's continue with the ideal. The baby comes home from the hospital (unless he or she was born at home) and life as a member of the family begins. At first baby and caregiver parent(s) experience what seems to be an unending cycle of very basic functions. Time is spent signaling and fulfilling needs—sleeping, eating, eliminating. Each of these needs is communicated by baby to caregiver parent(s) in a variety of individual ways, which the caregiver(s) must learn to read in order to respond appropriately.

As caregiver parent(s) and baby become more and more in tune with each other, the attachment grows. The vision that the parents carried while the baby was in the womb may be transferred onto the person before them. However, some parents recognize early on the difference between their own vision and the real live individual who has come into their lives. The baby helps them do that differentiation task by not quite fitting the expectations. Sensitive parents recognize when their vision is getting in the way of the baby's growing into the unique individual he or she is.

SIGNS OF PARENTAL ATTACHMENT

Some parents show signs of attachment right away. They're smitten. They feel close to their offspring. They find parenting pleasurable—even the hard and frustrating parts. Some cultural rituals are related to attachment. Giving a name to the baby and calling him or her by that name is a way of acknowledging the child as an individual.

Buying possessions for the new baby is also a way of recognizing individuality and personhood. These are so expected that they don't seem to relate to attachment, but when they don't occur, it can be a sign that something is wrong with the attachment.

SIGNS OF INFANT ATTACHMENT

Babies take longer to show signs of attachment, although careful research shows that signs exist from birth. Babies just a few hours old can distinguish their mother's smell and her voice, for example. [5] Before long, babies begin to act differently around their primary caregiver (who may or may not be the mother). They may be more animated, less fussy, more interested and alert.

Eventually some babies begin to show distress when someone they don't know arrives in their field of vision. The distress may accelerate if the stranger approaches. This shows that the baby can distinguish between the person(s) he or she is attached to and others.

However, some babies never show stranger anxiety, not because they are not attached, but because they have had a secure and trusting life with multiple caregivers (either at home or in childcare). If babies skip this milestone, some parents and even some experts become distressed because they think it shows lack of attachment. That's not necessarily true.

For some babies, the next milestone is separation anxiety, as the baby protests at being away from the caregiver. (More about this subject in the next chapter.)

Attachment behaviors can be seen in both of the preceding situations—as the baby looks or moves toward the primary caregiver for comfort and reassurance. Clinging, crying, fussing, whining, and following after are all attachment behaviors that can show the emotional bond between the child and someone else. Although they are indicators of attachment, an absence of these behaviors does not necessarily signal a lack of attachment in children with multiple caregivers.

OBSTACLES TO BONDING

Sometimes the attachment process doesn't start with bonding and follow such a perfect progression. For many reasons, parents may not feel an emotional connection to their unborn baby. They may be unhappy about the pregnancy or with each other, and those feelings may influence their feelings for the baby. The father may not be in relationship with the mother—so any feeling for the baby on his part will necessarily be "long-distance." Even for the mother, the reality of the baby may be fuzzy. It's hard to love someone you can't see or touch or interact with.

Then, at birth, the time may still not be right. The birth itself may not be a pleasant experience, and that unpleasantness can carry over into the period after. Or the birth may be complicated. If the baby or the mother are in any kind of physical distress, medical procedures may take precedence over time alone together. For one reason or another, baby and parents often miss out on the initial bonding.

Even if it is arranged so that parents and baby can spend the first hour or so together, there may be worries or disappointments that cast an emotional overlay over the bonding process and prevent the magical happy moment from occurring.

Adoption presents another obstacle to bonding. The new parents may not have been a part of the birth or the bonding period immediately afterward.

Attachment can proceed very well in spite of all these obstacles to early bonding, as long as the relationship grows and flourishes, preferably in the first year—the earlier the better. If you think back to what you know about your own birth, the chances are that you didn't experience "bonding" immediately there in the delivery room (if you had a hospital birth). Allowing parents and babies time together is a relatively new procedure in standard medical practice in this country. Perhaps your life might have been different if your parent(s) had been given a chance to fall in love with you at first sight immediately after your birth. Or perhaps it wouldn't have made a difference.

OBSTACLES TO ATTACHMENT

Attachment may be delayed for many reasons. If the infant is very sick, parents may unconsciously protect themselves from getting attached by putting an emotional distance between themselves and the baby. Sometimes the difficulty is that, for whatever reason, the baby remains unresponsive to the caregiver's initiations. Some infants don't have the kinds of behaviors that draw adults to them. They're not cute, or cuddly, or smiley. They don't make eye contact. These infants, who don't reward the adults around them, need adults who make a conscious effort to attach. Even mismatches of temperament can delay attachment as the quiet placid parent gets used to a highly active baby, or the reverse.

If babies experience early lengthy separation, the attachment process can be disrupted. Babies in foster care may be moved around; changing caregivers can disrupt attachment. These delays or disruptions in attachment can influence future life in drastic ways if a sense of basic trust is not established. The child may put up barriers so that no one can get close. The hurt from loss is too great to chance again.

TEMPERAMENT AND ATTACHMENT

Temperament can affect attachment in either a negative or positive way, depending on the temperamental match between the infant and parent. Temperament is built in and can be detected early in a child's life. Genetically determined, temperament becomes obvious as infants show differing levels of activity, emotionality, and sociability that tend to remain the same over time. Thomas, Chess, and Birch, [6] the pioneers in the temperament research, categorized babies as "easy," "slow to warm," and "difficult." Their work helps today's parents and caregivers understand how temperament affects behavior and shapes personality. J. Ronald Lally and his colleagues in the Program for Infant-Toddler Caregivers renamed the categories "fearful," "flexible," and "feisty," which puts them in a more objective light. A good match between parent temperament and child temperament promotes attachment; a mismatch may hinder it. If the two aren't a natural fit, the parent must adjust to the baby rather than expecting the reverse.

What would a mismatch look like? If an active and intense mother with a high energy level finds herself with a slow, calm, mild baby, she may be disappointed. She may even wonder if something is wrong with her baby, even though the baby is perfectly normal. If this high energy mother is not aware of what she is doing, she may overstimulate her baby. She has to learn to read the signs that the baby has had enough. Some parents keep on after the baby turns away or closes her eyes. A serious mismatch occurs when the mother interprets this behavior as bored and continues to try to "wake the baby up and make her more lively."

Or imagine a calm, relaxed father who loves things done on schedule and appreciates predictability in his life. He'll find a mismatch with a highly active, intense baby who never seems able to regulate his rhythms or body needs. Some babies don't keep any sort of routine, even eating at a different time every day. Napping is as unpredictable as appetite and never follows a schedule. If the father of such a baby doesn't accept that his son is different from himself, he may have trouble being sensitive to the child's needs.

Parents who have children whose temperaments don't match their own have to adjust their expectations, accept their babies as is, and learn to understand them. They have to be flexible about how and when they respond. They have to be supersensitive so that they can meet their baby's needs. All that may be hard for a parent whose temperament isn't flexible, or sensitive.

LEARNING TO COPE WITH FEELINGS OF LOSS

Babies who are attached experience feelings when separation occurs. Separation is the other side of the coin of attachment. Each human has the lifelong task of coming to grips with separations and coping with the feelings that occur as people come into and go out of one's life. Each broken relationship, physical departure, or death brings into play all the coping skills learned earlier. The skills for dealing with separation begin to develop in infancy.

You can perhaps get in touch with the power of the feelings surrounding separation by thinking back to a time in your own life when you were apart from someone you cared about. Perhaps it was the first day of school, or a trip to the hospital, or even the first time you were left with a baby-sitter. It may be a less significant event—but one that sticks in your memory—like the time you took the wrong turn in the grocery store and were "lost" for a minute or two. It might be an even more significant event like the day your father walked out, never to return, or the day your mother died. All of us have experience with separation, and those experiences start earlier for some than for others.

Jeremy

Jeremy's mother took drugs when she was pregnant. No one was aware of this problem until the day Jeremy was born. He arrived in the world full of the harmful substances his mother had ingested, and his first days of life were spent in withdrawal. He suffered and so did the hospital staff who tended him.

"Poor little guy!" said a nurse, as she tried to make him more comfortable.

Getting the drugs out of his system didn't end his problems. Jeremy was a difficult baby from the beginning. He cried incessantly—it seemed sometimes as if he would never stop. He'd scream and scream until he finally wore himself out; he'd sleep restlessly for a period and then start again. It was hard to be around Jeremy.

His foster mother, a patient woman, understood how hard life was for Jeremy just now. Although she had other babies to care for, she spent special time with him, trying to give him the message that he was cared about—that he was loved. It wasn't easy. When an adoptive family came along that knew Jeremy's history and his problems, she was relieved because she felt he deserved a permanent home and parents—a family of his own who could give him a good deal of time and energy—the time and energy she had were stretched so thin!

Jeremy's new parents were special people. They didn't go into the adoption blindly expecting to rescue a child and have him forever grateful to them. They knew something about the kinds of problems that Jeremy had at the time and the kinds he was likely to have in the future. They were prepared to deal with these problems.

They started out right away to establish an attachment with Jeremy. It wasn't easy—he wasn't an appealing baby. When his new parents picked him up, he stiffened and shook. He didn't cuddle like lots of babies. He seldom seemed relaxed; in fact, his movements were jerky and uncontrolled. He twitched, jiggled, and shook as he lay in his crib.

Jeremy didn't like to be touched; often he screamed louder when he was touched than when he wasn't. It was tempting to leave him alone, since picking him up seemed agonizing to him. But his parents knew that leaving him in his crib wasn't the answer, so they did some observing and brainstorming to discover what ways they could pick him up that would cause him the least discomfort. They felt proud when they were able to discover some. It became more rewarding to pick him up.

Jeremy didn't look at anyone very often. Even when his parents tried to get his attention, he tended to look away. It's hard to develop a relationship with someone who doesn't make eye contact—but they managed. They just kept on trying until the day came that Jeremy looked his mother right in the eye. What a moment that was for her—worth waiting for. That was the beginning of the development of a series of positive behaviors that made Jeremy easy to love. The big day when Jeremy smiled for the first time, his father grinned back as if his face would split in two. "You're going to be okay, Jeremy," he said, patting his son.

Since happily-ever-after stories only occur as fairy tales, I have to tell you that Jeremy did continue to feel the influence of his early drug exposure into his preschool years. But with the help of his parents and their love for him, he was able to cope with the cards that life had dealt him.

Learning to cope with feelings of loss: Children who are attached experience feelings when separation occurs.

If you can remember your feelings surrounding these experiences, you can probably get in touch with one or more of the following: panic, fear, anxiety, misgivings, apprehension, qualms, terror, horror, bewilderment, confusion, annoyance, irritation, anger, outrage, fury, wrath, frenzy, desperation, indignity, sadness, loneliness, desertion, and abandonment. The feelings come from the need for security as well as a sense of loss of control over the situation.

The memory of your pain may be intense or it may have muted over time. Or perhaps you have a fuzziness around the feelings or even an absence of feeling. You may even dredge up a sense of depression when you get in touch with this early separation experience.

There are all kinds of separation experiences in infancy—some that help the child grow to independence, others that leave scars and long-lasting aftereffects. One common separation infants experience comes when they are put into cribs to sleep by themselves. In cultures where independence is a high priority, this physical separation from the beginning is regarded as important. Learning to sleep alone as an infant is a skill that is valued by many in this country. It's an important step for children coming to see themselves as separate individuals. Some parenting experts are adamant about babies sleeping alone. Some experts, including Dr. Ferber, who wrote *Solve Your Child's Sleep Problems*, say that babies can't get a good night sleep if they have to "interact" all night with someone else.

Ironically, some new information on Sudden Infant Death Syndrome (SIDS, or crib death) indicates that an undisturbed night's sleep may put infants at risk. In cultures where infants are held, jostled, and put to bed with an adult or another child, the rate of SIDS is dramatically lower than in cultures where infants sleep apart from the hustle and bustle of family life in cribs in their own rooms. [7] All cultures don't value sleeping alone, even if they had the space and means to do so. They aren't as interested in their children becoming independent individuals as they are in creating a spirit of interdependence and connectedness to others. In many families both in this country and around the world, infants and toddlers sleep with the mother or both parents until the next baby comes, then move into the bed of siblings or grandparents. Some European-Americans have made an attempt to change the way they were raised by instituting what is called the "family bed." [8]

A number of articles and books have been written about getting babies to sleep by themselves, because it isn't as easy to accomplish as it might seem. Many babies comfort themselves while alone in the crib by developing an attachment to a particular object. This process fits right in with being part of an object-oriented culture. Most parents and caregivers are delighted when a child attaches to a favorite blanket or a stuffed animal. Experts see this particular way of self-comforting as a sign that the child has coping skills.

Learning to put oneself to sleep and stay by oneself is a step toward independence and is a valued behavior in many families. It's a healthy sign that infants are able to handle separation.

VARYING ATTACHMENT PATTERNS

Many look at attachment from the view of some research designed to assess it. Mary Ainsworth set out to study how attached babies are to their mothers. She used something she called "the Strange Situation" in which a baby is observed in an experimental room with toys designed to entice. The situation involves the mother and a stranger in a series of comings and goings. How the baby reacts to the separation, the stranger, and the reunion are used to judge the type of attachment.

From her research Ainsworth came up with three types of attachment. One, the baby is securely attached and uses the mother as a base to move out from and explore the interesting toys in the room. You can see this happening in any setting where there are toys and a baby with enough mobility to get to them. Babies move away from their mothers, checking back periodically to see where they are, and crawling back to get a snuggle, hug, or a bit of comfort when needed. If the mother leaves, securely attached babies are delighted to see her when she returns.

Not so with insecurely attached infants. They either ignore or avoid their mothers when reunited or they resist their mother in a kind of push-pull fashion. They may alternately cling and kick away.

One criticism of this way of judging attachment is the unnatural setting. Do babies and mothers behave the same in a laboratory as they do at home or somewhere else?

Another criticism of the Strange Situation as a way of assessing attachment is that it is based on a particular model of mother-child attachment. There are a lot of variations on that model. What if the baby has been in childcare and used to multiple caregivers? Is he really showing insecure attachment if he avoids the mother when she returns or just used to having an interesting environment and being separated from his mother? Or what if the baby comes from a large family where the mother isn't the only caregiver? What if the mother isn't the person the baby is most attached to?

Ainsworth and other researchers focused on attachment as it relates to the insular or nuclear family. Today we know better. We can see with our own eyes that, even in the nuclear or insular family, caregiving may be shared between mother and father or between one parent and another relative or childcare provider. Under these circumstances, attachment is not just between mother and baby, although often the mother remains the primary attachment.

So far we've been looking at attachment as it relates to the insular or nuclear family with mother, father, and child. This, however, isn't the only kind of family. Another type of family is the single-parent family. Sometimes the parent(s) and baby are not a unit by themselves but are part of a larger extended family. According to Carol Stack, some families are "an extended cluster of kinsmen (related chiefly through children but also through marriage and friendship) who align to provide domestic functions. This cluster, or domestic network, is diffused over several kin-based households, and fluctuations in individual household composition do not significantly affect cooperative arrangements." [9] The single-parent family that finds itself in this type of network may be thought of as "embedded" rather than alone.

A woman once told me a story about how she had changed her perspective on her family. This person was a single parent with two children who lived with her parents in their house. She thought of her situation as two families living in one house, until she decided to have a family portrait taken. She included all five family members, deciding for herself that this was one family, rather than two. [10] The concept of an embedded family is a more positive and realistic one. In an embedded family the attachment might be quite different because of shared caregiving. The child can become attached to several caregivers or to a group rather than to just one or two individuals. When you are used to looking at attachment as an exclusive relationship, you may be concerned about the infant who is attached to multiple caregivers. However, cultures all over the world raise their children this way. Shared care has advantages over one parent carrying total responsibility for a child's well-being. What a burden that much responsibility can be, especially for a new parent who may have had little previous experience with babies!

Some childcare programs function as a family support system, rather than as just a place to leave children during the day. These programs are able to provide families with the kind of support they would find in embedded families if they had them.

ATTACHMENT AND INFANT MORTALITY

Sometimes attachment patterns are influenced by infant mortality rates. When families have the expectation that the infant may die before the first year is up, they treat babies differently from families who don't consider their babies at risk for survival.

Adults with fears about survival concentrate on ways to save the baby, rather than worrying about attachment or emotional development. The goal of saving the baby is so ingrained into the childrearing practices that it isn't thought of in those terms. In fact, even a generation or more after the danger is past—say the family climbs up the economic ladder and/or moves to a location where the infant mortality rate is vastly improved—the childcare practices continue. Here are examples of caregiving behaviors when survival is the priority: [11]

1. The infant is on or near a caretaker's body at all times day and night, so he or she can be monitored. It is important to determine whether the baby is getting sick. It is also important to keep the baby out of danger when families live in conditions where there is no safe place for babies to be free to move about.
2. Crying is quickly attended to and becomes relatively rare. Caregivers know that it is important to eliminate other causes if they are to determine whether crying is a sign that the baby is getting sick.
3. Feeding is a frequent response to crying. The constant feeding helps prevent dehydration, which is the most common cause of death in infants throughout the world. Infants easily get diarrhea, which by itself isn't necessarily a killer, but the diarrhea causes the dehydration, which is.
4. There is relatively little treatment of the infant as an emotionally responsive individual (as in eye contact, smile elicitation, or chatting). The concern is to save the child's life. It may even be that attachment in the sense that we are discussing it in this chapter is delayed until the child gets through the difficult period when so many children are lost.

These are adaptive responses and they influence attachment. Behavioral patterns such as those in the preceding list become customs that are ingrained in the cultural approach to infant care. It is hard to separate these survival practices from cultural values and attachment patterns.

JUDGING ATTACHMENT IN A CROSS CULTURAL SITUATION

When a mother doesn't seem sensitive to the baby's emotional signals, seldom speaks to the baby, and/or never holds the baby in a face-to-face position so adult and baby can make eye contact, it is not clear whether these are functional or dysfunctional behaviors. Do they fit customs and expectations and make sense if viewed in cultural context? Or are they left over from a time when survival was the main issue? Or do they have another explanation? For example, in a situation where the baby is never called by the given name, it is not immediately evident what is going on, unless you are of the same culture and social class as the family you're wondering about. If you don't thoroughly understand the culture and perhaps even the individual family, you can't make judgments about the way people are raising their children and whether or not they have a healthy attachment.

Language is another area where an outsider may misjudge what is happening. European-American middle-class families are very vocal, and all this vocalization is part of the attachment process. Watch most middle-class European-American parents and you'll see that they talk face-to-face with their babies—chattering away as if the baby understands. They even wait for a response, creating a turn-taking situation that imitates real conversations in which both participants talk. Research (done by European-Americans on European-Americans for European-Americans) shows the value of this kind of behavior, not only for attachment but also for future development as well. For example, this early emphasis on verbalization makes a difference later in school performance; children with good verbal skills do better academically.

In contrast, some families rarely speak to their infants. What is not clear to the outsider is how much the family is using *nonverbal* communication that the observer isn't aware of. Because a family doesn't behave the same as a European-American middle-class family toward babies doesn't necessarily mean that there is an attachment problem—it may be more a matter of cultural difference.

CHILDCARE AND ATTACHMENT

A major concern of many who come from the tradition of mother-child attachment as an exclusive relationship is the question, What does childcare do to attachment? The term *maternal deprivation* rings in the ears and sends chills down the spine. Horror stories of old-time orphanages come to mind—babies left to themselves in rows of cribs along sterile walls. The picture is heartbreaking. Those babies had no attachment, few interactions, little power to influence anyone in their lives, a feeling that no one cared about them, and a great lack of any kind of sensory stimulation. No wonder many died and the rest were left impaired.

Childcare is an entirely different picture and story. Children in childcare are not orphans. They have families who are raising them. Childcare is supplemental to these families, not a replacement for them.

Children in childcare not only have one person who cares about them—a parent—but often two or more. They usually arrive in childcare already firmly attached to their own family, and may well acquire a secondary attachment or two in childcare. As far as sensory deprivation goes, childcare usually has more than enough stimulation—not too little—especially for babies. The problem is cutting down to appropriate limits rather than raising stimulation to make up for other lacks.

A look across the seas to Israel reassures us that parents and children can remain attached even if the parents never live with their children or are never responsible for their day-to-day care. In some of the kibbutzim in Israel, where communal living is a norm and a value, children are raised from infancy separate from their parents. They visit their parents, but they don't live with them. Full-time caregivers/teachers are in charge of childrearing and education rather than the parents.

There is no lack of attachment between parents and children in the kibbutzim. Attachment looks different because children split their attachment between parents and peer group. However, each child is well aware of his or her identity as a member of his or her own family—and each feels a sense of belonging.

When looking at the question of how attachment might be affected by childcare, one has to ask, What kind of family—in what kind of care? Obviously if a family is overwhelmed by stress and the members are not functioning well, and a baby is born into the family at this point, the baby is at risk.

Let's say that a single mother, living by herself in a one-room apartment, doesn't have money to make ends meet, so she drinks herself into a stupor and the baby cries from hunger constantly. How will putting this child into childcare influence his attachment? It's hard to tell, because it depends on what kind of childcare. If the baby goes into a program where he gets consistent loving care, finds attachments, and gets the food he needs, and his mother gets connected to the community resources she needs to get back on her feet, obviously the baby will do far better in childcare than if he is left crying in that one room twenty-four hours a day. *In this situation childcare is a lifesaver.*

There are such programs. Some childcare and early-education programs in the United States today not only give quality care to children but also give families the support they need to get on their feet so they, themselves, can provide for their children's needs. These kinds of programs are cost effective because they deal with attachment and other needs at the beginning rather than trying to fix problems that arise later (which is much more expensive). We could use many more of these kinds of programs! *Prevention* is a key word when looking at early deprivation and attachment problems.

Unfortunately, these kinds of comprehensive programs are too few in number. If the baby in the example is placed in a childcare program where he never gets to know any of his caregivers and his mother gets little or no support, it's a different story. Attachment may be delayed because caregivers come and go too fast. Not one of the adults gets to know him well enough to read his signals, understand his uniqueness, become fond of him. Childcare may save his life, yet still not provide for his attachment and trust needs. Because of underfunding, that's the tragedy of the state of many childcare programs in the United States today. The turnover rate of caregivers and teachers in underfunded programs is shocking.

You can't know exactly how childcare affects attachment without taking into consideration countless variables that have to do with the quality of the care and the way the family works.

What about the question of when to put a child into childcare. Is there an optimum period? There is more than one way to look at this question. If you are to avoid the period of stranger anxiety and separation distress, putting a baby into childcare before the age of six months or after a year or so may help the adjustment. In other words, *avoid* choosing nine months as the age to start out-of-home care. However, at the same time, consider the establishment of attachment. Some parents worry that if they don't have enough time with the new baby—if they go back to work right away—they won't really become attached as firmly as they might. According to Bettye Caldwell, "If a baby has an insecure attachment to the mother, being placed in childcare at an early age may cause this already shaky relationship to become more so." [12]

Some parents don't have much choice and won't until parental leave becomes a societal policy. It may reassure them to know that most studies have shown that babies become attached to their own parents even when childcare is begun quite early.

Quality Care Is Vital to Attachment

Quality care is examined in greater length in chapter 6. Here it is discussed in relationship to attachment.

Good caregivers have many of the qualities of good parents, and those qualities promote attachment. One vital quality is sensitivity. When a caregiver learns to read each infant's signals, he or she can respond appropriately and in a timely fashion (if the staff-child ratio is good). Infants learn that they can give messages. They can influence the people in their world. They have personal power. They become attached. The attachment not only grows out of the sensitivity and the ability of the caregiver to communicate but also promotes further communication. The infant becomes better at sending signals when someone is trying to read them. The caregiver gets better and better at reading them as he or she grows to know the baby as an individual. A synchronous relationship results.

Good caregivers and good parents have many similar behaviors and goals, but they also have some differences. The caregiver's attachment is necessarily short term, and it's important for him or her to remember that fact. This childcare arrangement isn't forever; the caregiver has little control over the future. It's the

When a parent or caregiver learns to read the infant's signals, attachment grows.

parents' job to have a vision for the child's future, just as they have the knowledge of the past. It's the parents—the family—who connect the child in time, giving a sense of continuity. The child has a life beyond childcare; that's a fact that is important for the caregiver to keep in mind.

Parents and caregivers differ in the degree of closeness that's appropriate. The goal of *parental* attachment is to establish *optimum closeness* with the child; the *caregiver's* goal is *optimum distance.* The child benefits from attachment to both, but it's a different kind of attachment. The caregiver must put limits on the degree of attachment; after all, the family may move out of town tomorrow. In addition, caregivers usually have other children to consider; they can't allow themselves to get completely wrapped up in just one to the neglect of the others.

"Fairness" is another category in which parents and caregivers differ. Parents can be advocates for their own children. They don't have to be fair and consider all the children in the program. It's appropriate for parents to focus on their own children. Caregivers can't afford to favor one child over another, but that doesn't mean that they must treat all the children in their care alike. Similar treatment in the face of differing needs doesn't create fairness. [13]

SUMMARY

Trust and attachment are lifelong issues. When conditions are right, parents and babies get "hooked" on each other right from the beginning. The relationship that results serves both well. It not only ensures the baby the nurturing and protecting he or she needs at the beginning but also sets the stage for later relationships. Being attached feels good. It offers security.

This security is just what the baby needs to move out from the parent and become a fully functioning individual. That subject is the focus of the next chapter.

FOR DISCUSSION

1. Give an example of synchrony and explain how attachment grows from it.
2. What are your own views about why attachment is important?
3. Have you been aware of attachment occurring? Tell about that experience.
4. What are your ideas about the difference between bonding and attachment?
5. Tell about how an infant shows he or she is attached.
6. What are your experiences with obstacles to bonding? To attachment?
7. What story can you tell about "separation"?
8. Compare two different attachment patterns.
9. Have you ever known anyone whose baby had a life-threatening illness? Do you know anything about how attachment worked in that family?
10. Have you had any experience with how childcare might affect attachment? What are your ideas or thoughts about this subject?

PERSONAL REFLECTIONS

Thinking about your personal reactions and experiences will help you better understand and integrate the material in this chapter. Use these questions to interface between you and what you read. Use the pertinent ones to reflect on, write about, or discuss with others.

> ❯ On page 7 are two scenes written from an infant's perspective under the heading "Building basic trust in infancy through meeting needs." Read the two scenes aloud. What is happening in each? Could you retell each from the adult perspective? Which scene do you prefer and why?
>
> ❯ Are you a person with "trust issues"?
>
> ❯ The chapter states that adults with unresolved trust issues seek relationships with other adults that mimic their early caregiving experience. Do you agree with this idea? If no, why not? If yes, why do you think this is so?
>
> ❯ Babies are often different from what the parents expect. Did you live up to your parents' expectations as a baby? As an adult?
>
> ❯ What do you know about your own attachment process?
>
> ❯ Can you relate to the list of feelings triggered by "loss" and "separation" described on pages 13 and 15?
>
> ❯ What are your experiences with attachment, separation, and childcare?
>
> ❯ Could you relate to Jeremy's parents (see p. 14)?

NOTES

1. Erik Erikson explains that each child struggles to resolve a conflict between trust and mistrust during the first year of life. Erik Erikson, *Childhood and Society* (New York: Norton, 1963).

2. Harville Hendrix, *Getting the Love You Want* (New York: Harper Perennial, 1990).

3. Emmy E. Werner, "Research in Review: Resilient Children," *Young Children* (November 1984): 68–72.

4. Providing for bonding at birth is an excellent idea and is encouraged for many reasons, one of which is the supposition that child abuse and/or neglect is more likely in families where there is no attachment. In a good number of cases in modern American society, caregiving may depend on feeling some attachment to the baby rather than on a deep sense of obligation that compels one to fulfill a caregiving role from which attachment grows. The American mainstream cultural tradition demands that emotion precede commitment. Love comes first, then marriage. Attachment (love for a baby) produces commitment to the baby, which ensures that he or she will be taken care of. All cultures don't work that way. In some, marriage comes first (arranged for the couple) and love follows. The baby is born and then cared for because with the role of parent comes commitment, whether attachment comes early on or not. Attachment grows from the commitment.

5. Anthony J. DeCasper and William P. Fifer, "Of Human Bonding: Newborns Prefer Their Mothers' Voices," *Science* 208 (1980): 1174–1175; J. M. Cernoch and R. H. Porter, "Recognition of Maternal Axillary Odors by Infants," *Child Development* 56 (1985): 1593–1598.

6. Alexander Thomas, Stella Chess, and Herbert G. Birch, *Behavioral Individuality in Early Childhood* (New York: New York University Press, 1963).

7. J. K. Grether, J. Shulman, and L. A. Croen, "Sudden Infant Death Syndrome Among Asians in California," *Journal of Pediatrics* 116 (1990): 525–528; James J. McKenna, "SIDS Research," *Mothering* (Winter 1992): 45–51.

8. Tine Thevenin, *The Family Bed* (Garden City, NY: Avery, 1987).

9. Carol Stack, "Sex Roles and Survival Strategies in an Urban Black Community, in *The Black Family: Essays and Studies*, 4th ed., ed. Robert Staples (Belmont, CA: Wadsworth, 1991).

10. This story of the family portrait started me thinking about my own family situation as I grew up. My mother, my sister, and I lived most of my childhood in the house of my grandparents. We never had a family portrait taken. We didn't see ourselves as a unit; rather we were two families—an intact one (my grandparents) and a "broken" one (my mother and her two children). Nowadays, of course, we would call ourselves a single-parent family rather than a broken one, but many would still see us as deprived without a father in the household, rather than enriched because of grandparents and the uncles who lived there for periods during my growing up.

11. Robert A. LeVine, "Child Rearing as Cultural Adaptation," in *Culture and Infancy: Variations in the Human Experience*, eds. P. Herbert Leiderman, R. Steven Tulkin, and Anne Rosenfeld (New York and San Francisco: Academic Press, A Subsidiary of Harcourt Brace Jovanovich, 1977).

12. Bettye M. Caldwell, "The Tie That Binds," *Working Mother* (April 1987): 106.

13. Lilian Katz, "Mothering and Teaching: Some Significant Distinctions," in *Current Topics in Early Childhood Education*, vol. 3, ed. L. G. Katz (Norwood, NJ: Ablex, 1980), 47–63.

REFERENCES

Ainsworth, M. D. S., and S. Bell. "Infant Crying and Maternal Responsiveness." *Child Development* 48 (1977): 1208–1216.

Ainsworth, M. D. S., M. C. Blehar, E. Waters, and S. Wall. *Patterns of Attachment: A Psychological Study of the Strange Situation*. Hillside, NJ: Erlbaum, 1978.

Barnard, K., and T. B. Brazelton, eds. *Touch: The Foundation of Experience*. New York: Bantam, 1990.

Bowlby, J. *Attachment*, vol. 1 of *Attachment and Loss*. London: Hogarth, 1969.

Brazelton, T. B., and B. G. Cramer. *The Earliest Relationship: Parents, Infants, and the Drama of Early Attachment*. New York: Addison-Wesley, 1990.

Brazelton, T. B., M. Yogman, H. Als, and E. Tronick. "The Infant as a Focus for Family Reciprocity." In *The Child and His Family*, eds. Michael Lewis and Leonard A. Rosenblum. New York: Plenum, 1979.

Buss, A. H. "The EAS Theory of Temperament." In *Explorations of Temperament*, eds. J. Strelau and A. Angleitner. New York: Plenum, 1991.

Caldwell, Bettye M. "The Tie That Binds." *Working Mother* (April 1987).

Caudill, W., and H. Winstein. "Maternal Care and Infant Behavior in Japan and America." *Psychiatry* 32 (1969): 12–43.

Chang, Hedy. *Affirming Children's Roots: Cultural and Linguistic Diversity in Early Care and Education*. San Francisco: California Tomorrow, 1993.

Chang, H. N. L., A. Muckelroy, and D. Pulido-Tobiassen. *Looking In, Looking Out: Redefining Child and Early Education in a Diverse Society*. San Francisco: California Tomorrow, 1996.

Clark, A. L., ed. *Culture and Childrearing*. Philadelphia: F. A. Davis Company, 1981.

Comer, J. P., and A. F. Poussaint. *Black Child Care*. New York: Simon and Schuster, 1975.

Cortez, Jesus, ed. *Infant-Toddler Caregiving: Guide to Culturally Sensitive Care for Infants and Toddlers*. Sacramento, CA: California State Department of Education, 1992.

Derman-Sparks, Louise. "The Process of Culturally Sensitive Care." In *Infant/Toddler Caregiving: A*

Guide to Culturally Sensitive Care, ed. Peter Mangione. Sacramento, California: Far West Laboratory and California Department of Education, 1995.

Erikson, E. *Childhood and Society*. New York: Norton, 1963.

Ferber, R. *Solve Your Child's Sleep Problems*. New York: Simon and Schuster, 1985, 38–9.

Fisher, Roger, and William Ury. *Getting to Yes: Negotiating Agreement Without Giving In*. New York: Penguin Books, 1991.

Fox, N. "Attachment of Kibbutz Infants to Mothers and Metapelet." *Child Development* 48 (1977): 1228–1239.

Gerber, M. *Resources for Infant Educarers*. Los Angeles, CA: Resources for Infant Educarers, 1991.

Gonzalez-Mena, Janet. "Cultural Sensitivity in Routine Caregiving Tasks." In *Infant/Toddler Caregiving: A Guide to Culturally Sensitive Care*, ed. Peter Mangione. Sacramento, California: Far West Laboratory and California Department of Education, 1995.

Gonzalez-Mena, J. *Infant/Toddler Caregiving: A Guide to Routines*. Sacramento, CA: California State Department of Education, 1990.

Gonzalez-Mena, Janet. "Taking A Culturally Sensitive Approach in Infant-Toddler Programs." *Young Children* 47(2) (January 1992): 4–9.

Gonzalez-Mena, Janet, and Anne Stonehouse. "In the Child's Best Interests." *Child Care Information Exchange* (November 1995): 17–20.

Greenman, Jim. "Living in the Real World: Diversity and Conflict." *Exchange* (October 1989).

Greenman, Jim, and Anne Stonehouse. *Prime Times: A Handbook for Excellence in Infant and Toddler Programs*. St. Paul: Redleaf, 1996.

Grether, J. K., J. Shulman, and L. A. Croen. "Sudden Infant Death Syndrome Among Asians in California." *Journal of Pediatrics* 116 (1990): 525–528.

Hale-Benson, Janice E. *Black Children: Their Roots, Culture, and Learning Styles*. Baltimore, MD: The Johns Hopkins University Press, 1986.

Hall, Edward T. *Beyond Culture*. Garden City, NY: Anchor Press/Doubleday, 1981.

Hess, Robert. "Social Class and Ethnic Influences upon Socialization." In *Carmichael's Manual of Child Psychology*, ed. Paul Mussen. New York: John Wiley and Sons, 1970, 457–549.

Honig, Alice Sterling. "Meeting the Needs of Infants." *Dimensions* (January 1983): 4–7.

———. "The Eriksonian Approach: Infant-Toddler Education." In *Approaches to Early Childhood Education*, eds. J. Roopnarine and J. Johnson. Upper Saddle River, NJ: Merrill/Prentice Hall, 1987, 49–69.

———. "Quality Infant/Toddler Caregiving: Are There Magic Recipes?" *Young Children* (May 1989): 4–10.

Hughes, R. "The Informal Help-Giving of Home and Center Childcare Providers." *Family Relations* 34 (1985): 359–366.

Hutchinson, Janice. "What Crack Does to Babies." *American Educator* (Spring 1991).

Kagan, Jerome. *The Nature of the Child*. New York: Basic Books, Inc., 1984.

Kagan, S. L., D. R. Powell, E. F. Zigler, and B. Weissbourd, eds. *America's Family Support Programs*. New Haven and London: Yale University Press, 1987.

Karen, R., *Becoming Attached*. New York: Warner Books, 1994.

McKenna, James J. "SIDS Research." *Mothering* (Winter 1992): 45–51.

Katz, L. G. "Mothering and Teaching: Some Significant Distinctions." In *Current Topics in Early Childhood Education*, vol. 3, ed. L. G. Katz. Norwood, NJ: Ablex, 1980, 47–63.

LeVine, Robert A. "Child Rearing as Cultural Adaptation." In *Culture and Infancy: Variations in the Human Experience*, eds. P. Herbert Leiderman, Steven R. Tulkin, and Anne Rosenfeld. New York and San Francisco: Academic Press, A Subsidiary of Harcourt Brace Jovanovich, 1977.

Pawl, Jeree H. "The Therapeutic Relationship as Human Connectedness: Being Held in Another's Mind." *Zero to Three* 15(4) (February-March 1995).

Peters, D., and J. Benn. "Day Care: Support for the Family." *Dimensions* 9 (1980): 78–82.

Phillips, Carol Brunson, and Renatta M. Cooper. "Cultural Dimensions of Feeding Relationships." *Zero to Three* (June 1992): 10–13.

Powell, D. R. "Day Care as a Family Support System." In *America's Family Support Programs*, ed. S. L. Kagan, D. R. Powell, E. F. Zigler, and B. Weissbourd. New Haven and London: Yale University Press, 1987, 115–132.

————. *Families and Early Childhood Programs.* Washington, DC: National Association for the Education of Young Children, 1988.

Stack, C. B. "Sex Roles and Survival Strategies in an Urban Black Community." In *The Black Family: Essays and Studies,* 4th ed., ed. Robert Staples. Belmont, CA: Wadsworth, 1991.

Stern, Daniel N. *Diary of a Baby.* New York: Basic Books, 1990.

————. *The Interpersonal World of the Infant.* New York: Basic Books, 1985.

Thevenin, Tine. *The Family Bed.* Garden City, NY: Avery, 1987.

Thomas, Alexander, Stella Chess, and Herbert G. Birch. *Behavioral Individuality in Early Childhood.* New York: New York University Press, 1963.

Thonman, E. B., and S. Browder. *Born Dancing.* New York: Harper and Row, 1987.

Weissbourd, B., and J. S. Musick, eds. *Infants: The Social Environments.* Washington, DC: National Association for the Education of Young Children, 1981.

Weissbourd, B., and D. Powell. "For Children's Sake: Family-Centered Childcare." *Family Resource Coalition* 9 (1990): 1, 2-3, 18.

Werner, Emmy E. "Resilience in Development." *Current Directions in Psychological Science* (June 1995): 81–85.

Werner, E. E., and R. S. Smith. *Overcoming the Odds: High Risk Children from Birth to Adulthood.* Ithaca and London: Cornell University Press, 1992.

Whiting, B., and C. Edwards. *Children of Different Worlds.* Cambridge, MA: Harvard University Press, 1988.

Young, V. H. "Family and Childhood in a Southern Georgia Community." *American Anthropologist* 72 (1970).

Zimmerman, L., and L. McDonald. "Emotional Availability in Infants' Relationships with Multiple Caregivers." *American Journal of Orthopsychiatry* 65(1) (1995): 147–152.

AUTONOMY

CHAPTER **2**

TEST YOURSELF

Look for the answers to these questions as you read the chapter:

1. How can you tell that a child is beginning to develop autonomy?
2. What are self-help skills and why do some people think they are important to learn early?
3. What is the difference between independence and interdependence?
4. Why are toddlers called "doers" but not "producers"?
5. What are three signs of readiness for toilet training, or toilet learning, as it is usually carried out in Western society?
6. What do toddler behaviors have to do with power?
7. How can you empower toddlers?
8. What are the effects of a prolonged good-bye when parents feel ambiguous about leaving their children?
9. What are some ways that young children cope with their feelings about separation?

TODDLERS AND AUTONOMY

Sometime around the first birthday the baby pulls herself to her feet and staggers forward. That first shaky baby step represents a huge developmental leap. The baby is now a toddler, and the central task of his or her life is to become a separate independent being. Erik Erikson calls this the stage of autonomy. [1]

Many adults find the way that toddlers carry out this task to be a headache. They see the behaviors that come along with this push for independence—for autonomy—as difficult to manage. The theorists (who generally see things from a European-American perspective) explain the meaning behind the behaviors and expect adults to understand and put up with the difficulties while they promote independence. The labels put on this stage by parents (*the terrible twos*) and by experts (*the terrific twos*) reflect the various ways to look at the behaviors of this stage.

SIGNS OF DEVELOPING AUTONOMY

What are the behaviors that indicate a child is becoming an autonomous individual who will one day be self-sufficient and self-reliant? [2] The most notable are negativity, exploration, self-help skills, and a sense of possession.

Negativity

The first sign of the coming of one of these behaviors that signal developing autonomy is when the darling baby who happily opened his mouth for each bite of cereal or strained vegetables suddenly one day clamps his lips shut and turns aside. His meaning is clear. Without a word spoken, this is the beginning of "No!"

The theory says that the child can now begin to see himself as an individual separate from his mother or other object of attachment. He finds power in his difference—he's not the same person as this adult in his life. He finds power and he uses it.

This is only the beginning. By two years of age this child is likely to be contrary about everything. If his mother likes peas, he hates them. If his father wants to take him for a ride, he balks. He refuses to get into the bathtub, and when he is finally coaxed in, he refuses to get out again. Life becomes a struggle because he is so busy asserting his individuality.

Sometimes toddlers say "no" so much because they hear the word all the time. If parents or caregivers use the word *no* as the primary means of controlling behavior, the first *no's* of their children may be imitations of adults.

However, even if adults use a variety of means of controlling behavior and minimize the number of *no's* in their child's life, toddlers still learn to say that magic word.

It's important to realize that learning to say "no" is a vital skill. What would your life be like if you never said "no" to anything? Do you remember the temptations of your teen years? Do you wish you had learned to say a good strong "No!"

It's important to realize that saying no is a vital skill, even if you don't like the manner in which it is being said.

earlier? What are your temptations now? Do you find saying "no" a useful skill in your life today? How much do you remember about your own toddler years? Did the adults who were in your life regard your *no's* as skill building or did they take them as defiance of their authority? Their perception of you then may influence *your* perception of children in the toddler stage now.

Exploration

Exploration grows out of attachment and increases as children move toward autonomy. It may seem ironic that a child who is firmly attached explores more than one who is not. But it makes sense if you think of the attachment as providing a secure base to move out from. In fact, you can even see this phenomenon in action by watching a parent and a young child who are in a strange environment. The child will move out from the parent, but will check back regularly. Sometimes it's just a glance; other times he or she runs back to the parent and clings for a moment before venturing out again.

Toddlers move around a lot when they feel secure. They spontaneously explore the space around them. In my classes I've asked students to observe a toddler in childcare and to map the territory he or she moves through. The maps that come out of these observations are amazing. A toddler can cover miles in a single day just by toddling back and forth across a room or a play yard.

Independence and Interdependence

Newborn babies are faced with the two major tasks of childhood: (1) to become independent individuals and (2) to establish connections with others. The parents' job is to help their children with these tasks. Most parents focus more on one task than the other. Some even ignore the other and leave its accomplishment to chance.

European-American parents and researchers focus on independence and individuality, which is also the focus of this chapter. Parents from other cultures are more concerned about their children's ability to create and maintain connections. These parents have a different view of practically everything because of their focus on *interdependence,* or mutual dependence, instead of independence.

Parent's whose primary goal is to establish and keep connections may have little concern about teaching their children self-help skills. For example, self-feeding may be postponed because feeding is a time in which connections are nourished. They may continue spoon-feeding way past infancy into toddlerhood and beyond. This practice can get them in trouble if their child enters childcare. Teachers may be shocked when a three-year-old sits down at breakfast the first day and waits to be fed. Parents can be quite surprised and disappointed when they learn of a program's policy on self-help skills.

Although parents who stress independence look down on the idea of "coddling" children, to the parent focused on making connections, there's nothing negative about doing things for children. These parents see no reason to keep from prolonging babyhood and continuing the closeness. Their attitude makes sense if you understand their goal. They worry about too much independence, so they try to discourage it. Independent-minded parents have the opposite worry. They fear that if they don't encourage independence their children will remain dependent on them, maybe forever!

Parents who stress connectedness expect their children to be independent as well, but they believe it will happen naturally. In fact they worry that the drive for independence is too strong; that's why they have to work so hard to maintain connections.

Toddlers explore with their hands—and use their other senses as well. Given something new, they'll bang it, smell it, try to pull it apart, maybe throw it, and quite often taste it. They are little scientists. They want to know what everything can do—how it works.

Toddlers are "doers," but not "producers." They explore, experiment, and try things out to see what will happen. That means if you give them a toy or an activity that is designed to be used in a certain way, they're sure to try a dozen other ways to use it. They are not interested in outcomes or products. They enjoy the process of exploring and experimenting for its own sake, and they don't need anything to show for it.

Janice and Tracy

Janice is seventeen and she has an eighteen-month-old, Tracy, who is driving her crazy. Janice has just started in a teen parent program that allows her to continue her high school education. Tracy is taken care of at the school in a portable building that has been set up for infants and toddlers. Although Tracy protests at being left in the morning, which really bothers Janice, she quickly becomes contented while playing with the other babies. Janice misses her, so she pops in briefly between her classes—which almost always results in another crying spell when she has to leave again. That annoys Janice. Why can't she just come and go without all this fuss!

Whenever she is around Tracy, the child clings to her, making it impossible for her to even walk from one place to another. Janice doesn't like this.

Janice also doesn't like it when the childcare teachers assure her that Tracy was fine all day and didn't miss her at all. That doesn't feel good. And she doesn't like the way Tracy is beginning to hang around one of the teachers, and even hugs her good-bye when they leave at the end of the day. Janice wonders if Tracy still loves her when she shows affection toward the teacher.

Some of Tracy's other behaviors bother Janice as well. She doesn't like the defiant look Tracy gets in her eye when she tells her to do something. That makes Janice feel angry and she gets just as stubborn as Tracy has become.

Sometimes she feels like hitting Tracy, but she talks about that feeling in her parenting class, where she is learning a variety of ways to guide Tracy's behavior. Somehow talking about hitting helps her control herself, so she doesn't do it. She's seen another child in the center whose mother got carried away with spanking and ended up abusing her daughter. It was pretty awful, both how the child looked, and what happened to her mother. She ended up losing her baby. Janice couldn't stand to lose Tracy, and she cries at the thought that she might ever hurt her. So she is careful to never spank her, no matter what.

Another thing that bothers Janice is how dirty Tracy gets. She insists on doing things for herself—like feeding herself. She isn't very neat! And the childcare staff doesn't seem to understand how important it is to Janice that Tracy look like a sweet little doll. They let her feed herself, which means that often her clothes get messed up. Sometimes Janice comes in and finds Tracy in the center's old beat-up clothes, because they ran out of changes for her. Janice doesn't like seeing her like this.

And the sand! Can't they understand how hard it is for Janice when Tracy gets sand in her hair? It seems that whenever they go out in the yard Tracy ends up with her head full of sand. It's a lot of trouble to wash that out and redo her hair. Besides, Tracy *hates* to have her hair washed and puts up quite a fight.

This is all so different from when Tracy was younger and she used to just lie around and laugh and look cute. It was a lot easier then. But this is a different stage and it isn't so easy!

Janice knew that none of this would be easy when she decided to keep Tracy. She had lots of warnings about the life of a teen mother. But with her family's support and the help of the center staff, she's making it. And Tracy is an important part of her life!

Enjoying an exploratory sensory experience.

Self-Help Skills

Another behavior that indicates growing autonomy is the push for self-help skills. How the adults respond to this and to the exploring behavior will determine to some extent the child's adult behavior. Children who aren't allowed to touch or to try things on their own get a message about their own capabilities. When restricted to an extreme, they can lose their curiosity, their willingness to take risks, and their drive to be independent of others and do things for themselves.

Consider the difference between these two scenes:

Little Sarah has unbuckled herself from her car seat and is demanding that she be allowed to climb out of the car by herself. "Sarah do it!" she proclaims loudly.

She has never done this before and nobody knows if she can do it safely or not. Her father, annoyed by her demands, steps back out of reach and says in a sarcastic tone: "Go ahead, little girl, show me how grown up you are!" True to her father's expectations, she falls out the door and onto the ground. Crying, she reaches for her father. He picks her up and comforts her. Brushing away her tears, he tells her that she's too little to do things by herself. He makes it clear that she needs him. Later he tells the story and the whole family laughs at the little girl who is "too big for her britches." It becomes a family joke—the "Let Sarah do it" joke.

Let's replay that scene.

Here's Sarah, unbuckled from her car seat, demanding, "Sarah do it!" Her father, instead of trying to prove to her that she is too young, decides to help her find out what she can do, but he will protect her while she's making the discovery. Instead of being sarcastic and stepping back, he says: "I'm here if you need my help." He stands far enough away that Sarah can maneuver, but close enough to help her if she needs it. She does fine until the slick sole of her shoe slips on the door frame. She starts to fall and reaches out a hand. Her father grabs it and restores her balance. She lets go of his hand, holds on to the armrest, and climbs the rest of the way out safely. They both rejoice at her accomplishment. Later her father tells the family proudly, "Sarah climbed out of the car by herself today!"

Consider the difference in the messages of scene one and scene two. Scene one: "You're too uppity and you need a good lesson. When you learn it, you'll know that you're too young to try things on your own." In scene two, the father encour-

"Look, I can do it all by myself!"

aged self-help, but provided the protection needed for Sarah to be successful. The Sarah of scene two sees her father as a facilitator of her independence; the Sarah of scene one does not.

When independence is a strong cultural priority, the first stirrings of it prompt adults to begin to encourage and facilitate it. However, in some cultures *interdependence* is the priority and signs of independence may trigger a push on the part of the adult to work harder to promote the cultural goal. For example, in Japan some parents find their children too independent from the start, so they begin right away giving lessons in dependence. The goal is to help children see themselves as connected, not separate. When at about nine months of age children begin to assert themselves, pushing away the adult hand trying to feed them, for example, the lessons in interdependence intensify. The specific objective is to teach the child to graciously accept help, even if they can do it for themselves.

Sometimes adults share responsibility for the same child and one pushes independence while the other struggles against the same behaviors. These two adults may be parents in a cross cultural marriage or teacher and parent. If they are in disagreement about their goals and priorities for the child, they need to sit down and talk about their differences. It's hard on a child to have two conflicting approaches to deal with.

Self-Feeding

Take, for example, self-feeding. The caregiver who values independence encourages self-feeding as soon as the baby grabs for the spoon or can pick up a teething biscuit and get it to her mouth. This caregiver gives the baby her own spoon and lets her help, and before long lets her feed herself—as soon as she can get enough in her mouth to count. Also, she cuts up small bits of appropriate finger foods and makes them available for the child to self-feed. Because what this caregiver does is considered developmentally appropriate practice among early-childhood practitioners, she won't feel a conflict until she runs into a parent who see things differently. Some parents have different priorities for toddlers. Self-feeding is not one of them. Their goal for their children is learning to help others rather than helping oneself. Therefore they model helping skills by spoon-feeding children into the preschool years. They may justify their actions in a number of ways, including their desire to keep things neat and clean and not waste food, for example. When a caregiver and a parent see something like self-feeding from very different perspectives, arguments and angry feelings can result.

Toilet Training

Toilet training is another area where values of independence and interdependence can collide. Just as no culture produces adults who are unable to feed themselves, no matter how late they start, no culture produces adults unable to toilet themselves. But the approach and the timing are different depending on whether your stress is independence or interdependence.

Most experts discuss toilet training only from the independence perspective. The advice is to watch for signs of readiness, which fall into three general categories: physical, intellectual, and emotional. Physical readiness means the ability to hold on and let go. A first sign is when a child goes for longer and longer periods with a dry diaper. Physical readiness also is determined by the child's ability to handle his or her own clothing—pulling down pants, for example. A sign of intellectual readiness is when a child tells the adult *after* eliminating or in other ways indicates that he or she knows there's more to the process than letting go in one's diapers. Emotional readiness comes when the child shows a willingness to use a potty or a toilet instead of diapers. The timing for these signs varies with each individual, but in general they seldom appear before the second birthday.

An adult with a priority of interdependence may look at toilet training from a entirely different point of view. This person won't wait for a couple of years to start, but may start as early as a few months or even at birth to try to "catch" the baby and hold him or her over a potty. Readiness takes on a whole different meaning when the goal is interdependence.

Here's how it works. Timing is crucial. Sometimes the caregiver can predict based on the baby's regularity. "Time to hold her over the potty," says the caregiver periodically. Also, the caregiver learns to read subtle body messages that indicate the baby is about to wet. The baby learns to let the caregiver know, and the caregiver trains the baby to let go at a signal—perhaps a whistling sound. It's truly amazing to a caregiver whose only experience is from the independence perspective how young babies and their caregivers can manage dry, clean diapers most of the time.

"It's the adult who's trained, not the baby!" is a common reaction to this interdependence approach. Caregivers who use the first approach, waiting until after age two to begin, are sometimes critical of those who use the other—and vice versa—yet each works well for the adults and children who are using it. Both approaches eventually result in fully trained children who are able to handle all of their own toileting.

Toilet training becomes difficult when the child perceives that his or her autonomy is being usurped and fights back. Some children even feel that the adult is depriving them of something that is rightfully theirs—their body products! The resulting power struggle can be ugly and its effects long lasting. Some children with an unfortunate toilet-training history may be left with big control issues that pop up in a variety of arenas. Whatever method you use, it is important to tread gently and avoid the use of harshness or force.

A Sense of Possession

In a culture that prizes possessions, a sense of ownership and its counterpart—a willingness to share—become important developmental steps. What many adults of this culture don't realize is that the one must come before the other. Without a firm sense of possession, children can't understand the concept of sharing. [3]

There's quite a difference between the infant who doesn't have a sense of possession and the toddler who does. Most of us have seen babies receiving gifts that they have no feeling for or interest in. The adults have the concept of ownership—the baby doesn't. That picture is a contrast to the toddler holding a toy as far out of reach as possible and screaming "Me! Mine!" at an advancing playmate.

The immediate adult inclination is to rush in with a lesson on sharing. However, it's a little too soon for the lesson to be truly effective. This toddler is just beginning to get the concept of ownership. She is starting to see herself as a person with possessions. She needs to grasp that idea fully before she can understand the idea of sharing. She'll just harbor a grudge if you take the toy away and insist that she share it. Anger and grudges are not involved in the true spirit of sharing, which is the lesson most adults want to get across when they teach the behavior.

At this point the conflict between the two children over a toy is more a momentary power issue than anything else, and there are feelings on both sides. An effective way to intervene in this situation is to reflect the feelings of both parties rather than to discuss issues of sharing or fairness. For example, here's a scene between Joy and Jacob, both two-year-olds:

> Joy is triumphantly holding a rag doll in her arms. Jacob is standing near her, crying his eyes out. An adult is squatting beside them.
>
> "You both want that same doll and Joy has it," says the adult.
>
> Jacob sits down on the floor and screams in response to the adult intervention.
>
> "I see how unhappy you are, Jacob," says the adult.
>
> Joy flaunts the doll in front of Jacob's face, saying again, firmly, "Mine!"
>
> Jacob grabs for the doll, connects, and jerks it away. Joy is the one screaming now.
>
> "Jacob has the doll now," says the adult, announcing the action rather than making any judgment about it. Then the adult reflects the feelings. "You don't like it when he grabs things from you. You can tell him 'No!'"
>
> Joy screams "No!" at Jacob's departing back. A moment later Jacob drops the doll to pick up a cloth book that is lying at his feet. Joy starts for the dropped doll, then changes her mind and grabs a page of the book, yelling, "Mine!" Jacob starts to cry.
>
> The adult says, "You don't like that, Jacob! You don't like it when she grabs things. Tell her 'No!'"

And so it goes.

Look at these two a couple of years later:

> They are painting side by side at an easel. Joy reaches for the brush that Jacob has in his hand—the one that goes in the green paint. "That's mine," says Jacob firmly.
>
> "No, it's not, it's the school's," says Joy, "and I need it."
>
> "I'm using it," says Jacob.
>
> Joy continues to reach for the brush, and grabs hold of it so Jacob can't paint.
>
> "Stop that!" says Jacob.
>
> "I need the brush!" insists Joy.
>
> "Can't you wait until I'm through?" asks Jacob.
>
> "No," says Joy.

"I have an idea," says Jacob. "There's another green brush on the other side of the easel. Let's get that one."

Joy lets go long enough for him to reach to the other side and retrieve the brush and the paint container. "Here," he says, handing it to her.

"Thanks," she replies.

Later in the same year, at the same easel, Joy asks Jacob for the brush he is using. He says to her, "I'm almost finished. You can have it in a minute." She waits until he is finished, uses it, then gives it back to him.

These two have learned the behaviors of sharing and also the spirit. They have experienced the benefits. They understand the concept of possession and ownership.

In cultures where private ownership is not an issue and personal possessions do not play a large part in people's lives, this sequence might be very different.

DEALING WITH ISSUES OF POWER AND CONTROL

The behaviors discussed—saying "no," exploring the world, learning self-help skills, and gaining a sense of possession—all have to do with issues of power and control. Just as the *infant* came to experience a sense of power through signaling his needs and satisfying them by means of the adults around him, so does the *toddler* need to experience a sense of power through these typical toddler behaviors.

There is much an adult can do to facilitate this empowerment and the controls that need to go with it to keep the toddler and others safe and secure.

Set Up a Developmentally Appropriate Environment

A developmentally appropriate environment will provide freedom for exploration with few prohibitions. Think of the difference between a toddler in a playroom set up for her versus spending an hour in Grandma's living room, trying to keep her hands off all the precious knickknacks. Yes, toddlers need to learn that there are some things they can't touch, but you can limit this lesson to a few times when it's important and spend the rest of the time teaching them that there are many things in the world that they *can* touch.

When toddlers spend their time in an environment that is appropriate for their age, they are freer to explore. They won't be faced with so many *no's*. If they don't have to hear the word *no*, they may decrease their own usage of the word. It is worth thinking about what kind of environment says "yes!" to toddlers and then arranging things so that where they spend their time affirms their developmental needs. At this stage they touch, explore, try things out, and use their bodies to learn about the world. Their natural inclination is to climb, push, poke, prod, and perform a huge variety of other movements. They need a safe place to do all this— a place where they feel empowered rather than prohibited. [4]

Provide a developmentally appropriate environment for toddlers.

Encourage Self-Help Skills

Encourage children to do for themselves what they are capable of; don't do for them what they can do for themselves. [5] This way of empowerment starts in infancy as the adult includes the child as a full partner in caregiving routines. For instance, diapering is a teamwork affair, and the baby is treated as a whole person worthy of respect, not just as a bottom that must be tended to while the top half is being entertained with something else. [6] This attitude of teamwork makes the toddler feel a little less rebellious because the adult is sometimes seen as a partner rather than as an adversary. It isn't a cure-all for rebellion, of course, because the struggle to defy the adult is a mark of the toddler stage.

Give Choices

Help toddlers feel powerful by giving choices. Instead of saying, "Get in that bathtub now!" you can offer a choice such as, "Do you want to take a bath before supper or after?" When after supper comes and the child still balks, you can say, "After you get in you can choose between the boats or the blocks." And if the child still balks and it's time for a showdown, you can still give a choice: "Do you want to climb in by yourself, or should I put you in?" This way the child still feels empowered and you are able to do what you perceive he needs to do. You're not being wishy-washy. The child *will* take a bath, but he has some choices about when, with what, and how he will enter the bathtub. [7]

Provide Control

Provide the control toddlers need. Here are two scenes to illustrate that principle. Let's go back to Joy and Jacob as two- year-olds:

> They are playing happily and the phone rings. The adult turns her back to answer it, and Jacob grabs the toy Joy has in her hand. Joy, who hasn't learned to express her feelings in words yet (though the adults have been working on that) expresses her anger and frustration by sinking her sharp little baby teeth into Jacob's arm. Jacob lets out a yell, and the adult comes running. She scolds Joy, telling her it isn't nice to bite, then puts her in a time-out chair. Joy keeps getting up, so the adult continually puts her back, scolding her each time. Finally she hugs her, lets her up, and warns her not to bite again.
>
> Later that afternoon, when Joy is tired and a little lonely for her mother and the adult is busy with another child, Joy walks up to Jacob and bites his arm again. She remembers the stir it caused this morning, and she enjoys a repeat performance this afternoon. However, she feels vaguely uncomfortable because she knows that she should control that urge.

Contrast that scene with this one:

> Joy and Jacob are playing together when the doorbell rings. The adult knows that Joy has the urge to bite when she gets frustrated, so rather than taking the chance of leaving her alone with Jacob for even a minute, she takes Joy with her to open the door.
>
> Later that morning, when Joy and Jacob are playing together, Joy gets frustrated. She makes a move toward Jacob's arm; before she can connect, the adult's hand covers her mouth gently. "I know you are unhappy, but I won't let you bite Jacob," she says in a clear tone that doesn't imply judgment—just fact. "You can bite this teething ring," she adds. "Or this plastic toy." She offers the choice. Joy grabs the teething ring and bites down hard. "You really are upset," affirms the adult.

This adult wisely provides the control that Joy lacks at this age. She prevents the biting from occurring instead of dealing with it afterward in a way that rewards Joy with extra attention.

Of course it isn't realistic to assume that the adult will be there 100 percent of the time. Even with careful vigilance, Joy might get her teeth into Jacob sometime. If that were to happen, the adult would then deal with the situation as a failure to control on her part—not as badness on Joy's part. After all, Joy is using her mouth to express her feelings in the only way she knows how. She lacks control—the control that it's up to the adult to provide.

If the bite occurs, the adult responds in much the same way she responded over the toy-grabbing incident earlier in this chapter.

> She approaches both children, modeling gentleness by touching them both lightly and lovingly. She says, "That really hurts, Jacob." To Joy she says, "Jacob is unhappy because you hurt him." As she says the words, she touches gently the red

place on Jacob's arm. Then she touches the same place on Joy's arm. After the demonstration of gentleness and the words indicating the feelings, she deals with any first aid needed. She is careful not to give either child a great deal of the kind of extra attention that hooks children on either the victim or the aggressor role. She doesn't turn her back on Joy and say, "Oh, poor little Jacob, let's put some ice on that bite—poor baby" because she knows that ignoring Joy may make Jacob feel it's worth it to get bitten in order to enjoy this lavish sympathy. And Joy is not left with the uncomfortable feeling of being ignored while realizing that she doesn't have the control she needs to keep from hurting someone. Being out of control is as scary for the person experiencing it as it is for the victim.

Set Limits

Setting limits and enforcing them also empowers children by giving them freedom within those limits. You can think of limits as a fence around a pasture. The horse is free to graze within the fence. Without the fence his freedom would have to be limited by a rope, by vigilance, or by training, none of which gives the freedom of the fence.

Limits for toddlers work the same way. The limits may be environmental boundaries, such as a barricade across the stairs, a lock on the toilet lid, or a gate on the driveway. Or they may be human boundaries, such as consistently taking a child off a counter he insists on climbing up on, stopping a child from throwing toys, or holding a kicking child who threatens to hurt others.

Children will test limits until they find that they hold. The child locked out of the bathroom pounds on the door, jiggles the doorknob, tries to poke something into the keyhole. He gives up when the physical barrier holds. Human boundaries are the same way. The child may continue to climb on the counter, and if the adult gives up and quits stopping him, he gets the message that this isn't a real limit—it doesn't hold if he's persistent enough. If the child is allowed to throw toys sometimes, he doesn't know there's a limit. His test shows that it doesn't hold up.

So in order to empower a child and provide security at the same time, it is necessary to set limits and hold to them. Because toddlers are persistent and are still discovering things about the world, you can also expect those limits to be tested until the toddler is satisfied that they're firm. The testing makes sense if you understand what's going on. If you don't, it seems as if the child is just trying to make you unhappy with his persistently unacceptable behavior. Don't get unhappy—just outpersist him!

COPING WITH LOSS AND SEPARATION

Separation issues start in infancy and continue into toddlerhood and beyond; they are never handled once and for all. The infant who has learned to sleep alone may well become the toddler who, because new fears arise, balks at going to bed and staying there. Even though a toddler copes very well with separation and independence during waking periods, she may resist sleep because she must give up the control she has. Lack of control can be very scary because it means that coping mechanisms don't work in the same way they do during waking periods. In addition, dreams, which can also create fear, enter in. Parents and childcare teachers who recognize this fact will be more understanding when children develop sleeping problems at home or react badly to sleeping away from home.

Taking Separation in Small Steps

It is easier for children if they first experience separation in small steps. Sleeping alone is one of these steps. Having a baby-sitter or being away from the person(s) they are attached to for short periods are other examples of steps of separation.

With a succession of periods away from the parent(s), either at home or away from home, children come to trust that the attachment holds, and that they will be reunited.

Be aware of the dangers of giving children more to cope with than they can handle. If parents feel a need to take an extensive vacation away from their child, they should realize the possible effects of a prolonged separation during the toddler period. Obviously, if the child has someone else he or she is attached to, the effects of such a separation won't be as serious as if the only person or two people in the world the child feels close to suddenly disappear for a few weeks. Such an interruption in attachment can be devastating to the child's sense of trust.

Some sudden and prolonged separations can't be helped, of course. If the child must undergo an extensive hospitalization, he or she will get through it better if parents stay at the hospital with the child or at least visit frequently. Visiting isn't the perfect solution because of the continual anguish of painful good-byes; it's better if a parent can stay with the child. When this isn't possible, visiting is preferable to nothing, even though parents may be tempted to cut down on their visits because of the pain their departures cause the child. But children who feel deserted can experience depression. [8]

When both parents work, sometimes separation problems can be minimized by hiring a nanny if the family can afford it. With a nanny, the child can stay in a familiar setting with one familiar person. The problem is that the child may get overly attached to someone who is an employee rather than a friend or a relative. Employees come and go, in most cases without causing too many disruptions. However, when a nanny quits, the child can experience untold grief.

ENTERING CHILDCARE

When a separation such as going into childcare is on the horizon, it's best to prepare the child. Imagine being the child of a mother who has been with you day and night for the first two years. Mom suddenly decides to go back to work, and one day she drives you to a strange place and leaves you there for the entire day. How would you feel?

It's far gentler to visit first and to keep the first experiences short, so the child gets to know the place and the people. Being left for only an hour or so at first, the child learns that the parent will return after a time. If the day is gradually lengthened, the child gets used to it and it's not such a shock. [9]

Helping Children Adjust

Some children walk right into childcare without batting an eye. They're so intrigued with the new setting that they forget their fears. Other children cling and suffer greatly. In this case it helps to let the child make the decision to separate rather than peeling him off and walking out the door, leaving him screaming.

One program has a room for the use of parents whose children hesitate to leave them. [10] The doorway just beyond the separation room is open and is filled with the sounds and sights of children playing, which serve to entice the child to leave the parent's side. Parents are asked to be patient about the separation process, and they're given some help and support in order to make it a healthy coping experience for both parent and child. Of course, everyone doesn't have the option of a slow departure. However, if more people understood the value, they might find ways to open up their options.

When the good-byes come, it helps to make things predictable. When parents sneak out and leave the child playing without saying good-bye, trust issues arise.

If possible, ease a child into child care. By keeping the first experiences short, she learns to trust that her parent will return.

Some children walk right into childcare without any fear. Other children are less brave about the new situation.

How can the child feel any power in the world if there's no way to predict what will happen? Saying good-bye may bring tears and protests, but it's the open, honest way of helping the child understand what's happening.

Accepting Feelings

When strong feelings are a part of the good-byes, it's important to acknowledge and accept the feelings rather than distracting the child from them. If the adult has leftover issues of separation and loss from childhood, it may be very hard for him or her to deal with the child's feelings. It's just too painful. If that's your problem, it's important to recognize how your own unresolved issues may be influencing your ability to deal with a child in the throes of a separation. Separation experiences remain with us—especially the unexpressed and unresolved feelings. Bringing these to awareness can help us cope with them in ways that are healthy for us and allow us to be available to the child who needs us.

Many adults who find separation painful because of their own experiences do whatever they can to distract the child and not acknowledge what he or she is feeling. Far better to put the child's feelings into words: "You're upset that your mother left you." It's also important to emit a sense of confidence that the child will be all right and that she will be reunited with the loved one. Don't go overboard, however. If you constantly reassure the child, she'll begin to wonder if you're reassuring yourself because what you're saying is not true. Better to be empathetic about the feelings and reassuring without discounting them.

It's also important to recognize that parents may have strong feelings about separation. It may hurt to leave their child with someone else. They may feel guilty. Some parents prolong good-byes because of their own feelings of ambiguity. These slow departures can be torture to everyone, especially if the child has shown willingness to be left, but has second thoughts because of the way the parent is dragging his or her feet. In these situations, caregivers sometimes have to help parents see how the child's feelings are affected by their reluctance to leave. Caregivers need to support parents and accept their feelings in the same way they do with children, without supporting detrimental actions such as agonizing, lingering departures.

Helping Children Cope

Some children are comforted and reassured by what's called a "transition object"—some kind of comfort device, such as a stuffed animal or a favorite blanket. Having something from home that they're attached to provides a link between

Some children are comforted and reassured by what's called a "transition object" such as this boy's blanket.

home and childcare. Leaving something of the parents at childcare can help, too. One child was comforted when his mother left her purse (she carried her wallet with her) because he figured if she forgot to come back for him, she'd at least remember her purse. He knew how important it was to her.

Providing something to do that's compelling and interesting is a good technique for helping the child cope with feelings of loss. Often the child will migrate to an interesting activity or a friendly person after the pain of arrival is beginning to pass. Don't hurry this process of moving to an activity or other person, however. Give time for the feelings. There's a fine line between helping children cope with feelings and distracting them from those feelings. It is important that the feelings be accepted and acknowledged.

In addition, allow the child to play out the feelings. Often you can see children over among the dolls or out in the sandbox, working through what's on their minds. This is a healthy way to deal with feelings that may be hard to express directly in words.

SUMMARY

This chapter explored the variety of behaviors that accompany the task of developing autonomy. It looked at exploration and self-help skills as well as examining ways of handling behavior that is difficult, ways of empowering children, and helping children cope with separation and loss. It ended with a quick look at the value of play, which is carried on as an important theme in the next chapter.

FOR DISCUSSION

1. Do you agree that negativity, exploration, self-help skills, and a sense of possession are indeed signs of developing autonomy? Can you think of other signs?

2. How do you feel about encouraging self-help skills from infancy on?

3. Have you ever known a family that valued interdependence over independence?

4. How do you feel about the statement, "Toddlers are doers, but not producers"?

5. What experience do you have in determining when a child is ready for toilet learning? Does your experience fit what the text says?

6. Give an example of a toddler behavior that relates to power issues.

7. Give an example of how an adult can empower a toddler.

8. The chapter lists five ways in which adults can empower children. Do you agree with them? Can you add some to the list?

9. What experience do you have with the effects of a prolonged good-bye with toddlers?

10. What are some ways you have seen young children cope with their feelings about separation?

PERSONAL REFLECTIONS

Thinking about your personal reactions and experiences will help you better understand and integrate the material in this chapter. Use these questions to interface between you and what you read. Use the pertinent ones to reflect on, write about, or discuss with others.

> Do you remember anything about being a toddler? What?
> How do you respond to negativity? How do you feel about it?
> Are you an adult who says "no" when appropriate? What does saying "no" mean to you?
> What messages did you get as a child about your capabilities? How did those messages affect you?
> Are you an "explorer" today? Do you think the fact that you are or aren't relates more to your early childhood experiences or to your temperament?
> What do you know or remember about your own toilet training (learning)?
> Which is your priority, independence or interdependence? Why? How much does what you answered relate to your culture?
> In a scene on page 38, Joy and Jacob are squabbling over a doll. What were your feelings about how the adult handled the situation?
> What do you think about offering children choices of things they *can* do instead of ordering them to not do something?
> What memories do you have of significant "separations" in your childhood? Are you still experiencing any lingering aftereffects of those memories?
> Could you relate to Janice and Tracy (see p. 33)?

NOTES

1. The stage of autonomy versus shame and doubt was named by Erik Erikson in *Childhood and Society* (New York: Norton, 1963).
2. The words the theorists use to label the process are *seeking autonomy, separating,* and *individuating.* Experts are willing to concede that the behaviors associated with this stage are sometimes "difficult." The words parents commonly use are *stubborn, obstinate,* and sometimes even such loaded terms as *brat* and *spoiled.*
3. It is important to note that not all cultures are object-oriented to the same extent, and that not all regard personal possessions as important.

4. See *Infant/Toddler Caregiving: A Guide to Setting Up Environments* (Sacramento, CA: California State Department of Education, 1990); Jim Greenman, *Caring Spaces, Learning Places: Children's Environments That Work* (Redmond, WA: Exchange Press, Inc. 1988); Louis Torelli, "The Developmentally Designed Group Care Setting: A Supportive Environment for Infants, Toddlers and Caregivers," *Zero to Three* (December 1989).
5. This bit of advice comes from an author with a cultural priority on independence and may not apply to those from cultures who see early independence as a threat to interdependence.

6. This idea of respect as exemplified in diapering and caregiving tasks came to me from Magda Gerber, who discusses it in all her writings, including *Educaring,* a quarterly publication from her group, Resources for Infant Educarers, and also what she calls the RIE Manual: *Resources for Infant Educarers* (Los Angeles, CA: Resources for Infant Educarers, 1991).

7. This is also a culturally specific approach based on the concept of life as a series of choices. When you regard learning to make choices as important, you give children practice when they are young so that as they grow up they have had experience with making choices and living with the consequences. In cultures that don't see life in this light and don't regard learning to make choices as important, giving toddlers choices doesn't make as much sense.

8. J. Bowlby, *Separation: Anxiety and Anger* (New York: Basic Books, 1973).

9. Resources for learning more about helping children with separation include Carolyn Harmon, "In the Beginning: Helping Parents and Children Separate," *Young Children* (May 1996): 72; Kathy Jarvis, ed., *Separation* (Washington, DC: National Association for the Education of Young Children, 1987); Janet Brown McCracken, *So Many Good-byes: Ways to Ease the Transition Between Home and Groups for Young Children* (Washington, DC: National Association for the Education of Young Children, 1986); and the video, *First Moves: Welcoming a Child to a New Caregiving Setting, Child Care Video Magazine* (Sacramento, CA: California State Department of Education, 1988).

10. Described in Eleanor Griffin's book about her program, *Island of Childhood* (New York: Teachers College Press, 1983).

REFERENCES

Balaban, N. *Learning to Say Goodbye: Starting School and Other Early Childhood Separations.* New York: New American Library, 1987.

Bowlby, J. *Attachment,* vol. 1 of *Attachment and Loss.* London: Hogarth, 1969.

———. *Separation: Anxiety and Anger.* New York: Basic Books, 1973.

Caudill, W., and D. W. Plath. "Who Sleeps by Whom? Parent-Child Involvement in Urban Japanese Families." *Psychiatry* 29 (1966): 344–366.

Clark, A. L., ed. *Culture and Childrearing.* Philadelphia: F. A. Davis Company, 1981.

Derman-Sparks, Louise. "The Process of Culturally Sensitive Care." In *Infant/Toddler Caregiving: A Guide to Culturally Sensitive Care,* ed. Peter Mangione. Sacramento, California: Far West Laboratory and California Department of Education, 1995.

"Easing Separation: A Talk with T. Berry Brazelton, M.D." *Scholastic Pre-K Today* (August/September 1991).

Erikson, E. *Childhood and Society.* New York: Norton, 1963.

Gerber, Magda. *Resources for Infant Educarers.* Los Angeles, CA: Resources for Infant Educarers, 1991.

Gonzalez-Mena, Janet, and Dianne Eyer. *Infants, Toddlers and Caregivers.* Mountain View, California: Mayfield Publishing Company, 1997.

Gonzalez-Mena, Janet. *Multicultural Issues in Child Care.* Mountain View, California: Mayfield Publishing Company, 1997.

Gonzalez-Mena, Janet. "Cultural Sensitivity in Routine Caregiving Tasks." In *Infant/Toddler Caregiving: A Guide to Culturally Sensitive Care,* ed. Peter Mangione. Sacramento, California: Far West Laboratory and California Department of Education, 1995.

Gonzalez-Mena, Janet. *Program for Infant Toddler Caregivers: A Guide to Routines.* California Department of Education, Child Development Division, and The Center for Child and Family Studies, Far West Laboratory for Educational Research and Development, 1990.

Gonzalez-Mena, Janet. "Taking a Culturally Sensitive Approach in Infant-Toddler Programs." *Young Children* (January 1992).

Gottschall, Sue. "Understanding and Accepting Separation Feelings." *Young Children* (September 1989): 11–16.

Greenberg, Polly. *Character Development: Encouraging Self-Esteem and Self-Discipline in Infants, Toddlers, and Two-Year-Olds.* Washington, DC: National Association for the Education of Young Children, 1991.

Greenman, Jim, and Anne Stonehouse. *Prime Times: A Handbook for Excellence in Infant and Toddler Programs.* St. Paul: Redleaf, 1996.

Harmon, Carolyn. "In the Beginning: Helping Parents and Children Separate." *Young Children* 51(4) (May 1996): 72.

Honig, Alice Sterling. "Quality Infant/Toddler Caregiving: Are There Magic Recipes?" *Young Children* (May 1989).

Jervis, K., ed. *Separation: Strategies for Helping Two to Four Year Olds.* Washington, DC: National Association for the Education of Young Children, 1987.

Kagan, Jerome. *The Nature of the Child.* New York: Basic Books, Inc., 1984.

Keenan, Marjory. "They Pushed My Buttons: Being Put Up against Myself." *Young Children* 51(6) (September 1996).

Lieberman, A. F. *The Emotional Life of the Toddler.* New York: The Free Press, 1993.

McCracken, J. B. *So Many Good-byes: Ways to Ease the Transition Between Home and Groups for Young Children.* Washington, DC: National Association for the Education of Young Children, 1986.

Mangione, Peter L., ed. *Infant/Toddler Caregiving: A Guide to Culturally Sensitive Care.* California Department of Education and the Far West Laboratory for Educational Research, 1995.

"National Association for the Education of Young Children: Linguistic and Cultural Diversity Position Paper." *Young Children* 51(2) (January, 1996).

Shigaki, Irene. "Child Care Practices in Japan and the United States: How They Reflect Cultural Values in Young Children." *Young Children* 38 (May 1983): 4.

Stonehouse, Anne, ed. *Trusting Toddlers: Programming for One to Three Year Olds in Child Care Centres.* Australian Early Childhood Association, 1988.

———."Toddlerhood." *Early Childhood Diversity Series.* Barrington, IL: Videos Magna Systems, 1995.

Whiting, B., and C. Edwards. *Children of Different Worlds.* Cambridge, MA: Harvard University Press, 1988.

INITIATIVE

CHAPTER **3**

In this chapter you'll discover:

> Whether young children have a conscience
> How guilt helps or harms children and what determines which it does
> When guilt appropriately controls behavior and when it squelches initiative
> Whether children should be encouraged to fantasize
> What children get out of playing
> The difference between a child with high energy and one who is hyperactive
> Whether all shy children are shy for the same reason
> How some children learn to be aggressive
> What can be done about aggression in young children
> Some ways to reduce tension in young children

TEST YOURSELF

Look for the answers to these questions as you read the chapter:

1. Erikson's stages always have a conflict. They are labeled something *versus* something else. What are the two stages mentioned in this chapter?
2. How does conscience work in a four-year-old?
3. What happens when a child grows up with an exaggerated sense of guilt?
4. How do children use fantasy?
5. What do children get out of playing?
6. How does the environment contribute to a sense of initiative in a four-year-old?
7. What are five dimensions of a play environment for children age three to six?
8. How can adults support the development of initiative in young children?
9. What are the five causes of aggression mentioned in this chapter?
10. What are some ways to empower the preschool-age child?

America is built on individual initiative, which has a high value for many in this country. When does initiative begin to develop? What factors facilitate its development? How do adults socialize children to have initiative?

According to Erik Erikson, initiative is the developmental task of the three- to six-year-old. [1] The child of preschool age, whether in a program or at home, is usually bursting with initiative. Sometimes the behavior behind these urges gets the child in trouble, especially around adults who don't understand developmental ages and stages. Take a look at Briana, a four-year-old who shows initiative.

WHAT INITIATIVE LOOKS LIKE IN A FOUR-YEAR-OLD

Briana runs in the door of her childcare center, leaving behind her mother, who is still coming up the steps. She flings a hasty "Hi" at the teacher seated by the door, glances at the interesting "science" display set out to capture the interest of the arriving children, tosses her coat at a hook on the rack by the door, and runs into the classroom with her teacher on her heels.

"Whoa," says her teacher good-naturedly. "Let's go back and do that again." She gently guides Briana back toward her coat on the floor, where her mother waits. Briana kisses her mother good-bye, then starts to take off again. Her teacher grabs her as she goes by. She patiently reminds her again to hang up her coat, which Briana does hastily. Then, released from the teacher's grasp, the lively girl takes off again into the classroom at a fast clip. She heads straight for the art table, which is set up with wood scraps and glue. She elbows her way into a spot at the table, finds an interesting assortment of wood within reach, and begins applying glue to various pieces, which she stacks one on another. She works busily for quite a while, absorbed in what she is doing. After her flighty entrance, the focused attention is quite a contrast. At last she looks up from her project. Turning to a boy sitting next to her, she remarks, "I'm making a house."

He answers, "I'm making a spaceship. See how it launches?" He waves his creation in the air several times. Briana ducks and then turns to the boy on the other side of her. "My mommy's gonna have a baby, and I'm making her a bed," says Briana. The boy ignores her, concentrating on his gluing. Briana goes back to work on her project, concentrating her whole attention on the wood in front of her.

"I need scissors," says Briana to the teacher, who is seated at the end of the table. "I need to put something here," she says, indicating a spot on her wood project. The teacher looks interested and says, "You know where the scissors are."

Briana gets up with her creation in her hand and dances to a nearby table set up with scissors, crayons, various kinds of paper, hole punches, and tape. She sits down at the table and carefully chooses a piece of yellow paper. She painstakingly cuts the paper into an irregular shape, folds it in half, and glues it on a piece of wood sticking out at right angles from the central core of her work. It takes her about ten minutes to complete this task. She gets up to leave, then turns back to the table and picks up the paper scraps she left there and hurriedly glues them on too. Then she grabs a pencil, writes a *B* on the paper, then another *B*, then a third. She then "flies" her sculpture over to the art table and passes it under the nose of her teacher, saying, "I wrote my name on my art."

She gives her teacher a hug. The teacher hugs her back. "I see," is the response. Then, "If you're finished, put your art in your cubby."

Briana flies her sculpture to a row of lockers by the coat rack, pokes it inside one of them, and takes off running to the dramatic play area. She ignores the children already there and pulls out a frilly smock from a box of clothes, puts it on, pats it down the front, looks in the mirror, and turns away satisfied. She flounces over to the little table, sits down, picks up a small empty teacup, and pretends to drink.

"You can't play," announces a girl already seated at the table. Briana ignores her and continues slurping noisily into the cup. Then she gets up and takes the cup and the pot with her to the sink, where she swishes them around in the soapy water she finds there. She stands there for a long time, relishing the sensory experience. "Let's play house," suggests a boy, thrusting his hands into the soapy water.

"Ok," agrees Briana. "I'll be the mom," she says.

"*I'm* the mom," says the girl who told her she couldn't play.

"Then I'll be the *other* mom," says Briana, squeezing a sponge out and carrying it over to wipe off the table. "You're my baby," she announces to the boy, who immediately falls to the ground and clings to her foot, clawing at her legs and making a whimpering sound.

"Stop being bad!" Briana scolds him in a harsh voice. "Bad baby, bad, bad, bad!" she screams angrily. The boy cries louder. A teacher passing by smiles at them and continues on her way.

"Pretend I have to spank you," Briana tells the boy. He responds by crying even louder.

She gives him a couple of dramatic whacks, which only connect lightly. He screams in agony. Then she gives him a third whack, which accidentally lands hard.

"Hey, stop that! You hurt me." The boy jumps to his feet and his voice becomes his own. He looks mad.

A quick look of surprise, a touch of fear, then remorse comes across Briana's face. She hastily retreats to where four children are lying on cushions looking at books. She flings herself to the ground and takes a book out of the hand of the only child within reach.

"Don't!" protests the child, reaching to grab it back. Briana holds up a hand as if to slap her, then slowly lowers it. She turns two pages of the book carefully and deliberately, then tosses it back toward the waiting child, gets up, and leaves.

Seeing the door open, she runs toward it, snatching off the smock and dropping it on the floor as she runs. She stops, looks around to see if a teacher has spotted the smock on the floor. No teacher is around. Briana hesitates. Then she goes back, picks up the smock, and takes it over to the box where she found it. She dumps it in and hurries back to the open door. She pauses in the doorway for a moment, glancing around. Then she shouts "Sarah!" joyfully and runs down the ramp into the play yard.

ANALYZING INITIATIVE IN A FOUR-YEAR-OLD

Let's examine that scene in terms of initiative. Because Briana is now four years old, she is able to use her fertile imagination quite effectively, and she can solve problems. She is also becoming increasingly more competent in her physical abilities and communication skills. Her attention span has lengthened and she can spend long periods in concentrated focus. She's active, curious, and energetic. A phrase that describes Briana is *get-up-and-go*. She's got it!

What does she do with all this energy and newly developed ability? She uses it to make decisions about what she wants to do. She is so interested in everything that you could almost describe her as in an "attack mode." It's not a negative kind of attacking, but a thrusting kind of energy that propels her toward activities and materials that seem to draw her. Briana needs no motivation from her teachers to get involved. She has her own inner motivation.

Much of what Briana undertakes is spontaneous, but that doesn't mean that she is incapable of planning and executing a plan. For example, she had something definite in mind when she asked the teacher for scissors at the wood-gluing table. The teacher, understanding the value of encouraging initiative, responded in a positive way instead of restricting Briana to what was available on the table for that particular project. Briana also had something definite in mind when she scanned the play yard, found Sarah, and headed over to play with her.

It's important to note that some children are as active as Briana but lack her ability to focus attention and concentrate on any one thing. They don't plan out what they want to do, but impulsively rush from one thing to another, destroying things in their path. These children are not displaying the normally high energy that goes with the stage of initiative. Instead they are hyperactive and have what is known as an attention deficit disorder (ADD).

DEVELOPMENTAL CONFLICTS

With all the energy and activity that this stage of initiative brings with it, Briana is bound to run into trouble—at least occasionally. How she handles adult guidance and corrections has to do with her stage of development.

Autonomy versus Shame and Doubt

As a toddler, Briana learned about getting into trouble. In her constant search for autonomy, two-year-old Briana got into trouble all the time. She learned to look for one of her parents or a caregiver when she did something she knew was wrong. She reacted to their reactions by showing shame for what she had done. If they weren't watching, however, and she didn't get caught, she didn't show signs of remorse.

Erikson [2] defines the major task for toddlerhood as working out the conflict between autonomy and shame or doubt. Briana has done that and come out with a sense of what she can do that is not greatly overshadowed by a sense of shame. She has managed a positive resolution for this conflict.

Initiative versus Guilt

Briana has now moved into Erikson's next stage, which signifies a new conflict—that of initiative versus guilt. She's a big girl with a beginning sense of responsibility *and* a budding conscience. She has taken the watchful eye of her parents and teachers inside herself and can now begin to judge her own behavior. She can feel the kind of guilt whose nagging warns her when she's about to violate some behavior standard and gives her a sense of remorse when she carries out the action anyway. Her guilt is useful because it helps keep her in control sometimes. It guides her toward positive and acceptable behavior.

Briana now has an internal government that dictates the ideals and standards of behavior that are requirements of society. Her government is a benevolent one. Her guilt serves as a little warning sign when her parents or teachers aren't present. She needed reminding to hang up her coat, but she knew not to leave the smock lying on the floor. She stopped herself from hitting the child who was trying to grab the book back.

Briana's guilt is not expected to always control her actions. She still needs adults close by to help her control herself when she can't manage. They do this without making too big a fuss, knowing that Briana has the beginning of control within her.

Briana's guilt is only a small sign—a signaling device. It's not a battering ram hitting her over the head or an acid eating away her insides.

Not all children are as fortunate as Briana. Some are governed by an inner tyranny. They judge themselves so harshly in order to enforce the standards of those around them that they lose their initiative. They're afraid to act. Their energy is sapped by the overkill methods of their inner government. [3]

This situation happens when adults go overboard and use heavy-handed punishment, accusations, threats, or torments on young children. Children who grow up in this atmosphere develop an exaggerated sense of guilt, and they torture themselves even for trivial offenses.

What's perhaps most notable about the stage of initiative is the way children work their imaginations and use fantasy.

IMAGINATION AND FANTASY

What's perhaps most notable about the stage of initiative is the way children work their imaginations and how they use fantasy. What was Briana doing when she was playing house? She was doing just what adults do with dreams and daydreams. She was experiencing hopes and fears by dealing with the past symbolically and rehearsing for the future. She tried on roles and feelings in the same way she tried on dress-up clothes. Fantasy play gives Briana practice in interacting with others while in these roles. She also uses fantasy play to express fears and anger and to discover ways to adjust to painful situations.

THE VALUE OF PLAY OF ALL SORTS

Play is an arena where children learn new skills and practice old ones, both physical and social. Through play they challenge themselves to new levels of mastery. They gain competence in all areas of development, increasing language, social skills, and physical skills, for example. [4] Briana not only practices such important skills as eye-hand coordination but also at times uses her whole body to improve balance and coordination.

Play provides for cognitive development, which is tied in with physical and social interactions.

Julie and ADHD

Julie is a four-year-old who has just been diagnosed as having an attention deficit hyperactivity disorder (ADHD). In a way, her mother, Shannon, is glad to get the diagnosis because it confirms her idea that Julie is not "bad." She has been worried about her for a long time. It seems as though Julie was born kicking. She was an irritable baby who cried a lot. She seemed to sleep very little. She was in constant motion and she hasn't slowed down yet. Once she got on her feet, life got even harder, if that was possible. Julie was into everything. She never sat still for a minute. Shannon compared her with a neighbor child, Hannah, and saw that Julie was very different. By age four, Hannah would sit for periods of time looking at books or drawing with crayons. Julie never did that. When she looked at a book, she flipped through at a rapid rate, threw the book down, grabbed another one, threw it down, and was off to something else in the space of less than a minute. In fact none of Julie's activities lasted more than a minute. What was wrong?

Shannon decided to send Julie to preschool, but that didn't help much. Although it gave Shannon a few hours of peace each day, the reports from school kept her in a constant state of tension. Every week it was something new. "What can we do about Julie's behavior?" the teachers kept asking. "She so impulsive that she constantly makes decisions that result in unfortunate consequences. But she doesn't seem to learn from her mistakes. She just keeps jumping into things and making rash decisions." Shannon felt discouraged that they called her in for her ideas and opinions. Why didn't they know how to handle Julie? They were the trained experts!

When the school called a meeting and the teachers and Shannon sat down and did some brainstorming, things improved. They all shared ideas and information about what worked best at home and what worked best at school for Julie. One of the problems was that preschool was so stimulating. There was just so much to do that Julie was overwhelmed with the number of choices. She ended up constantly running around and not doing anything. Also, the room tended to be noisy and sometimes a little chaotic when all the children were inside. Julie reacted to the high energy level of the classroom by losing what little control she had.

At home two things captured her attention: television, sometimes, and video games, almost always.

When the director of the preschool finally suggested that testing Julie might be in order, Shannon felt relieved. When she got the results, she felt even more relieved. However, then she was faced with the question of whether or not to medicate Julie. That's where she is right now. She has joined a parent support group and is discussing the decision of whether or not to go for medication.

Play also provides for cognitive development, which is tied in with physical and social interactions in the preschool years as children are constructing a view of the world and discovering concepts. There's nothing passive about play—even if the body is passive for a time, the mind is busy working.

Children at play are active explorers of the environment as they create their own experience and grow to understand it. In this way they participate in their own development.

Through play, children work at problem solving, which involves mental, physical, and social skills. While playing, they can try on pretend solutions and experience how they work. If they make mistakes, those mistakes don't hurt them as they would in real life. They can reverse power roles and be the adult for a change, telling other children what to do. They can even tell adults what to do, if the adults are willing to play along.

Play enables children to sort through conflicts and deal with anxieties and fears in an active, powerful way. Play provides a safety valve for feelings. Children can say or do things while pretending that they can't do in reality.

Play makes children feel powerful and gives them a sense of control as they create worlds and manipulate them. Watch children playing with blocks, or dolls and action figures, or even in the sandbox. Think about how they create the worlds they play in. What power!

Children also get a sense of power by facing something difficult and conquering it, like finding a place for a puzzle piece that just won't fit anywhere or climbing higher on the jungle gym than they've ever climbed before. Think back to your own childhood. Think of a time when you were challenged in play. What was your feeling as you overcame obstacles (including perhaps your own fear) and met the challenge?

HOW THE ENVIRONMENT CONTRIBUTES TO A SENSE OF INITIATIVE

The environment reflects whether the adults in charge of it regard developing a sense of initiative to be of value or not. [5] If initiative is a value, then the environment in which children spend most of their time will be set up to give them a range of options so they can choose how to spend that time. Not only will there be choices of developmentally appropriate activities, toys, and materials, but they will be enticingly arranged to attract attention and draw children to them.

Not all adults see giving children choices as valuable. Some people expect children to adapt to what is and to entertain themselves in the environment of adults, rather than selecting from a number of options that have been provided for them. They disagree with the notion of a child-oriented environment isolated from the real world of adults. According to Jayanthi Mistry, some adults do not believe in creating learning situations to teach their children; they put their children in adult-oriented environments and expect them to learn by observation, not from playing in an environment specially set up for them. [6]

If initiative is a value, then the environment in which children spend most of their time will be set up to give them a range of options so that they can choose how to spend that time.

"DIMENSIONS" OF PLAY ENVIRONMENTS

Elizabeth Jones and Elizabeth Prescott [7] at Pacific Oaks College in Pasadena, California, have looked at children's play environments in terms of what they call "dimensions." To create an optimum environment for the kind of play that enhances initiative, Jones and Prescott advocate a balance of these dimensions: *soft/hard, open/closed, intrusion/exclusion, high mobility/low mobility, simple/complex.*

Balancing the *soft/hard* dimension means that the environment is both responsive and resistant. Softness in play environments comes from things like rugs, stuffed animals, cozy furniture, grass, sand, play dough, water, soft balls, pads, and laps, to name a few. Hardness comes in the form of vinyl floors, plastic and wooden toys and furniture, and concrete.

The *open/closed* dimension has to do with choices. Low open shelves displaying toys to choose from are an example of openness. Some closed storage is also appropriate, so that the number of choices are manageable. Closed storage also gives a sense of order and avoids a cluttered feeling. Balance between open and closed is important.

The open/closed dimension also has to do with whether there is one right way to use a toy or material (like a puzzle, a form board, or graduated stacking rings) or whether it encourages all kinds of exploration. A doll, finger paint, and play dough are open; so is water play. Children need both open and closed toys, materials, and equipment.

The environment should provide for both optimum *intrusion* and optimum *exclusion* or *seclusion*. Desirable intrusion comes as the children have access to the greater world beyond their play space through, for example, windows that allow them to see what is happening outside but protect them from dangers and noise. Desirable intrusion also occurs as visitors come into the play environment.

Seclusion should be provided so children can get away by themselves. Think of the hideaways you had as a young child. Given a little freedom, children will find these kinds of places for themselves; however, in a childcare center or home, they sometimes need to be provided. Lofts, large cardboard boxes, and tables covered with sheets provide semi-enclosed private spaces in which children can make "nests" in order to hide from the world.

A balanced play environment provides for both *high-mobility* and *low-mobility* activities. Children need quiet and still occupations as well as opportunities to move around freely and engage in vigorous movement.

We all know that young children can be satisfied with the simplest things. A baby can be fascinated with something that an adult wouldn't give more to than a glance. This fact relates to the *simple/complex* dimension. As children grow older, they need complexity, which they often provide for themselves by combining simple toys with other materials. Watch a child who finds sand, water, and utensils conveniently close to each other. The park designers may never have thought of how that drinking fountain close to the sandbox would be used, but the four-year-old who finds an empty soda can is almost certain to think of using it to carry water to the sand. Complexity presents increased possibilities for action. Preschool teachers know this, so they put a dripping hose in the sandbox on warm days, and give the children scoops, buckets, cups, spoons, and a variety of other implements to use. They know that attention span lengthens when children find or create complexity in the environment. The more complex a material or toy (or combination of materials and toys), the more interesting it is. Blocks are fun. Blocks with small figures and wheel toys are even more fun!

HOW ADULTS CONTRIBUTE TO CHILDREN'S INITIATIVE

Adults contribute to the development of children's sense of initiative in several ways. They are responsible for setting up the environments for children's play. As just stated, the kind of environment they set up determines to some extent whether or not initiative is a value. Adults are the ones who must guide and control children's behavior in these environments. How they do that also contributes to a sense of initiative. Discipline methods that encourage children to continue to explore, to try things out, and to solve problems contribute to their growing initiative. Methods that squelch children's interest, inhibit their behavior, and make them afraid to try things because they might make a mistake take away their confidence in themselves and work against bringing out each child's own initiative. In addition, adults encourage initiative in children by modeling it themselves. (Chapter 7 examines this subject at length.)

THE SHY CHILD

Some children don't show a lot of initiative. They seem to lack get-up-and-go. They may be labeled *shy,* or perhaps they are looked at as withdrawn.

Let's look at one of these children:

> Molly has always been the quietest child in the preschool she attends. She hangs out on the fringes of things and seldom talks or even smiles. When someone talks to her, she lowers her eyes and stares at her shoes. She follows the routine of the program, but never really joins in with anything that is going on. She's so quiet that sometimes she's almost invisible.

What could be going on with Molly?

Some children are born extra cautious. This trait may even be in their genes. They don't enjoy putting themselves out in the world, taking risks, trying new things. Sometimes this trait doesn't really hinder them, because it's more a matter of timing than a deficiency. Some children are observers; they learn a good deal by watching for long periods before they try something themselves. When they do try something, they make rapid progress because of their careful observations. They may be thought of as being slow to warm up. Other children jump in with both feet without giving a thought to the consequences. If these more-impulsive children are successful in their endeavors, they may be valued for their speed and compared with children like Molly. (*Bright* and *quick* are sometimes thought to be synonymous with *intelligent.*) Thus, Molly's slow, cautious way of doing things may be undervalued, both in the family and in the school setting. It may look as though she lacks initiative when indeed it's more a matter of timing than initiative. And maybe it's even an unfamiliar environment that slows her down. Molly at home with a sibling or a playmate may be much more secure and outgoing, and not look so shy and cautious. Shyness and caution are sometimes situational.

The teachers at Molly's school have discovered that pushing her doesn't do any good. She's very resistant to joining an activity until she decides on her own to do so. She has the ability to absorb by watching—far more ability than any of her teachers, who think she must be bored, because they are projecting their own needs on to her. She isn't bored. In fact, she is getting much more out of preschool than anyone realizes; but she's doing it in her own way. The teachers have decided to be patient with her and to respect her style. They also, when they can, arrange for her to be in smaller groups and play alone with one or two children rather than always urging her to join into large-group activities.

The teachers have been rewarded to discover that this quiet, cautious child has grown into something of a leader in the class. The other children are drawn to Molly and are influenced by her. In fact, the day doesn't truly begin until Molly arrives. The teachers were really surprised when they discovered that Molly's quiet presence now influences the activities in the classroom.

Factors other than those that influence Molly may be at work on another child who exhibits the same behavior. Take Brandi, for example:

Brandi is shy and cautious for entirely different reasons—she has a history of abuse and attachment issues. As a result, she has a great deal of trouble separating from her foster-mother, who delivers her to school. She cries loudly and must be peeled off, so that the foster-mother, who has other children to deliver to another school, can leave. Once Brandi quits crying, she goes into mourning. She stands by the art table with one finger in her mouth and her eyes staring vacantly. The teachers have decided that she isn't even really "there" most of the time. She stares into space. She sits in circle time silently. She doesn't seem to have learned a single song (compared with Molly, who never sings at school, but at home can go through every word of every verse, complete with hand movements). Brandi is withdrawn, and it isn't just that she has a slower pace than most children. She has a problem. In fact, this child might well have been born quick, lively, and a willing risk-taker, but her life circumstances have beaten her into the child she is now— one who needs more help than her teachers alone can give her. Under ideal circumstances, Brandi's teachers, foster-parents, and biological family are working with social workers and therapists to help her family get back together, help her resolve her attachment issues, and heal the raw scars of her abuse. If all goes well and everyone cooperates, Brandi will get her life back together and her spark will come back. She'll be the child she really is rather than the child she has become.

The vital difference between Molly and Brandi is that Molly is the child she is and Brandi is not—she's been damaged.

A LOOK AT AGGRESSION

Let's examine the subject of aggression in the preschool-age child—where it comes from and what to do about it.

We'll start with Cory. He's a four-year-old who attends an all-day preschool in which he is one of a group of thirty children. He gives his teachers a lot of trouble because he seems always to be hurting someone. Someone is constantly having to deal with the aftermath of his aggressive behavior. What's going on with Cory?

Causes of Aggression

It's not easy to say what's going on with Cory. There are many possible reasons for his aggressive behavior—some simple and fairly easy to solve, and some much more complex. It could be simple—Cory has just not learned any other way to behave. In that case he needs to be taught. Or it could be that Cory was rewarded for this behavior in the past, and is continuing to be rewarded for it, so he continues his aggressive behavior. It could also be that Cory's behavior is the result of bottled-up emotions. Maybe something is going on at home and he's feeling very upset by it. He's letting off steam at school. His behavior might even stem from a physical source—either his own body chemistry or influences of the environment interacting with his physical makeup. Or his aggression can come from an extreme defensiveness. (The following section explores these sources of aggression more closely.)

Extreme Defensiveness

According to Selma Fraiberg in her classic book, *The Magic Years*, [8] some children imagine danger everywhere and interpret every little action of playmates as threatening to themselves. They are defensive to an extreme. Out of their fear, they attack first, rather than waiting to be attacked and then striking back. They need help to change their perspective and come to see the world as a nonthreatening place. Their world view may be due to attachment or abuse issues, in which case those are the areas in which they need help. That help may need to come from a trained therapist rather than a lay person, though teachers may carry out whatever program the therapist suggests. All by themselves, the teachers probably can't solve the problem of Cory's aggression if that problem comes from damage inflicted on him.

Physical Influences on Aggression

Teachers *can* work on the problem of physical influences on aggression. For example, Cory's diet may be terrible. Perhaps some parent education is in order. Careful observation can determine whether low blood sugar is influencing his behavior. Is he particularly aggressive when he's hungry? Steps can be taken to remedy that situation, both with a change of diet and with increased high-protein snacks. If physical problems are suspected, a visit to the doctor is in order.

It's easy to see how environment can influence behavior. If Cory is part of a group of thirty children and they spend much time together in one classroom, he may well be overstimulated, which can easily result in a lack of control on his part. Crowding is a clear cause of aggression in animals. I think we, as a society, try to ignore this problem in people because crowding is a part of our daily lives and we just expect children to adjust to it.

Other environmental influences can be heat, lighting, and environmental pollution. Even weather can make a difference. If you've ever been with a group of children on a windy day, you know how it can affect their behavior.

Aggression as the Result of Bottled-Up Feelings

Some children react to tension with aggression. Their feelings are bottled up inside them, and even a little incident can "uncork" them. What "pours out" is more than the provoking incident calls for. That's a clue to tension as a cause of aggression. Any little frustration can cause "the top to blow off the bottle." When tension is behind the aggression, it is best to work on the source of the tension. However, that may be a job for a social worker and a therapist. If you're Cory's teacher, for example, you don't have the opportunity to work on his home tensions and you're not a trained therapist. What you *can* do is reduce frustration for him at school. You can also give him outlets for his angry feelings. Some examples of outlets are:

1. Vigorous physical activity can serve as an outlet—for example, running, jumping, and climbing.
2. Aggressive activities are also beneficial—for example, pounding punching bags, digging in the dirt, hammering nails, and even tearing paper.
3. Soothing sensory activities can help calm the aggressive child—activities like water play, clay work, and finger paint. Cornstarch and water available as a paste to play in is a wonderfully soothing sensory activity.
4. Art and music activities also serve as outlets for emotional expression. Many children paint picture after picture, covering every inch of the easel paper with paint. From the looks on their faces, you can tell that they are finding the activity soothing.

Learned Aggression

Children can learn aggression from watching others get what they want through aggressive means. They can also learn it from firsthand experience.

For example, a child wants a toy. She grabs it from another child, and pushes him when he fights back. She has the toy—she gets her reward. Or, if adult attention is the reward she's looking for, she gets it when the adult marches across the room, grabs the toy out of her hand, and holds her arm tight while squatting down to look her in the eye and give her a good long scolding. She gets even more when she is marched over to apologize. Her final rewards come when placed in a time-out chair and brought back every time she gets up. She has the adult's full attention—including eye contact, touch, and a long stream of words. She can get the adult to notice her even from clear across the room simply by her behavior. If she still wants more reward, all she has to do is push one of the adult's buttons. Spitting at her will probably do it. A "bad word" will usually do it too.

If this child has learned this way of getting attention, the only solution is to give her the attention she needs in other ways and to make her "unlearn" the ingrained behaviors. Behavior modification is the answer. The adult must unlink the behavior and the reward by withdrawing attention rather than pouring it on. This is not easy to do while keeping everyone safe. Sometimes it is a matter of providing physical control while giving the least attention possible. Other times just ignoring the behavior will eventually make it go away. However, if this is a long-time pattern, it will probably get worse before it gets better, until the child learns that the attention she so desperately needs will come, but linked to a different kind of behavior.

The problem is that most adults who have to deal with this kind of aggression in a child are sorely tempted to turn to punishment; they want to hurt the child either physically or emotionally. What they may not realize is that hurting children doesn't work. You don't make a child less aggressive by hurting her—you make her more aggressive. [9]

Power may be behind the child's need for aggression. Power issues are never solved by being overpowered, which is the message behind punishment.

TEACHING YOUNG CHILDREN PROBLEM-SOLVING SKILLS

The roots of violence start in the first years of life. You can spot children in preschool who are at risk for becoming violent teens. They are the four-year-olds who solve all their social problems physically. If they want a truck, they grab it, then sock the little kid who had it first. If accidentally bumped, they shove the offender back harder.

Of course, all children who grab, hit, and shove won't become violent teens. After all, this is normal behavior for young children. Some will outgrow it, but others won't. Instead they will develop deeply ingrained ways of approaching problems, which can lead directly from preschool aggression to teenage violence.

Four weakness in problem-solving skills are exhibited by teenage offenders:

1. They make assumptions about a situation and neglect to get further information.
2. They seldom give anyone the benefit of the doubt, but see everyone as a potential adversary. They think people are "out to get them."
3. They have a narrow vision of alternative solutions but rely mainly on violence.
4. They fail to consider consequences when they lash out.

Adults can help young children develop problem-solving skills before the weakness becomes ingrained. They can help children clarify situations, consider consequences, and explore alternatives to aggression.

In order to help, the adult must be on the spot when difficulties arise between children. It's important to intervene **before** the action gets physical. For example, as the four-year-old grabs for the truck in the other child's hands, the adult can stop him and say, "You really want the truck. I wonder what you can do besides grabbing it." If the child's response shows he can't think of anything but grabbing, the adult can list some other ideas.

It's important that adults not be critical or judgmental when they intervene. This approach is about talking it through, not giving lectures on being nice. Tone of voice and attitude are all important as the adult guides the talking. The goal is for the children to begin to see the other's perspective and consider alternative solutions.

Four qualities are important when helping children talk to each other in a conflict situation:

1. Firmness should come through—"I won't let you grab or hurt."

2. Empathy also should come through—"I know how much you want that truck."

3. A problem-solving attitude rather than a power play must be part of the exchange—"He might give it to you if you ask him."

4. Persistence is critical—"Well, asking didn't work, I wonder what else you could try."

The objective is not to solve the problem in a particular way for the child, but to help him discover his own alternatives to violence.

Adults often short-circuit this kind of learning by putting children in time-out. Or they solve the problem themselves: "He had it first, give it back to him." "If you're going to fight over that toy, you can't play with it." Those adult actions don't teach the problem-solving skills so necessary for the future.

Skillful intervention makes a difference. We can teach children nonviolence in the preschool years. Of course, teaching alone won't eliminate violence. Other factors come into play. If the child sees violence at home, on the streets or on TV, the modeling effect comes in. Or if the child is a victim of abuse, the likelihood of his becoming a perpetrator is increased.

There is no one solution. If we are to create a peaceful world to live in, we must take a many-pronged approach. But a good prong to start with is to help children learn effective nonviolent problem solving in the early years.

EMPOWERING THE PRESCHOOL-AGE CHILD

Think of a time you felt powerful as a child. Avoid focusing on those times when you were overpowering someone; [10] concentrate instead on personal power that gave you the feeling of being able to be yourself and of having some effect on the world or the people in it.

When I ask students to give examples of times they felt powerful as a child, they come up with a variety of situations in which they demonstrate effectiveness. Sometimes the situation has to do with carrying out some responsibility; some remember a time when they were particularly competent at something; others remember a moment of strength or courage—particularly in relationship to being challenged and conquering their fear. Some felt powerful because of their affiliations—the support people in their lives. Some people got a sense of their own power simply from being able to make choices—even when the consequences weren't what they expected.

One way that children gain a feeling of power is by "dressing up" and trying on powerful roles. They do this by itself or in conjunction with creating their own world and then playing. That puts them in the role of creator—a very powerful position indeed.

Even something as simple as physically changing perspective makes children feel powerful. One young woman remembered spending time as a child squatting on the top of the refrigerator, looking down from her vantage point at the world and the people beneath her. Another had a secret hideout on the garage roof, under the shelter of a tall spreading tree.

One less-than-desirable way that children gain power is by misbehaving and making adults angry. Only when you watch a scene of a little child sending an adult into a frenzy do you realize what a feeling of power the child must get from this reaction. It's a little like being the person who pushes the button that sends a rocket into space. Wow!

Sometimes a child in a preschool situation will cause a good deal of trouble. This child manages to affect everyone around him. It gets so that everyone breathes a sigh of relief on the days he is absent because things are so different. Children who behave like this are often so needy for power that they get it in the only way they know how—by making a big impact on the environment, including the people in it.

If you recognize power as a legitimate need, it seems reasonable to find ways to empower children so that they won't need to manipulate or disrupt to feel a sense of their own power. The following are some ways that adults can empower children:

- Teach children effective language and how to use it. Even very young children can learn to hold up a hand and firmly say "Stop!" to someone threatening them. They won't need to hit or shove once they learn to use the power of words. They can learn to express feelings. [11] They can learn to argue their point. They can become effective language-users. (More information on this subject is given in chapter 8.)

- Give children the support they need while they are coming to feel their personal power. Don't let them continually be victimized until their personal power becomes so trampled that it threatens to disappear from sight altogether. Use your personal power *for* them so they can come to use their own eventually. Don't rescue them. Instead, teach them ways to protect themselves—with your support at first; later they can do it without your support.

- Teach them problem-solving skills (see chapter 9).

- Help children tune in on their uniqueness [12] and appreciate their differences. Help each child become more fully who he or she really is rather than trying to cast them into some preset mold.

We can't leave the preschool-age child without a discussion of early learning. The scene with Briana showed a developmentally appropriate preschool setting with activities and approaches that encouraged initiative. Unfortunately, everyone doesn't understand the value of such a program. Many well-meaning adults take the position that academics rather than play should be the focus of the preschool curriculum. They base their view on the facts that the early years are important ones and that most young children are equipped with a good memory and a will-

*Children gain feelings of
power by trying on powerful
roles.*

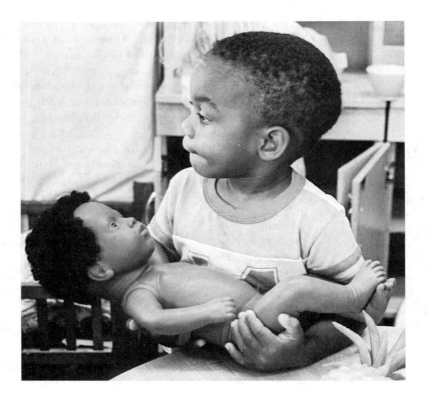

ingness to please. A response to this view is: Just because children *can* do some-thing doesn't mean that they *ought* to. [13]

When children are pushed to engage in rote learning or to perform for adults, their initiative can be squashed. Their need to please the powerful others in their lives conflicts with their own inner motivation. The need to please often wins out and children take to heart the message that adult-directed learning is more valu-able than child-directed activity. [14]

SUMMARY

This chapter focused on the preschool-age child, who, according to Erik Erikson, has the task of developing a sense of initiative and grappling with feelings of guilt when faced with social restrictions. We examined how adults provide for initiative in children by setting up an appropriate environment and by their own actions. We also looked at shy and aggressive children and explored the roots of these behaviors, as well as ways to respond to them. We ended with an examination of personal power and how to encourage it in children.

The next chapter continues with the subject of personal power and looks at it from a slightly different vantage point, under the label of *self-esteem*.

FOR DISCUSSION

1. What do you think Briana's racial or ethnic background is? What makes you think what you think?

2. In the scene with Briana, she pretends to spank a boy. If you were the teacher, how would you know that it was just "pretend"? Would you stop that behavior?

3. How would you describe a child who had a high level of initiative but was different from Briana?

4. What is the difference between a high energy child and a child with attention deficit disorder (ADD) who is also hyperactive (ADHD)?

5. How do you react to the idea of an "internal government"? Do you believe it is better for children to always have someone in authority watching them and taking charge of their behavior?

6. The chapter says that children "create the worlds they play in." What does that mean?

7. Is a sense of initiative a European-American value or do other cultures in this country also see initiative as something to nurture in children?

8. Analyze the environment you're in right now in terms of the five dimensions named by Elizabeth Jones and Elizabeth Prescott. Is it an appropriate environment for 3- to 6-year-old children to play in?

9. What are some adult discipline methods that squelch initiative?

10. What is the difference between Molly's shyness and Brandi's?

11. What are some physical influences on aggression?

12. What are some ways to reduce tension in four-year-olds?

13. How do children learn to be aggressive?

14. The book states: "You don't' make a child less aggressive by hurting her—you make her more aggressive." Do you agree with that statement?

15. This chapter looked at the importance of play as the center of preschool curriculum. However, some adults take the position that academics rather than play should be what young children do during their preschool day. What is your experience and opinion?

PERSONAL REFLECTIONS

Thinking about your personal reactions and experiences will help you better understand and integrate the material in this chapter. Use these questions to interface between you and what you read. Use the pertinent ones to reflect on, write about, or discuss with others.

> Do you remember a time during your childhood when you showed some initiative? How much were you like or unlike a four-year-old?

> What did you think of Briana's behaviors?

> What did you think of the teacher's behaviors?

> How do you use fantasy? How much are you like or unlike a four-year-old?

> Think back to a time during your childhood when you were playing. Relive that experience. What benefits did you derive from what you were doing?

> Can you remember an early play experience in which you were challenged? Did you gain some benefits from that experience?

> The chapter says that children learn through playing. It puts much importance on play. Do you agree that playing is so important for children's learning? What other ways do they learn?

> How do you feel about mud, sand, water, finger paint, and other messy activities that are sometimes found in preschools and considered valuable by some teachers?

> What is your experience with shy people? Are you one? How do you feel about shyness?

> What are some situations that trigger aggressiveness in you?

> What are some outlets you have for reducing tension?

> Can you remember a time during your childhood when you felt powerful?

NOTES

1. Erik Erikson, *Childhood and Society* (New York: Norton, 1963).
2. *Ibid.*
3. Selma H. Fraiberg, *The Magic Years* (New York: Charles Scribner's Sons, 1959), 248–49.
4. Judith Van Hoorn, Patricia Nourot, Barbara Scales, and Keith Alward, *Play at the Center of the Curriculum* (Upper Saddle River, NJ: Merrill/Prentice Hall, 1993).
5. Individual initiative, like independence, is not a universal priority. In some cultures, individual initiative is less important than going along with the group spirit.
6. Jayanthi Mistry, "Culture and Learning in Infancy: Implications for Caregiving," in *Infant/Toddler Caregiving: A guide to Culturally Sensitive Care*, ed. Peter L. Mangione (California Department of Education and the Far West Laboratory for Educational Research, 1995).
7. Elizabeth Jones and Elizabeth Prescott, *Dimensions of Teaching-Learning Environments*, vol. 2 of *Focus on Day Care* (Pasadena, CA: Pacific Oaks, l978).
8. Selma H. Fraiberg, *The Magic Years* (New York: Charles Scribner's Sons, 1959), 21–2.
9. Barclay Martin reviewed twenty-seven studies on the effects of harsh punishment and concluded that children were likely to store up frustration from being punished and vent it later, using the violence that was used on them. Barclay Martin, "Parent-Child Relations," in *Review of Child Development Research*, vol. 4, ed. Frances Degen Horowitz (Chicago: University of Chicago Press, 1975).
10. *Over*powering children often leads straight to power struggles, which are the antithesis of *em*powering children. Power struggles are to be avoided rather than encouraged if you are working on empowerment.
11. Some cultures have a different view of teaching children to express their feelings. The goal is group peace and harmony over individual expression of feelings. It is important to recognize this difference when working with children who come from these cultures. How

would you know? Ask the parents' opinions about personal expression of feelings.

12. Not all cultures see uniqueness and individuality as a value. Some emphasize downplaying any characteristics that make one stand apart from the group.

13. I've heard Lilian Katz, professor at the University of Illinois, make this statement a number of times.

14. Polly Greenberg, "Why Not Academic Preschool?" *Young Children* (January 1990).

REFERENCES

Bergen, Doris, ed. *Play as a Medium for Learning and Development.* Portsmouth, NH: Heinemann, 1988.

Berk, Laura E. "Vygotsky's Theory: The Importance of Make-Believe Play. *Young Children* (November 1994) 30–39.

Cajete, Gregory. *Look to the Mountain: An Ecology of Indigenous Education.* Durango, Colorado: Kivaki Press, 1994.

Chang, Hedy. *Affirming Children's Roots: Cultural and Linguistic Diversity in Early Care and Education.* San Francisco: California Tomorrow, 1993.

Chang, H. N. L., A. Muckelroy, and D. Pulido-Tobiassen. *Looking In, Looking Out: Redefining Child and Early Education in a Diverse Society.* San Francisco: California Tomorrow, 1996.

G. Chud, and R. Fahlman. *Early Childhood Education for a Multicultural Society: A Handbook for Educators.* Vancouver, BC: Pacific Educational Press, 1990.

Dodge, K. A. "Studying Mechanisms in the Cycle of Violence." In *Violence: Basic and Clinical Science,* eds. C. Thompson and P. Cowas. Oxford: Butterworth-Heinemann, 1994.

Erikson, E. *Childhood and Society.* New York: Norton, 1963.

Fraiberg, S. H. *The Magic Years.* New York: Charles Scribner's Sons, 1959.

Gardner, Howard. *To Open Minds: Chinese Clues to the Dilemma of Contemporary Education.* New York: Basic Books, 1989.

Gonzalez-Mena, Janet. "Do You Have Cultural Tunnel Vision?" *Child Care Information Exchange* (July 1991).

Greenman, Jim. "Living in the Real World: Diversity and Conflict." *Exchange* (October 1989).

Greenberg, Polly. "Why Not Academic Preschool?" *Young Children* (January 1990).

Hale, Janice. "The Transmission of Cultural Values to Young African American Children." *Young Children* 46(6) (September 1991): 7–15.

Jones, Elizabeth. "The Play's the Thing: Styles of Playfulness." *Child Care Information Exchange* (January/February 1993): 29–31.

Jones, E., and G. Reynolds. *The Play's the Thing: Teachers' Roles in Children's Play.* New York: Teachers College Press, 1992.

Kagan, Jerome. *The Nature of the Child.* New York: Basic Books, Inc., 1984.

Lubeck, Sally. *The Sandbox Society: Early Education in Black and White America.* Philadelphia: The Falmer Press, 1985.

Martin, B. "Parent-Child Relations." In *Review of Child Development Research,* vol. 4, ed. Frances Degen Horowitz. Chicago: University of Chicago Press, 1975.

Mistry, Jayanthi. "Culture and Learning in Infancy: Implications for Caregivng." In *Infant/Toddler Caregiving: A guide to Culturally Sensitive Care,* ed. Peter L. Mangione. California Department of Education and the Far West Laboratory for Educational Research, 1995.

Piccigallo, Philip R. "Preschool: Head Start or Hard Push?" *Social Policy* (Fall 1988).

Van Hoorn, J., P. Nourot, B. Scales, and K. Alward. *Play at the Center of the Curriculum.* Upper Saddle River/NJ: Merrill/Prentice Hall, 1993.

Weiss, B., K. Dodge, J. Bates, and G. Pettit. "Some Consequences of Early Harsh Discipline: Child Aggression and a Maladaptive Social Information Processing Style." *Child Development* 63 (1992): 1236–50.

Zeece, Pauline Davey, and Susan K. Graul. "Learning to Play: Playing to Learn." *Day Care and Early Education* (Fall 1990).

Zimbardo, P. *The Shy Child.* Garden City, NY: Dolphin, 1982.

SELF-ESTEEM

CHAPTER 4

In this chapter you'll discover:

> Some ways to promote self-esteem
> Changing a negative self-image
> What criticism, labels, and name calling do to self-esteem
> What happens when the media stereotypes in negative ways
> What's wrong with praise
> That always being positive is not a way to raise children's self-esteem
> How "scaffolding" a child's learning works toward the development of self-esteem
> How rescuing children from their problems works against the development of self-esteem
> How cultural differences affect the way parents perceive self-esteem

TEST YOURSELF

Look for the answers to these questions as you read the chapter:

1. What is a definition of self-esteem?
2. What is the difference between self-image, self-concept, and self-esteem?
3. What are four dimensions of self-esteem?
4. What are two determinants of self-esteem?
5. What is a self-fulfilling prophecy?
6. How does the home environment affect the development of self-esteem in children?
7. How does the greater society affect the development of self-esteem in children?
8. What's the difference between encouragement and praise?
9. What is "scaffolding"?
10. How is scaffolding different from rescuing a child who has a problem?
11. Is failure always bad for children?
12. How can adults teach children to "celebrate differences?"
13. What does it mean to "create an antibias environment" for children?

Who am I? That's a question asked over and over throughout each person's lifetime. The first "askings" start nonverbally in infancy, as the child begins to define the boundaries between herself and the rest of the world. She learns where she ends and the world begins. She learns about her separateness. [1] She also learns about her personal power by discovering that her actions have consequences—she cries and someone responds, for example. Self-esteem development continues in toddlerhood and in the preschool years as children learn to observe themselves, which gradually helps them become more and more aware of themselves as separate, individual people. The answer to the question Who am I? reflects our *self-concept*, which is our self-definition. How we *feel* about how we define ourselves reflects *self-esteem*. Much attention is being given nowadays to promoting high self-esteem in children because a link is seen between achievement, behavior, positive growth patterns, and high self-esteem. This chapter looks at the development of self-esteem.

PORTRAIT OF A PERSON WITH HIGH SELF-ESTEEM

What does a person with high self-esteem look like? On the surface, this seems like a fairly simple question to answer. Without much thought it's easy to come up with a portrait that's something like this:

People with high self-esteem have self-confidence that shows in the way they dress, groom themselves, walk, and talk. People with high self-esteem are secure and happy. They're outgoing, energetic, brave, strong, and proud. They're also motivated, successful, independent, and assertive. The list could go on and on. [2]

However, if you think of a specific person who seems to have high self-esteem, the picture changes. That person is not likely to be a walking example of this list of culturally specific ideal traits. Rather, that person is more likely to be herself. And if you compare that person with another one with high self-esteem, they may be very different from each other, because the second person is also likely to be herself.

High-self-esteem people aren't necessarily happy, though we would like to think that happiness comes from boosting self-esteem. Often people who are themselves and feel good about it run into problems when they are in circumstances that challenge their ability to express who they are and have their needs met. A person in a refugee camp may have high self-esteem, but probably won't be too happy. More is said about this later in the chapter, but here let me just point out that part of being who you are has to do with feeling your feelings, which means that you'll have a wide range—not just constant sunshiny happiness.

High-self-esteem people also aren't necessarily talented, good looking, strong, or financially successful. If that were true, ordinary people wouldn't have much of a chance, and disabled people would have even less of a chance. Just look around you and you'll discover that a person's looks, abilities, possessions, or wealth aren't necessarily related to self-esteem. Some of the best-looking people in the world feel inferior. They either think they're not *really* good looking, or they worry that all they have is their looks—which are destined to fade. If they feel significant or powerful based on looks alone, they're in trouble.

Actually, if you scratch the surface of people who seem to have high self-esteem, you'll find that some are covering up perceived inadequacies. [3] People are often the opposite of what they seem. The extremely assertive person may be hiding a shy, scared child underneath. The paragon of virtue may have a core of hidden vices. Judging self-esteem in others isn't easy! There's lots of room for error. People just aren't always what they seem.

So instead of trying to judge the degree of self-esteem in adults, let's look at where it comes from in childhood. Let's start with some definitions.

DEFINITION OF SELF-ESTEEM

What is self-esteem anyway? Self-esteem is a valuing process and results from an ongoing self-appraisal in which traits and abilities are acknowledged and evaluated. Self-esteem is made up of self-image—the pictures we carry of ourselves—and self-concept—the ideas we have about ourselves.

High self-esteem comes when, after a realistic appraisal of pluses and minuses, a person decides that she has more positive attributes than negative ones. High self-esteem means that a person feels good about herself—she holds herself in esteem. Overall, she likes herself, warts and all. Low self-esteem means that a person lacks a global sense of self-worth.

This concept of self-esteem or self-worth is entirely tied to culture. For example, in a culture that values independence, self-assurance, self-help, competence, and being "special," self-esteem rises when the individual is proud to perceive herself as being in possession of those traits. However, the proud, independent, self-assured individual who stands out in a crowd in some cultures will be given strong messages about the importance of fitting in, belonging, and putting others first. Culture makes a difference in one's view of what comprises self-esteem. In some cultures the very notion of holding oneself in esteem is abhorrent, and pride is a no-no. Instead, humility and humbleness are valued. People in those cultures find other ways of feeling worthy. Conflicting cultural messages can tear down self-esteem. Although some people can rise above cultural messages and continue to feel good about themselves, other can't. Self-esteem isn't just deciding that you're great just as you are and giving that message to the world.

Children sometimes have an exaggerated sense of their own power that doesn't reflect self-esteem at all, but rather their stage of cognitive development. Take, for example, the three-year-old who feels angry about having been dethroned by a baby sister. He makes ugly wishes concerning the baby. Then the baby gets sick—or worse, *dies*—and the three-year-old thinks he caused the tragedy by willing it. The child's misconceptions aren't caused by the degree of his self-esteem, but rather by thinking himself capable of willing things to happen. He lacks logic at this age.

Self-perception must relate to reality to create true self-esteem. Exaggerated misperceptions that aren't stage-related as in the example above are delusions. A picture that appeared on the cover of *Newsweek* [4] depicts this problem: A pitiful-looking man stands in front of the mirror and the reflection he sees is the opposite of what he is. The mirror shows a strong, well-built, handsome, self-assured man, whom we can assume to be talented and intelligent as well. Nothing in the reflection is the same as the man creating it—nothing relates to reality. That's not self-esteem!

If, in the name of promoting self-esteem, you try to fool a child by painting her a false picture of herself, it won't work. (If it did, it wouldn't be healthy anyway.) Take a child who is miserably aware of her lack of ability, who feels unloved, who has little power to control anything in her life, and is behaving in unacceptable ways. You can't raise her self-esteem by telling her none of what she is experiencing is true. She simply won't believe you. If there is no reality to back up what you're saying, you're wasting your breath. Even if you point out her good traits, if she's focused on what she perceives to be her bad ones, she won't pay attention.

It's harder to change someone's self-esteem than it seems. In fact, only when the person herself decides to change her perceptions will she allow someone else to be effective in helping her. *Building self-esteem involves a collaboration, not a deception.* The goal is to help the child build a sense of self that is both valued and true.

DIMENSIONS OF SELF-ESTEEM

Self-esteem has at least four dimensions: significance, competence, power, and virtue. [5] Your self-esteem depends on what you value, which is likely to be influenced by what your family and culture values for you (which may depend on gender) and where you perceive that you fall in each category. Let's take a look at each of these dimensions in turn.

Significance has to do with a feeling of being loved and cared about, the feeling that you matter to someone. You can't instill this feeling in a child. You can try to influence it with words and deeds, with nurturing and protection, with caring, and with meeting needs, but you can't ensure that the messages you send are the ones the child will receive. A feeling of significance, the feeling that you are important because you are cared about, is a choice the individual makes.

It is vital to understand that children are active participants in the development of their sense of self. No matter what hand fate deals, it's not the events themselves that determine self-esteem—it's how the child reacts to those events. Obviously some children are born into more fortunate circumstances than others, yet there are children who have everything going for them who don't feel good about themselves. Other children are just the opposite. They manage to emerge from a series of traumas with self-esteem intact and, indeed, growing. These children seem to be able to use adverse circumstances to their own advantage. They grow and learn from their experiences and come out stronger than ever. They seem to take the negative and twist it around to have a positive effect.

You can influence *competence* in a child by helping him become increasingly skilled in a number of areas. But whether the child *feels* competent depends on whether he compares himself with someone who is more competent than he is.

It's a decision the child makes, not one that you make, though you can push him toward this decision by making comparisons yourself or demanding perfection. If competence is particularly important to him, he may experience lower self-esteem, even though he is highly competent, simply because he doesn't see himself as competent *enough*. There's a discrepancy between where he thinks he should be (or wants to be) and where he is. He doesn't meet his own standards (which may or may not have come from his family or his culture).

Let's look at *power*, the third dimension of self-esteem. Feeling that you have some control over being who you are, making things happen in the world, having an effect on the people and events in your life, and living your life satisfactorily gives a sense of power. If power is of major importance to you, having a feeling of it can raise your self-esteem. Notice that power is not defined here as having control over other people—it's not a matter of *overpowering*, but power in the pure sense of the word—personal power, which reflects the root meaning of the word—"to be able." Power has to do with effectiveness.

Virtue is the fourth dimension of self-esteem. Being good is important to some people. Their self-esteem relates to how much of a gap there is between how good they perceive themselves to be and how good they want or need to be. Virtue is not a supreme value to everyone.

So suppose that self-esteem depends on two things: the dimensions that are of utmost importance to the individual, and the gap between where this person perceives herself to be and where she wants to (or feels she should) be. Take the housewife who sees herself as good and loved (excels on the scales of virtue and significance), yet values only power and competence, where she sees herself sadly lacking. In this case her self-esteem may be quite low.

The housewife is a contrast to, for example, a monk who values virtue above all and derives his self-esteem from being obedient to his faith. He doesn't care about power, competence, or significance. These are extreme examples, granted, but they make the point. A discrepancy between where you are and where you want to be on the scale(s) most valuable to you is what counts in self-esteem.

Although self-esteem eventually becomes established and relatively stable over time, it's not forever fixed and static. Creating and maintaining self-esteem is a lifelong process—it gets shaped and reshaped. It changes as children develop. It changes when circumstances change. It can even change instantly. The wife who is a competent driver may watch her self-esteem slide down the scale in the area of driving skills when her husband gets in the passenger seat.

Self-esteem brings with it self-confidence, which is a vital trait for development. What a child *believes* he can or cannot do sometimes influences what he *can* or *cannot* do. Children who perceive that they lack competence, for instance, may not try something because they've had bad experiences in the past, or simply because they have no confidence in themselves. What we *believe* influences our behavior greatly. Our beliefs create a self-fulfilling prophecy. What we expect is what we get for no other reason than that we expect it.

Past experience can play a big part in raising or lowering expectations. The research on learned helplessness is eye opening. Dogs who were shocked when they tried to get out of their cages learned to stay in even after the shocks stopped and the cages were left open. They were free to leave, but they didn't perceive it that way. They continued to act on past experience even though the circumstances of the present were different. Their perceptions didn't relate to reality. [6]

Picture this cartoon: A man stands in a cage, gripping bars in both hands with his face pressed up against them. But those two bars are the only ones holding him in the cage—there are no other bars. His perceptions are what are trapping him, not the reality of the situation. Perceptions make up self-esteem. They may be wrong perceptions.

WHERE DOES SELF-ESTEEM COME FROM?

Self-esteem comes along with self-identity from early experiences and continues up through the school years into adolescence and adulthood. Children define themselves partly by looking at the images that they see reflected in the people around them. [7] If they develop close attachments with people who love and value them, the reflection they see is positive and they're likely to have positive feelings about themselves. They decide that they are lovable. If they create an impact on the world—starting as babies when they cry and are responded to in ways that meet their needs—they develop a sense of self-efficacy, which they then include in their self-definition. If they develop a wide variety of competencies that are well received by those around them, they are likely to decide that they are competent. If they learn acceptable ways to behave and are given recognition for their good

Self-esteem comes from early experiences and continues up through the school years into adolescence and adulthood.

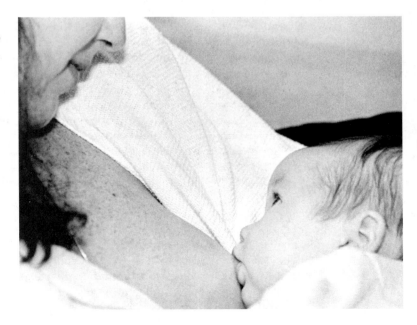

behavior, they are likely to decide that they are virtuous. Put all together, the child who sees more positive reflections of himself is likely to develop a global sense of self-worth—self-esteem.

So it seems as though a child who has someone who cares about him and meets his needs and creates positive reflections will likely develop a healthy sense of self-worth. But what if the outside world gives you a different set of messages because of your color, your gender, your ethnicity, or your physical/mental abilities? What if the reflection you see in the eyes of those outside your home depict you as somehow inferior? What if you go to the movies or watch TV and you see people like you either not depicted at all or depicted in negative ways? What will all that do to your self-esteem?

What if the people and/or institutions you encounter outside your home give you differential treatment and act as if you are inferior? Further, what if those people or institutions create insensitive or even assaultive environments and you find yourself in those environments?

Under these circumstances can the positive messages you get from home counteract the negative ones you get from outside? Maybe. Surely what you get at home will make you stronger and perhaps more able to withstand the negative images that are being thrust on you. But what about children whose self-esteem is already a bit damaged? What happens to them when they enter an insensitive or assaultive environment outside the home? The results can be devastating.

Children define themselves partly by looking at the images that they see reflected in the people around them.

PROMOTING SELF-ESTEEM

This section examines some general ways to promote self-esteem. It also examines some that are specific to changing those negative messages just mentioned to positive ones.

One way to promote self-esteem in children is to work on closing the gap on the four scales representing the dimensions of self-esteem. Be careful about putting expectations on children that are beyond their reach. Help them examine their own expectations and where they came from. Above all, help children to feel lovable, capable, powerful, and good.

Start by getting rid of critical attitudes, labeling, and name calling. Even in the name of socializing a child, *you can't make him feel better about himself by making him feel bad about himself.* That doesn't mean to move right to "LaLa Land," where everything is sweetness and light and nothing connects to reality. Of course children misbehave, make adults angry, and act in less than loving ways. They need guidance and protection. They need honest feedback. But the form in which you guide, protect, and give honest feedback matters a good deal.

Just consider for a moment whether your methods *overpower* children or *empower* them. Do correction methods help children see themselves as good people or bad ones? Are they given confidence in their abilities, or is it torn down by the correction methods? Do they come to see themselves as unloved? Chapter 7 gives many ways of guiding behavior that build self-esteem rather than tearing it down.

Give Honest Feedback and Encouragement, Not Praise

Some adults in the name of self-esteem building vow always to be positive and to praise children at every possible opportunity. They replace honest feedback with constant overblown praise. Praise is no cure for low self-esteem. All it does is create a need for the child to look to the adult for a judgment of everything he does. Children need coaches rather than cheerleaders. [8] If you overdo praise, your words become meaningless. For example, if you say "Great job!" about every little thing, it becomes an empty phrase. It's more effective and less damaging to use encouragement instead of praise. Call attention to children's legitimate successes, but don't butter them up with heavy judgments. Compare past performances with present ones, but not with those of other children—"You picked up more blocks this time than last time" rather than "You're the best block picker upper I've ever seen." Better yet, explain why this behavior is valuable. [9]

Give Children Opportunities to Experience Success

Even more important than just talking is to give children many chances to experience success of all sorts. Challenge them so that when success comes they've worked for it—it didn't just arrive on a platter. Do this by creating a manageable, yet challenging, environment that is developmentally appropriate. [10] Further, provide what's called scaffolding. [11] *Scaffolding* is a process that can be viewed as similar to the temporary structure one puts up to paint a building. In other words, the adult provides the support the child needs, allowing him to problem solve at new levels. The scaffolding helps the child experience success, which encourages the child to challenge himself further, thereby meeting with the possibility of new success. Scaffolding, because it is temporary, can be built for a specific need on each occasion and can easily be remodeled to serve changing needs.

Optimum challenge and risk-taking is the secret to development, to learning, and to skill-building. Scaffolding supports children so they have experiences with positive results when challenged to take a risk. When children encounter a problem, or an obstacle, and are about to get stuck in the problem-solving process, instead of rescuing them, adults can provide help—not heaps of help—the smallest amount necessary. In this way they facilitate the continuation of the problem-solving process. They provide the missing link in the chain that allows children to move forward toward solutions. Thus children's success is eventually their own, not the adult's. Experiencing personal success in the face of obstacles gives children messages about their abilities, about their self-worth. [12]

Look at the difference between helping through scaffolding and helping through rescuing:

Jamie, 4, has rolled off the path and gotten his tricycle stuck in the sand. He's upset and angry as he tries to pedal forward and can't move. He pushes and twists so hard that the tricycle tips over, depositing him on his back in the sand. An adult comes over to his side and squats down, talking calmly about his experience, giving him support, and accepting his feelings. Jamie, calmer now, gets up and rights the bike. He prepares to get back on it when the adult points out how hard it is to ride in the sand and then wonders out loud what Jamie can do to get the trike back on the path. Jamie goes around to the front of the trike and tugs at the handlebars. The trike moves forward a bit. Jamie puts more effort into his work. He's rewarded by getting the bike back over to the path. He continues to tug forward, but the wheel catches on the edge of the cement. "Try lifting it," says the adult, just as Jamie is getting ready to throw a fit and give up. Jamie lifts the wheel up and over, and pulls it forward; the back wheels follow and he experiences success! He gets back on and continues riding down the path. "Hooray," says the adult. Jamie turns around and grins at him.

Contrast that scene with this one:

Jamie lies in the sand, crying. The adult comes up, picks him up, dusts him off, sets him back on his feet on the path, then retrieves the bike and places it beside Jamie. He pats Jamie on the back and tells him how great he is. What did Jamie learn? How does Jamie feel about his ability to solve problems like this one?

Give honest feedback and encouragement.

Rescuing doesn't promote self-esteem.   It's more important to build real skills and remark about them than it is to try to boost self-esteem through empty words and pretending to be excited about nonexistent successes.

While you're thinking about skill-building, don't neglect social skills. They are as important as physical and intellectual ones. When a child doesn't have a clue as to the effect of his or her behaviors on others, help that child come to see what is effective and what is not. Teach the skills the child may lack.

Children Learn from Failure

One of the best feedback devices we have is failure. When we try something and it doesn't work, that's clear feedback. Of course, children need an array of positive experiences every day of their lives. However, in the name of success we sometimes go overboard in protecting children from failure, thus cutting them off from valuable learning experiences.

Travis

Travis is four-years-old and he's big for his age. His size alone commands attention, but what he does with it commands even more. He pushes kids around every chance he gets. He walks with a swagger and with a challenge on his face. "Just try to get the better of me," his expression seems to say. He's also loud and sometimes unruly. What he wants he wants *now* and he lets everybody know it.

One day at staff meeting one of his teachers confessed her discomfort about Travis and his attitude. "I don't like him very much," she said in a quiet voice. "I try, but his behavior just gets in the way of the warm feelings I *want* to have for him. It seems like self-esteem is just oozing out all over him, and I don't like that."

The rest of the staff was silent for a moment, amazed at her confession. Then her co-teacher spoke up. "I don't see Travis as a high-self-esteem child," he said cautiously. "Sure, he acts like he's got all the confidence in the world, but I think he's just making up for what he thinks he lacks."

"What do you mean?" asked the first teacher.

"Well, his bullying, for instance. When kids bully, it's not a mark of high self-esteem. Rather, it's a mark of low self-esteem. Kids who feel good about themselves—who they are and their capabilities—don't have to push other kids around."

"What else makes you think that Travis doesn't feel good about himself?" asked the first teacher. "I always thought that he felt *too* good about himself."

"The way he avoids doing anything that would show he's not as capable as the other kids. I think that because of his size people always expect more out of him than he can manage. It must be hard for him. I know I keep forgetting that he's not as old as he looks. So, if it's a problem for me, it's probably a problem for other people too."

"I've noticed that," acknowledged another teacher. "He puts a lot of energy into avoiding things. But he's so loud about his demands that we pay attention to those and not to the fact that he rarely gets involved in much of anything."

"I wonder if he has picked up my negative feelings," worried the first teacher. "It won't help him much to be around someone who admits she doesn't like him."

"I like him," said her co-teacher. "But he probably doesn't know it because I'm always dealing with his negative behavior. That's when he gets attention from me. I think I'll work on changing that situation."

"I wonder how we can help him have more positive experiences in our program," mused the first teacher out loud. "Maybe we can gently move him toward

The problem with failure is that it often comes accompanied with heavy value judgments, spoken or unspoken. For example, many of us were called "dummy" as children when we made a mistake. It's hard not to pass on that kind of response to children when they make mistakes. However, if children are to learn from mistakes as well as emerge from failure with an intact sense of self-worth, it is important that adults be supportive rather than critical. After all, a mistake is just that. We all make them and we all stand to learn from them.

activities that particularly interest him. I saw him trying to fold a paper airplane yesterday. Maybe I can get him to help me set up a project of paper airplanes for all the kids. That might give him some recognition."

"We could focus more on giving him some social skills, so he can quit bullying," was another suggestion.

"I wonder what would happen if we used the video camera and showed him what he looks like when he bullies," was still another suggestion. "Or maybe that would be too threatening at this point."

"I think what he needs is a friend," came another suggestion. "I've noticed he seems drawn to Paul. Maybe we could encourage that relationship."

"Well," said the first teacher, "I'm glad I brought the subject up. I see Travis differently now, and I'm already beginning to like him better!"

CELEBRATING DIFFERENCES: AN ANTIBIAS APPROACH

How adults react to differences in people affects how children react to differences, which influences self-esteem. Louise Derman-Sparks and her antibias curriculum task force have brought awareness of issues of bias that were hidden from many until recently.

The tendency in early childhood education and mainstream cultural childrearing has been to be blind to both privilege and injustice. The motto of many is that "Children are children," by which they mean differences such as skin color and gender don't matter. (Although the expression "Boys will be boys" dispels the gender-blindness myth). Many people who are "blind" to differences are those who don't carry a number of bruises and scars left by unfortunate remarks and by the biased behavior of those who promote stereotypes and practice unfair treatment. Conscious and unconscious racism, classism, sexism, and ableism are areas of bias still with us in spite of the fact that many assume that the way to equality is to ignore differences.

Instead of disregarding differences, we should celebrate them. Celebrate differences—What does that mean? A loving attempt to do just that occurs regularly as well-meaning adults bring "culture" into children's lives in order to teach them about people who are different from themselves. I remember a Japanese "tea party" put on in the classroom of one of my children. I attended as a parent guest and happened to sit next to a Japanese parent, who was also a guest. She was aghast at what she saw. "There's nothing Japanese about this!" she whispered to me, insulted by the whole proceeding. What had happened was that the teacher, based on what she had read and on her own ideas, had created a strange conglomeration of stereotypes and fantasy, which she believed was promoting cultural knowledge in the children.

Michael Dorris writes about this phenomenon as it occurs with Native-American children who may know nothing about their own heritage other than the mistaken stereotypes they encounter everywhere. Stereotypes of fighting savages come televised year round from sports arenas across the country. Thanksgiving arrives every year, and cute little savages come out of the woodwork and get pinned on the bulletin boards, complete with feathers and tomahawks. Throughout the rest of the year, children are told not to act like "wild Indians" (a stereotype), but to sit quietly "Indian style" (another stereotype) and sing songs that are deeply insulting to Native Americans, such as "Ten Little Indians" (dehumanizing). How can Native-American children get a sense of who they are and of their worth if their culture is so stereotyped, devalued, and misrepresented? [13]

Many mistakes and insults occur in the name of "celebrating differences." What is largely unrecognized or at least little discussed is that differences are connected with privilege and power. Differences carry values. It shouldn't be that way, but it is; and until that fact is recognized, there is little hope for change. That's where the antibias approach comes in. Adults must begin to recognize that value messages, both spoken and unspoken, are constantly sent and received about color, language, gender, and differences in physical abilities. Once they become aware of the messages, they can begin to intercept them and change things. They can stop teaching children to ignore differences, and instead teach them to respond positively and appropriately to differences.

Bias Is Bad for People

Bias is bad for children and it's bad for adults. It's bad for those who are the target of bias. It not only harms self-esteem, but it sucks energy from the developmental process. It hurts to feel inferior. To be disempowered influences your life course.

Bias is also bad for those who are regarded as superior. When you see others as beneath you, you're out of touch with reality. It's dehumanizing to act superior and to enjoy unearned privilege, even when you are not aware of what's happening. [14]

It may seem easier to just pretend we're all alike in the name of equality. It may be easier to say to someone who is a different color than you are, "I don't think of you as different from me." But we're not all alike, and to pretend we are is to ignore the truth. That kind of ignorance can be very insulting. If you are a woman, how would you like it if a man said to you, "I never think of you as female," meaning that remark as a compliment. Personally, I would be shocked if someone looked at me and didn't see me as a female. If you are a man, reverse the situation. Can you imagine yourself without your maleness? What if someone thought it was a compliment to you to remain ignorant of the fact that you are a male. How would you feel?

People want others to respond to who they are—not some blind, misguided version of who they should be. They want to be valued for who they are. For example, we would all be very uncomfortable around those who pretend to be "gender blind," if, indeed, such a thing were possible. But adults pretend to be "color blind" all the time in the name of equity. *Discriminating* on the basis of skin color is immoral. *Recognizing differences* in skin color is not, as long as you don't present one color as better than another.

I want people to respond to who I am—not to some blind, misguided version of their own idea of who I should be. I want to be valued for who I am. I would be very uncomfortable around "gender-blind" people, if, indeed, there is such a thing.

So, how can you teach children to respond positively in the face of differences if they've been taught to be blind to them? How can they respond positively if they've been exposed to biased attitudes and behaviors?

Start by modeling *antibias* behaviors. Become aware that the white able-bodied male is the norm in the society, then try to get beyond that. Acknowledge the existence and experience of others by creating an antibias environment; expose children to pictures, books, and experiences of adults and children both like themselves and unlike themselves.

Point out stereotypes in the media when they occur. For example, remark about that fact that women can be strong, intelligent people capable of doing many things, when a book or a TV program shows weak, helpless women in limited roles.

Make it clear that bias is unacceptable. Children understand the concept of fair and unfair. Bias is definitely not fair. It is only fair that people of all races, religions, cultures, and physical abilities be treated with equal respect. It is only fair that both genders be allowed and indeed encouraged to expand beyond the limits of narrow gender roles. It is not fair to exclude someone from playing because of skin color or gender. Children need to understand that biased behavior is unacceptable.

CULTURAL DIFFERENCES AND SELF-ESTEEM

Who am I? Each of us continues to explore that question throughout our lifetime. The answer we come up with and the value judgment we make about that answer make up our self-esteem.

As children grow they develop an idea of themselves. This idea influences the behavior of the actual self—the one that operates in the world. The actual self in turn influences the self-concept, which continues to influence behavior. Thus the actual self and the self-concept are forever tied together, and the self-esteem grows from the interaction of the two.

Self-esteem is culturally based and depends on the basic concept of what makes up a person. One culture looks at each person as a unique, potentially self-sufficient individual; another de-emphasizes individuality and regards each person as an inseparable part of a greater whole. How parents focus their socialization efforts depends on which view they take.

Parents whose goal is individualism see their baby arriving in the world connected and dependent. The responsibility of the parent then is to help the baby learn that he or she is separate and apart. So those parents concentrate their efforts on autonomy, stressing self-help skills as the baby is ready.

Parents who are more concerned about their children's ability to maintain connections have a different goal. They perceive an independent streak in their baby and see that independence as getting in the way of the close life-long relationship to family that is their goal. So they focus on showing the baby in every way that dependence is a value and relates to connections—the greatest value. They know that some independence is inevitable, but they want to be sure that the baby is forever connected before he discovers autonomy. These parents focus on interdependence instead of independence.

How you build self-esteem in the early years is influenced by your view of the individual. However, realize that both views are valid. They are not mutually exclusive. It isn't an either/or situation. When two people disagree about which is most important—individuality or group embeddedness—it's a matter of *where* they are placing the emphasis and *when* they see independence as an issue. It isn't independence versus interdependence. We all need both to survive. It is a matter of timing. One person may see the importance of *early* independence and its relationship to later getting along in a group. Another may feel that only through subduing early independent urges can the child be truly part of the group, which will *later* lead to his or her developing or finding the *individual* skills, feelings, dreams, and desires that contribute to furthering group goals.

A valid goal of self-esteem is to enable children to stand on their own two feet as well as to stand together, indeed lean on each other. It is important to get and give support and to feel good about it.

Who am I? Each of us continues to explore that question throughout our life time. The answer we come up with, and the value judgment we make about that answer, make up our self-esteem.

A True Story from the Author

When I was a new teacher faced with the job of educating parents, I had great enthusiasm for sharing all that I had learned in my teacher training, plus what I knew from experience. My energy was boundless, matched only by my zeal.

I will never forget trying to explain the concept of self-esteem to Teresa, a Mexican immigrant mother. Teresa kept insisting that there was no such concept in Spanish. I didn't give up. I kept trying to explain it to her. She stood there the whole time with a blank look on her face. She wasn't getting it. Finally she said in complete bewilderment, "*Self-esteem* doesn't make any sense at all. You can't esteem yourself, you can only esteem others."

I've been thinking about that exchange for twenty-five years. She didn't get what I was saying, but I didn't get what she was saying either.

I've become less zealous in my parent education efforts as I've gotten older. I am much more willing to accept parents as they are; and if they want to "get better," I'll help—but only when I know what they perceive their weaknesses are. Mainly I just support them in the good things they are doing. I don't decide where they need to improve, that's their decision. I help parents sort out what isn't working for them rather than tell them what I think and give advice. My motto is, The less advice the better.

But I still try to teach concepts. Self-esteem is one I haven't given up on; however, I've broadened my view of what I mean when I define self-esteem. I include the fact that though the concept fits European-American culture, it probably doesn't fit everybody in the same way.

That's why I am not surprised when my students and I don't agree on what the term *self-esteem* means. For example, a student described a child who thought only of himself, never of others. He had a fierce temper and got out of control when he didn't get his way. He even hit his parents. His parents' efforts to guide his behavior didn't work. This little boy didn't get along with anybody and didn't have any friends either.

The student concluded that the child's problem was his self-esteem; he had too much of it. That isn't the way I see self-esteem. You can't get too much. When you have a good strong sense of self-worth, you are more able to see others as being worthy too. That's the point. Esteem breeds esteem.

Maybe it was just a translation problem with this student. Like Teresa, this student was a Spanish speaker. However, I suspect that it wasn't a simple language difference. I believe our mismatch went deeper than that.

I decided to start with language as the path to understanding. I looked in my husband's huge Spanish-English dictionary. It had 196 entries under *self* in English and only 13 entries in Spanish. The concept of "self" is different in Spanish, and that difference influences the way people feel about the word *self-esteem*.

My experience with some parents, especially those from cultures where interdependence is more important than independence, is that focusing on "self" is a negative thing to do. To them, any word that has *self* connected to it is suspicious. They don't want to raise "self-ish" children. They want to raise children who put others first and think of themselves last.

I didn't understand that when I was trying to teach Teresa about self-esteem. I did understand it when I read my student's self-esteem paper. This latest time I put less effort into trying to teach her my way of looking at self-esteem and more into trying to understand her way.

Values show through misunderstandings. Every day I live I discover new ways of conceiving reality. The older I get the less I try to change people in general and parents in particular, and the more I try to tune in on their realities.

SUMMARY

We all ask ourselves the question "Who am I?" periodically, beginning in infancy when we must learn to distinguish ourselves from the environment around us. As we answer that question, we become more and more aware of ourselves as individuals. We learn about our personal power.

The answer to "Who am I?" reflects our *idea* of ourselves—our *self-concept.* How we *see* ourselves reflects our *self-image,* which is related to *self-concept.* How we *feel* about our self-concept and self-image reflects our *self-esteem.* Children are in a malleable state; and their self-esteem is, to some extent, in the hands of the adults in their lives. Those adults need to see the importance of keeping self-esteem intact so that children can grow to their fullest potential.

FOR DISCUSSION

1. The text says that people aren't always what they seem. Do you believe that statement? Has that been your experience? Do you have some examples to back up your opinion?

2. Is the idea of self-esteem universal?

3. If you have high self-esteem, does that mean you are proud of yourself?

4. Building self-esteem in a child involves a collaboration not a deception. What does that sentence mean?

5. No matter what hand fate deals, it's not the events themselves that determine self-esteem; it's how the individual reacts to those events. Explain. Do you agree?

6. Can you think of any examples of a self-fulfilling prophecy?

7. In what ways might the greater society outside the family tear down self-esteem?

8. "You can't make children feel better about themselves by making them feel bad about themselves." What does that mean? Can you give some examples?

9. What are some examples of ways to encourage children?
10. Give an example of an adult "scaffolding" a young child's learning.
11. In what ways do well-meaning adults sometimes promote stereotypes while trying to teach children to "celebrate diversity?"

PERSONAL REFLECTIONS

Thinking about your personal reactions and experiences will help you better understand and integrate the material in this chapter. Use these questions to interface between you and what you read. Use the pertinent ones to reflect on, write about, or discuss with others.

> Ask yourself the question "Who am I?" Your answer reflects your self-concept. How do you FEEL about your self-concept?

> Did your parents love you? Did you feel loved as a child?

> Do you know someone who seems to be able to face adversity, regard it as a challenge, and grow from the experience into a stronger, wiser person?

> The dimensions of self-esteem have been defined as significance, competence, power, and virtue. Which of these dimensions are most important to you personally? To your family?

> Has the notion of a self-fulfilling prophecy influenced your life? How?

> How did others in your early life reflect or not reflect your worth to you?

> How did the greater society as you were growing up reflect or not reflect your worth to you?

> As a child were you encouraged and supported more than you were criticized?

> Were you praised as a child? What effect did praise have on you?

> Could you relate personally to the discussion about Travis on pages 85 and 86?

> Can you remember a time that you learned something from failure?

NOTES

1. Concepts of separateness are influenced by culture. One culture sees the infant born into the world unable to differentiate herself from the rest of the world. In this culture, the infant's task is to learn to draw lines and discover her separateness—to discover herself as an individual, independent human being. Another culture sees the infant as separate and independent to start with. That culture wants to blur the lines and de-emphasize the independence. Jerome Kagan says: "The Japanese, who prize close interdependence between child and adult . . . believe they must tempt the infant into a dependent role . . . in order to encourage the mutual bonding necessary for adult life." Jerome Kagan, *The Nature of the Child* (New York: Basic Books, Inc., 1984), 29.

2. An exercise I do with my students is to ask them to list the characteristics of someone with high self-esteem. This list is a summary of the one my students compiled from their separate lists. Each semester, only one or two students catch a glimmer of the fact that these are ideal traits of the mainstream culture, not a list that relates to high self-esteem.

3. Dorothy Corkille Briggs, *Your Child's Self-Esteem* (New York: Dolphin Books, 1975).

4. *Newsweek* (February 17, 1992).

5. This discussion about the dimensions of self-esteem is my interpretation of a lecture by Lilian Katz and comes from the work of Stanley Coopersmith, a pioneer in self-esteem research; Stanley Coopersmith, *The Antecedents of Self-Esteem* (San Francisco: W. H. Freeman, 1967). Other researchers use similar ideas but employ different words. Harter, for example, uses the words *acceptance, power and control, moral virtue, and competence*; S. Harter, "Developmental Perspectives on the Self-System," in *Handbook of Child Psychology*, vol. 4, *Socialization, Personality, and Social Development*, 4th ed., ed. E. M. Heatherton, and series ed. P. H. Mussen. New York: Wiley, 1983, 275–386.

6. M. E. P. Seligman, *Helplessness: On Depression, Development and Death* (San Francisco: W. H. Freeman, 1975).

7. Dorothy Corkille Briggs, *op. cit.*

8. Nancy E. Curry and Carl N. Johnson, *Beyond Self-Esteem: Developing a Genuine Sense of Human Value* (Washington, DC: National Association for the Education of Young Children, 1990), 92.

9. R. Hitz and A. Driscoll, "Praise or Encouragement? New Insights into Praise: Implications for Early Childhood Teachers." *Young Children* 43(5) (1988): 12.

10. Sue Bredekamp, ed., *Developmentally Appropriate Practice in Early Childhood Programs Serving Children from Birth Through Age 8* (Washington, DC: National Association for the Education of Young Children, 1987).

11. L. S. Vygotsky, *Mind and Society: The Development of Higher Psychological Process* (Cambridge: Harvard University Press, 1978).

12. Magda Gerber, infant specialist, constantly demonstrates how this linking works in her program, Resources for Infant Educarers, in Los Angeles, California, and also in the movie, "On Their Own with Our Help," Bradley Wright Films.

13. Michael Dorris, "Why I'm NOT Thankful for Thanksgiving," *Interracial Books for Children Bulletin* 9(7) (1978): 6–9.

14. Louise Derman-Sparks, *Anti-Bias Curriculum: Tools for Empowering Young Children* (Washington, DC: National Association for the Education of Young Children, 1989), ix.

REFERENCES

Bernhard, Judith K. "Child Development, Cultural Diversity, and the Professional Training of Early Childhood Educators." *Canadian Journal of Education* 20 (1995): 4.

Billman, Janet. "The Native American Curriculum: Attempting Alternatives to Tepees and Headbands." *Young Children* (September 1992).

Bredekamp, S., ed. *Developmentally Appropriate Practice in Early Childhood Programs Serving Children From Birth Through Age 8*. Washington, DC: National Association for the Education of Young Children, 1987.

Briggs, D. C. *Your Child's Self-Esteem*. New York: Dolphin Books, 1975.

Cajete, Gregory. *Look to the Mountain: An Ecology of Indigenous Education*. Durango, Colorado: Kivaki Press, 1994.

Chang, Hedy. *Affirming Children's Roots: Cultural and Linguistic Diversity in Early Care and Education*. San Francisco: California Tomorrow, 1993.

Chang, H. N. L., A. Muckelroy, and D. Pulido-Tobiassen. *Looking In, Looking Out: Redefining Child and Early Education in a Diverse Society*. San Francisco: California Tomorrow, 1996.

Coopersmith, S. *The Antecedents of Self-Esteem*. San Francisco: W. H. Freeman, 1967.

Curry, N. E., and C. N. Johnson. *Beyond Self-Esteem: Developing a Genuine Sense of Human*

Value. Washington, DC: National Association for the Education of Young Children, 1990.

Derman-Sparks, Louise. *Anti-Bias Curriculum: Tools for Empowering Young Children.* Washington, DC: National Association for the Education of Young Children, 1989.

Derman-Sparks, Louise, and Kay Taus. "We're Different and . . . " *Scholastic Pre-K Today* (November/December 1989): 40–44.

Dorris, M. "Why I'm NOT Thankful for Thanksgiving." *Interracial Books for Children Bulletin* 9(7) (1978): 6–9.

Early Childhood Diversity Series, videos Magna Systems, Barrington, IL, 1995.

Fernea, Elizabeth Warnock. *Children in the Muslim Middle East.* Austin: University of Texas Press, 1995.

Garcia, Eugene E. "Bilingualism in Early Childhood." *Young Children* (May 1980): 52–66.

Gardner, Howard. *To Open Minds, Chinese Clues to the Dilemma of Contemporary Education.* New York: Basic Books, 1989.

Gergen, Kenneth J. *Realities and Relationships: Soundings in Social Construction.* Cambridge: Harvard University Press, 1994.

Gonzalez-Mena, Janet. "Learning to See Across a Cultural Gap." *Child Care Information Exchange* (May 1994).

Gonzalez-Mena, Janet. "When Values Collide: Exploring a Cross Cultural Issue." *Child Care Information Exchange* (March 1996).

Greenberg, Polly. "Teaching About Native Americans or Teaching About People, Including Native Americans?" *Young Children* (September 1992).

Hale, Janice E. "An African-American Early Childhood Education Program: Visions for Children." In *Reconceptualizing the Early Childhood Curriculum: Beginning the Dialogue,* eds. Shirley A. Kessler and Beth Blue Swadener. NY: Teachers College Press, 1992, 205–224.

Hale, Janice E. "Culturally Appropriate Pedagogy." Paper presented at the National Black Child Development Annual Conference, Washington, D.C., 1995.

Hale, Janice. "The Transmission of Cultural Values to Young African American Children." *Young Children* 46(6) (September 1991): 7–15.

Harter, S. "Developmental Perspectives on the Self-System." In *Handbook of Child Psychology,* vol.

4, *Socialization, Personality, and Social Development,* 4th ed., ed. E. M. Heatherton, and series ed. P. H. Mussen. New York: Wiley, 1983.

Hitz, R., and A. Driscoll. "Praise or Encouragement? New Insights into Praise: Implications for Early Childhood Teachers." *Young Children* 43(5) (1988): 6–13.

Hopson, Darlene Powell, and Derek S. Hopson. *Different and Wonderful: Raising Black Children in a Race-Conscious Society.* Upper Saddle River, NJ: Merrill/Prentice Hall, 1990.

Kagan, Jerome. *The Nature of the Child.* New York: Basic Books, Inc., 1984, 29.

Kawagley, A. Oscar. *A Yupiaz Worldview: A Pathway to Ecology and Spirit.* Prospect Heights, IL: Waveland Press, 1995.

Kendall, Frances E. *Diversity in the Classroom: A Multicultural Approach to the Education of Young Children.* New York: Teachers College Press, 1996.

Kitayama, Shinobu, Hazel Rose Markus, Hisaya Matsumoto. "Culture, Self, and Emotion: A Cultural Perspective on 'Self-Conscious' Emotions." In *Self-Conscious Emotions: The Psychology of Shame, Guilt, Embarrassment, and Pride,* eds. June Tangney and Kurt Fisher. New York: Guilford, 1995, 439–463.

Knight, George P., Martha E. Bernal, and Gustavo Carlo. "Socialization and the Development of Cooperative, Competitive, and Individualistic Behaviors Among Mexican American Children." In *Meeting the Challenge of Linguistic and Cultural Diversity in Early Childhood Education,* eds. Eugene E. Garcia and Barry McLaughlin, with Bernard Spokek and Olivia N. Saracho. New York: Teachers College Press, 1995, 85–102.

Ladson-Billings, Gloria. *The Dreamkeepers: Successful Teachers of African American Children.* San Francisco: Jossey-Bass, 1994.

Lee, Joann. *Asian Americans.* New York: New Press, 1992.

Mecca, A. M., N. J. Smelser, and J. Vasconcellos. *The Social Importance of Self-Esteem.* Berkeley, CA: University of California Press, 1989.

Medicine, Beatrice. "Child Socialization Among Native Americans: The Lakota (Sioux) in Cultural Context." *Wicazo Sa Review* 1(2) (Fall 1985): 23–28.

Mintzer, D., H. Als, E. Z. Tronic, and T. B. Brazelton. "Parenting an Infant with a Birth Defect: The Regulation of Self-Esteem." *Psychoanalytic Study of the Child* 39 (1984): 561–589.

Phillips, Carol Brunson. "Culture: A Process that Empowers." In *Infant/Toddler Caregiving: A Guide to Culturally Sensitive Care,* ed. Peter Mangione. Sacramento, California: Far West Laboratory and California Department of Education, 1995.

Phillips, Carol Brunson. "Nurturing Diversity for Today's Children and Tomorrow's Leaders." *Young Children* (January 1988): 42–47.

Phinney, J., and M. Rotherman, eds. *Children's Ethnic Socialization: Pluralism and Development.* Beverly Hills, CA: Sage Publications, 1987.

Rael, Joseph. *Being and Vibration.* Tulsa, Oklahoma: Council Oak Books, 1993.

Rashid, Hakim M. "Promoting Biculturalism in Young African-American Children." *Young Children* (January 1984): 13–23.

Rogoff, B., and J. V. Wertsch, eds. "Children's Learning in the Zone of Proximal Development." *New Directions for Child Development.* San Francisco: Jossey-Bass, 1984, 23.

Ross, Allen. C. (Ehanamani). *Mitakuye Oyasin: We Are All Related.* Denver: Wichoni Waste, 1989.

Sapon-Shevin, Mara. "Teaching Children About Differences: Resources for Teaching." *Young Children* (January 1983): 24–31.

Spence, M. B., G. K. Brookins, and W. R. Allen, eds. *Beginnings: The Social and Affective Development of Black Children.* Hillsdale, NJ: Erlbaum, 1985.

Tedla, Elleni. *Sankofa: African Thought and Education.* New York: Peter Lang, 1995.

"Ten Quick Ways to Analyze Children's Books for Racism and Sexism." New York: Council on Interracial Books for Children, 1986.

Wardle, Francis. "Are You Sensitive to Interracial Children's Special Identity Needs?" *Young Children* 42(2) (1987): 53–59.

Wardle, Francis. "Endorsing Children's Differences: Meeting the Needs of Adopted Minority Children." *Young Children* (July 1990): 44–46.

Werner, Emmy E. "Resilience in Development." *Current Directions in Psychological Science* (June 1995): 81–85.

Werner, E. E., and R. S. Smith. *Overcoming the Odds: High Risk Children from Birth to Adulthood.* Ithaca and London: Cornell University Press, 1992.

Vygotsky, L. S. *Mind and Society: The Development of Higher Psychological Process.* Cambridge: Harvard University Press, 1978.

PART 2

The Family: Socialization for High Self-Esteem in Healthy Families

Part 1 looked at the child in a developmental context. Part 2 examines the child in a family context. The next eight chapters explore specifics on families and socialization.

TOWARD A DEFINITION OF FAMILY

What is meant by the word *family*? Close your eyes and imagine a family. Does this family fit your *concept* of a family? Look around at symbols of families. Think of logos of agencies that serve families. What is the image conveyed by most? The images I usually see are a male, a female, and one or two children. Perhaps the balance and symmetry cause this type of family to be chosen as a logo—it's visually attractive. Or perhaps we're still living in the aftermath of the "Leave It to Beaver" tradition. Whatever the reason, many of us carry in our heads an image that doesn't apply to a large number of families in the United States today.

What are some of the many different ways a family can vary from the mother-father-child model? It can have more children or fewer. It can involve a marriage or not. The members can be all the same gender. Its members can vary greatly in age—vary by more than just two generations. It can include a number of people who are not related but are living under the same roof. It can include people who are related by blood and marriage along with those who are not related and who do not live under the same roof. (This kind of family is called a kinship network.) Its members can share the same bloodlines or name, or both, or neither. Its members can share the same history or not. The family can be blended—that is, composed of individuals coming together as a couple who each have children of their own. The blended family can live all together or not. The family can be composed of people who have traditional relationships to each other, but were not born into them. Children may come into the family from outside—through adoption, through fostering, or through less formal arrangements.

There are numerous traditional names for these varying kinds of families. They include nuclear, insular, extended, embedded, single parent, step, blended, adoptive, foster, communal, kinship networks, gay, and lesbian.

Families can vary infinitely in their makeup. Each variation has an effect on the socialization of any children in them. Families may originate through interracial or interreligious unions. Families may have members who are differently abled. Families may come about through marriages or affiliations that cross generational lines.

FAMILY CORE FUNCTIONS: PROTECTION, COMMUNICATION, AND SELF-ESTEEM

The family's job is to turn any children in it into well-functioning citizens for tomorrow's world. To do this job, families must provide for protection, communication, and the promotion of self-esteem. Self-esteem has a chapter all to itself; communication and protection are not set apart in separate chapters, but are discussed throughout the book. A few additional words here may shed further light on the subject of protection when it needs to come from the society because the family no longer functions as protection from the outside, or harm to the children is coming from the inside family itself.

It used to be that wives and children belonged to men as possessions. A man could own property, a herd of cattle, a horse and buggy, and a house and furnishings. His family fell in the same category with the rest of his belongings. The law supported such a notion. No one interfered with what a man did to his property. If he destroyed what he owned, it was his business, until around the turn of the last century when the Society for the Prevention of Cruelty to Animals (SPCA) stepped in to protect his pets, his work animals, and his livestock. In those days, wives and children still had no legal recourse if they were abused by the man who owned them. A man's home was his castle and no one could penetrate it. Eventually the SPCA took on the task of protecting children too. Ironically, it was originally the only agency available to respond to child abuse!

Times have changed. Women managed to gain status as citizens in their own right; however, protection under the law has been slow in coming. Many battered women through the second half of the twentieth century appealed to the law for help but were reprimanded for their part in their own victimization and sent back to their abusing husbands.

It has also taken a long time for children to gain rights as human beings entitled to protection under the law. It has been hard for the society to decide that intervention was necessary to provide protection to children from their own parents. The idea that a family "owns" their children is still with us, though the law is now clear that abuse is illegal.

Of course, when a family is functioning well, they don't abuse their children and the children don't need outside protection. But when things break down, intervention is necessary. The Child Abuse Prevention Act passed in 1974 made such intervention possible. The law becomes clearer and clearer, and now there are legal sanctions for those who are considered "mandated reporters" (such as childcare workers, teachers, and counselors) and fail to report suspected abuse.

As a society we are still new at intervening when families fail to function properly. Sensitivity is sometimes missing, and legal red tape can cause more problems than it solves. But we must step in. Far too many children have been permanently damaged, physically and emotionally, and sometimes killed, by abuse. It's time to stop that kind of treatment and help families and children to heal.

One big problem concerns the question, Where does the society stop when it comes to intervention? How much and under what circumstances should the authorities step in and interfere? The newspapers every day carry accounts of families resisting governmental attention to what they consider their business. For example, differing views of medical treatment can end with a court case. If the medical establishment's views of what a child needs and the parents' views differ, the issue goes to a judge to decide if the parents are withholding medical treatment or just looking at the child's condition from a different point of view.

Another issue is, To what extent can parents protect their children by making demands of the society's institutions? For example, do parents have the right to demand that certain books, some considered classics, be banned from school libraries because they don't want their children to read them? Should censorship be instituted in the media at the insistence of parents who want to insure children won't watch certain programs on television? We, as a society, are dealing with these issues every day and haven't come to a clear understanding about where parents' rights end and society's rights begin in certain matters, such as censorship.

OTHER FAMILY FUNCTIONS

Besides providing for protection, communication, and self-esteem, families perform a variety of other functions. Those functions may include financial support, emotional support, concepts of authority, housing, elderly care, childcare and childrearing, education and intellectual stimulation, carrying on of traditions, religious education, and training in matters of the spirit.

Not all families perform all of these functions directly. Some use sources outside the family; others provide all of the above and more.

One of the most important family functions is teaching about intimate and personal relationships. Through the early experiences described in chapters 1 through 4, children develop the capacity to establish relationships with others. They learn what it means to get along in a family setting. They learn to share space, possessions, time, attention, and any available resources. From their family life, children learn ways of cooperating and competing and how those ways either fit or don't fit in their family's value system. They learn what to do when what they want or need conflicts with what other family members want or need. They learn about feelings and authority, and about being protected or not being protected.

Patterns of interactions among family members become a model for children. They learn about closeness and distance (between parents and children and between males and females). Each child experiences the patterns of his or her own homelife and, as a result, is socialized in certain ways. Children learn what to expect from an alcoholic parent, for example. Children of alcoholics are socialized differently than those who do not have to deal with alcoholism. Loving or indifferent parents affect socialization; so do domineering or submissive siblings. Socialization is different if a child lives in a relaxed household where interactions tend to be good natured instead of where tension prevails.

THE SHIFTING SHAPES OF TODAY'S FAMILIES

Today's family may come in a variety of changing forms and shapes. Living patterns are shifting and those shifts change family structure. The changes aren't necessarily good or bad—they just are.

We are in a period of change regarding the family—its definition, its functions, and its structure. The family in some ways is in transition from an older system in which members played specific roles based on their position in the family to a newer one in which division of labor is agreed upon rather than dependent on roles and in which decision making is not the realm of a single authority. Some families today are tied together more by companionship, mutual affection, and communication than by legal ties and traditional mandates. In some cases commitment lasts as long as the arrangement is working. When it breaks down, the configuration of the family may change as well.

The reality is that many children (more in some cultures than in others) will live in a single-parent family for some period of their childhood. And of those, many will live in blended families, as stepchildren or half brothers and sisters.

This reality means that not only will they have to learn to be flexible but also many will live in poverty for at least part of their childhood. When couples split up, the children usually go with the mother (though that tendency has changed slightly in recent years). A woman's standard of living drops drastically when she is supporting herself and her children without other sources of income.

Some of the patterns may seem new, but aren't. For example, the divorce rate among today's parents isn't much different from the death rate of parents a century ago. Many children in those days were raised in single-parent families, by grandparents, in step- and blended families, just as today's children are. We often put a glow on the past that makes it seem much kinder, healthier, and happier than the present—a glow that doesn't relate to reality.

RELATIONSHIP OF FORM TO FUNCTION

There's a lot of talk today about the family breaking down. When a family is not functioning well, raising children who aren't functional, there's cause to be concerned. However, the definition of *functional* varies from culture to culture. It's tempting to see a family as dysfunctional when its patterns or structure are different from your image of what they should be; but family structure alone doesn't tell you how well the family functions. It only tells you that it's different from what has been regarded as traditional—the white middle-class family.

For too long society has been regarding the mythical white middle-class family as the standard by which all other families are to be judged. For too long those families that differed were thought not to measure up and were labeled as lacking or deprived. It's time to give legitimacy to cultural differences and alternative lifestyles.

A good start is to get rid of the term *broken family*, which sounds as if something is wrong, when in reality the so-called broken family may be quite functional. You can't tell by family structure whether a family functions in healthy ways or not. The single-parent family in apartment A may be quite functional compared with the two-parent, *intact*, but highly dysfunctional, family in apartment B next door.

You have to be very careful about making generalizations about family structures. For example, some African-American family structures have been portrayed as deficient. Those who have studied the African-American family have unfortunately been "literally inundated by visions of domineering mothers; absent fathers; disorganized families; abusive, neglectful, interpersonal relations; routine psychological self-defamation; and frustrated, hopeless, intellectually barren lives." [1]

It's time to quit looking at differences as deficits, rather than as legitimate forms in themselves. Families of all types and sizes are fully capable of producing healthy children and providing a support system for all of the people who comprise the family. You can't judge the degree of functionality of a family by its structure, patterns, or makeup.

Instead of automatically labeling some family structures as deficient and looking at them as social problems, it's time that we started to see their strengths. We should be supporting diversity in family structure. When we, as a society, come from a point of view that the family is breaking down, rather than changing in form, we put all of our resources into looking at causes of the breakdown. We already know something about what causes stress in families. We know that you can't separate the way families function from the social, economic, and political realities that influence their lives.

MAKING CHANGES

It is time to look at how we, as a society, can change some of the factors that work against family health and functionality. These factors include racism, classism, and educational, social, economic, and political inequalities.

We also need to discover the strengths of families in stress who manage to successfully socialize their children to discover their strengths. What enables these families to function effectively under difficult or demanding circumstances? Why do some families remain organized and supportive of each other under extreme pressures? How can we promote that same kind of togetherness in families that lack it?

We need to understand more about how the effects of class are different from the effects of race, gender, culture, and ethnicity.

You can't take families out of their cultural context. We need now to spend more time and money understanding cultural patterns of childrearing as they relate to socialization. We need to give up the idea of universals when it comes to parenting. It's important to recognize that the cultural imperatives of families determine which competencies it is appropriate to foster in children. We need to know more about how the socialization techniques and childrearing practices promote the survival of any given culture. We must not equate cultural survival with family breakdown.

Although parts of the next seven chapters have the slant of a white middle-class perspective, please read them with an eye to cultural sensitivity. Childrearing is not the same in all cultures, and what works for one culture may not be right for another. We need to know more about all the varieties of socialization in a multicultural society. We need to know more than will fit into one book. Some day, perhaps, we will have a multitude of books describing the many different cultural processes of socialization for high self-esteem in healthy families.

I must hasten to add that even though part 2 is written from a white middle-class perspective, it is not the traditional white middle-class view of socialization. Rather, it is written from a developmental, research-oriented perspective (done mostly by white middle-class researchers). Raising your children traditionally, that is, as you were raised, is not necessarily better or worse than what is advocated here, but it may well be different.

NOTES

1. Walter Recharde Allen, "Race, Income, and Family Dynamics: A Study of Adolescent Male Socialization Processes and Outcomes," in *Beginnings: The Social and Affective Development of Black Children*, ed. Margaret Beale Spencer, Geraldine Kearse Brookins, and Walter Recharde Allen (Hillsdale, NJ: Lawrence Erlbaum Associates, 1985), 273.

REFERENCES

Allen, W. R. "Race, Income, and Family Dynamics: A Study of Adolescent Male Socialization Processes and Outcomes." In *Beginnings: The Social and Affective Development of Black Children*, ed. Margaret Beale Spencer, Geraldine Kearse Brookins, and Walter Recharde Allen. Hillsdale, NJ: Lawrence Erlbaum Associates, 1985.

Cicchetti, D. and S. L. Toth, eds. *Child Abuse, Child Development and Social Policy: Advances in Applied Developmental Psychology*, vol. 8. Norwood, NJ: Ablex Publishing, 1993.

Flaherty, M. J., L. Facteau, and P. Garver. "Grandmother Functions in Multigenerational Families: An Exploratory Study of Black Adolescent Mothers and Their Infants." In *The Black Family: Essays and Studies*, ed. Robert Staples. Belmont, CA: Wadsworth, 1991, 192–199.

Kozol, Jonathan. *Savage Inequalities: Children in America's Schools*. New York: Crown Publishers, 1991.

Powell, G. J., ed. *The Psychosocial Development of Minority Children*. New York: Brunner/Mazel Publishers, 1983.

Sandoval, M., and M. De La Roza. "A Cultural Perspective for Serving the Hispanic Client." In *Cross-Cultural Training for Mental Health Professionals*, eds. Harriet Lefley and Paul Pedersen. Springfield, IL: Charles C. Thomas, Publisher, 1986.

Scott, J. W., and A. Black. "Deep Structures of African-American Family Life: Female and Male Kin Networks." In *The Black Family: Essays and Studies*, ed. Robert Staples. Belmont, CA: Wadsworth, 1991, 201–209.

Skeen, P., B. E. Robinson, and C. Flake-Hobson. "Blended Families: Overcoming the Cinderella Myth." *Young Children* (January 1984): 64–74.

Starr, R. H., and D. A. Wolfe, eds. *The Effects of Child Abuse and Neglect: Issues and Research*. London: Guilford, 1991.

Washington, Valora, and Ura Jean Oyemade. "Changing Family Trends." *Young Children* (September 1985): 12–19.

Sue, Stanley, and Thom Moore, eds. *The Pluralistic Society*. New York: Human Sciences Press, Inc., 1984.

Staples, Robert, ed. *The Black Family: Essays and Studies*. Belmont, CA: Wadsworth, 1991.

Goals, Values, and Culture

CHAPTER **5**

In this chapter you'll discover:

> Why a salad bowl is pluralistic and a melting pot is not
> The goals for a pluralistic society
> How unconscious culture is
> Two contrasting cultural patterns that affect childrearing
> Why one parent teaches her child pride while another criticizes her child for being proud
> A particular way of approaching problems called "RERUN"
> How children learn morals and values
> Prosocial behaviors and how adults teach them to children

TEST YOURSELF

Look for the answers to these questions as you read the chapter:

1. What is cultural pluralism?
2. How much of culture is unconscious?
3. Why doesn't the text list various cultural childrearing practices instead of just comparing two patterns?
4. How might sleeping arrangements differ for a pattern one and pattern two family?
5. Which pattern is more likely to have parents teaching their children to be humble instead of proud? Why?
6. How might a pattern one parent differ from a pattern two parent in approaching toilet training?
7. Which parent, pattern one or pattern two, is more likely to emphasize manners over honest self-expression?
8. What does the acronym RERUN stand for?
9. Besides using RERUN for problem solving, what else could you do if you should find yourself in a cultural conflict over childrearing? The chapter lists seven further suggestions. What are they?
10. When children are making a decision about how to behave in a situation in which there is a potential for right and wrong, what kinds of questions do they ask themselves?
11. What are "prosocial behaviors" and what are some ways to promote them in children?

RELATIONSHIP OF GOALS AND VALUES TO CHILDREARING PRACTICES

A worthwhile exercise for all parents, caregivers, and teachers is to examine their values, see how they relate to their goals, and decide whether or not what they are doing with their children is in tune with what they believe in. Take, for example, a family who highly values peace. Their goal is that each child be raised to always pursue nonviolent solutions to problems. If a parent in this family spanks as a means of controlling behavior, the childrearing practice is out of tune with the value and the goal.

Anyone who works with other people's children, for instance as a teacher, childcare provider, or social worker, should understand the values and goals of the parents of those children. They should examine their own behaviors to see if what they are doing with the children, or with the families, is in harmony with what the families want for themselves and their children.

Recognizing that cultural learning starts at birth and is mostly nonverbal, it is imperative that those who work with families familiarize themselves with cultural differences. The ideal is that families and the agencies that work with them are involved in a joint process that ensures that each child will become and remain a member of his or her own culture through a steady developmental progress toward cultural competence. The child may become bicultural in the process, but taking on another culture should be adding to what they already have—not replacing the original culture of the family.

This view is based on cultural pluralism as a value. "Cultural pluralism" is the label for the idea that groups should be allowed, even encouraged, to hold on to what gives them their unique identities while maintaining their membership in the larger social framework. The old idea of America was of a melting pot, where all cultures blended into one. The new image, for those who believe in cultural pluralism, is of America as a salad bowl, where each of the many ingredients retains its own unique identity, but the parts combine into a "delicious" whole.

CULTURAL DIFFERENCES IN GOALS AND VALUES

Our culture affects everything we do, from determining the precise way we move our arms and legs when we walk to deciding the objectives we're moving toward. [1] Culture rules how we position our bodies, how we touch each other, what we regard as mannerly, how we look at the world, how we think, what we see as art, how we sense time and perceive space, what we think is important, and how we set immediate and lifelong goals.

Because culture is ninety percent unconscious, most people find it hard to talk about their own culture until it bumps up against one that's different. Culture is so much a part of our lives that we don't see it or pay attention to it. Yet it determines our values, which are also so much a part of our lives that they too remain invisible most of the time. Values are behind everything we do and every decision we make. They guide us in childrearing.

Contrasting Cultural Patterns

What are some cultural differences? [2] Because one culture is best seen in contrast to another, I've taken the approach of pointing out cultural patterns that are quite different from each other, rather than listing characteristics of various cultures. It is important to point out that to make a contrast I've exaggerated differences. Although some families may fit neatly into one category or the other, many defy categorization. As you read about pattern-one and pattern-two families, you'll probably find that your family fits somewhere between the two. The point is not to fit families into categories, but to show contrasts and differences by highlighting them.

Pattern one values people as unique individuals, starting at birth. Stress is on independence of both thought and action. Members of this culture regard the individual's feelings highly and encourage expression of those feelings. Individuals in this culture are perceived to have personal power, and they are taught assertiveness from an early age. If you're not a pattern-one person yourself, you probably know some people who are.

Pattern two sees the group as more important than the individual. Individual uniqueness is valued only as it serves the group. Children are taught to blend in, to fit. They learn to see the group as the basic unit and themselves as a part of it, rather than seeing the individual as the basic unit. In other words, the individual is nothing by himself or herself—the individual counts only as a part of the group.

This pattern stresses interdependence (mutual dependence) and obedience. Obedience has to do with the group will, which is expressed by a hierarchy of authority.

The sense of identity of a pattern-two person comes from membership in the group rather than from personal competence, power, significance, lovability, or virtue. The behavior of an individual is never just a reflection of himself or herself; instead it reflects on the group and either adds to or detracts from the group identity.

The two patterns also differ in their view of the attachment process. The pattern-one person sees early attachment as very important—something that must happen to ensure that the baby will be properly cared for. Attachment and separation cannot be divided and are viewed as two parts of a single process that follows a progression leading to later independence from the family of origin. Indeed, the separation part of the process is as important as the attachment part and occurs in stages throughout childhood, then finally culminates in "leaving home" at some point after adolescence. After he or she leaves home, the individual is expected to take full charge of his or her own life and no longer look for parental advice or support more than just occasionally.

The pattern-two person sees attachment differently. The focus is on keeping the child in the family/group rather than on teaching separation skills. Attachment is not such an issue at the beginning because group expectations ensure that each baby will be taken care of properly—if not by the mother, then by another mem-

How Do Independence and Interdependence Goals Show?

What do parents who focus on independence actually do that shows their focus? They encourage early self-help skills, for one thing. They expect toddlers to feed themselves and soon after to dress themselves. They teach their children to sleep alone in their own beds. They may take them into their bed for short periods, but their goal is to get the child back to bed. If they "baby" their children, they feel guilty.

Parents who focus on interdependent relationships are less adamant about babies learning to sleep through the night alone. The idea of "babying" children is viewed in a positive light, not a negative one. Babies and parents tend to have strong connections, so prolonging babyhood makes sense if your goal is *inter*dependence. These parents are more worried about maintaining relationships than creating an independent individual, so they see nothing wrong with coddling children.

It's a completely different way of looking at getting needs met. Children who grow up in an individualistic home learn that it's each person's job to take care of his or her own needs. But children who grow up in "other-centered" homes, learn that the needs of the others are their problem. They still get their needs met, because while they are taking care of others, they are being taken care of. In both kinds of homes, basic needs get met, but the process is different in each.

Of course, most people, no matter how they were raised, do become BOTH independent individuals AND people who create and maintain relationships. Children accomplish both the major tasks even if their parents only focus on one. Parents expect their children to be both independent and connected, but they work harder on what they believe to be most important. They leave to chance what they are less concerned about or work toward it in random bits and pieces.

ber of the group. It's not up to the individual to be drawn to the baby and therefore give it the care it needs; instead, it's up to the group member to fulfill an expected role that is unquestioned.

Attachment in the pattern-two culture is a lifetime process; the child is expected to remain unto death a viable member of the family into which he or she is born. Each person in the group is connected to and interdependent on the other members of the group.

How might these themes of individual versus group, attachment versus separation, and independence versus interdependence show up in childrearing practices? Where might the conflicts lie if a pattern-one person married into a pattern-two family? Or if a pattern-one person were the teacher or childcare provider of a pattern-two person?

WHEN PARENTS AND/OR CAREGIVERS OR TEACHERS HAVE CONFLICTING GOALS AND VALUES

Pattern-one parents might put their baby daughter to sleep in a crib in a room away from their bedroom. In fact, if they could afford it, they might give her a room of her own from the beginning. A goal would be to get her to put herself to sleep in her own bed and stay there asleep all night long. Families might vary about when they would expect this to occur—and some would "baby" the child longer than others—but eventually the child is expected to show her ability to manage on her own by sleeping alone.

Pattern-two parents might sleep with their daughter from birth on, never buying her a crib or planning to provide her with a room of her own. They might move her out of the parental bed when another baby came along, but most likely would move her into another sibling's bed, or perhaps in with her grandmother. Being alone, even when asleep, is not sought after by most members of a pattern-two culture.

A pattern-one caregiver or teacher may expect to raise each child's self-esteem by emphasizing individuality. He or she may purposely set out to praise accomplishments—drawing attention to individual behavior. Phrases like "You did that all by yourself!" illustrate this emphasis on the individual. Along the same lines, the caregiver or teacher may provide for each child a storage cubbie that is decorated with the child's name in bold print and a picture of him or her. The idea is for the child to gain a sense of his or her own personal identity while experiencing private ownership, even in the group situation.

A pattern-two caregiver or teacher may put energy into being sure no one child is singled out, but that all remain firmly fixed in the group. He or she will point out group accomplishments rather than individual achievements. He or she will focus on rewarding cooperative efforts instead of individual efforts. This caregiver or teacher will downplay individual achievement by refusing personal credit when given a compliment. He or she will teach "modesty" to those children who "brag" about themselves.

In a pattern-one culture, the emphasis is on helping oneself; in a pattern-two culture, the emphasis is on helping others. This difference shows up in the attitude about training for self-help skills. A pattern-one parent, teacher, or caregiver is in a hurry for the child to learn to feed himself, for example. When the baby first grabs the spoon, most pattern-one people will get another spoon and let the baby begin to help. Finger food is given early so the child can feed independently.

A pattern-two parent, teacher, or caregiver is too busy modeling "helping," in keeping with the goal of interdependence, to worry about teaching the baby to "do it himself." Needless to say, pattern-one children are able to do things for themselves at a surprisingly young age; and pattern-two children are able to do things for other children at a surprisingly young age. In some cultures around the world with pattern-two tendencies, preschool-age children take charge of their younger siblings, doing for the baby what was done for them only a short time before.

Toilet training is another area where the two patterns may conflict. The pattern-one caregiver, teacher, or parent puts the emphasis on self-help, so he or she doesn't see signs of readiness for toilet training until the child is somewhere around two years of age. To this adult, toilet training starts when children are able to control bladder and bowels, handle clothing, and get to the toilet or potty on their own.

A pattern-two caregiver, teacher, or parent has a very different view. With the de-emphasis on self-help and the emphasis on interdependence, the adult is part of the child's elimination processes from the beginning. The adult watches from the early months on for signals preceding bowel and bladder activity. When the signals appear, the adult responds immediately. Eventually the two set up a system of signals that allows the adult to get the child barebottomed to the proper place, then trigger the elimination response. If you've never seen this, I can assure you, it's impressive!

A pattern-two caregiver, teacher, or parent may view manners as much more important than self-expression. Learning manners reflects the goal of becoming a good group member. Pattern-two caregivers, teachers, or parents may be horrified as they watch a pattern-one adult encourage children to speak out, to express anger, or to assert themselves.

To illustrate the difference in the early months, contrast these two approaches. One adult touches a screaming baby lightly on the shoulder and says, "I know you're mad. It's okay to cry!" After reviewing the situation—he's not tired, hungry, or in need of a change—she leaves him alone to express himself, checking in periodically to let him know that he hasn't been deserted. She doesn't try to distract him or lull him with words or touch because she thinks that his expression of emotion is healthy.

Another adult, rocking and lulling, holding the baby tight, says, "There, there, quiet down, it's okay! You're upsetting everyone else. Please don't cry!" She tries to stop the crying, using all the verbal and nonverbal techniques she has. She doesn't regard displays of anger as healthy. She doesn't feel that the baby has the individual right to destroy the peace of the household. She tries to teach him to consider others, even though she understands that he's too young to learn this lesson.

A pattern-one caregiver, teacher, or parent is understanding when a four-year-old cries when away from home or parents for the first time. But the expectation is that this child needs to learn to cope with separation, and that this experience is good for him. The crying may go on for a while, but the adult is confident that the child will gain coping skills and will eventually adjust. The adult sees this period as just one in a long series of separation experiences.

On the other hand, the crying of a pattern-two child may be devastating to the adults in his life because they don't see that being away from family is in his best interests, even though circumstances have dictated the separation. They may be less willing to look at this situation as good for him. They may have less knowledge about teaching coping strategies or helping with separation because they don't value separation.

A pattern-one caregiver, teacher, or parent says, "Call me by my first name," in her eagerness to be friendly. She values casualness. The pattern-two adult is uncomfortable with such informality and insists on using titles. She doesn't see this first-name business as creating closeness, but only showing a lack of respect.

WHAT TO DO WHEN CONFLICTS ARISE

Conflicts constantly arise—in families, between parents, and between parents and professionals who serve them. In some cases these conflicts have cultural differences at their bases.

In America today the professionals in most areas of expertise, regardless of their home culture, are trained from a white European middle-class American perspective. However, many of the families they deal with are not of this mainstream culture. Sensitivity to, understanding of, and respect for differences is vital if we are to fulfill the dream of a pluralistic society based on equity and justice. [3]

What do you do when you are having a cultural conflict? First of all, become aware that you are in a cultural conflict. Because we all tend to look at any situation from our own point of view, it may be very hard to understand another person's frame of reference, which, of course, is cultural. All of us are ethnocentric—that is, we look out of our own cultural eyes and measure others with our own cultural yardstick. It takes awareness and skill to move from our ethnocentric position.

Dialoguing is an approach to problem solving a conflict that is effective at helping the disagreeing parties see each other's point of view. Rather than trying to convince someone of their own viewpoint, people engaged in dialogue try to understand the other perspective. The idea is not to win, but to find the best solution for all concerned.

The following list summarizes the differences between an argument and a dialogue:

> The object of an argument is to win; the object of a dialogue is to gather information.

> The arguer tells; the dialoguer asks.

> The arguer tries to persuade; the dialoguer seeks to learn.

> The arguer tries to convince; the dialoguer, discover.

> The arguer sees two opposing views and considers hers the valid or best one; the dialoguer is willing to understand multiple viewpoints.

Most people are better at argument than they are at dialogue. When faced with a conflict or problem, almost nobody considers starting a dialogue. Especially when it is an emotional conflict, many people are likely to jump feet first into an argument rather than begin a dialogue. When they do argue, they are anxious to win, and that makes them leap to conclusions.

If you watch people arguing, you can see some types of body language that show each person is trying to convince the other of something. When arguing, many people tend to stand firm and tough when listening—assuming a defensive position. They are anything but open. They seem to be just waiting for their turn. When they talk, they lean forward and make aggressive gestures with their hands. Just by looking at them, even if you can't hear their words, you can tell that they are fighting about something. The body language of someone in a potentially win-lose situation is different from someone who is truly trying to understand another point of view, such as happens when people enter a dialogue. Gestures reflect their attitude—hands especially. Instead of waving fists or making strong, tense movements, dialoguing people tend to let their hands remain open.

So how does one switch from an argument to a dialogue in the heat of the moment? Start by noticing your body language. Sometimes you can just change your body language and an energy switch will follow. Then it's a matter of doing one simple thing: listening to the other person. To truly listen, one must suspend judgements and focus on what's being said rather than just gathering ammunition for the next attack. Really hearing someone is extremely simple, but it's not easy.

From then on it's a matter of working through a problem-solving procedure. To help remember the elements of problem approach think of the word *rerun*. RERUN stands for Reflect, Explain, Reason, Understand, Negotiate. To explain further:

> > *REFLECT.* This is the action of acknowledging what you perceive the other person is thinking or feeling. If you understand where the person is coming from, tell him: "I think you're looking at it this way . . . " Or if you perceive that the person is full of emotion, acknowledge your perception: "You really sound upset." Those two openers are invitations for the person to talk some more. People who know that their feelings and thoughts are received and accepted by you are liable to be more open to listening—if not right away, eventually.

> > *EXPLAIN.* Remember, we have two ears and only one mouth; that's a reminder that we should listen twice as much as we talk. Only after you have listened, listened, and listened is it time to explain your point of view.

> > *REASON.* Part of the explanation should include the reason you have for your perspective.

> > *UNDERSTAND.* Next comes the hardest part. Tune in to both thoughts and feelings and try to understand the situation from both points of view. You don't have to say anything out loud at this point, just be sure you have clarity. You may have to talk inwardly to yourself to get it. And while you're going inward, make sure you understand yourself as well as the other person. Then you're ready for the next step.

> > *NEGOTIATE.* Now is the time for the finale. Try brainstorming together until you can find a mutually satisfying solution. Don't give up. Refuse to take an either-or attitude. (It's either my way or your way and it can't be both ways.) If you don't get stuck in a dualistic frame of mind, you can probably find a third or fourth solution that is different from or combines both your stances on the matter. Creative negotiators can open up new avenues of action that no one ever thought of before.

The finale is seldom final. In only the simplest situations do you negotiate an agreement without communications breaking down. When feelings arise, return to the beginning. Go back through the first four (R-E-R-U) parts. You may have to R-E-R-U-N many times before the problem is solved. Be patient.

Instead of taking time to really work through something, we get impatient and reach into the old hip holster and pull out a power play if we have one. It's unfortunate when that happens because one-upmanship destroys relationships rather than strengthening them. It may take a long time to solve a particular problem when the conflict is deep and serious, but a positive outcome in the form of a win-win solution is worth the time and effort it sometimes takes.

Though the RERUN device seems to be steps, or a sequence to follow, nevertheless, the elements are more holistic than that. They come as a package and may occur in a different order or all mixed up as one. The fact that the acronym spells *rerun* serves as a reminder that you can repeat the process as often as necessary until the problem is solved—you come to an agreement or you agree to carry on while disagreeing.

The suggestions that follow are designed to help further when in a cultural conflict involving values and goals. [4]

BUILD RELATIONSHIPS

People who have good relationship are more likely to work on their conflicts in more healthy ways. Relationships sometimes just happen, but more often, they need to be initiated and then nurtured. Commit yourself to working constantly on the total relationship not just the conflict.

Know Yourself

Be clear about what you believe in. Be aware of your own values and goals. Check to see if your behavior reflects your values and goals. If you are in tune with yourself and are clear about what you believe in, you're less likely to present a strong defensive stance in the face of conflict. It is when we feel ambiguous that we come on the strongest.

Work to Bring Differences Out in the Open

Be sensitive to your own discomfort in response to the behavior of others. Tune in on something that bothers you, instead of just ignoring it and hoping it will go away. Work to identify what specific behaviors of others make you uncomfortable. Try to discover exactly what in yourself creates this discomfort.

You need to be honest with yourself and to do some soul-searching to get your prejudices out in the open. None of us likes to do that, but it's an important part of relationships and clear communication.

While you're looking at yourself, look for signs of discomfort in other people in response to your behavior. When you discover discomfort, talk about it!

A Cultural Conflict

Helen is a vegetarian. When she put her daughter, Sissy, into childcare, she had a talk with the director to explain her dietary beliefs. The director explained to her that the center's food was catered and that the protein was usually a meat dish. She suggested that Sissy be served everything but the meat and that Helen supplement with some kind of protein dish. Helen agreed, and everything went well for a while.

Then the director moved on and a new director was hired. Sissy moved up from the younger group to the older group, and that meant a new teacher. Helen got busy one morning and forgot to send Sissy's protein dish. No one complained, including Sissy, so before long Helen was dropping her daughter off in the morning without the supplemental food. She assumed that her daughter was getting enough to eat without it.

Then one day Helen took the afternoon off and arrived at lunchtime to pick up her daughter. She was horrified to find Sissy sitting at the table with the other children, chewing happily on a chicken drumstick. She looked around to see who was responsible and found a substitute in charge. She complained to the substitute, and then thought the matter was settled.

However, a few weeks later Sissy talked about the fish sticks she had had for lunch. Helen stormed into the center, demanding to see the director.

The director pushed herself back from her desk and its huge pile of paperwork, and invited Helen to sit down. Angrily, Helen threw herself into a chair, then launched into a bitter tirade. When she finally paused for breath, the director said with concern in her voice and in her facial expression, "I see how upset you are about this!"

That got Helen going again. When she paused, the director said that she wanted Sissy's teacher in on the discussion, and went to get her.

When the three of them sat down together, Helen was calmer. "Why did you feed Sissy meat?" she demanded of the teacher.

"I didn't—only fish. I know she doesn't eat red meat," answered the teacher.

"She doesn't eat any kind of meat," Helen shot back.

The teacher looked surprised. "I didn't realize you considered fish meat."

"And chicken!" added Helen.

"Oh!" responded the teacher, biting her lip. "I'm sorry," she went on. "It's just that Sissy always seems so hungry, like she can't really get full on the fruits and vegetables alone. I feel sorry for her."

The conversation went on—give and take—and slowly the facts and feelings on both sides began to emerge. The teacher's misunderstanding about what Helen considered meat gave way to her feelings about Sissy feeling hungry and left out as the other children enjoyed hamburgers and hot dogs and other foods forbidden to

Sissy. She was obviously not committed to vegetarianism herself, and it was hard for her to see why Helen felt so strongly about it. She even questioned whether a vegetarian diet was a properly nutritious one for a child.

Helen in turn confessed that she had some resentment that children with food allergies were carefully monitored and given special consideration, yet no one seemed to care what Sissy ate. She felt the program should individualize more.

For a while it looked as if these two might never see eye to eye; yet once the feelings got out in the open, the atmosphere began to change. It became obvious that both were concerned about Sissy, and once they realized that they had that in common, they found it wasn't so hard to sort out the problem and solve it. Respect and communication were the keys, they decided; and when the conversation ended, they both left with good feelings about each other.

Discuss Differences

Discussing differences isn't easy to do. Some people shy away from direct discussion of sensitive areas. Many want to cover up differences because they perceive that recognizing them will complicate the relationship. Others avoid discussion of differences in hopes of promoting equality and harmony. Some have never thought about values until they bump up against a set that is different from their own.

Become an Effective Cross-Cultural Communicator

Learn how to open up communication instead of shutting it down. Work to build a relationship with the person or the people with whom you're in conflict. You'll enhance your chances for conflict management or resolution if a relationship exists. Be patient. These things take time.

Learn about communication styles that are different from yours. Teach your own communication styles. Become aware of body language, voice tone, posture, and position. All of these carry cultural messages that are open to being misinterpreted across cultures. For example, if you're a parent and a caregiver stands too close to you when carrying on a conversation, you may feel that she is pushy, or at least strange, while she thinks she is conveying warmth and friendliness. If you are a teacher and a parent is very late to an appointment and then arrives and fails to apologize, you may make assumptions about his priorities or his manners. But he may have a very different time sense from yours and not consider himself late at all. He may have no idea that he has offended you.

If you tend to talk in a high-pitched voice when you are excited, and others interpret your tone of voice as anger, explain to them what you're really feeling. (Pitches and tones carry emotional messages that are culturally based and not the same across cultures.)

Sensitivity to, understanding of, and respect for differences is vital.

Problem Solve

Use a problem-solving approach to conflicts rather than a power approach (if you're the one with the power in the situation). Dialogue. Communicate. Be flexible when you can. Negotiate when possible. (See chapter 9 for examples of how to use this approach with children.)

Commit Yourself to Education

Learn about other cultures. Become a student of culture if you are in a cross-cultural situation. Observe, listen, and read, but don't believe everything you read or are told. You'll hear lots of generalizations about particular cultures. Don't get sucked into promoting more stereotypes! Check out what you are learning. Be a critical thinker.

HELPING CHILDREN UNDERSTAND AND VALUE CULTURAL PLURALISM

Just as adults are ethnocentric, so are children. Ethnocentrism relates to the ego-centrism that young children struggle with as they slowly learn to see the world from more than one point of view. Adults need to help children work through both their ethnocentrism and their egocentrism. They can do that only if they have grappled with their own ethnocentrism. It's a matter of getting children to communicate with each other, accept the reality of another as valid, and learn what it's like to walk in another's shoes.

Some children come from a multicultural background and have firsthand experience with cultural pluralism. This can be a great benefit for them and for those around them who can use them as models. When we see a person who is comfortable operating out of more than one culture, we gain an idea of how it works.

Here is an example of a bicultural child:

David was born in this country of a Mexican father and an Anglo-American mother. The family traveled frequently to Mexico and enjoyed extended visits with the father's family. By the time David entered preschool at the age of four, he was already bilingual and bicultural. He could perform amazing feats, such as making a judgment about which language to speak with someone he met for the first time. He was seldom wrong. He could also switch midstream from English to Spanish when the occasion demanded. For example, if he was playing in the sand with an Anglo child and a Spanish-speaking child approached, David would speak English with one and Spanish with the other, while playing with both. David fits very well in an all-Anglo group or an all-Mexican group or a Mexican-American group. He has chameleonlike qualities. He is a truly bicultural person.

Help children understand and appreciate cultural pluralism.

Children have the ability to compartmentalize—that is, to understand that one set of behaviors is appropriate at Grandmother's, another at childcare, and still another at home. Although we, as adults, may try hard to make most of the environments children find themselves in consistent, that's not the way the world works. One set of behaviors is expected in the bank, another at the park. Part of socialization is learning how to behave in each of the many environments in which children find themselves. Learning culturally appropriate behavior is one aspect of this same skill.

TEACHING MORALS AND VALUES TO CHILDREN

How do children come to know what's important in life and set their goals accordingly? How do children come to know right from wrong? Although the two questions are in many ways the same, the answer to the first mostly concerns values; the answer to the second mostly concerns morals.

Our values begin to come to us in our cribs (or our parents' bed) when we are infants. They are absorbed along with the breast milk or the formula we drink. They come hand in hand with our culture. They are the *shoulds* and *shouldn'ts* that guide our footsteps through life and the beliefs we feel compelled to stand up for. They tell us what to respect and what to oppose.

Some values are simply absorbed in infancy; others come later in the form of little lessons. "Don't hurt the caterpillar" may reflect a value of life. "Be gentle with your brother" may reflect a value of peace and harmony. "Don't let people push you around" may reflect a value of self-assertion. "Work hard at school" may reflect a value of individual success, or possibly a value of being an asset to your family. As children grow, they continually define, appraise, and, sometimes, modify their values. In a pattern-one culture, children are expected to do some deep soul-searching at some point, usually in adolescence. They are expected to examine the set of values they've grown up with and come to their own conclusions about whether to embrace those values or to redefine them and come up with their own set. Upset as parents may be at the possibility that their children will reject their values, pattern-one parents aren't entirely surprised, because the culture expects people to make up their own minds about values. After all, independence is a value—independence of thought as well as of action.

Pattern-two parents may be far less tolerant if their children threaten to deviate from the set of values the family embraces. The younger generation is not supposed to question the older one. Deciding values is not an individual matter for children—or for adults either, for that matter.

TEACHING MORALS BY HELPING CHILDREN EXAMINE THEIR DECISION-MAKING PROCESS

We—children and grownups alike—deal with morals and values with every decision we make. Each time we are forced to choose an action (and each action is a choice, whether we realize it or not), we go through a process of determining whether we're making the right decision. The impulsive person puts less thought into decisions than the more considered one; however, unless the person is reacting from reflexes alone, there is a flash of thought behind each decision.

If you could tune in on the flash, you'd find some of the following questions:

> Will I be punished if I decide to do this (either by my own bad feelings or by someone else in a physical or emotional way)?

> Will I be rewarded? (Will I gain some benefit, including feeling good about doing this?)

> Will this action or decision make someone whom I care about happy— thus making *me* happy (another form of reward)?

> Is there a rule (or a law) that requires or forbids it? And if I break the law and get caught, what is the punishment? And if I break the law and don't get caught, how will I feel?

> Is this what I would want someone else to do? (This calls into play the Golden Rule: "Do unto others as you would have others do unto you.")

> What's the right thing to do? (Using my highest reasoning abilities—is this the best decision, most right, highest good, or least bad thing to do?)

> Who might be hurt by my decision or action? [5]

We don't always ask these questions consciously, but on some level they govern each and every one of our decisions. We're more aware of that fact when the decision concerns a situation where there is a good deal at stake.

We can help children bring these questions into the open and examine them. Looking at the questions as a hierarchy helps us determine which ones are most likely to be of importance to younger children. [6]

Most children under the age of seven are only able to think in concrete terms. Although they may feel emotions related to such abstract concepts as love, honesty, and justice, they don't think or reason about them. [7] Instead of using sophisticated cognitive processes, young children are more likely to make judgments about right and wrong actions based on their past experience of the reactions of those around them. They consider the possibility of punishment or reward when trying to decide on the "right thing to do."

TEACHING MORALS BY PROMOTING PROSOCIAL DEVELOPMENT

How do caregivers, teachers, or parents promote prosocial development in the children they rear or care for? It helps to be clear about which prosocial behaviors are important to you. Start by making a list of some behaviors you want to encourage in children. Your list will probably include such items as sharing, nonviolent conflict resolution, consideration for others, sensitivity to feelings, cooperation, involvement with and responsibility to others, kindness, reverence for life, and respect for self, others, and the earth (nature). You will probably have these values on your list regardless of whether you are a pattern-one or a pattern-two person.

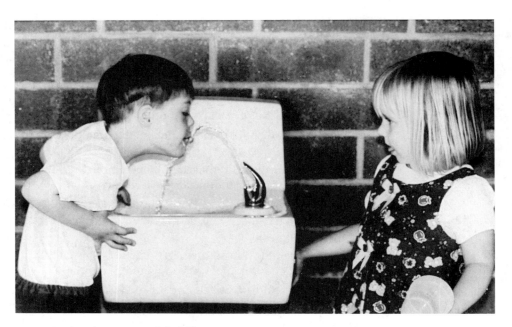

Cooperation is a prosocial skill.

Here are some tips about how to encourage those behaviors listed above:

1. Model them yourself. If you want children to share, they need to see you share. If respect is important, they need to see you being respectful. Modeling is the most powerful way to convey your messages. You'll see your own behaviors reflected in the children around you. If honesty is a value, be honest. If cooperation is important to you, show yourself to be cooperative—don't just expect it from children.

2. Use the power of your attention. A scene of a meal at a childcare center comes to mind. One child said gruffly, "More toast!" Another child said, "May I please have more toast?" The teacher immediately responded to the second child, ignoring the first, who quickly rephrased his question as "Please, may I have more toast?" Pay attention to children who exhibit the behaviors you're looking for. Notice how gently big sister is stroking the baby. Remark on how nicely Johnny is waiting for his turn.

3. Always explain why you are setting limits. Say "I can't let you throw the blocks; you might hurt someone," rather than "The rule is no block throwing!" Children need to know the effects of their behaviors. They need to know the reasoning behind your prohibitions.

4. Encourage cooperation by finding ways to get children to work and play together. Every picture doesn't have to be individually drawn—how about painting a mural? Collage can be a group effort. Play hospital—stretchers take two people to carry them! A set of large wooden blocks that are too big for one child to transport encourages cooperation.

5. Take a problem-solving stance when dealing with conflicts, rather than a power stance. Help children talk to one another, explain their feelings, and brainstorm solutions. Don't rescue, but let them talk it through. If they don't have the words, provide the words for them. (Chapter 9 deals with this subject at length.)

6. Avoid punishment as a way of disciplining. Although punishment may suppress some behaviors, it doesn't eliminate them—they go underground. Besides, punishment doesn't teach prosocial behaviors—it models antisocial ones. (See chapter 7 for ideas of ways to guide behavior without punishing.)

7. Examine your power relations with children. Do you *overpower* them rather than *empower* them? Don't rob them of opportunities to develop skills and experience their own competence by doing things for them or to them. Use your power, your superior size and skills, to bring out their own sense of power—their sense of themselves—who they are and what they can do. Empowered people have less need to use force and violent means of solving problems than do people who feel powerless. When you find yourself in power

Encourage cooperation by finding ways to encourage children to work and play together.

struggles, take a close look at why the parties concerned need to feel power. Take steps to empower them (and yourself, if you are one of the parties).

8. Avoid using competition to motivate. If you value competition, you probably think that starting early to teach children to compete with each other won't hurt. But it does. Even though we live in a competitive society, we do a disservice to children if we start too young to teach them about competition. Young children are still figuring out who they are. Even though you may see competition as a motivation device, you may be setting up comparisons that damage self-esteem and relationships. Avoid questions like "Who is the smartest?" "Who is the neatest eater?" or "Who is the fastest cleanerupper?" Also avoid win-lose situations. When you play games with young children, you don't need a winner and losers. You don't have to make a big deal over who gets bingo first. You can continue playing until everyone gets bingo. No young child can afford to be stuck with the label "loser"! Losers have poor self-images and they behave according to their labels.

9. Help children appreciate the world they live in and the people they share it with by "being with" them rather than lecturing or instructing. [8] Adults can do this best by feeling the sense of wonder children feel and encouraging the awe they experience at the beauty and mystery of nature. It's vital to help children perceive their connection to the earth and to all her creatures, including other humans.

10. Give choices. Only by experiencing the effects of their own actions on the world around them can children understand how things work. When they are faced with choosing from alternatives, they get practice in becoming good decision makers.

11. Teach children to solve conflicts without violence. Conflict is natural and is to be encouraged, but violence is never an appropriate response to conflict. Especially never use violence as a last resort, because the message then is that when all else fails, you can always fall back on violence. Do allow children their violent feelings—it's healthier to feel them than to deny them. Make it clear, however, that children won't be allowed to act on those feelings. Teach a number of ways to express those feelings in ways that do no harm. (See chapter 8 for further explanation.)

12. Teach children to be peacemakers. [9] Peacemaking is a vital part of moral education. Peace is not an absence of tension or conflict. Creating peace is an active process of balancing opposing forces and dealing with conflicts and tensions. True peace cannot be imposed. Peacemaking requires resourcefulness in using a number of skills, including confrontation, debate, dialogue, and negotiation. The goal of peacemakers is to bring conflicts to the surface and to respect differences while resolving or managing those conflicts in ways that preserve the self-esteem of everyone involved. Children learn both the philosophy and the skills of peacemaking from the adults around them who daily help them settle the numerous disputes that occur in the natural course of life, both at home and in early-childhood programs.

Teach children to be peace-makers.

SUMMARY

This chapter looked at goals and values, including the differing ones reflected in cultural conflicts. The chapter also looked at how children learn morals and values from living day to day with adults who pass them on. Some priorities are specific to the family's culture, but universal values can also be found in most early-childhood-education settings. This chapter examined the relationship of goals and values to childrearing in both the home and the childcare center. The next chapter focuses specifically on the childcare setting.

FOR DISCUSSION

1. What do goals and values have to do with childrearing?
2. How is a pattern-one person different from a pattern-two person?
3. Which pattern is more likely to have parents emphasizing modesty over pride? Why?
4. Which parent, pattern-one or pattern-two, is more likely to emphasize manners over honest self-expression?
5. If you should find yourself in a cultural conflict over a childrearing practice, what could you do?
6. How might a pattern-one parent differ from a pattern-two parent in his or her approach to toilet training?

7. How do you teach morals by helping children examine their decision-making process?

8. What do you think of the suggestions for promoting prosocial development on page 122?

PERSONAL REFLECTIONS

Thinking about your personal reactions and experiences will help you better understand and integrate the material in this chapter. Use these questions to interface between you and what you read. Use the pertinent ones to reflect on, write about, or discuss with others.

> Do you speak the language of your ancestors? Why or why not?

> We all belong to a particular culture, but some are more aware of that fact than others. Do you realize that you belong to a culture? What is the name of your culture?

> If someone walked into your home and looked around, what would they know about you just based on what they saw inside your home? Would they discover something about your culture?

> Have you ever learned something about your culture because someone compared yours with theirs? If yes, what?

> Are you more of a pattern-one person or a pattern-two person?

> Are there some things about you that don't fit the pattern you just chose? What are they?

> What is an example of something from your culture that is different from other cultures?

> Do you find yourself on one side or the other of the cultural conflict between Helen and the childcare center in the box on page 114–115?

> Are the questions that children ask themselves as laid out on page 119 the same ones you ask yourself when facing a moral dilemma?

> Which of the suggestions for promoting prosocial development on pages 120–122 appeal to you most? Which are new to you?

NOTES

1. Culture has been carefully studied. Ray L. Birdwhistell and others have analyzed and coded body movement, adding to the body of knowledge concerning communication and linguistics. Birdwhistell turned his studies of body movement into an exact science, calling it *kinesics*. Behavior has been coded by kinesists from blinks and head nods to body position and gross movements.

Others have studied larger sets of behaviors. Edward Hall, an anthropologist, has spent a lifetime observing and recording cultural information. He studied cultural differences in perceptions of space and time, among other things.

Other writers have concentrated on contrasting one culture with another. Thomas Kochman, in his little book, *Black and White, Styles in Conflict* (Chicago: University of Chicago Press, 1981) contrasts, among other things, the white European middle-class American way of what is seen as straightforward communication with the African-American approach called "signifying." He says, "Because blacks regard direct questions as confrontational, intrusive, and presumptuous, they are virtually obliged to 'ask' others for personal information in a way that avoids what black etiquette considers inappropriate. This can be done by signifying. Signifying . . . means intending or implying more than one actually says." In other words, African Americans, according to Kochman, hint rather than ask directly.

2. Because cultural differences comprise such a huge subject, I'm going to greatly simplify it. That means I might be making huge generalizations—which could well promote even more stereotypes than we already have in this society. For that reason, I'm not going to talk about specific cultures or name names, but rather discuss contrasting cultural patterns. I'm also going to ask you to remember that within any cultural pattern there are individual differences.

3. Stanley Sue and Thom Moore's book makes a good case for why America should be a pluralistic society, and does a good job of defining and describing such a society. Stanley Sue and Thom Moore, eds., *The Pluralistic Society* (New York: Human Sciences Press, Inc., 1984).

4. The tips that follow were inspired in part by the work of Louise Derman-Sparks and her Antibias Curriculum Committee.

5. The questions were inspired by the work of Lawrence Kohlberg and of Carol Gilligan. Kohlberg created a hierarchy of stages that relates to stages of cognitive development. Gilligan and others (Nell Noddings, for example) have come up with an ethic of caring. For them the question is not "Which principle is higher?" but "How can I act so that those around me—those I care about—will get hurt the least?" The Gilligan view is more of a net than an ascending scale or ladder. In her book, *In a Different Voice,* she makes it clear that although her research focused on women, both males and females may "speak in a different voice."

6. As stated in note 5, Kohlberg set forth stages of moral development as a hierarchy. Kohlberg, following the work of Jean Piaget, saw a pattern of organization of moral thought, which he laid out in progressive stages from children determining what's right and what's wrong by whether they were rewarded or punished, to obeying rules in order to uphold a social order, and finally to a personal commitment to an abstract hierarchy of principles. In Kohlberg's scheme, intellectual development, specifically the ability to reason, is vitally linked to moral development. It is important to note that Kohlberg did his research on men and boys.

7. However, children are quick to state what is "fair" and what is "unfair" from their own point of view.

8. Michael True states this concept very well in his book, *Ordinary People: Family Life and Global Values* (Maryknoll, NY: Orbis Books, 1991).

9. Michael True also discusses "peace-making" in his book.

REFERENCES

Allen, Judy, Earldene McNeill, and Velma Schmidt. *Cultural Awareness for Children.* Menlo Park, CA: Addison-Wesley, 1992.

Bernhard, Judith K. "Child Development, Cultural Diversity, and the Professional Training of Early Childhood Educators." *Canadian Journal of Education* 20(4) (1995).

Bredekamp, Sue, ed. *Developmentally Appropriate Practice in Early Childhood Programs Serving Children from Birth Through Age Eight.* Washington, DC: National Association for the Education of Young Children, 1987.

Chang, Hedy Nai-Lin and Laura Sakai. *Affirming Children's Roots: Cultural and Linguistic Diversity in Early Care and Education.* California Tomorrow, San Francisco, CA, 1993.

Chang, H. N. L., A. Muckelroy, and D. Pulido-Tobiassen. *Looking In, Looking Out: Redefining Child and Early Education in a Diverse Society.* San Francisco: California Tomorrow, 1996.

Derman-Sparks, Louise. *Antibias Curriculum.* Washington, DC: National Association for the Education of Young Children, 1989.

Derman-Sparks, Louise, and Kay Taus. "We're Different and . . . " *Scholastic Pre-K Today* (November/December 1989): 40–44.

Dorn, Lois. *Peace in the Family.* New York: Pantheon Books, 1983.

Fernea, Elizabeth Warnock, *Children in the Muslim Middle East.* Austin: University of Texas Press, 1995.

Garcia, Eugene E., and Barry McLaughlin, eds., with Bernard Spokek and Olivia N. Saracho. *Meeting the Challenge of Linguistic and Cultural Diversity in Early Childhood Education.* New York: Teachers College Press, 1995.

Gergen, Kenneth J. *Realities and Relationships: Soundings in Social Construction.* Cambridge: Harvard University Press, 1994.

Gilligan, Carol. *In a Different Voice.* Cambridge, MA: Harvard University Press, 1982.

Gonzalez-Mena, Janet and Dianne Eyer. *Infants, Toddlers and Caregivers.* Mountain View, CA: Mayfield Publishing Company, 1997.

Gonzalez-Mena, Janet. "Learning to See Across a Cultural Gap." *Child Care Information Exchange* (May 1994).

Gonzalez-Mena, Janet. *Multicultural Issues in Child Care.* Mountain View, CA: Mayfield Publishing Company, 1997.

Gonzalez-Mena, Janet. "When Values Collide: Exploring a Cross Cultural Issue." *Child Care Information Exchange* (March 1996).

Greenman, Jim. "Living in the Real World: Diversity and Conflict." *Exchange* (October 1989).

Hale, Janice E. "An African-American Early Childhood Education Program: Visions for Children." In *Reconceptualizing the Early Childhood Curriculum: Beginning the Dialogue,* eds. Shirley A.

Kessler and Beth Blue Swadener. New York: Teachers College Press, 1992, 205–224.

Hale-Benson, Janice E. *Black Children, Their Roots, Culture, and Learning Styles.* Baltimore, MD: Johns Hopkins University Press, 1986.

Hale, Janice. "The Transmission of Cultural Values to Young African American Children." *Young Children* 46(6) (September 1991): 7–15.

Hall, Edward T. *Beyond Culture.* Garden City, NY: Anchor Books, 1977.

Hall, Edward T. *The Dance of Life.* Garden City, NY: Anchor Press/Doubleday, 1984.

———. *The Hidden Dimension.* New York: Anchor Books, 1966.

———. *The Silent Language.* Greenwich, CT: Fawcett Publications, Inc., 1959.

Heath, S. B. *Ways with Words: Language, Life, and Work in Communities and Classrooms.* Cambridge: Cambridge University Press, 1983.

Kendall, F. *Diversity in the Classroom.* New York: Teachers College Press, 1996.

Kitayama, Shinobu, Hazel Rose Markus, and Hisaya Matsumoto. "Culture, Self, and Emotion: A Cultural Perspective on 'Self-Conscious' Emotions." In *Self-Conscious Emotions: The Psychology of Shame, Guilt, Embarrassment and Pride,* eds. June Tangney and Kurt Fisher. New York: Guilford, 1995, 439–463.

Knight, George P., Martha E. Bernal, and Gustavo Carlo. "Socialization and the Development of Cooperative, Competitive, and Individualistic Behaviors Among Mexican American Children." In *Meeting the Challenge of Linguistic and Cultural Diversity in Early Childhood Education,* eds. Eugene E. Garcia and Barry McLaughlin, with Bernard Spokek and Olivia N. Saracho. New York: Teachers College Press, 1995, 85–102.

Kochman, Thomas. *Black and White, Styles in Conflict.* Chicago: University of Chicago Press, 1981.

Kohlberg, Lawrence. "Moral Stages and Moralization. The Cognitive-Developmental Approach." In *Moral Development and Behavior,* ed. T. Lickona. New York: Holt, Rinehart & Winston, 1976.

Lee, Joann. *Asian Americans.* New York: New Press, 1992.

Lefley, H., and P. Pedersen, eds. *Cross-Cultural Training for Mental Health Professionals.* Springfield, IL: Charles C. Thomas, Publisher, 1986.

Liederman, P. H., Steven R. Tulkin, and Anne Rosenfeld. *Culture and Infancy: Variations in Human Experience*. New York: Academic Press, 1977.

Lynch, Eleanor W., and Marci J. Hanson. *Developing Cross-Cultural Competence: A Guide for Working with Young Children and Their Families*. Baltimore, MD: Paul H. Brookes Publishing, 1992.

Makin, Laurie, Julie Campbell, and Criss Jones Diaz. *One Childhood, Many Languages*. Pymble, NSW, Australia: HarperEducational, 1995.

Mallory, Bruce, L., and Rebecca S. New, eds. *Diversity and Developmentally Appropriate Practices: Challenges for Early Childhood Education*. New York: Teachers College Press, 1994.

Morelli, G., B. Rogoff, and D. Oppenheim. "Cultural Variation in Infants' Sleeping Arrangements: Questions of Independence." *Developmental Psychology* 28(4) (July 1992): 604–619.

Medicine, Beatrice. "Child Socialization Among Native Americans: The Lakota (Sioux) in Cultural Context." *Wicazo Sa Review* 1(2) (Fall 1985): 23–28.

"National Association for the Education of Young Children: Linguistic and Cultural Diversity Position Paper." *Young Children* 51(2) (January 1996).

Neugebauer, Bonnie. *Alike and Different: Exploring Our Humanity with Young Children*. Redmond, WA: Exchange Press, 1987.

Outsama, Kao. *Laotian Themes*. Philadelphia: Temple University, 1977.

Phillips, Carol Brunson. "Culture: A Process That Empowers." In *Infant/Toddler Caregiving: A Guide to Culturally Sensitive Care*, ed. Peter Mangione. Sacramento, CA: Far West Laboratory and California Department of Education, 1995.

Phillips, Carol Brunson, and Renatta M. Cooper. "Cultural Dimensions of Feeding Relationships." *Zero to Three* (June 1992): 10–13.

Phillips, Carol Brunson. "Nurturing Diversity for Today's Children and Tomorrow's Leaders." *Young Children* (January 1988): 42–47.

Ramsey, P. *Teaching and Learning in a Diverse World*. New York: Teachers College Press, 1986.

Rashid, Hakim M. "Promoting Biculturalism in Young African-American Children." *Young Children* (January 1984): 13–23.

Saracho, Olivia N., and Bernard Spodek. "Preparing Teachers for Early Childhood Programs." In *Meeting the Challenge of Linguistic and Cultural Diversity in Early Childhood Education*, eds. Eurene Garcia and Barry McLaughlin. New York: Teachers College Press, 1995, 154–166.

Shigaki, Irene. "Child Care Practices in Japan and the United States: How They Reflect Cultural Values in Young Children." *Young Children* 38(4) (May 1983).

Stephens, William N. *The Family in Cross-Cultural Perspective*. New York: Holt, Rinehart & Winston, 1963.

Sue, Stanley, and Thom Moore, eds. *The Pluralistic Society*. New York: Human Sciences Press, Inc., 1984.

True, Michael. *Ordinary People: Family Life and Global Values*. Maryknoll, NY: Orbis Books, 1991.

Wagner, D., and H. Stevenson. *Cultural Perspectives on Child Development*. San Francisco: W. H. Freeman and Company, 1982.

Werner, E. *Cross-Cultural Child Development: A View from the Planet Earth*. Monterey, CA: Brooks/Cole Publishing Company, 1979.

Whiting, B., and C. Edwards. *Children of Different Worlds*. Cambridge, MA: Harvard University Press, 1988.

Whiting, B., and J. Whiting. *Children of Six Cultures*. Cambridge: Harvard University Press, 1981.

Whiting, J. W. M. *Child Training and Personality*. New Haven, CT: Yale University Press, 1953.

Young, V. H. "Family and Childhood in a Southern Georgia Community." *American Anthropologist* 72 (1970).

Childcare: An Extension of the Family

CHAPTER 6

In this chapter you'll discover:

> Why childcare can be considered childrearing
> Three things that influence quality in childcare
> How the home can be a model for childcare programs
> Some arguments about breaking large centers into small groups
> Some ideas about bridging the gap between the childcare program and the home
> Advantages and disadvantages of matching teachers to the children's language and culture
> Some roadblocks to respect between parents and teachers

TEST YOURSELF

Look for the answers to these questions as you read the chapter:

1. Why does the text insist that childcare is childrearing?
2. What are some alternatives for parents who work outside the home and are concerned about someone else rearing their children?
3. What are the three variables that influence quality in childcare?
4. What are some disadvantages of large, closed-structure programs?
5. What are some advantages of using the home as a model for childcare?
6. What are examples of adult behaviors that pressure children to comply?
7. What are examples of adult behaviors that are facilitative?
8. What are some arguments for breaking larger centers into smaller self-contained groups?
9. Continuity between home and school has some advantages. Is there ever a situation when continuity might not be the best goal?
10. What are the advantages of aiming for racial and cultural similarities between children and caregivers or teachers? Are there ever any disadvantages?
11. What are some roadblocks to mutual respect, appreciation, and support between parents and childcare providers?

Who is rearing America's children and how are they being reared? That is an increasingly compelling question. It was a nonquestion just a generation or two ago, because America's children were mostly reared by their own parents, or by specific substitutes whom the parents designated. Childrearing belonged to the family. Business, education, and government mostly stayed out of the picture, except for a period during World War II, and except for protective and remedial reasons.

Today the picture has changed. The number of single-parent families where the parent trains or works outside the home steadily rises. In a majority of two-parent families, both parents work outside the home. Childrearing is now shared as families use an array of childcare services, and business and government have become part of the picture.

Who is raising America's children? Perhaps you are or will be—either as a parent or as a teacher/childcare worker. As the need for childcare expands and services struggle to keep up with the need, more and more childcare workers, teachers, caregivers, family day-care providers, in-home care providers, and nannies supplement parent care.

CHILDCARE AS A CHILDREARING ENVIRONMENT

Why does this text keep equating childcare with childrearing? After all, the United States doesn't have a communal childrearing system where children are taken out of the home and socialized into a model consisting of a single set of ideals. We don't believe in political indoctrination for our children. Childrearing is an individual matter of individual families and always has been. As a society, Americans agree to disagree. Diversity has always been a key theme as well as a strong point of America's people. However, these days individuals and families must look outside themselves for supplementary care. They can no longer do all the childrearing themselves.

But is childcare really childrearing? Yes. You can drive your car to work, park it in a garage, and come back and pick it up in the afternoon and, except for a new layer of dust, it is almost always in the same condition you left it in. You can even leave your car at home in the garage, take the bus or the train to work, and come back and find it just as you left it.

But you can't park your children. Wherever your children are, they are growing and learning, being changed by their experiences. They are being reared. How they are being reared is a big question. They can be reared in accordance with parental expectations and values, or they can be reared in ways that are quite contradictory.

The challenge for our society in these times is to offer enough choices so that parents can find childcare in tune with what they want and need for their children. The choices could include both nonparental care solutions such as center care, family childcare, and in-home care, as well as creative alternatives that allow working parents a greater role in caring for their own children. Flextime, one of these alternatives, allows parents to stagger their work schedules and manage to be with the child, doing the childrearing mostly themselves. Part-time work also allows more parental involvement in childrearing; job-sharing is one way to become a part-time worker. In some countries, workers are subsidized to stay home with their children instead of working a full day or a full workweek. Flexible benefits plans and flexible leave and transfer policies can also be creative alternatives that allow parents to spend more time with their children.

AFFORDABILITY AND AVAILABILITY

Two *A* words loom up when we look at requirements for nonparental childcare— *affordability* and *availability*. When we, as a society, work to create both cheap and widespread childcare, quality often gets lost. We get into a double bind when we deal with both quality and cost: Most parents can't afford to pay what quality child-care really costs, and as a society we can't afford not to pay it, especially for low-income families. After a lengthy, extensive research, the classic Lazar study [1] showed that for every dollar spent in quality early-childhood education for poor children, seven dollars was saved in later remedial work and social services. Quality costs, but it saves in the long run.

As a society we haven't learned that lesson yet. We aren't willing to pay what childcare really costs. We say we can't afford it. As a result, childcare in our country isn't as good as it could be.

Status and salaries of childcare teachers are two problems related to quality and cost that haven't been solved yet. Childcare teachers are still underpaid. Their salaries put them at poverty level, and their status puts them in the same category as parking lot attendants. Not a pretty picture! A campaign called "Worthy Work, Worthless Wages" is under way to bring these facts to public attention. In the meantime, turnover rates soar. According to Marcy Whitebook in the National Child Care Staffing Study Revisited, though the turnover rate was high when the study was first published in 1989, it continued to climb. In 1993, four years after the first study, 70 percent of the teaching staff interviewed the first time had left and were no longer available to be interviewed in the second study. The researchers found that the lower the salary, the higher the turnover rate. Turnover rate for childcare teaching staff is three times the 9.6 percent annual turnover rate of U.S. companies and well above the 5.6 percent turnover rate of public school teachers. [2]

If all these teachers are leaving the field, what does this mean to children? It means that they are constantly disrupted by changes in their routines. It means that rules switch as teachers come and go. It means that just as the children get to know a teacher, he or she disappears suddenly and is replaced by a new person. Separation issues don't get resolved. The consistency of the stable environment that children need to flourish is a sought-after vision, but seldom a reality.

We need to find ways to solve these problems. It isn't just up to the parents and the childcare teachers to work toward solutions. Indeed, many parents are paying

Worthy Wages and Quality Care

Kayla is in a quality childcare center with a stable staff that know her well and can provide just the kind of care and education she needs. It's a sensitive, well-trained staff that has the time and energy to arrange the environment in appropriate ways, and to set out a variety of interesting and worthwhile activities that promote growth and development. They are there to guide, protect, and teach her by relating to Kayla on an individual basis and supporting her development in numerous ways. Kayla is happy in her school and her mother is happy that she is there. The whole picture is happy, but what about the teachers?

If the teachers are happy, it's because they love teaching and/or work in a very well-funded program in which they are paid well and have adequate support through staff and other resources. Or perhaps they are happy because they have other sources of income and have figured out how to scrounge up the resources they need. Or they may get so many rewards from teaching that money isn't an issue with them. Many good teachers remain in the field despite the low pay.

However, in most childcare programs, the staff is underpaid and if any of them are the sole support for their families, they have a hard time managing on childcare teacher wages. Childcare teachers' wages reflect their status, which, according to the Bureau of Labor statistics, is equated with parking lot attendants. Some refuse to leave the field, even though they are being paid less than prison guards and animal tenders. These dedicated souls are raising the nation's children—raising them at the point of their lives when they are very impressionable.

What does it mean to children and families that childcare teachers are underpaid and undervalued? It means a lot. It means that many people will never even consider going into the field—people who have a lot to offer children. It means that anyone who isn't totally dedicated to the profession and wants to make an adequate living will look elsewhere. It means that few men, especially those who have families to support, will look to childcare as a career option. This limits the field drastically.

The problem of low status and salary is reflected in the turnover rate. Many people enter the field only to leave it in a short time, when they find the demands of the job too much and the pay too little. One-third to one-half of the people working in childcare are new every year. That means that children see their teachers constantly changing—continually coming and going. As soon as they get to know and trust someone, that person leaves. Eventually children stop developing relationships with their childcare teachers—it's just too painful to keep saying good-bye for good.

That's not good for children.

Quality is tied to status, salaries, and training. Who is going to spend the money to get themselves trained if the status and salaries are so low?

We are in a crisis situation. We have a great need, as a nation, for childcare, and it can be a very satisfying career. Yet the money for quality care just isn't there. Many parents couldn't possibly afford what quality care costs. They need subsidies. A few get them from the government; others get them from employers. But an enormous number receive their subsidies from the teachers who work for so little. It's time that changed.

Childcare has become a necessity for many families.

more than they can afford now. A low-income family can pay as much as 26 percent of the family budget for childcare. And teachers, by working for poverty wages, are subsidizing childcare themselves. No, it's not up to parents and teachers to solve this problem alone. It is in the public interest to help in raising other people's children to the extent that they need it. Children are the future of America.

Even without platitudes, you can look at the situation from a very personal point of view. When you reach retirement age, you will be dependent on a strong, healthy, productive workforce to keep the society and the economy going. You won't be able to sit back and enjoy the fruits of your own labor if there is no one to carry on.

Even more personally, imagine yourself in a retirement home being cared for by men and women whose own upbringing left much to be desired. If today's society allows its future citizens to be neglected at home or warehoused in an institutional setting, how well will they treat you if and when you need their care in your old age?

THE STATE OF CHILDCARE IN AMERICA TODAY

What is the state of childcare in America today? The study called The Cost, Quality, and Child Outcomes in Child Care Centers [3] found the following:

> Childcare at most centers is poor to mediocre and infant care is the worst (40 percent of infants are cared for in centers that rate less than minimal quality).

> Children in higher quality programs display greater cognitive and social skills, have more positive self-perceptions, and are more likely to have warm, open relationships with their teachers and caregivers.

> Quality of childcare is related to teachers' wages, education, specialized training, and staff-child ratio.

> Programs that meet higher standards than those set by their respective states have higher quality.

> Good quality services cost more than mediocre quality, but not a great deal more.

(Recommendations based on this study are found in chapter 15.)

In addition to this study, an earlier study conducted by The National Panel on Child Care Policy [4] came up with seven findings and conclusions after extensive study:

1. Existing childcare services in the United States are inadequate to meet current and likely future needs of children, parents, and society as a whole.

2. A large number of children are presently cared for in settings that do not protect their health and safety and do not provide appropriate developmental stimulation.

3. Irrespective of family income, childcare has become a necessity for the majority of American families, yet many lack access to services.

4. Problems in arranging for quality childcare are compounded for low-income families who lack time, information, and economic resources. For these families, the choices are often more limited, and the consequences of inadequate care are likely to be more severe.

5. The most striking characteristic of existing childcare services is their diversity, which is both a strength and a challenge to the development of a coherent system that meets the needs of all children and all families.

6. There is no single policy or program that can address the childcare needs of all families and children.

7. Responsibility for meeting the nation's childcare needs should be widely shared among individuals, families, voluntary organizations, employers, communities, and government at all levels.

LOOKING AT QUALITY

Defining, measuring, and monitoring quality of childcare is very hard, because to some extent the definition of quality is highly subjective and personal. However, the National Day Care Study [5] came up with three variables that influence quality: *group size, caregiver-child ratio,* and *caregiver qualifications.* This study helped justify and substantiate the laws and regulations governing childcare. However, it is important to recognize that in many places in the United States childcare remains unregulated, and that even where it is regulated, laws and regulations provide only a bottom line (i.e., they define *minimal* standards). Various national and state professional organizations have provided more optimal guidelines. [6]

Although it may be hard to define quality beyond health and safety issues, ratios, group size, and square feet per child, it's fairly easy to see what *isn't* quality childcare, even if your personal tastes aren't quite like most people's. We all deplore mass-produced, institutionalized care. No one wants to see children warehoused in dehumanizing kinds of situations.

Let's now look at quality by examining some research done in the late 1970s—research that is as valid today as when it was done. Researchers [7] at Pacific Oaks College in Pasadena, California, spent hours and hours observing children [8] and coding their behavior in centers, family childcare homes, and in their own homes. The centers and family childcare homes were all quality settings as defined by licensing regulations, and further, all had community and parental recognition for quality.

The centers were divided into two kinds by the researchers: those where the adults initiated most of the activities (called by the researchers "closed-structure" centers) and those where the children initiated most of the activities (called "open-structure" centers).

In the closed-structure center, which tended to be larger and more school-like, adults made 58 percent of the decisions for children about the activities they were involved in. Adults started and ended the activities. In open-structure centers, adults made those decisions only 20 percent of the time. In family childcare, children made most of their own decisions about initiating and ending activities; adults made decisions 13 percent of the time. The children in their own homes made almost all of their own decisions about what to do, how to do it, and for how long. Adults made those decisions for them only 7 percent of the time. In other words, children in their own homes and in family childcare homes learn a lot more about how to structure their own time, follow their own interests, and pace themselves than children in larger, school-like childcare programs. That's what childhood is for—discovering who you are and what you like, and developing a sense of time. Children in open-structure centers also learned to structure their time and make choices. It seems as though the home and the homelike environment encourage these early learnings more than large groups of children in a school-like environment. Large centers give children the least opportunity to follow their own interests and structure their own time.

Advantages to Using the Home as a Model for Childcare

What follows is more information from this same research, which shows many advantages to a home setting for childcare (childrearing). However, before I go on let me hasten to say that the message is not that we should get rid of centers, but that *we should reexamine the goal of modeling childcare centers after schools*. There is even a push now to make family childcare programs more like schools.

My proposal is that we rethink our models and consider making centers *more like homes and less like schools.* What follows are the facts from the Pacific Oaks research that support my proposal.

Consider this: In closed-structure centers the children spend *24 percent* of their time *waiting*—in lines, at tables for meals, to use the toilet, to wash their hands, and so forth. Open-structure programs require only half that waiting time. At home (both family childcare and in children's own homes), the waiting time is less than 3 percent.

Given that many children have great difficulty controlling their behavior during waiting periods, you can see the potential for behavior problems that wouldn't exist if the child weren't required to spend nearly a quarter of his or her childcare day in transitions.

If you add waiting time in closed-structure programs to sleeping time and television time at home, you find that the average child in a large school-like childcare program spends a rather small proportion of his or her life actively involved in learning about and enjoying the world and a rather large proportion passive or waiting for the next event to happen. Children should spend their days actively involved in exploring and learning about the world, with a helpful adult close by to provide resources, input, and guidance. That's what mostly happens in homes and in open-structure smaller programs where, according to the research, there is a five times greater chance that children have an adult to themselves for short periods—or share an adult with only two or three other children. Yet, in the larger school-like programs, children are much more apt to be in groups of ten to twelve children for most of the day. Think of the implications of raising children with little privacy, few one-to-one interactions, and very little personal access to adult attention.

Adult behavior.   The researchers didn't look just at the amount of adult input, they also examined the type of input. They looked for adult input in two categories: pressure for compliance versus facilitation. In the larger school-like centers, adults were much more likely to use pressure—issue demands, give orders, and quote rules. In homes and in smaller centers, adult input was more likely to be facilitative—encouraging, helping, and suggesting, rather than demanding.

Not surprisingly, children's access to adults was significantly higher in home care. Where there are large numbers of children, adults are less able to focus on relationships, because their concern must be crowd control. Of course many centers are able to give children the individual time and attention they need, but it gets harder and harder as numbers rise.

In homes and small centers, children have more individualized adult attention, which results in quality interactions that encourage the development of autonomy and initiative, which, according to Erik Erikson, [9] is vital to healthy development in the early years.

Child behavior.   Child behavior also differed markedly in each setting studied. Children in large school-like programs spent much more time resisting or responding to adult expectations as the adults made demands, issued orders, and asked questions. Children in open-structure smaller centers and homes exhibited a greater variety of healthy behaviors. They initiated as well as responded. They were more likely to be physically and socially engaged, as they gave orders, chose activities, playfully and aggressively intruded on each other, asked for help, and gave opinions.   Children in home settings were lowest in distressed behaviors such as frustration, rejection, thumbsucking, crying, and so forth.

The home is a more natural, less artificial childrearing environment. The home environment is the one best suited to teach children how to function in a home—a worthy goal, considering that they will grow up to establish their own homes some day. Centers should strive to be more like homes rather than the reverse.

Making changes.   We already have a large system of home care in place, though it is generally ignored by the media and the public, except when some unfortunate piece of publicity brings a family childcare program into the headlines. We also have a number of small open-structure centers already in place. Many of these centers are modeled after home environments. More could follow their lead if they understood the importance. They should be encouraged to do so, instead of being pushed into a school model, as the trend is now. A problem is that larger centers are growing in number because they are more cost effective than smaller centers.

According to Elizabeth Prescott, one of the Pacific Oaks researchers: "I would propose limiting the size of centers. Centers that get to be much larger than sixty children do not, despite the intentions of well-qualified staff, seem to stay as warm and personal as smaller centers." [10]

A challenge.   The challenge is either to find ways to make large centers more homelike or to redefine cost effectiveness. We could say that small centers are more cost effective in the long run because they tend to produce more autonomous citizens with initiative.

At the very least, every effort should be made to break centers into smaller, self-contained groups. Group size is a vital factor to quality. The National Day Care Study [11] showed that group size has more effect than any other factor on teacher and child behavior and on intellectual development. Yet at present, fewer than half the states regulate group size. [12]

To summarize.   Quality care provides a safe, healthy, and nurturing learning environment designed to meet the needs—physical, emotional, intellectual—of the individual and the group. Good care, like good childrearing, enhances each child's development as a unique and powerful person who is capable of cooperating with others and living in a group situation. The goal is to establish a sense of being an individual while incorporating a growing sense of community. This happens most easily with a stable, consistent, trained staff, available at least some of the time to interact with children one on one and in small groups. Another contributing factor is plenty of play time during which the child is actively engaged with peers, and practices decision making, problem solving, and conflict resolution. Quality care can occur in a variety of environments, including home and center settings.

QUESTIONS CONCERNING CONTINUITY BETWEEN CHILDCARE AND HOME

How much should the childcare program, whether in-home, home based, or center based, reflect the methods, the approaches, and the values of the parents? This subject was discussed in the last chapter; however, following are some more questions to consider.

Is continuity between home and program always valuable? A look at a cross-cultural example gives one view. In China today, [13] couples are allowed to have only one child. Yet China is very family oriented; so all the energy that went into the many children of the large families of the past is focused today on a single child. As a result, this child gets a good deal of attention—"spoiling," if you will—from two parents and four grandparents. Six adults are all vitally concerned with this one small child. So childcare is set up to purposely counteract this effect. Child-to-adult ratios are large, so that adults cannot focus very much time on any one child. Group expectations are heavy—the child must learn to be a good group member, which happened easily at home in the old days of big families. It doesn't happen at home easily now. So the child is learning away from home what is very hard to teach at home. Childcare is set up to create a gap between home and program—one is designed to counterbalance the other.

Quality care provides a safe, healthy, nurturing learning environment designed to meet the needs—physical, emotional, intellectual—of the individual and the group.

Choosing Childcare: Debbie and Walt

Debbie is a physical therapist in her middle thirties. She and her husband, Walt, delayed having children, but now they have eighteen-month-old Jason. Debbie took a six-month leave when Jason was born, but when it came time to go back to work, she had such strong feelings about leaving him that she and Walt worked out a time-share plan. She went back to work half time, and he rearranged his work schedule so that he could be home when she wasn't. So far they haven't had to use childcare. But now they've decided that their city apartment isn't the right place for Jason to grow up, so they're in the market for a house. In addition, Walt, who has two teenage children from his first marriage, is feeling some pressure because his oldest daughter is applying to expensive colleges. It's time for Debbie to go back to work full time. She is looking for childcare. Here's her story.

She started by calling a friend at work, who recommended the childcare center that she uses. Debbie went over right away. She was appalled at what she saw. The place seemed like a madhouse—furniture overturned, paper on the floor, children everywhere yelling and screaming. Debbie couldn't imagine her precious little Jason here! A harried-looking teacher showed her around, but was interrupted every ten seconds by some squabble or a child demanding something. After ten minutes the teacher handed Debbie a fistful of papers, told her that all the information she needed was on them, and left her standing wide-eyed by the door. She made a fast exit, depositing the papers in the trash can in the parking lot.

Next Debbie checked the phone book. At random, she picked another place, close to her work. She was astonished to find this center just the opposite of the first one. She arrived to find the children waiting in line to go outside. Although they were talking quietly and wiggling just a bit, they were not unruly. The room was immaculate, a little cold, and on the bare side. Debbie tried to imagine exuberant Jason in this setting. She couldn't. She left without talking to anyone.

The next place Debbie tried was down the street from her apartment. "At last!" she thought as she stepped inside a pleasant, well-lighted room alive with healthy child activity. She liked what she saw—clusters of children playing busily, adults on the floor with them. "Good energy here," she concluded. But when she talked to the director, she discovered that this center took only low-income children and even for them it had a waiting list with 100 names on it. She left disappointed!

"Your turn," she told Walt when she got home that night. "I'm just too discouraged."

By the end of a week she and Walt had learned a lot about childcare. They found out there was a local resource and referral agency that gave them information about centers as well as family childcare providers—people who use their own homes for childcare.

By the end of two weeks they had visited a number of centers and family childcare homes and found two that suited them that had openings. They sat down to make a decision.

First Walt brought up an earlier discussion about in-home care. "Are you sure you don't want to reconsider looking for someone to come here? If we could find someone it would be easier."

"Yes, it would be easier, but I want Jason to be with other children. I can't imagine him here all day every day by himself with someone who isn't me or you."

"So what will it be, Mrs. Watson's house or the River Street Center?" asked Walt, ready to settle this question. "They both have pros and cons. The center is more convenient and cheaper. It's warm and homelike. I like the way they plan curriculum around the children's interests. The staff seems stable—I asked each how long he or she had been there, and was impressed at the low turnover rate. What do you think?"

"Well," Debbie was hesitant. "I liked the center too, but I wonder how Jason would fit in with those kids. They are so much older than he is."

"Mrs. Watson has a five-year-old and a four-year-old," said Walt.

"Yes, but the group is so small that the older kids are an asset rather than a liability. I don't worry that he will get lost in a crowd of big kids."

"But Mrs. Watson's is twice as far away."

"True, but I really like the fact he'd be sort of part of a family. He has so many years to be in school, I'd rather he experience family life at this point. And when he's older he could go to the preschool down the block from Mrs. Watson, so he could have a larger group experience before he goes to kindergarten."

"I think you've made up your mind."

"I guess I have. What about you?"

"I think Mrs. Watson's house is great! Let's call her."

Is the ideal to aim for racial and cultural similarities between caregivers and children or to aim for diversity? The advantage in similarity is that when children see adults of the same race as themselves, they identify with these people. When children of color see adults of their race in positions of authority and competence, they see models, which can be valuable for their self-esteem.

When consistency exists between family and program, cultural competence is more likely. All children, no matter what race, culture, or ethnicity, should be in settings that increase their cultural competence. However, there are advantages when children experience interracial, multicultural staff and children in their childcare settings. They can learn early to respond in positive ways to diversity. Children in America today need to learn to adapt to people who are different from themselves.

Choosing Childcare: Sean

Sean is a single parent and a physical therapist who works with Debbie. He has custody of his four-year-old daughter, Chelsea. And now he too is looking for childcare.

When Chelsea was born, Sean's mother, Barbara, offered to care for her on a daily basis. The arrangement worked out very well until just recently. Barbara inherited some money, and she's gotten the travel itch. This itch came at a convenient time, because Sean was just thinking that Chelsea needed to expand her horizons a bit. Not that she didn't get what she needed in her grandmother's home, but Sean wants her in a program with teachers and other children.

Sean started his childcare search about six months after Debbie did. He felt a good deal of pressure from Debbie to check out Mrs. Watson's, where Jason was so comfortably settled, so he did. He liked what he saw, but it wasn't what he wanted for Chelsea. Mrs. Watson was warm and kind, and obviously knew how to provide developmentally appropriate activities for the children in her care. She was also motherly to Sean, but he bristled at that. "I don't need another mother," he told himself.

It was easy to decide against Mrs. Watson's family childcare home. What Sean wanted for Chelsea was a center.

He visited a number of places, including the ones that Debbie had gone to. Sean wasn't as appalled as Debbie at the variety of programs he found.

Sean knew what he wanted. It's just a matter of finding it, he told himself. He wanted a place where Chelsea could experience children and teachers of other cultures—one where teachers were trained to treat four-year-olds as four-year-olds and provide a rich variety of creative activities. It was hard for Barbara to open her house to easel painting, clay and play dough, carpentry, and other messy kinds of projects.

Barbara and Sean have discussed this subject before. They are in agreement. "Those are the kinds of experiences a childcare center should provide—ones it's hard to set up for at home," Sean told Barbara.

Barbara agreed. "It will be nice for Chelsea to be with other children too, instead of all by herself with just me."

Sean found several programs that he liked. The one he liked best was in a church. He worried at first that they might teach religion there, but was assured that the program was only renting the Sunday-school rooms, and that it wasn't affiliated with the church itself.

What Sean particularly liked about this program was the racial mix of the staff, and the atmosphere. He made a couple of visits and was pleased to see the variety of creative activities, including a sensory table and water play, available for the children. When he brought Chelsea to visit, some children were finger-painting. Chelsea dived right in and was soon up to her elbows in oozing reds and yellows. She was having a glorious time smearing paint around. No one got upset that she went beyond the paper a couple of times.

Chelsea loved circle time and was the first to grab some streamers and start dancing to the music. She beamed as the teacher sang her name in a good-morning song. There wasn't anything that Chelsea didn't love.

"This is the place for us," Sean told the teacher as he walked out the door, Chelsea in tow, protesting.

"Can't I just stay a few more minutes?" his daughter begged.

"You can come back tomorrow and spend all day!" Sean answered.

PARENT-PROVIDER RELATIONS

An important aspect of childrearing is *care*—the feeling and the function. We can't legislate the feeling, only the function. But we can make it more likely that the feeling will follow if we have well-trained, well-paid, recognized staff and providers who are not overworked or burned out. This means that as a society we have to place a value on childcare and on those who provide it.

Childcare workers and parents, who together equal the full picture of childrearing, must be partners. Most parents today can't do it alone. But a childcare system can't do it alone either, no matter how good it is. What parents give (most of them) is passionate feeling, highly personalized, that comes with a history and a future. Watch a power struggle between a parent and a child and you'll see emotion seldom seen between two other people. Although providers and teachers are often critical of the passionate exchanges they witness from time to time, it is important to recognize that that's what parenting is about. It's about connectedness, which results in intense interactions. Parenting is passionate business—the anger as well as the love. Parenting is a long-term affair—much longer (excluding certain circumstances) than any childcare arrangement. The parents provide the continuity through the child's life as he or she passes from program to program or from childcare to school. Caregivers and teachers come and go, but children need continuity in their lives, and it's up to the parents to provide it.

Parent and caregiver are partners in childrearing. Therefore, it is vital that they appreciate and respect and support each other.

Roadblocks to Mutual Appreciation, Respect, and Support

What gets in the way of this mutual appreciation, respect, and support? One roadblock on the part of some caregivers, teachers, and childcare providers is the "savior complex." I remember my own period of being a savior. I was a beginner, and I thought I knew everything. And besides, I had a great desire to rescue children from their parents—especially the parents I didn't like much or understand very well. I went even further—I saw myself saving the world through the work I was doing with young children. Can you imagine how it must have felt to be a parent trying to communicate with me way up on my high horse?

Another roadblock I've encountered in others I've worked with is anger and resentment. Tune in on the following scene, which takes place in the living room of a modest home:

> The sun is still just a hint in the eastern sky as the doorbell rings. A family child-care provider in her bathrobe, who has barely managed to get her hair combed at this early hour, rushes to the door, followed by her fussing baby, who keeps raising his arms to be picked up. She is greeted by a mother who is dressed in a lovely print dress with jacket and jewelry to match. Hiding behind the woman is a sniffling toddler who is wiping her nose on the sleeve of her pajamas. After a rapid exchange of greetings, the mother explains briefly that she will be late tonight because she is taking an important client to dinner. She says a quick good-bye, then turns on her high heels and leaves.
>
> The provider closes the door with a slight slam and leans up against it for a moment before she faces the two needy children who are both fussing at her. Although reminding herself that she made a conscious decision to stay home while her own child is a baby, she is nevertheless resentful of the nice clothes, jewelry, and makeup, as well as the freedom to attend power lunches and client dinners. All of that is totally unrelated to her own day of picking up messes, wiping noses, and changing diapers.
>
> Meanwhile, in the car at the curb, the mother sits for a moment trying to rid herself of the distress she feels at leaving her daughter like this. She wonders if the sniffles are the beginning of an illness. She wishes she could be there to watch her daughter closely and take care of her. She's resentful that the provider can be in her bathrobe at this hour and not have to worry about makeup or clothes. She starts up her car, thinking about how nice it would be to have all day to play with children instead of deal with clients and coworkers in a dog-eat-dog world.
>
> Neither really wants to trade places with the other, but they both harbor resentments. Consider how these resentments might influence communication between the two. Imagine how the provider will feel tonight if the mother arrives later than she promised. Imagine how the mother will feel if the provider calls in the afternoon and says the child has a fever and must go home regardless of the important dinner scheduled. Will either one feel very understanding? Probably not, with all that resentment that was brewing earlier in the day.

A major issue between parents and childcare workers is competition of all kinds, but especially competition for the child's affection. Because children are likely to be attached to both their parents and their providers, the competition is often intensified. Although in most cases childcare workers remain only secondary attachments for children, parents can feel quite insecure about what they perceive as the threat of being replaced as number one in their child's eyes. It is up to both parents and providers to be aware of the feelings generated by this situ-

Children can grow and develop in a variety of settings, including their own homes, family childcare homes, and childcare centers.

ation and to learn to respect and relate to each other in supportive ways. This is accomplished most easily when all parties involved remind themselves that the child's welfare is at stake.

We have a model for sharing the care of a child: the extended family so prevalent in many cultures. In this model, the child experiences several simultaneous attachments instead of an exclusive one with the parent alone. There may be a single primary attachment, but the child is usually parented by more than one person.

SUMMARY

At the end of the twentieth century, America has a long way to go as a society to solving the many problems of raising children, but we are at least becoming aware of the problems. A key term in childrearing today is *shared care.* We'll make great strides when parents and childcare workers, teachers, and caregivers become true partners and when all the adults concerned with any one child come to respect, appreciate, and support each other. We know now that children can grow and develop in a variety of settings, including their own homes, family childcare homes, and childcare centers. The key word in any setting is *quality*!

We know too that early childhood programs, including Head Start and childcare, can break the cycle of poverty and disadvantage. [14] Not all programs that serve young children are equally effective. Programs that manage to break the cycle have particular characteristics: They are small, flexible, and interdisciplinary. They provide more than just early-childhood education and childcare; they also deliver comprehensive services to meet the child's needs in the family, and the family's needs in the community.

It is time for this society to make children a national priority. The Federal Childcare bill passed at the beginning of the 90s is a step in the right direction.

This chapter took a look at childcare as a childrearing setting, and dealt with a broad range of childcare/early-childhood education issues. The next chapter looks at one specific aspect of childrearing that occurs in both homes and centers—*discipline*.

FOR DISCUSSION

1. Do you agree that children are actually "reared" in childcare? Can you give the view of someone who agrees? Can you give the view of someone who disagrees?
2. Do you know a working parent who found an alternative to having someone else take care of his or her child? What alternative was it? How do you feel about it?
3. Of the three variables that influence quality care, which do you think is most important and why?
4. Compare a large, closed-structure program with a small, open-structure one.
5. Why should the home be used as a model for childcare programs?
6. What are examples of adult behaviors that pressure children to comply?
7. What is the behavior of an adult who "facilitates" development?
8. What do you think about breaking up larger groups into smaller ones?
9. What do you think about trying to match teachers to children's cultural and language background?
10. What are your experiences with mutual respect, appreciation, and support between parents and childcare providers?

PERSONAL REFLECTIONS

Thinking about your personal reactions and experiences will help you better understand and integrate the material in this chapter. Use these questions to interface between you and what you read. Use the pertinent ones to reflect on, write about, or discuss with others.

> What are the characteristics of the childcare system in the United States today, as far as your experience goes?
> If you had all the power in the world, what kind of childcare system would you create? How would it be similar to or different from the one in the United States today?

> Have you had experiences in choosing childcare from among several alternatives?

> What is your personal reaction to the statement that parents and childcare teachers are partners in childrearing?

> How do you react when someone pressures you to conform, makes demands, and quotes rules? How do children react, in your experience?

> Have you ever been in childcare yourself as a child? What are your memories and experiences? How does your own experience affect the way you think about childcare?

NOTES

1. I. Lazar, R. B. Darlington, H. Murray, J. Royce, and A. Snipper, "Lasting Effects of Early Education: A Report of the Consortium for Longitudinal Studies," *Monographs of the Society for Research in Child Development* 47(195) (1982): 2–3.

2. M. Whitebook, C. Howes, and D. Phillips, *The National Child Care Staffing Study revisited.* (Oakland, CA: Child Care Employee Project, 1993).

3. *Cost, Quality, and Outcomes in Child Care Centers, Technical Report,* Center for Research in Economic and Social Policy (University of Colorado at Denver, 1995).

4. Cheryl D. Hayes, John L. Palmer, and Martha J. Zaslow, eds., *Who Cares for America's Children? Child Care Policy for the 1990's* (Washington, DC: National Academy Press, 1990).

5. R. Ruopp, J. Travers, F. Glantz, and C. Coelen, *Children at the Center: Final Results of the National Day Care Study* (Boston: ABT Associates, 1979).

6. Three examples are: (1) Sue Bredekamp, ed., *The Accreditation Criteria and Procedures of the National Academy of Early Childhood Programs,* (Washington, DC: National Association for the Education of Young Children [NAEYC], 1984); (2) *Safeguards: Guidelines for Establishing Programs for Four Year Olds in the Public Schools* (Washington, DC: National Black Child Development Institute [NBCDI], 1987); and (3) Program Quality Review of the California State Department of Education, Child Development Division.

7. Elizabeth Prescott, "Is Day Care as Good as a Good Home?" *Young Children* (Washington, DC: National Association for the Education of Young Children, January 1978).

8. The research included 112 children ranging in age from two to five, each for a total of 180 to 200 minutes.

9. Erik H. Erikson, *Childhood and Society* (New York: Norton, 1963).

10. Prescott, *op. cit.,* page 18.

11. Ruopp, *op. cit.*

12. Hayes, *op. cit.*

13. Joseph J. Tobin, David Y. H. Wu, and Dana H. Davidson, *Preschool in Three Cultures: Japan, China, and the United States* (New Haven, CT: Yale University Press, 1989).

14. L. B. Schorr with D. Schorr, *Within Our Reach: Breaking the Cycle of Disadvantage* (New York: Doubleday, 1988).

REFERENCES

Bellum, Dan. *Breaking the Link: A National Forum on Child Care Compensation.* Washington, DC: National Center for the Early Childhood Workforce, 1994.

Bernhard, Judith K. "Child Development, Cultural Diversity, and the Professional Training of Early Childhood Educators." *Canadian Journal of Education* 20(4) (1995).

Bernhard, Judith, Marie Louise Lefebvre, Gyda Chud, and Rika Lange. *Paths to Equity: Cultural, Linguistic, and Racial Diversity in Canadian Early Childhood Education.* Toronto: York Lanes Press, 1995.

Bowman, Barbara T., and Frances M. Stott. "Understanding Development in a Cultural Context: The Challenge for Teachers." In *Diversity and Developmentally Appropriate Practices: Challenges for Early Childhood Education*, eds. Bruce L. Mallory and Rebecca S. New. New York: Teachers College Press, 1994, pp. 119–133.

————. *Breaking the Link: National Forum on Child Care Compensation.* National Center for the Early Childhood Workforce, April, 1994.

Bredekamp, Sue, ed. *Developmentally Appropriate Practice in Early Childhood Programs Serving Children from Birth Through Age 8.* Washington, DC: National Association for the Education of Young Children, 1987.

Carter, M. "Face to Face Communication: Understanding and Strengthening the Partnership." *Child Care Information Exchange* 60 (1988): 21–25.

Carter, Margie and Deb Curtis. *Training Teachers: A Harvest of Theory and Practice.* St. Paul, MN: Redleaf Press, 1994.

Chang, Hedy Nai-Lin and Laura Sakai. *Affirming Children's Roots: Cultural and Linguistic Diversity in Early Care and Education.* San Francisco, CA: California Tomorrow, 1993.

Chang, H. N. L., A. Muckelroy, and D. Pulido-Tobiassen. *Looking In, Looking Out: Redefining Child and Early Education in a Diverse Society.* San Francisco, CA: California Tomorrow, 1996.

Chud, G. and R. Fahlman. *Early Childhood Education for a Multicultural Society: A Handbook for Educators.* Vancouver, BC: Pacific Educational Press, 1990.

————. *Cost, Quality, and Outcomes in Child Care Centers, Technical Report.* Center for Research in Economic and Social Policy, University of Colorado at Denver, 1995.

Delpit, L. "The Silenced Dialogue: Power and Pedagogy in Educating Other People's Children." *Harvard Educational Review* 58(3) (1988).

Derman-Sparks, Louise, and the ABC Task Force. *Anti-bias Curriculum: Tools for Empowering Young Children.* Washington, DC: National Association for the Education of Young Children, 1989.

Derman-Sparks, Louise. "The Process of Culturally Sensitive Care." in *Infant/Toddler Caregiving: A Guide to Culturally Sensitive Care*, ed. Peter Mangione. Sacramento, California: Far West Laboratory and California Department of Education, 1995.

Erikson, Erik H. *Childhood and Society.* New York: Norton, 1963.

Fenichel, Emily S. and Linda Eggbeer. *Preparing Practitioners to Work with Infants, Toddlers, and Their Families: Issues and Recommendations for the Professions.* Arlington, VA: National Center for Clinical Infant Programs, 1990.

Fong Yun Lee. "Asian Parents as Partners." *Young Children* (March 1995): 4–8.

Gallinsky, Ellen, and Bernice Weissbourd. "Family Centered Child Care." *Yearbook in Early Childhood Education.* Champagne-Urbana: University of Illinois, 1992.

Gallinsky, Ellen, Carollee Howes, and Susan Kontos. *The Family Child Care Training Study: Highlights and Findings.* New York: NY: Families and Work Institute, 1995.

Genishi, Celia, and Margaret Borrego Brainard. "Assessment of Bilingual Children: A Dilemma Seeking Solutions." In *Meeting the Challenge of Linguistic and Cultural Diversity in Early Childhood Education*, eds. Eugene E. Garcia and Barry McLaughlin, with Bernard Spokek and Olivia N. Saracho. New York: Teachers College Press, 1995, 49–62.

Gonzalez-Mena, Janet, and Anne Stonehouse. "In the Child's Best Interests." *Child Care Information Exchange* (November 1995).

Gonzalez-Mena, Janet. "Do You Have Cultural Tunnel Vision?" *Child Care Information Exchange* (July, 1991).

Gonzalez-Mena, Janet, and Dianne Eyer. *Infants, Toddlers and Caregivers.* Mountain View, CA: Mayfield Publishing Company, 1997.

Gonzalez-Mena, Janet. "Cultural Sensitivity in Routine Caregiving Tasks." In *Infant/Toddler Caregiving: A guide to Culturally Sensitive Care,* ed. Peter L. Mangione. California Department of Education and the Far West Laboratory for Educational Research, 1995.

Gonzalez-Mena, Janet. "Learning to See Across a Cultural Gap." *Child Care Information Exchange* (May 1994).

Gonzalez-Mena, Janet. *Multicultural Issues in Child Care.* Mountain View, CA: Mayfield Publishing Company, 1997.

Gonzalez-Mena, Janet. *Program for Infant Toddler Caregivers: A Guide to Routines.* California Department of Education, Child Development Division and The Center for Child and Family Studies, Far West Laboratory for Educational Research and Development, 1990.

Gonzalez-Mena, Janet. "Taking a Culturally Sensitive Approach in Infant-Toddler Programs." *Young Children* (January 1992).

Gonzalez-Mena, Janet. *Tips and Tidbits for Family Day Care Providers.* Washington, DC: National Association for the Education of Young Children (NAEYC), 1991.

Gonzalez-Mena, Janet. "When Values Collide: Exploring a Cross Cultural Issue." *Child Care Information Exchange* (March 1996).

Greenman, Jim, and Anne Stonehouse. *Prime Times: A Handbook for Excellence in Infant and Toddler Programs.* St. Paul, MN: Redleaf Press, 1996.

Hughes, R. "The Informal Help-Giving of Home and Center Childcare Providers." *Family Relations* 34 (1985): 359–366.

Kendall, Frances E. *Diversity in the Classroom: A Multicultural Approach to the Education of Young Children.* New York: Teachers College Press, 1996.

Kessler, S., and B. Swaderner. *Reconceptualizing the Early Childhood Curriculum, Beginning the Dialogue.* New York: Teacher's College Press, 1992.

Kontos, Susan. *Family Day Care: Out of the Shadows and Into the Limelight.* Washington DC:

National Association for the Education of Young Children, 1992.

Lally, J. Ronald. "The Impact of Child Care Policies and Practices on Infant/Toddler Identity Formation." *Young Children* 51(1) (November, 1995).

Lazar, I., R. B. Darlington, H. Murray, J. Royce, and A. Snipper. "Lasting Effects of Early Education: A Report of the Consortium for Longitudinal Studies." *Monographs of the Society for Research in Child Development* 47(195) (1982): 2–3.

Leach, William. "Child-World in the Promised Land." In *The Mythmaking Frame of Mind: Social Imagination and American Culture,* eds. James Gilbert, Amy Gilman, Donald Scott, and Joan W. Scott. Belmont, CA: Wordsworth, 1993.

Lynch, Eleanor W., and Marci Hanson. *Developing Cross Cultural Competence: A Guide for Working with Young Children and Families.* Baltimore, MD: Brookes, 1992.

Mallory, Bruce L., and Rebecca S. New, eds. *Diversity and Developmentally Appropriate Practices: Challenges for Early Childhood Education.* New York: Teachers College Press, 1994.

Mangione, Peter L., ed. *Infant/Toddler Caregiving: A Guide to Culturally Sensitive Care.* California Department of Education and the Far West Laboratory for Educational Research, 1995.

Miller, Angela Browne. *The Day Care Dilemma: Critical Concerns for American Families.* New York: Plenum Press, 1990.

Mistry, Jayanthi. "Culture and Learning in Infancy: Implications for Caregiving." In *Infant/Toddler Caregiving: A Guide to Culturally Sensitive Care,* ed. Peter L. Mangione. California Department of Education and the Far West Laboratory for Educational Research, 1995.

Moore, Evelyn K. "Mediocre Care: Double Jeopardy for Black Children." *Young Children* (May 1995): 47.

Morgen, Gwen, and Sheri L. Azer. *Making a Career of It: The State of the States Report on Career Development in Early Care and Education.* Boston, MA: Center for Career Development in Early Care and Education, 1993.

———. National Black Child Development Institute. Paths to African American Leadership Positions in Early Childhood Education: Constraints and Opportunities, Washington, DC, 1993.

————. National Association for the Education of Young Children, Linguistic and Cultural Diversity Position Paper. *Young Children* 51(2) (January 1996).

Native American Parent Preschool Curriculum Guide. Oakland, CA: Office of Native American Programs, Division of Educational Development and Services, 1986.

Neugebauer, Bonnie, ed., *Alike and Different: Exploring Our Humanity With Young Children*. Washington DC: National Association for the Education of Young Children, 1992.

Peters, D. L., and S. Kontos. "Continuity and Discontinuity of Experience: An Intervention Perspective." In *Continuity and Discontinuity of Experience in Child Care*, ed. D. L. Peters and S. Kontos. Norwood, NJ: Ablex, 1987, 1–16.

Powell, D. R. "Day Care as a Family Support System." In *America's Family Support Programs*, ed. S. L. Kagan, D. R. Powell, E. F. Zigler, and B. Weissbourd. New Haven and London: Yale University Press, 1987, 115—132.

Prescott, Elizabeth. "Is Day Care as Good as a Good Home?" *Young Children*. Washington, DC: National Association for the Education of Young Children (January 1978).

Ruopp, R., J. Travers, F. Glantz, and C. Coelen. *Children at the Center: Final Results of the National Day Care Study*. Boston: ABT Associates, 1979.

————. *Safeguards: Guidelines for Establishing Programs for Four Year Olds in the Public Schools*. Washington, DC: National Black Child Development Institute (NBCDI), 1987.

Schorr, L. B., with D. Schorr. *Within Our Reach: Breaking the Cycle of Disadvantage*. New York: Doubleday, 1988.

Schweinhart, Larry. "The United States Needs Better Child Care," *Young Children* (May 1995): 48.

Sholtys, Katherine Cullen. "A New Language, A New Life: Recommendations for Teachers of Non-English-Speaking Children Newly Entering the Program." *Young Children* (March 1989): 76–77.

Diaz Soto, Lourdes, and Jocelynn L. Smrekar. "The Politics of Early Bilingual Education." In *Reconceptualizing the Early Childhood Curriculum: Beginning the Dialogue*, eds. Shirley A. Kessler and Beth Blue Swadener. NY: Teachers College Press, 1992, 189–203.

Tobin, Joseph J., David Y. H. Wu, and Dana H. Davidson. *Preschool in Three Cultures: Japan, China, and the United States*. New Haven, CT: Yale University Press, 1989.

Whitebook, Marcy, and Robert C. Granger. "Assessing Teacher Turnover." *Young Children* (May 1989).

Whitebook, Marcy. *Salary Improvements for Head Start: Lessons for the Early Care and Education Field*. Washington, DC: National Center for the Early Childhood Workforce, 1995.

Whitebook, Marcy. "What's Good for Child Care Teachers is Good for Our Country's Children." *Young Children* (May 1995) 49–50.

Wong Fillmore, Lily. "When Learning a Second Language Means Losing the First." *Early Childhood Research Quarterly* 6 (1991): 323–346.

Youcha, Geraldine. *Minding the Children: Child Care in America from Colonial Times to the Present*, New York: Scribner, 1995.

Zinsser, Caroline. *Raised in East Urban: Child Care Changes in a Working Class Community*. New York: Teacher's College Press, 1991.

Disciplining for High Self-Esteem

CHAPTER **7**

In this chapter you'll discover:

› How you can prevent kids from needing discipline

› What's wrong with punishment

› Guidelines for disciplining young children

› Ways to prevent misbehavior

› The common themes that underlie child abuse

› How to respond positively to negative behavior

› The difference between punishment and consequences

› When time out is useful and when it's not

› Why you might want to ignore unacceptable behavior

TEST YOURSELF

Look for the answers to these questions as you read the chapter:

1. According to the text, what's wrong with punishment?
2. What are the five guidelines for disciplining young children explained in the text?
3. What are seven ways to prevent unacceptable behavior in young children?
4. How can the environment be used to prevent misbehavior?
5. From Carla's story, what can you say about the common themes that underlie most child abuse stories?
6. What are seven positive adult responses to a child's unacceptable behavior?
7. What is the difference between punishment and consequences?
8. What is the difference between a natural and a logical consequence?
9. What is time out and when is it useful?
10. Under what circumstances does ignoring unacceptable behavior make it go away?
11. What does it mean to "teach prosocial behavior"?

DEFINING THE WORD DISCIPLINE

Discipline is a loaded word. For years, early-childhood experts tried to remove it from the vocabulary of teachers, caregivers, and parents, substituting the word *guidance* instead. But too many parents and educators were uncomfortable with what they considered the lack of discipline being advocated by the experts (*guidance* just didn't do it); so the word has refused to die.

Why did the experts want to change the word *discipline* to *guidance*? It has to do with the associations connected with the word. For years I've been asking college students to draw symbols that show what the word *discipline* means to them. I consistently get pictures of jails, whips, gallows, electric chairs, and slapping hands. The least painful (in a physical sense) are the corners and stools with dunce caps on them. (No wonder educators tried to substitute the word *guidance*!)

Obviously, to many people, *discipline* means punishment, and punishment means pain or at least humiliation. It doesn't have to be that way!

My own symbol of discipline is a path with two people, a big one and a little one, walking along together—a master and a disciple. (*Discipline* and *disciple* come from the same root word.) In my book, *discipline* means guiding and controlling behavior, not through punishment, but by being attached to a more experienced partner. This partner is a man or a woman who is wiser, knows more, and has lived longer than the child. Eventually children internalize the master or the older partner and take charge of themselves. This development of *inner controls,* or self-discipline, is the goal of disciplining children. [1]

Unlike punishment, discipline doesn't have to hurt, but it may. Life isn't easy, and discipline involves *choices* that can sometimes lead to painful consequences. I don't want to mislead you into thinking that the path in my symbol is always smooth, easy, and covered with rose petals. It's not. Still, even discipline that hurts is different from punishment. Suffering the consequences of your own choices feels different from being punished because someone bigger or more powerful than you decides to do it.

PROBLEMS WITH USING PUNISHMENT TO TEACH YOUNG CHILDREN

One problem with punishment is the negativity that accompanies it. Often the adult uses punishment to get even, which triggers a spirit of retaliation on the part of the child. This starts a vicious circle that ends only when one or the other triumphs, usually leaving quite a path of destruction in the wake of the conflict. Children who are frequently punished become more devious, not more cooperative. They respond to the hurt, loss, or penalty (the punishment) with anger, resentment, and defiance. This does not build the good relationships that are the basis of effective discipline. Instead, it causes resentment and the urge to strike back. [2]

Children who are punished for trying things out and making mistakes in the process become inhibited in their development of autonomy and initiative. The urge to explore and experiment is squelched when punishment hangs over a child's head. Learning is reduced. Of course, childhood urges are strong, and many survive in spite of what adults may do to discourage them. However, it is important to understand how punishing young children affects their later development. Children come to see new situations as potentially "trouble making" rather than as opportunities to use their initiative to find out more about the world around them. The adults those children become are afraid to try anything new because they were punished for mistakes as children.

When punishments hurt, the teachable moment is lost. Children are most open to learning right after they've done something wrong or made a mistake. That's the time for helping them see what went wrong. If they are wrapped up in pain (physical or psychological), they can't concentrate on the "lesson" the adult has in mind, and may instead learn some other lesson that wasn't even intended.

Physical punishment is not an option in an educational setting, but for those adults who still use it at home it can be especially problematic because it models aggression. [3] Parents who are trying to keep their children from hurting others or using violence to solve problems work against their own goals when they use physical punishment. The message the children get is that it is okay to hurt people if you are bigger and have a good reason.

Worst of all, physical punishment can lead to child abuse when adults go further than they intend to. [4] When a parent first starts using physical punishment, the result of even a little is often resentment. Just as modern germs build up resistance to medicine, so does the resentful child become resistant to punishment. The parent finds it takes more and more punishment to get the same effect. Some children are willing to take a lot, so the parent continues to escalate. It's a vicious circle. Some parents end up abusing their children when they get caught up in this ugly pattern.

The discipline I'm advocating is not punishment, but it's not a bed of roses either. Adults who use the approaches to discipline that I advocate do not allow their children to do whatever they want regardless of anyone else's needs. That's permissiveness. Permissiveness is not good for either children or the adults who are in charge of them.

The discipline I'm advocating is far from permissiveness. It also *isn't* a simplistic, manipulative reward system. It *is* a complex approach that involves meeting needs, understanding developmental issues, expressing feelings, and, above all, preventing problems and using a *problem-solving process* when you can't prevent them. [5]

When examining any discipline approach, it's vital to look at your goals. One important goal is to find ways to guide and control behavior without lowering children's self-esteem. They need a positive perspective of themselves if discipline is going to have beneficial long-term effects. [6] Consider the difference between teaching blind obedience and producing thoughtful children who are both cooperative and responsible.

Ask yourself this: When you are faced with misbehavior, are you more interested in changing the behavior than you are in winning, controlling, and coming out ahead or in making the child suffer? It's important to understand your own motives before you begin to discipline.

GUIDELINES FOR DISCIPLINING YOUNG CHILDREN

Here are some general guidelines for disciplining young children:

> Communicate what you are doing and why. Don't reason at length, but always provide reasons. If you do this, children will eventually do their own reasoning.

> Check communication to see if it is clear. If it is not, you may have ambiguous feelings—in which case you have to do something about them. An example of ambiguous feelings shows in the parent who wants her children to go to bed, but feels guilty about being away from them all day; so she puts them to bed and tells them to go to sleep, but doesn't insist or follow through and then gets mad when they keep bouncing out of bed or calling her. They pick up on and respond to her ambiguity. Bedtime is a big problem in many homes where there are toddlers or preschoolers.

> Trust children. They have a drive toward health, wholeness, and goodness. Misbehavior often comes as a result of their being thwarted in having their needs met. Look closely at any pattern of misbehavior; take the attitude

Build good relationships. Discipline is more effective if it comes from a loving place.

that this behavior is trying to communicate something. Trust the child to know what he or she needs even though on the surface the behavior may look just plain troublesome or contrary. Just because he seems to be "out to get you" doesn't mean that there aren't needs behind the behaviors.

> Trust yourself. You also have needs. You can only make good choices about disciplining children when your own needs are met. When your needs clash with children's needs, strive to find a balance, so that no one's needs are neglected. Convey the message to children that everyone's needs are important—theirs and yours too.

> Build good relationships. Whatever approach you take to discipline will be more effective if it comes from a loving place.

What follows are fourteen concrete examples of ways to discipline that lead to high self-esteem in healthy families.

DISCIPLINE AS PREVENTING UNACCEPTABLE BEHAVIOR

Start with prevention. The following sections present seven things to do *before* the unacceptable behavior occurs. Though they may not seem like discipline techniques, they are because they are a means of guiding and controlling behavior. The first two have to do with the environment, the third with modeling, the fourth and fifth with redirection and control, the sixth with feelings, and the seventh with needs.

Set Up an Appropriate Environment

The younger the child the more he or she needs freedom to move, things to explore, and something to do. For example, you can predict unacceptable behavior when you have a toddler for any length of time in a fancy restaurant, an elegant living room, or a department store. You are more likely to find acceptable behavior when children are in an environment that is age-appropriate as well as suited to their needs and interests.

Let the Environment Provide the Limits

Fence off dangerous areas from young children. Most communities have laws about swimming pools, but they don't expect rules alone to prevent drownings. The same approach could be used in the home or childcare center. Put breakables out of reach. Lock doors to rooms that are off limits to children.

This principle works beyond childhood. Freeways and throughways are good examples of how the environment provides the limits. Most are designed so you *can't* go off the on ramp. Center dividers make it impossible to cross into oncoming traffic. The safety principles used by highway designers are a good model to keep in mind as you design appropriate environments for children.

Set up an appropriate environment. The younger the child, the more he or she needs freedom to move, things to explore, and something to do.

Model Appropriate Behavior

Model gentleness in the face of aggression. Model courtesy, kindness, sensitivity, sharing, and caring. It works! [7] You may be surprised how much children pick up. If you yell at children to stop yelling, or if you're aggressive in response to aggression, they'll follow your actions instead of your words. Modeling is powerful. It works, either for you or against you.

Redirect Energy

Much unacceptable behavior is just exuberance. It doesn't need to be curtailed, it just needs to be redirected. Find ways to turn potentially unacceptable actions into acceptable ones. Provide time outdoors for a child who wants to run, for example. If exuberance becomes overstimulation, try some calming activities—water play is a good one for the younger child. Playing with "goop" (a mixture of cornstarch and water) will calm almost anyone. Baths are a time-honored calming device.

Provide Physical Control When Needed

For the very young child, physical guidance may prevent problems. Stop the hitting hand unless you're sure words alone will trigger the control the child needs to stop

Child Abuse: A Story

Carla is dealing with the consequences of abusing her child. Right now she is in a group session with other abusing parents, listening to their stories. She's surprised that some of the themes are the same as hers, though the details are different.

As she listens to the others, she involuntarily goes back to the moment before she threw Cody against the wall, fracturing his skull. She gets a sick feeling in her stomach as the memory floods her.

She had reached the end of her rope that evening—she knew it then and she knows it now. "How much do you think I can take?" she had screamed at Cody, who was standing over a broken plate he had just thrown down from the counter in anger. She remembered the series of incidents that had led up to this confrontation better than she remembered what happened afterward. It had been a bad day!

The problem was that she was so alone. Since her husband had left her, she found herself with fewer and fewer social contacts. She knew she needed friends, but it was so hard to make them with two children to support and raise. They took up all her time. And they drove her crazy sometimes. Like that awful rainy Saturday when Cody ended up breaking the plate.

As the other parents in the circle continued talking, it became obvious that being isolated was a theme for most of them. Another problem for Carla was that Cody was so immature. She had told him time and again that now that his father was gone he was the man of the house. But he just didn't live up to any of her expectations. Sure, he was only four, but still . . .

Carla didn't know it yet, but this was another common characteristic of parents who abuse their children. They don't understand developmental stages and often have unrealistic expectations for their children. Carla will learn about this subject from the class she is enrolled in.

She will also learn some techniques for guiding and controlling her children's behavior in positive ways. She knows she needs those techniques. Discipline has always left her feeling helpless. She only knows what she learned from her own parents, who used belittling, sarcasm, and, above all, beating on Carla when she was little.

Carla never thought of herself as an abused child. She figured that all children were punished in the same way she was. She knew that she had more scars than some of her childhood friends, but she accepted that as a fact. She never considered that she could question her parents' methods, and indeed she couldn't—she just would have been beaten harder for talking back.

It's not that her parents didn't love her—Carla knows that they did. In her mind they showed their love by hitting her—in fact, they even told her that. In Carla's experience, love and hurt were linked together.

Carla knows now that she *must stop* abusing Cody. No matter what problems she has, there's no excuse for not controlling herself—she knows that now. She also knows that she's not alone anymore. She's getting help—in the form of education, therapy, and, above all, support. Things will be different now, and eventually Cody and his sister, Candace, will be back home again.

Carla breathes a sigh of relief as she sits back in her chair, ready to talk. It's her turn now. The group looks at her expectantly.

"I have lots of feelings . . . " she starts out.

his or her own hand. Words may work fine, but don't depend on them by themselves, especially with toddlers. Back up words with touch. Eventually you can use words alone; perhaps just a look will do it. But they need to know you really mean it—which you show by consistently providing physical control when needed.

In order to provide this physical kind of guidance, you need to be nearby when trouble threatens. It also helps to know the rule of thumb of interaction distance that early childhood teachers have been using for years. Speak to a child from the distance of one foot for each year. When you ask a two-year-old at two feet to control his hitting hand, you're close enough to reach out and control it for him if necessary. Children can hear you shout from across the room, but most won't listen. It takes your close physical presence for any words they might not want to hear to register.

Teach Appropriate Expression of Feelings

Feelings are important and should be not only allowed and accepted but also appreciated—by yourself and by children. Children need to learn how to express the feelings they have in ways that don't harm themselves, anyone else, or the things around them. Teach them to say, "I'm mad!" Teach them how to show those feelings. [8]

Redirection may come in handy as you guide a child from hitting another child to hitting a pillow or pounding clay. Art, music, dance, and physical exercise are classic ways of expressing feelings that should be available to children. You don't have to provide anything elaborate. Some children can get rid of a lot of anger simply through tearing paper into very small bits and throwing them into the wastebasket.

Meet Needs

A good deal of undesirable behavior can be prevented when children (and adults too) are feeling satisfied because their needs are met. Basic needs like food, rest, and exercise come first; but beyond the basics lie higher needs such as security, protection, love, and closeness. [9] When any of these needs are unmet, discipline problems can result.

DISCIPLINE AS RESPONDING TO UNACCEPTABLE BEHAVIOR

When unacceptable behavior occurs in spite of your efforts to prevent it, an appropriate and effective response is in order. The response should not include name-calling, belittling, or global judgments of worth, because such responses lower self-esteem. It's not effective to make children feel bad about themselves in order to motivate them to behave better. In fact, that approach usually works at cross-purposes. [10] Children who feel bad about themselves are less likely to behave in acceptable ways unless they are dominated by fear. If you rule by fear, you damage relationships, which does not lead to healthy families or high self-esteem.

The following sections offer seven effective and healthy ways to respond to unacceptable behavior. They include giving feedback, allowing consequences, using time-out, rewarding some behaviors and ignoring others, teaching desired behaviors, and meeting needs.

Give Feedback

If the problem belongs to the children involved, and you can keep your feelings out of it, the best kind of feedback is "sports announcing." [11] For example, when

Protect children by using physical control when necessary, but also do "sports announcing." Explain what you see happening without judgments and encourage children to solve their own problems.

children are fighting over a toy, you can step in and narrate what you see, express the feelings you pick up, and get the children to talk to one another. This kind of sports announcing leads to problem solving on the part of the children.

If, on the other hand, you have strong feelings because your needs are being trampled on, state them in a sentence that starts with *I* and contains a feeling word. [12] The sentence should also encapsulate the behavior in question. For example, if children are screaming their lungs out and it bothers you, say, "I feel nervous (upset, tired) when I hear you scream." Feedback is different from judgmental criticism or blame, which diminishes self-esteem.

Allow Children to Experience the Consequences of Their Actions

Natural consequences don't have to be arranged. [13] It's a matter of stepping back and not rescuing a child from a decision he or she has made. When a child chooses not to wear a sweater when going out to play, the natural consequence is to feel cold.

Logical consequences are set up by adults and reflect the reality of the social world. [14] Logical consequences are a direct result of the child's own actions. When children leave their clothes on the floor instead of in the hamper, the clothes don't get washed. If the child can't be trusted not to go into the street, he or she is taken into the house. Children talk during story time and the adult stops reading. The child who spills the milk sponges it up.

Consequences are different from punishment, even though they may cause anguish, because they are related to the child's own actions. They are reasonable, not arbitrary. Adults must be respectful when allowing or applying consequences. If adults are angry or harsh, consequences become punishment.

Use Time-Out

Time-out (sitting apart, being sent to another room or to a certain place in the same room) can be punishing if done in a punishing way (as can any of the approaches listed here). Used properly, time-out is a chance for children to gain control of themselves. This only works when the child is truly "out of control." Those are the times when the adult can become an ally, a helper to the child. The attitude is, "I see that you can't control yourself in this situation, so I am going to help you by taking you out of it and getting you into a peaceful, less stimulating situation." This is very different from a punishing attitude, where the adult is viewed as an adversary rather than as a partner. Time-out should be followed up with a problem-solving session between the child and the caregiver.

Unfortunately, time-out is overused by some adults, who respond to every misbehavior by sending the child off to sit in a chair. It is also abused. Instead of being a positive means of discipline, time-out often takes the place of the old-fashioned stool and dunce cap. Or it becomes a shunning technique. Children should be neither shamed nor shunned through time-out or any other device.

Reward Desired Behavior

Notice when children are "being good." Pay special attention when children are being kind, courteous, sensitive, and helpful. Unfortunately, these are the times when we are tempted to ignore children because they aren't causing any problems. This is the behavior we expect, so why should we go out of our way to make a fuss over it?

However, behaviorist learning theory points out the power of the reward—even if it's only adult attention. Behavior that's rewarded tends to continue. Behavior that's ignored tends to disappear. Be careful about going overboard, however. Constant gushing praise doesn't work. In his book, *Punished by Rewards,* Alfie Kohn wrote about how when we try to manipulate children's behavior through using incentives, side effects arise and our good intentions backfire. Using hundreds of studies, Kohn shows that the more we use rewards to get children to do what we want, the more they lose interest in doing it. Children don't perform as well and they aren't as creative when we entice them to do something by dangling a reward in front of their noses.

It's not manipulative to be honest and sincere. Use your powers of observation to notice behavior that deserves noticing.

For example, if you view a child treating her younger sibling in a gentle manner, you could say: "I see that you're being very careful when you touch your little brother." Just regular manners work too: "I appreciate it when you help me set the table." "Thanks for feeding the dog." (See chapter 10 for more on this subject.)

Ignore Misbehavior That Is Designed to Attract Attention

Everyone needs attention—it's like a life-giving substance. When children don't get the attention they need through positive behaviors, they develop negative ones that are hard to ignore. If the message behind these behaviors is "I'm here, notice me," the only way to change the behaviors is to ignore them, and then give the needed attention at times when the child is acting acceptably. Turn your back on arguing that is designed to get your attention (much arguing among children is for that very purpose). Walk out of the room when a child is trying to annoy you.

Teach Prosocial Behavior

Don't just teach what not to do through the aforementioned approaches. Take a proactive stance and teach what *to do* as well. Indirect teaching comes about through the already mentioned devices of modeling and rewarding. Direct teaching comes about through talking. Avoid lectures. Instead, use stories and role plays, and even actually practice prosocial behavior by trying it out in little dramas or puppet shows. (See chapter 5 for more about teaching prosocial behavior.)

Meet Needs

Children often behave in unacceptable ways because they are needy. Respond to behaviors from that source by meeting the needs. Don't yell at a boy who is

Using Consequences to Guide and Control Behavior

Jean is a mother who decided not to use punishment on her five-year-old, Trevor, anymore. She had learned about using consequences as a discipline method and was ready to try it. She had the perfect opportunity the day she got tired of trying to get Trevor to put his dishes in the dishwasher after eating.

Trevor was very lazy about this—lazy to the point of stubbornness. Up to now Jean would remind him, time after time, but he'd "forget." She began to feel like a nag. She finally got so frustrated that she resorted to threatening him, but that didn't work either. Nothing worked!

Of course, nothing worked because Trevor knew that if he waited long enough, his mother would put the dishes away for him. Besides, it didn't really matter to him if a few dirty dishes were left lying around. His next meal always arrived right on schedule. The only consequence for leaving dishes on the table was that they magically disappeared eventually anyway. Finally Jean decided she needed to get more creative about how to handle this problem, which she recognized as *her* problem. She decided that using a "consequences approach" would make it Trevor's problem as well.

She started by asking herself what the ultimate consequence of not putting dirty dishes in the dishwasher would be. She visualized a house full of molding dishes—it looked terrible. Would he mind that? She wasn't sure. Then she visualized an empty cupboard—no dishes for the next meal. That's the ultimate consequence. Even if the dirty house didn't affect him, the empty cupboard would if he didn't find his next meal, all hot and delicious, waiting for him on a clean plate.

So Jean explained to Trevor that she wouldn't remind or nag anymore about dirty dishes, but she wouldn't put them away either. She didn't. He didn't either. By bedtime the first day the place was a dump, but Trevor didn't seem to mind.

Jean was discouraged. She thought she'd see results quicker. How long was this going to take anyway, she asked herself, looking at the smeared glasses, sticky plates, and crusted forks lying here and there around the kitchen and the family room.

She had a brainstorm. "I'll hurry up the process by adding to the problem," she told her sister, whom she called for moral support. "I'll just quit putting my dishes away too."

"Do you think it will work?" was her sister's response.

"Yes," said Jean enthusiastically.

That night Jean left a plate on the coffee table, with a dirty glass beside it. The next morning she left her coffee cup on the newspaper by her rocking chair, her cereal bowl and juice glass on the table, and an empty water glass on the wood stove—next to the two empty glasses Trevor had left there the previous day.

It didn't take long. They never got to the point of the bare cupboard. Trevor didn't like the mess once it got really ugly. He picked up his dishes, Jean picked up hers, and that was the end of it.

So how was this different from punishment? For one thing, Jean didn't inflict it on Trevor. She merely quit doing what hadn't worked before and let his own actions show him what the problem was. He learned a lesson about the benefits of household order without being punished. Jean was a bystander—not a moralizer, judge, or jury. She even managed to refrain from saying, "I hope you learned your lesson."

A good deal of undesirable behavior can be prevented when children are feeling satisfied because their needs are met.

fussing because he's hungry; feed him. Don't give feedback to a tired girl who is out of control; put her to bed. Don't prevent restless children from wiggling; take them someplace where they can get the wiggles out. Of course you can't always meet each child's needs immediately, and it doesn't hurt them to learn to wait a bit—but not too long! [15] Do what you can to control the truly unacceptable behavior, and put up with that which is only expressing feelings about having to wait.

SUMMARY

This chapter discussed how to discipline so the effects are positive and enhance self-esteem rather than tear it down (as punishment is apt to do). A final word of advice: When you use any of these fourteen approaches, communicate what you are doing and why. Don't reason on and on, but give reasons. Children will internalize your reasons and will eventually do their own reasoning, which leads to self-discipline. Punishment and the resulting possible fear do not lead to self-discipline in the same way.

Because feelings and problem solving play such a prominent part in matters of discipline, the next two chapters focus specifically on those subjects.

What One Town Did About Child Abuse

A while back, in a medium-sized town in a Northern California valley, a baby died as the result of abuse. A group of citizens, led by one individual, decided to do something about child abuse. This was about the time that national awareness was beginning to grow, as emergency room doctors questioned where all those mysterious bruises and broken bones were coming from. It was the same time that psychotherapists were hearing adult stories of early beatings. Each person who dredged up these memories was convinced that he or she was a unique case. No one realized that child abuse was so widespread.

Now, of course, we have one glaring statistic after another showing that for many children, growing up is very dangerous business. As a nation we decided to change the statistics, and we passed laws prohibiting child abuse.

The laws were not enough for this particular group of citizens, who wanted to *prevent* abuse in their community, not just punish it. This motivation on their part coincided with some funding set aside for prevention, intervention, and treatment of child abuse. The group went to work.

First they established a hotline for parents to call, just to talk, when they felt as though they might not be able to control themselves. Then they began to educate the community about child abuse and about using the hotline. What they and the community were surprised to discover was that child abuse crosses all economic, cultural, and racial lines. No one is immune. We're all at risk for "losing it" and hurting our children.

These citizens and others soon discovered that what parents needed was a variety of support services. Some needed parenting information and skills, some needed relief childcare, some needed a job, some needed a place to live, and some just needed relief from the many stresses in their lives that led them to take out their frustrations on their children. The picture was much bigger than anyone had ever suspected.

Today many of these services are in place, but many more are needed. The original citizen group went on to establish relief childcare, an after-school "phone friend" for children who come home to an empty house, parent support and education groups, an emergency aid fund, and support services for children in foster care. They also provide part-time temporary home service, where parent aides go into the home to help with household and child management through support and role modeling.

A good deal of energy has gone into changing things for children and their parents in this community. The group continues to provide community education by making speakers available and through a regular newsletter. Through its twenty-year history, this organization has remained overwhelmingly a volunteer group, with a ratio of more than four volunteers to each paid staff member. Volunteer training is an ongoing focus as new recruits become involved, and old volunteers change from one program to another within the organization. The funding now comes from a variety of federal, state, and local sources.

FOR DISCUSSION

1. What do you think the word *discipline* means? What is the dictionary definition? What is the text's definition? How are they the same? How do they differ?

2. Give an example of how the environment can be used to curb behavior and restrict a child from doing something dangerous or unacceptable.

3. What are some problems with using punishment to teach?

4. What was your reaction to Carla's story of fracturing her son's skull on a rainy Saturday, the day she was "at the end of her rope?"

5. What is an example of learning from experiencing a consequence?

6. Can you give an example of a logical consequence versus a natural consequence?

7. Can you explain how a punishment is different from a consequence?

8. What's wrong with using "time-out" as a punishment?

9. What do you think about rewarding desired behavior and ignoring the rest of it? Can you think of any problems with this approach?

10. Why is there a section on "meeting needs" in a chapter on discipline?

11. Give examples of three "prosocial behaviors" you would want to teach young children.

PERSONAL REFLECTIONS

Thinking about your personal reactions and experiences will help you better understand and integrate the material in this chapter. Use these questions to interface between you and what you read. Use the pertinent ones to reflect on, write about, or discuss with others.

> What pictures, words, or images does the word *discipline* invoke for you?

> What are your thoughts, feelings, ideas, and experiences with using punishment to teach?

> Give an example from your own life where the environment prevented you from doing something dangerous or unacceptable.

> What are your thoughts, feelings, and ideas about child abuse, as well as your experiences with child abuse?

> When is a time you learned by experiencing a consequence of your behavior?

> Can you think of an example from your own life showing how a punishment is different from a consequence?

> Does "time-out" work for you? How? Under what circumstances?

> How do you feel when you perceive someone is "rewarding desired behavior" in you through incentives, praise, or other means?

> What if what they want in the name of "desired behavior" is not what you want?

> Can you give an example of a time you "misbehaved" because your needs weren't met?

> What are three prosocial behaviors that a young child could learn from you through modeling after you?

NOTES

1. Not all cultures aim for "inner controls" at an early age. Janice Hale-Benson says that adults in the black community play a social-control role, "making a network of significant adults who firmly correct undesirable behavior whenever it occurs and report such behavior to the parent." Therefore, parents are at the center of this social-control network. For the child, this means that he or she is always under the surveillance of adults. The significant feature of the control system is that it seems to operate externally to the child. Therefore, the child seems to develop external locus of control.

    "In the school situation, adults seem to behave as if locus of social control exists within the child. They do not function in ways that are consistent with the child's expectations of how adults should behave toward them in situations that require the enforcement of social controls." Janice E. Hale-Benson, *Black Children: Their Roots, Culture, and Learning Styles* (Baltimore, MD: The Johns Hopkins University Press, 1986), 85.

    In addition, Lonnie Snowden says: "The black community invests effective responsibility for control of children's behavior in an extensive network of adults. . . . Because of this extended parenting, children's behavior receives proper monitoring and more immediate sanctions than is the norm in American society. Children may be expected to develop more active exploratory tendencies and assertive styles, since respected external agencies can be counted on to reliably check excess. The school, however, exercises less direct and legitimate control, while expecting a relatively docile, immobile pattern of behavior.

    The cultural conflict is clearly drawn." Lonnie R. Snowden, "Toward Evaluation of Black Psycho-Social Competence," in *The Pluralistic Society,* ed. Stanley Sue and Thom Moore (New York: Human Sciences Press, Inc., 1984), 188.

    Sandoval and De La Roza describe the way extended family and interdependent network orientation work to provide external controls in the Hispanic community: "In grocery stores and other public places the mother is not inhibited from shouting directives to the young children to constantly remind them—even when engaged in no mischief—that her inquiring but protective eyes are on them. . . . By loudly verbalizing their directives they also mean to engage others in the social control of their children, seeking a sort of consensus protection. If I (the mother) were to see other children getting into trouble I would tend to them as if they were my own." M. Sandoval and M. De La Roza, "A Cultural Perspective for Serving the Hispanic Client," in *Cross-Cultural Training for Mental Health Professionals,* ed. Harriet Lefley and Paul Pedersen (Springfield, IL: Charles C. Thomas, Publisher, 1986), 167.

2. S. S. Brehm, "Oppositional Behavior in Children: A Reactancy Theory Approach," in *Developmental Social Psychology Theory,* ed. S. S. Brehm, S. M. Kassin, and F. X. Gibbons (New York: Oxford University Press, 1981), 96–121.

3. P. K. Trickett and L. Kuczynski, "Children's Misbehavior and Parental Discipline Strategies in Abusive and Nonabusive Families," *Developmental Psychology* 8 (1986): 240–260.

4. D. G. Gil, *Violence Against Children: Physical Child Abuse in the United States* (Cambridge, MA: Harvard University Press, 1970).

5. Thomas Gordon, *P.E.T., Parent Effectiveness Training* (New York: Peter H. Wyden, 1970).
6. Jane Nelsen, *Positive Discipline* (New York: Ballantine Books, 1987).
7. M. R. Yarrow, P. M. Scott, and C. Z. Waxler, "Learning Concern for Others," *Developmental Psychology* 8 (1973): 240–260.
8. All cultures don't view expression of feelings in the same way. In some cultures, group harmony is more important than individual expression of feelings. Jerome Kagan says about the cultures of Java, Japan, and China that respect for the feelings of elders and of authority "demands that each person not only suppress anger but, in addition, be ready to withhold complete honesty about personal feelings in order to avoid hurting another. This pragmatic view of honesty is regarded as a quality characteristic of the most mature adult and is not given the derogatory labels of insincerity or hypocrisy." Jerome Kagan, *The Nature of the Child* (New York: Basic Books, Inc., 1984), 244–245.
9. Abraham H. Maslow, *Motivation and Personality* (New York: Harper and Row, 1970), 72.
10. Nelsen, *op. cit.*
11. I learned about the concept of "sports announcing" as a means of giving feedback to young children from Magda Gerber, Los Angeles, California, infant specialist.
12. Thomas Gordon's "I" messages. Gordon, *op. cit.*
13. Rudolf Dreikurs and Vicki Soltz, *Children: The Challenge* (New York: Duell, Sloan, and Pearce, 1964); and Rudolf Dreikurs and Grey Loren, *Logical Consequences: A New Approach to Discipline* (New York: Dutton, 1990).
14. Dreikurs, *op. cit.*
15. Maslow says, "The young child needs not only gratification; he needs also to learn the limitations that the physical world puts upon his gratifications. . . . This means control, delay, limits, renunciation, frustration-tolerance, and discipline." Maslow, *op. cit.*, 157.

REFERENCES

"Avoiding 'Me Against You' Discipline." *Young Children* (November 1988).

Bluestein, Jane. *Twenty-First Century Discipline.* Rosemont, NJ: Modern Learning Press, 1989.

Clewett, Ann S. "Guidance and Discipline: Teaching Young Children Appropriate Behavior." *Young Children* (May 1988).

Dinkmeyer, Don, and Gary D. McKay. *The Parents Handbook: STEP.* Circle Pines, MN: American Guidance Service, 1982.

Dreikurs, Rudolf, and Grey Loren. *Logical Consequences: A New Approach to Discipline.* New York: Dutton, 1990.

Dreikurs, Rudolf, and Vicki Soltz. *Children: The Challenge.* New York: Duell, Sloan, and Pearce, 1964.

Elicker, James and Cheryl Fortner-Wood."Adult-Child Relationships in Early Childhood Programs." *Young Children* 51(1) (November 1995): 69–78.

Feshbach, N., and S. Feshbach. *Learning to Care: Classroom Activities for Social and Affective Development.* Glenview, IL: Scott Foresman, 1983.

Ginott, Haim. *Between Parent and Child.* New York: Macmillan, 1956.

Glenn, H. Stephen, and Jane Nelsen. *Raising Self-Reliant Children in a Self-Indulgent World.* Rocklin, CA: Prima, 1989.

Gordon, Thomas. *P.E.T., Parent Effectiveness Training.* New York: Peter H. Wyden, 1970.

Greenberg, P. *Character Development: Encouraging Self-Esteem and Self-Discipline in Infants, Toddlers, and Two-Year-Olds.* Washington, DC: NAEYC, 1991.

Honig, A. *Developmentally Appropriate Behavior Guidance for Infants and Toddlers from Birth to 3 Years.* Little Rock, AR: Southern Early Childhood Association, 1996.

Honig, A., and B. Pollack. "Effects of a Brief Intervention Program to Promote Prosocial Behaviors in Young Children." *Early Education and Development* 1 (1990): 438–444.

Kohn, Alfie. *Punished by Rewards: The Trouble with Gold Stars, Incentive Plans, A's, Praise, and Other Bribes.* Boston: Houghton Mifflin, 1993.

Marshall, Hermine H. "Beyond "I Like the Way . . . " *Young Children* 50(2) (January 1995): 26–28.

Maslow, Abraham. *Toward a Psychology of Being.* New York: D. Van Nostrand Company, 1968.

Miller, Cheri Sterman. "Building Self-Control: Discipline for Young Children." *Young Children* (November 1984).

Nelsen, Jane. *Positive Discipline.* New York: Ballantine Books, 1987.

Patterson, Gerald, and M. Elizabeth Gullion. *Living with Children.* Champaign, IL: Research Press Company, 1971.

Reynolds, Eleanor. *Guiding Young Children: A Child-Centered Approach.* Mountain View, CA: Mayfield Publishing Company, 1990.

Smith, C. *The Peaceful Classroom: 162 Easy Activities to Teach Preschoolers Compassion and Cooperation.* Mount Rainier, MD: Gryphon House, 1993.

Stone, J. G. *A Guide to Discipline.* Washington, DC: NAEYC, 1978.

Whiting, B. B., and C. P. Edwards. *Children of Different Worlds: The Formation of Social Behavior.* Cambridge, MA: Harvard University Press, 1988.

Accepting Feelings

CHAPTER 8

In this chapter you'll discover:

> How some people say "I feel" when they mean "I think"
> How children can be helped to cope with fear and anger
> The difference between expressing and acting on feelings
> How adults give children clues about how to feel in certain situations
> Why some adults react so strongly to children's sorrow
> What's good about anger
> Why there are no negative feelings

TEST YOURSELF

Look for the answers to these questions as you read the chapter:

1. What is "lopsided emotional development"?
2. What did Marcie do with the energy of her anger? How was she different when she learned to use the energy to advantage?
3. How do some people mix up thoughts and feelings?
4. What is the meaning of "all feelings are positive"?
5. What is "social referencing"?
6. When might social referencing create a problem?
7. What are cultural scripts?
8. Do all cultures have the same beliefs about how to deal with anger?
9. Why is "letting go" a parental task?

An important aspect of socialization is helping children recognize, accept, sort out, identify, label, integrate, express, and cope with their emotions. Perhaps the greatest task of all is helping children become socialized while fully experiencing their feelings. Part of the socialization process involves learning to know in each instance whether or how to express feelings appropriately. Finally, the socialized person must decide whether or how to *act* upon those feelings. This is an enormous lesson to learn.

Not all children grow up with adults who help them with the emotional aspects of development. Many adults promote lopsided emotional development in children. We all know adults who reached maturity skilled in some areas of feelings but unpracticed and unskilled in others. A person may be good at expressing anger and self-assertion and dealing with power relationships, but lack the abilities that lead to intimacy and closeness; they are unable to be sensitive, nurturing, loving, tender, vulnerable. Another person may be skilled in the nurturing mode, but lacking in self-assertion and fearful of his or her own power. These people may hold in their anger, fearing it as they would an untamed animal. They keep it all inside by tying it down, locking it in, because, in their minds, if this vicious animal gets loose, it will commit unspeakably violent acts as it rages out of control. This perception of anger as a wild, vicious animal hides deep within many tender, nurturing people.

Then there are the adults who see themselves as a mind walking around in a body; they avoid feelings altogether whenever possible. Many of these adults are so afraid of their feelings that they spend years denying them, and teach children to do likewise.

This chapter looks at counteracting lopsided development and the tendency to deny feelings. It focuses on encouraging children to feel their feelings, to decide whether and how to express and act on them, and, above all, to decide how to cope with them.

Using Anger

Marcie is a 35-year-old stepmother who has recently discovered how to use anger. As a child, she was taught to hide her feelings. She learned early that strong emotion bothered the adults in her life. "Mad is bad" was a motto of her family. She still hears her own mother's voice inside her head telling her "Don't be angry!" and "Oh, just don't think about it!"

And that's just what she learned to do—forget about what was bothering her. But just willing to forget isn't enough. She had to learn some distraction techniques. Those techniques worked well and she learned to stuff her feelings deep down inside, hiding them even from herself. One technique she used was getting out of her feelings into her head. She intellectualized when she stuffed.

But stuffing caused stewing. Grown-up Marcie is a master stewer. When she's upset, the simmering is practically audible.

Take the other day when her stepdaughter, Amy, screamed at her, "You can't tell me what to do. You're not my mother." Marcie felt a surge of anger rising, but as was her practice she stuffed it down inside herself and calmly responded to the five-year-old in a reasonable voice.

The same thing happened during dinner when Amy complained about the food, only picked at her plate, got up from the table, and fifteen minutes later asked for a snack. Marcie handled the situation well, but she was silent and sullen the rest of the evening. When Joe asked her what was wrong, she said, "Oh, nothing. Just tired."

But the problem with stewing is that the stuffed anger builds up until it eventually boils over. Then the rage comes pouring out unexpectedly.

That happened on the weekend. Marcie was still stewing when she emptied out Amy's dirty clothes basket and at the bottom, all wrinkled and smelling of dirty socks, was the little 100 percent cotton outfit that Marcie had hand washed and ironed for Amy the week before. Furious that Amy had put it in the dirty clothes without once wearing it, Marcie stomped into the living room where Amy was lying on the floor watching TV. "What's this doing in the dirty clothes?" she screamed at her startled stepdaughter.

"You told me to pick up everything on the floor. And that was on the floor," sassed Amy.

Marcie's reason left her. She began to rage. When she finally finished, she was exhausted and heartsick with guilt. She was extra nice to Amy to make up for her own lack of control. This pattern was familiar to both Marcie and Amy: to stuff anger, stew for a long period, suddenly rage, then feel guilty and try to make it up to Amy.

Marcie needs to learn to break that pattern. She needs to discover that she can recognize anger when it arises and that she can turn off the voices of her parents that tell her to ignore what she's feeling. She can stay with the feeling and fully experience it instead of distracting herself by becoming "intellectual" about it. She needs to know that she can still *think* while she's *feeling,* but she must be careful to accept and acknowledge the feelings.

If Marcie could focus on her anger, she would get a clarity that doesn't come when she's busy distracting and stuffing. Unfelt feelings can be damaging—physically and psychologically. Felt feelings, and the emotional energy they bring, could be used constructively to improve the relationship between her and Amy. Marcie's tension could be released periodically instead of being buried and then exploding. The tension from the anger could be turned into positive energy that would be useful for solving problems.

Let's suppose that Marcie has learned all that, and today she operates out of new patterns. She's learned to feel her anger and use its energy. The bystander might not notice the difference. Marcie still often decides *not* to express her anger directly to Amy. But now she acknowledges the feelings to herself and experiences them fully. She's replaced the models in her life who were so busy avoiding emotions with ones who make good decisions about feeling, expressing, and acting on their feelings.

Marcie does look happier and more relaxed now that she has learned that anger brings important energy that can be used for problem solving. Amy looks more relaxed too, since Marcie has left the stuffing, stewing, and boiling-over pattern behind.

Surprise! Children play with feelings.

WHAT ARE FEELINGS?

Let's look at the word *emotion*, which is what is meant by *feelings*. *Emotion* comes from the Latin word *emovere*, which means "to move out from, stir up, excite." So feelings indicate a stirred-up state of the individual. It is important to remember that the experience of this stirred-up state is subjective. The only way one can know about another's feelings is through communication (verbal and nonverbal), but the communication is not the feeling.

Feelings are complex subjective experiences that are different from but involve the physical and mental aspects of the self. [1] Feelings can be felt, expressed, acted on, and thought about, but each of those experiences of feelings is different.

Actions, thoughts, and feelings may be integrated, but they are not the same. Sometimes we mix them up. We say, "I feel that you aren't being as careful as you should be when you use my computer." That sentence is not about feelings; it's about thought. To discuss feelings one must use an emotion word such as *fear, anger,* or *sadness*. In the above sentence, substitute "I think" for "I feel" and the sentence is correct. To put feelings into that sentence, you have to add an emotion word. "I feel *upset* when I see that you aren't being careful when you use my computer." [2]

ALL FEELINGS ARE POSITIVE

If you made a long list of all the feelings you have ever experienced, it would be tempting to divide them into positive and negative feelings. However, all feelings have value and are useful, even the ones we wish would go away. They serve a purpose. Feelings are a reaction to experience; further, they help us define and organize experience. They give us direction for action. They give us cause for expression. Some of the greatest works of art, music, and dance have come from feelings—and not always pleasant ones.

LEARNING FEELINGS

Feelings come naturally. From the beginning, in some cultures, adults teach the labels for those feelings. Children come to understand concepts of emotional states; eventually they can think about feeling.

This labeling starts in infancy, when the adult begins to label the child's emotional state. "I see how unhappy you are that your mommy isn't here to feed you yet" or "That loud noise scared you!" Labeling feelings is part of the socialization process.

The socialization process is also involved in feeding children cultural information about feelings and their expression. There is a fine line between the kind of cultural explaining, shaping, and molding of feelings that adults do to socialize children and manipulating them with value judgments that cut them off from their true experience.

Placing values on feelings, teaching children *what* to feel and *what not* to feel, can do great harm. Carl Rogers wrote about this subject in his book *A Way of*

Children "try on feelings" like they try on dress-up clothes.

Being. [3] He wrote about how infants trust their experience. When they are hungry they want food. They are in touch with their deepest needs. But if as they grow their parents begin to tell them what to feel or not feel, they come to distrust their own experience. It's even worse if the parents connect love to the issue of feelings, saying things like, "If you feel that way I won't love you." Doing so can cut children off from their feelings. Adults have a tremendous responsibility for children's emotional development.

How do adults teach children what to feel? One way is through something quite innocent called "social referencing." [4]

Social Referencing

Have you ever noticed how a young child who is faced with an uncertain situation will turn to parent, caregiver, or teacher for clues about how to react? This is very helpful; the adult can calm fears, for example. The child is approached by Uncle Mario, a large man with a big beard and glasses. This child never saw a human who looked like this before. He turns to the trusted adult for cues. The adult smiles, puts an arm around him and walks confidently toward Uncle Mario, talking to the man as if she trusts him implicitly. Every child won't take the adult's cues, but some will, and what was a scary situation becomes an ordinary one—the meeting of a new relative. That's social referencing.

Anyone who has been around young children very much knows that when a young child falls down she will often look to her parent or other adult to see how she is supposed to feel. That's social referencing.

Adults use social referencing to calm children's fears, warn them of danger, help them like a new food, even infect them with joy. Children constantly receive unspoken messages about how to react to situations through adult facial expressions, body language, posture, and even muscle tone. They eventually build up what can be thought of as cultural scripts about how to respond to specific situations. [5]

However, a problem can occur when adults discover their power to influence children's feelings—to mold and shape their attitudes. Some adults overdo it.

Imagine a mother who has an overwhelming desire to make her child into her idea of the good, right, or perfect child; or a father who wants to make his child into a smaller version of himself—a person with the same interests, talents, personality traits. These parents may overuse social referencing. They make a fuss over what the child likes and dislikes when these leanings conform to the image of what they want their child to feel; otherwise they ignore the child's expressions of preferences.

Of course, some children resist this molding of their feelings mightily; they become their own person no matter what their parents desire for them. But others, anxious to please, take all the spoken and unspoken messages to heart and incorporate them into their personality. They feel what the parent feels. They like what the parent has indicated is worth liking. They're interested only in what interests the parent. They fear what the parent fears. They're angry when the parent is angry.

Most children have some tendency toward being influenced in their feelings by important people in their lives. That means adults must be very careful about wielding this influence or they'll put children out of touch with their real feelings. They'll cut them off from their true experience, as Rogers points out.

Recognize the power of social referencing and use it wisely. When a child looks to you for your reaction to something, decide whether it is beneficial to give it to him in that situation or not. Know that you can remain neutral and let the child decide for himself how to react. *After* he decides, a supportive verbal or non-verbal response from you is appropriate.

Remaining neutral eliminates the possibility of a mistaken response. Take these two examples of an adult mistake in influencing children's feelings. A toddler falls down. The adult acts as if everything is all right, but the child is hurt. The adult response discounts the child's feeling and makes him question his own reality. Or, conversely, if the adult makes a big fuss over what was only a little hurt, the child learns to ignore reality and exaggerate feelings to get attention.

Social referencing naturally starts in infancy, when babies look to adults to help them understand and interpret the world. The toddler also uses social referencing, but this approach should begin to fade in the preschool years. If it doesn't, its continuing presence may indicate a problem.

The outcome of the overuse of social referencing shows in the joke about the henpecked husband who asks his wife, "Dear, do I like custard?" But it involves more than simple likes and dislikes; it's a matter of a power differential. Take the example of the slave who when asked "How's the weather?" looks at the master's face rather than out the window in order to answer. No one wants children to grow up with a slave mentality, unable to express their own feelings and relate to their own perceptions in the face of powerful others.

CULTURAL SCRIPTS

All these warnings aside, it is important to recognize that feelings are influenced by cultural scripts that dictate the proper feelings for each occasion. [6] Scripts can be specific to individual families or cultures, telling their members what they are supposed to feel and how to convey it.

These scripts are useful in telling us what someone is likely to feel under certain circumstances. We know what emotion is "called for," for example, when someone close dies. Part of the socialization process is to learn these cultural scripts that dictate the correct emotional response to a situation. Even if we don't feel the way the script dictates, it is important to recognize that, in the eyes of others, the definition of *sane* or *normal* depends to some extent on knowing the cultural script.

One advantage of cultural scripts is that we get clues about how another person of our culture feels, even if they don't tell us. But a disadvantage, of course, is that though the unwritten script tells us how someone is *supposed to feel,* there is no guarantee that a person *will feel* as expected. And of course, our own script may not help us understand a person from another culture unless we know the script of that person's culture as well as our own.

Scripts differ greatly from culture to culture. For example, there is an enormous difference about when it is okay to get angry and express oneself.

In cultures such as the European-American culture, where individuality is stressed, everyone is encouraged to express feelings. The idea is that a person will function better as a group member if he or she enjoys the mental health that comes from expressing feelings. Good early-childhood practice requires that adults accept all feelings as valid and convey that message to children, as well as teaching them appropriate expression of those feelings. The adult's job is to teach the child to recognize and express all feelings, especially anger.

Anger gets a lot of attention in European-American culture. Therapists and some early-childhood practitioners see the importance of allowing a child to rage. The idea is for the child to fully experience the feeling in order to "work it through." These people see raging as a process that should not be interrupted until it is finished; otherwise the unexpressed feelings may remain unfelt and go underground, popping up again and again as a "leftover" instead of arising as a feeling that is clearly connected to the immediate situation and not to the past. These therapists and early-childhood practitioners assure the child that it is all right to feel whatever it is that he or she is feeling. They seek to prove to the child that expression of strong feelings won't result in abandonment.

Other cultures don't have the same view of feelings and their expressions. They are more concerned about group harmony than about individual expression of feelings, particularly anger. They don't see unexpressed feelings as dangerous to either individual mental health or the group.

Jerome Kagan says:

> Americans place greater value on sincerity and personal honesty than on social harmony. But in many cultures—Java, Japan, and China, for example—the importance of maintaining harmonious social relationships, and of adopting a posture of respect for the feelings of elders and of authority, demands that each person not only suppress anger but, in addition, be ready to withhold complete honesty about personal feelings in order to avoid hurting another. This pragmatic view of honesty is regarded as a quality characteristic of the most mature adult and is not given the derogatory label of insincerity or hypocrisy. [7]

Dorothy Lee says of the Hopi: "It is his duty to be happy, for the sake of the group, and a mind in conflict and full of anxiety brings disruption, ill-being, to the social unit." [8] And Trinh Ngoc Dung says that in Vietnamese families "children are taught at an early age to control their emotions. . . . " [9]

It sounds as though the mandate is to repress feelings, a situation that is regarded as unhealthy in white, Northern European-derived American culture. But there are other views, like that of Francis Hsu, who in his book *Americans and Chinese*, compares the

> prominence of emotions in the American way of life . . . with the tendency of the Chinese to underplay all matters of the heart. . . . Being individual-centered, the American moves toward social and psychological isolation. His happiness tends to be

unqualified ecstasy just as his sorrow is likely to mean unbearable misery. A strong emotionality is inevitable since the emotions are concentrated in one individual.

Being more situation-centered, the Chinese is inclined to be socially or psychologically dependent on others, for this situation-centered individual is tied closer to his world and his fellow men. His happiness and his sorrow tend to be mild since they are shared. [10]

THE IMPORTANCE OF ACCEPTING FEELINGS

In spite of cultural differences in how you teach children to express feelings, it is important that children be allowed to *feel* them. The first two years are important in socializing a child to feel or not feel. Children suffer when adults refuse to accept their feelings. [11]

Feelings are important to spontaneity, to being in touch with one's experience, and to mental health. We NEED our feelings to develop in healthy ways. If children are held back from reacting emotionally to harm being done to them, they may end up with psychological problems. [12]

Letting Go of Responsibility

Julie, mother of four-year-old Alexa, felt shattered when she learned that a friend's teenage son had committed suicide. "I can't believe it," she lamented to another friend, Laura. "She's such a good mother!" All Julie's own hopes and fears about how her parenting skills would ensure her daughter's happiness had come tumbling down around her ears.

"Being a good mother is no guarantee of anything," Laura spouted without thinking. She wanted to comfort Julie, but her words only made matters worse.

A tear rolled down Julie's cheek as she said, "I've always thought if you tried hard and were a good parent, you'd have control over how your children turned out. But this tragedy ruined that theory." She was weeping openly now—tears for her friend and tears for herself.

As the conversation continued, Julie realized she was feeling fiercely protective of her own Alexa. She kept trying to figure out how to keep her happy so that she'd never lose her. What good were parenting skills if they didn't guarantee the happiness and well-being of your child?

Laura wasn't able to comfort her because Julie had learned a cruel lesson about life: Even good parents suffer tragic disappointments and losses because of their children's decisions.

Parents can control (or at least try to control) what *they* do, but they can't control how their children receive, perceive, or react to what they do. They can love their children, but they can't ensure that they feel loved. They can't control their children's personal perspective on things. They can't control the decisions they make about how to act based on those perspectives.

A major task of most parents is to let go. Though the first obvious letting go comes at birth when the cord is cut, letting go continues throughout life, a snip at a time. The most important letting go, and perhaps the hardest, is relinquishing the responsibility for the child's happiness.

Of course a parent's job is to meet children's needs, and that job logically *should* lead to happiness. It sometimes happens that way, but not always, because life isn't logical and because cause and effect are never simple or clear cut in human development.

As the child gets older, the parent's ability and responsibility for meeting needs diminish and the child takes over the job. The parent no longer has the same degree of control of creating well-being or bringing about happiness (assuming he or she was able to do it in the first place). This is a hard realization for parents to swallow. Of course all parents want their children to be happy, but they can't *make* them happy!

Parents can only do the best they can—improve their parenting skills and take care of themselves and their children. Of course they'll have their expectations and hopes, but they must realize that too many factors are involved for them to take direct responsibility for their children's feelings and the decisions (even life-and-death ones) that result from those feelings.

Even if it were possible to control the feelings and decisions of others, would that be good? Think what loss of freedom that outside control would mean. Imagine feeling the way your parents wanted you to, or turning out exactly as they intended!

TEACHING CHILDREN HEALTHY EXPRESSIONS OF FEELINGS

Acceptable expression of feelings is culturally determined. Since I know middle-class European-American culture best, I will deal only with the range of ways approved by that culture. The rest of this chapter is written from that European-American perspective. Some of the information may apply beyond this one cultural perspective, but perhaps not all.

I will start by stressing the difference between feelings themselves, the expression of those feelings, and actions based on those feelings. It is never inappropriate to *feel* whatever one feels. That message should be given to children loud and clear. However, it is sometimes inappropriate to express those feelings, and part of the socialization process is to understand when it is appropriate and when it is not. Maturity is in part determined by being able to make good decisions in this area. Deciding when to act on feelings also takes some maturity. Because of all the energy feelings bring forth, the urge is to act each time. However, the young child learns soon enough that getting mad and slugging someone is not a socially acceptable action around most adults. Grabbing what you want has side effects, and taking a bite out of someone because you love them does not get a loving response.

It takes some children a while to learn these lessons. It is wise to be both kind and patient while the child is learning to control the actions brought forth by feelings and to find appropriate ways to express them. [13] While you're being patient, you can be teaching words to replace the actions. When the child begins to label feelings, you know he has now conceptualized them, bringing intellectual processes in to help with the emotional ones.

Once the mind comes into play, it isn't long until you see the child using "pretend" to help him further understand and cope with feelings. Now the child's mind and body are working in concert with feelings, thus helping the child integrate.

What are some appropriate ways for young children to express their feelings? Many adults encourage direct verbalization and teach children to say "I'm mad because you took my toy" or "I'm unhappy because my mommy had to go to work." They also teach children to say "I don't want you to do that" or "I don't like it when you hit me. It hurts."

Most adults agree in this approach—teaching one child to talk to another in a direct way. However, not everyone is comfortable with teaching children to talk so directly to adults. Some feel it is disrespectful for children to tell an adult they are mad at him or her. They are even more uncomfortable if the child translates "I'm mad at you" into "I hate you!" Other adults accept this form of expression, perhaps disregarding the actual words and responding to the feeling behind them. It is common for an adult trained in early-childhood education to reflect back the angry feeling by saying something like, "You're really mad at me right now."

Whatever ways of expressing feelings are acceptable to the adults in the child's life, those are the ways that should be taught to the child. Imagine how a parent who is very concerned that his child show respect to adults would feel if he walked into the center just in time to hear his child scream "I hate you" at the teacher. Although the teacher may find nothing wrong with this way of expressing anger, it is important to take the parents' perspective into consideration and find some way to accept the feeling and teach another mode of expression.

Examples of ways of expressing feelings that are acceptable to some adults and not to others are:

> Yelling and screaming
> Stating negative wishes or imagining violent happenings (for example, "I hope your new toy breaks." "Maybe you'll break your leg." "I wish my baby brother would die.")
> Taking out anger symbolically on toys or other objects (for example, spanking dolls or pounding pillows)

Most adults agree that name-calling and using obscenities are not appropriate ways for young children to express feelings. It's important, though, to realize that to a young child "bad words" have little meaning except that children know

It is never inappropriate to feel what one feels.

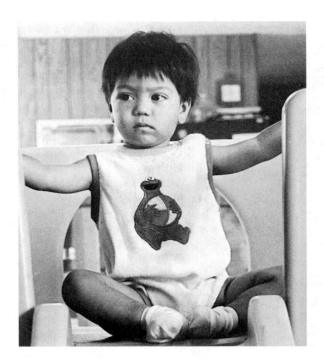

certain words hold power for adults. However, if you listen to young children trying to wield power over *each other,* they don't use adult words. They call each other "baby" or say, "I won't like you any more." Those expressions have more meaning and carry more weight than all the four letter words they may have ever learned.

TEACHING CHILDREN TO COPE WITH FEELINGS

Developing Self-Calming Skills

One of the greatest skills an adult working or living with young children can have is the ability to calm an upset child. Of course, the optimum is for children to learn to calm themselves, and for that reason adults should respect their attempts to do so. For example, when the crying infant finds a soothing thumb and pops it in, the adult should rejoice and not try to distract or substitute something else. The thumb is an example of a very effective self-soothing device.

If infants are to learn self-calming techniques, the adult must not jump up and respond to each little whimper or tiny demand. Timing is important; it takes skill to create a response gap that is just long enough to allow children to discover ways to meet their own needs. If the adult waits too long, children feel neglected; they may go beyond the place where they can calm themselves. Once the child gets overly excited and chaos sets in, the adult needs to be on hand to stop the momentum and help the child get reorganized. Sometimes this is merely a matter of being present and allowing the child to pick up your calm rhythms. Some adults have the natural instinct of tuning into the child's rhythms, flowing with them until the two are in tune, then slowing the combined rhythm until the child is once more relaxed and calm. [14]

There's usually an ideal time to intervene. Determining this ideal time is a skill adults who live and work with young children can acquire through experience.

Coping by Playing Pretend

Playing pretend is a way that children experience feelings in a way that they can control. In a sense, they *practice* emotions through playing. They're in charge of the environment and of themselves, which puts them in a very powerful position—often the opposite of their position when they are overcome by a feeling in real life.

Adults who understand how important pretend play is to emotional development encourage children to engage in it. They give them props to get them started. (That's what the "housekeeping corner" and all the "dress-up" clothes" are about in a childcare center.) When children don't automatically migrate to the housekeeping corner or other dramatic play area, adults can entice them there and even play with them to get them started. Adults who see the value of time spent pretending don't shove it aside for academic lessons. [15]

As children create their own worlds through pretend play, they gain a sense of power. They transform reality and practice mastery over it. No wonder pretend play is appealing.

In addition to personal power, children also gain communication skills. Through play with, for example, small figures, they deal with several levels of communication as the figures themselves interact, and the players who control them also interact. Children engaged in this type of play practice negotiation and cooperation in real life and on a pretend level. They can get very sophisticated at expressing feelings through this medium.

Coping with Simultaneous Feelings

It would be easier to teach children to accept, express, and cope with their feelings if all feelings came singly. However, almost no feelings come as a single pure and simple unit of emotion. Often, two feelings come simultaneously. For example, I feel sad that my dog has died, but I'm greatly relieved that his suffering is over; or I'm delighted about my contract to write a new book, but I'm worried about my ability to do it. Adults recognize those as mixed feelings. Having simultaneous feelings can be an advantage because we can focus on one to help us cope with the other.

However, it is a different story for young children, who can only focus on one feeling at a time; they aren't aware of mixed feelings. [16] We adults can help them

Adults can help children experience, express, think about, and cope with feelings.

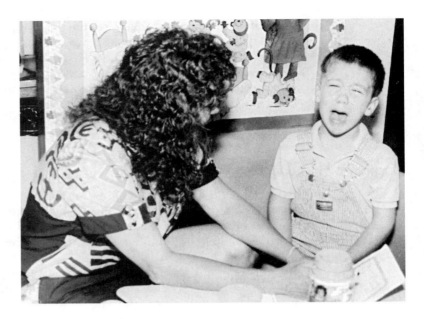

begin to experience more than one feeling by verbalizing for them when we perceive they might have mixed feelings (for example, "You're happy to stay overnight with your friend, but you're scared about being away from home.") Experiencing simultaneous feelings may take some time, since it only comes as the result of increasing maturity.

Coping with Anger

Sometimes anger carries good, clean, strong energy. Children can learn to use that energy to express themselves, to protect themselves, and, when needs or wants conflict, to work toward problem-solving solutions. The ultimate in problem solving is when the child is able to satisfy the need, thereby eliminating the source of the anger without tearing down or intentionally hurting other people. Anger can give extra strength or insight on how to get needs met and to aid this problem-solving process.

Teaching young children to express angry feelings without hurting anyone or anything is a goal for adults who live or work with them. Adults help children learn these skills by:

> *Accepting and labeling the feeling.* "I see how angry you are." "It really makes you mad when she grabs your doll!"

> *Redirecting the energy and helping the child get it out.* "I know you feel like biting your sister, but bite this washcloth instead." "Why don't you go out and run around the play yard three times and see if you still feel so mad."

Playing pretend is a way that children experience feelings in a way that they can control.

> *Calming the energy; soothing the chaos.* "I see how upset you are right now. Do you want to sit on my lap and rock a little?" (for the younger child). Or for the older child, a neck massage might help or a suggestion to "try messing around with this goop and see if it makes you feel better." (Time-honored substances for "messing around" are mud and its substitutes—wet clay, cornstarch and water, play dough. Water alone is a great soother in a water-play table, a tub, a sink, or a bathtub.)

> *Avoiding a reward for anger.* Some adults respond to a child's display of anger with so much attention that the behavior is reinforced. If a powerless child can achieve a powerful feeling by displaying anger, he is bound to continue to use the same approach unless someone helps him experience power in a different way.

> *Teaching problem solving.* When children learn to solve problems by communicating in a give-and-take negotiating kind of way, they feel less frustrated and have less need to try to get their way by using anger. [17]

Coping with Fear

Uncomfortable as they may be, fears are useful. They protect us from dangers. The problem is that sometimes fears get in our way of fully experiencing the world.

They can limit our explorations and discourage healthy risk taking, which gives us a fuller life and helps us expand our knowledge.

Adults can help children deal with fears by:

> *Taking them seriously.* What may not seem significant to an adult may be terrifying to a young child. It is important for the adult to be reassuring without discounting the feeling. Children need their feelings validated, even when the adult is convinced that there is no danger present.

> *Modeling.* Children can learn fears from other people. They can also learn to not be afraid by watching others interact with the object of their fear. The child who is afraid of dogs may be reassured when both an adult and another child pet the dog in a friendly, trusting way.

> *Playing out fears.* Sometimes an adult can find ways for the child to experience something in a safe environment that he or she is afraid of. Sometimes children will do this on their own through pretend play, either in a dramatic play setting or with small figures. Another example of playing out fears is when an adult encourages a toddler to play with a small amount of water in a dishpan or sink to help cope with bathtub fears. [18]

Many early-childhood practitioners also use a technique of children helping children cope with fears. The childcare teacher sends a gentle, outgoing child over

Adults can help children deal with fear by taking them seriously and not discounting the feelings.

Adults "Being Put Up Against Themselves"

It is hard for adults who grew up without fully experiencing their feelings to be around children who are able and willing to do so. A crying child can touch sore spots deep within adults who then react from their own pain as much as from the child's. Marjory Keenan calls this phenomenon "putting one up against oneself," as she tells her story of trying to contend with the lengthy separation agonies of three little girls in her care.

Marjory was professional, warm, caring, and supportive of these girls in their grief. She helped them write daily letters to their mommies telling them they were missed. But nothing worked for long to relieve them of the need to chant pitifully, "I want my mama." It took Marjory two months to finally face her own deep pain of her mother's death when she was just a little younger than these children. She realized what was happening one day in her classroom when the chanting started again. Marjory found herself thinking, "Shut up! You have a mommy and your mommy always comes and gets you." Marjory's mommy never came back again and the two-year-old inside of her was reacting. Marjory's feelings finally resurfaced when the three little girls "put her up against herself" with their nearly nonstop lamenting.

"The girls in my class were not consciously trying to upset me" Marjory says. "They were only expressing their true feelings of loss, and these were mirroring my deep pain. The more I listened to the child within me, the less my lamenters irritated me. I began to realize that they were speaking the words that I could only feel internally."[19]

to interact with the fearful child who is hanging back from participating in activities. Some childcare and preschool teachers have a real talent for linking up one child with another for the good of both. Some early-childhood educators go so far as to suggest to parents that so-and-so might be a good friend to invite over. The friendships that result from these linkages sometimes last for years.

SUMMARY

Helping a child recognize, express, and cope with feelings is not an easy job, especially for adults who were themselves emotionally stunted as children.

The child's feeling triggers a response in these adults that brings anger or fear and pain. For example, a child sobbing over her mother's departure from the childcare center may make her teacher so uncomfortable that the teacher will do whatever she can to distract the child from her feelings. Distraction works, but it doesn't allow the child to experience the full range of emotions and learn to cope with them in creative ways.

Some children seem to live life only on the surface. They are shut off from a full range of experience and emotions. Others show one set of emotions but not another. One child is assertive and powerful and shows a full range of the feelings that accompany those traits, but is unable to enjoy being close to people. Another child is good at intimacy and love, but shies away from any conflict because he is unable to be assertive or protect himself from those who are aggressive. Neither of these children possesses the ability to feel and use the whole range of human emotions.

The goal is for all children to gain feelings of independence and the security of belonging. But they must not do so by sacrificing all the deep and varied human emotions so vital to living life to its fullest and coming out a well-rounded person who embraces experience of all sorts.

This chapter explored feelings and some of the ways adults can help children experience, express, think about, and cope with them. Once children can separate feelings and thoughts, they can learn to be good problem solvers. This learning process starts early and is the subject of the next chapter, where problem solving is related to feelings, to discipline, and to empowerment.

FOR DISCUSSION

1. Give some examples of people who have "lopsided emotional development."
2. What does it mean to "use the energy" anger brings?
3. Give an example of a person who mixes up thoughts and feelings.
4. Explain how a feeling such as anger can be positive.
5. How does social referencing work? Can you give an example?
6. Why would you not want to use social referencing when responding to a toddler who has just taken a spill?
7. Can you give an example of a cultural script?
8. What are some cultural differences when it comes to expressing anger?
9. How can you help an angry child cope?
10. What does it mean that parents can love their children but they can't ensure that they feel loved?

PERSONAL REFLECTIONS

Thinking about your personal reactions and experiences will help you better understand and integrate the material in this chapter. Use these questions to interface between you and what you read. Use the pertinent ones to reflect on, write about, or discuss with others.

› Are you a person with lopsided emotional development? Explain your answer.
› How were feelings handled in the family you grew up in?

> ⟩ Can you remember a time in your childhood when you were influenced by "social referencing"?

> ⟩ Do you remember a time when someone said to you, "Oh, you're not hurt" and you were?

> ⟩ Are you aware of a cultural script that you have learned to help you deal with feelings?

> ⟩ What does your culture say about expressing anger?

> ⟩ What coping strategies do you have for dealing with anger?

> ⟩ Does the idea about parents "letting go of responsibility" fit your personal or cultural beliefs?

NOTES

1. Definition influenced by Greenspan and Greenspan's definition in the introduction of their book, *First Feelings*. Stanley I. M. D. Greenspan and Nancy Thorndike Greenspan, *First Feelings: Milestones in the Emotional Development of Your Baby and Child* (New York: Viking, 1985).

2. *Ibid.*, 6.

3. Carl R. Rogers, *A Way of Being* (Boston: Houghton Mifflin Company, 1980), 173.

4. R. B. Clyman, R. N. Emde, J. E. Kempe, and R. J. Harmon, "Social Referencing and Social Looking Among Twelve-Month-Old Infants," in *Affective Development in Infancy*, ed. T. B. Brazelton and M. W. Yogman (Norwood, NJ: Ablex, 1986), 75–94.

5. Michael Lewis, "Cultural Differences in Children's Knowledge of Emotional Scripts," in *Children's Understanding of Emotion*, ed. Carolyn Saarni and Paul L. Harris (Cambridge: Cambridge University Press, 1989), 350–74.

6. *Ibid.*

7. Jerome Kagan, *The Nature of the Child* (New York: Basic Books, Inc., 1984), 244–45.

8. Dorothy Lee, *Freedom and Culture*, a Spectrum Book (Upper Saddle River, NJ: Merrill/Prentice Hall, 1959), 21.

9. Trinh Ngoc Dung, "Understanding Asian Families: A Vietnamese Perspective," *Children Today* (March-April 1984): 12.

10. Francis L. K. Hsu, *Americans and Chinese: Purpose and Fulfillment in Great Civilizations* (Garden City, NY: The Natural History Press, 1970), 10.

11. Alice Miller, *For Your Own Good: Hidden Cruelty in Child-Rearing and the Roots of Violence* (New York: Farrar, Straus & Giroux, 1984).

12. *Ibid.*, 7.

13. Susan Isaacs's advice in 1930 to a parent of a "willful" three-year-old discusses the importance of patience: "Determination, obstinacy, and outbursts of temper are very normal and when we worry about them we get into a pattern that stimulates the behavior as the child either feels he has power as he gets us all upset, or he fears what we will do to him, so he gets frantic. The child has a big task before him in the way of accepting other people's ways and wishes, and learning control of his own. Don't expect perfection—work toward more and more control, reasonableness, and friendly agreement. Ignore screaming, stop hitting. Don't smack because the child can't see the difference between that and his own violence. If you try to rule by fear you'll only increase obstinacy. Avoid unnecessary demands—insist on only a few and don't ask anything you can't enforce. Give lots of choices on smaller matters. Be friendly and understanding, play with him. Nurture." Quoted in Lydia A. H. Smith, *To Understand and to Help: The Life and Work of Susan Isaacs* (Cranbury, NJ: Associated University Presses, 1985).

14. This approach can be used with a preschooler or even with a group of preschoolers. Experienced teachers and caregivers know how to go with the flow of energy and then bring it down to a less chaotic level. Thoman and Browder give specifics about how this can be done with a baby: "Sit in a quiet, softly lit room and hold your baby gently in your arms. . . . Breathe deeply. Feel all your muscles unwind. . . . Now tune in to your baby. Listen to his breathing. Feel his breathing against your chest. At first, try to match your breathing to your baby's breathing, so you're inhaling and exhaling in unison. Then slowly make your breathing deeper and see if your baby's breathing doesn't deepen too. E. B. Thoman and S. Browder, *Born Dancing: How Intuitive Parents Understand the Baby's Unspoken Language and Natural Rhythms* (New York: Harper and Row, 1987), 181–82.

15. Susan Isaacs says, "By means of imaginative play, children symbolize and externalize their inner drama and conflicts and work through them to gain relief from pressures. . . . Dramatic play provides children with the opportunity to create a make-believe situation, and to predict or hypothesize what might happen, and to play it out. They can act as if something were true, freed from the here-and-now of the concrete world. They re-create the past and hypothesize about the future." Smith, *op. cit.*

    Vivian Paley talks about the kind of pretend play she sees daily in her classroom of preschoolers. She says, "Whatever else is going on in this network of melodrama, the themes are vast and wondrous. Images of good and evil, birth and death, parent and child, move in and out of the real and the pretend. There is no small talk. The listener is submerged in philosophical position papers, a virtual recapitulation of life's enigmas." Vivian Gussin Paley, *Bad Guys Don't Have Birthdays: Fantasy Play at Four* (Chicago: The University of Chicago Press, 1988), 6.

16. Harter and B. J. Buddin, "Children's Understanding of the Simultaneity of Two Emotions:

A Five-Stage Developmental Acquisition Sequence," *Developmental Psychology* 22(3) (1987): 388–99.

17. For children who need more than the above approaches, Dowrick shows adults how to help children control impulsiveness or intensity by training reflectiveness and teaching acceptable reflex actions. He also explains what he calls self-instruction training, and he teaches perspective taking so children gain the ability to take another's role. Peter W. Dowrick, *Social Survival for Children: A Trainer's Resource Book.* (New York: Brunner/Mazel Publishers, 1986).

18. Dowrick offers further suggestions for training children to cope with fear, including "imaginal desensitization," in which he trains children in relaxation and helps them visualize themselves feeling brave in situations that scare them. He also talks about alleviating fear in children through helping them perform in graduated small steps following a carefully established hierarchy.

    Here is an example of such a hierarchy: A five-year-old greatly feared doctors and yet he needed to go to the dentist. The first step was to help him pretend to be a doctor with another child as patient. That was followed by getting him to play patient with another child as doctor. When he was comfortable with that, he was talked into allowing an adult "doctor" to pretend to inspect the inside of his throat. When he was finally able to allow a "pretend" adult doctor to put dental instruments in his mouth, he was ready for his visit to the real dentist.

    Each step of the play was recorded on videotape, then edited and reviewed by the child. Watching himself in repeated experiences in a benign environment strengthened his coping responses—a kind of self-modeling. In addition, the child was taught relaxation techniques, using positive imagery.

19. Keenan, Marjory, "They Pushed My Buttons: Being Put Up Against Myself," *Young Children* (51)6 (September 1996): 74–75.

REFERENCES

Clyman, R. B., R. N. Emde, J. E. Kempe, and R. J. Harmon. "Social Referencing and Social Looking Among Twelve-Month-Old Infants." In *Affective Development in Infancy*, eds. T. B. Brazelton and M. W. Yogman. Norwood, NJ: Ablex, 1986, 75–94.

Dowrick, Peter W. *Social Survival for Children: A Trainer's Resource Book*. New York: Brunner/Mazel Publishers, 1986.

Fraiberg, Selma. *The Magic Years: Understanding and Handling the Problems of Early Childhood*. New York: Scribner's, 1959.

Furman, Robert A. "Helping Children Cope with Stress and Deal with Feelings." *Young Children* 50(2) (January 1995): 33–51.

Greenspan, Stanley I. M. D., and Nancy Thorndike Greenspan. *First Feelings: Milestones in the Emotional Development of Your Baby and Child*. New York: Viking, 1985.

Harter, S., and B. J. Buddin. "Children's Understanding of the Simultaneity of Two Emotions: A Five-Stage Developmental Acquisition Sequence." *Developmental Psychology* 22(3) (1987): 388–399.

Honig, A. S. "Research in Review: The Shy Child" *Young Children* 42(4) (1987): 54–64.

Hsu, Francis L. K. *Americans and Chinese: Purpose and Fulfillment in Great Civilizations*. Garden City, NY: The Natural History Press, 1970.

Kagan, Jerome. *The Nature of the Child*. New York: Basic Books, Inc., 1984.

Keenan, Marjory. "They Pushed My Buttons: Being Put Up Against Myself." *Young Children* (51)6 (September 1996): 74–75.

Kitayama, Shinobu, Hazel Rose Markus, and Hisaya Matsumoto. "Culture, Self, and Emotion: A Cultural Perspective on 'Self-Conscious' Emotions." In *Self-Conscious Emotions: The Psychology of Shame, Guilt, Embarrassment and Pride*, eds. June Tangney and Kurt Fisher. New York: Guilford, 1995, pp. 439–463.

Kuebli, J. "Research in Review: Young Children's Understanding of Everyday Emotions. *Young Children* 49(3) (1994): 36–47.

Leavitt, Robin L. *Power and Emotion in Infant-Toddler Day Care*. Albany, NY: State University of New York Press, 1994.

Lewis, Michael. "Cultural Differences in Children's Knowledge of Emotional Scripts." In *Children's Understanding of Emotion*, eds. Carolyn Saarni and Paul L. Harris. Cambridge: Cambridge University Press, 1989, 350–374.

Lieberman, Alicia, F. *The Emotional Life of the Toddler*. New York: The Free Press, 1993.

Miller, Alice. *For Your Own Good: Hidden Cruelty in Child-Rearing and the Roots of Violence*. New York: Farrar, Straus & Giroux, 1984.

Paley, Vivian Gussin. *Bad Guys Don't Have Birthdays: Fantasy Play at Four*. Chicago: The University of Chicago Press, 1988.

Rogers, Carl R. *A Way of Being*. Boston: Houghton Mifflin Company, 1980.

Rosen, W., L. Adamson, and R. Bakeman. "An Experimental Investigation of Infant Social Referencing: Mothers' Messages and Gender Differences. *Developmental Psychology* 28 (1992): 1172–1178.

Smith, Lydia A. H. *To Understand and to Help: The Life and Work of Susan Isaacs*. Cranbury, NJ: Associated University Presses, 1985.

Solter, A. "Understanding Tears and Tantrums." *Young Children* 47(4) (1992): 15–20.

Thoman, E. B., and S. Browder. *Born Dancing: How Intuitive Parents Understand the Baby's Unspoken Language and Natural Rhythms*. New York: Harper and Row, 1987.

Trinh Ngoc Dung. "Understanding Asian Families: A Vietnamese Perspective." *Children Today* (March-April 1984): 12.

Walden, T. A., and Baxter, A. "The Effect of Context and Age on "Social Referencing. *Child Development* 60 (1989): 1511–1518.

Problem Solving

CHAPTER 9

In this chapter you'll discover:

> What's positive about having problems
> What parents can do when their needs conflict with those of their child
> What can be wrong with teaching children to obey
> What kind of parent is neither permissive nor authoritarian
> How to open up communication in the face of a problem
> Why sometimes you behave just like your parents even when you don't want to
> How problem solving relates to intellectual development

TEST YOURSELF

Look for the answers to these questions as you read the chapter:

1. What are some possible disadvantages to using direct orders to solve problems?
2. What are some disadvantages in making children afraid in the name of solving problems?
3. What are some issues around demanding obedience as an approach to solving problems?
4. What are the three parenting approaches mentioned in the chapter? How is each different from the other?
5. How is problem solving when the child has the problem different from when the parent has the problem?
6. What are the elements of a "RERUN" process for problem solving?
7. What does problem solving have to do with cognitive development?

Problems are an important part of life. [1] They are the way we learn. They provide the challenges to keep life interesting. Problems grow out of interactions, and they create situations in which we interact. They are inherent in family life, and they occur in childcare programs on a regular basis too.

PROBLEM SOLVING WHEN NEEDS CONFLICT

Problems occur when needs clash. Let's say a parent has the need for peace and quiet; she is overtired and has a headache. Her young children have the need for exercise and interaction. They are joyfully wrestling in the living room at the foot of the couch where she is trying to meet her need. How does she solve the problem?

The Direct Order and Its Disadvantages

One way is with heavy-handed authority. "Stop that right now. Go to your room and color or do something else quiet." What do you think the chances are that her children will listen to her and will obediently leave the room to go do something less active, especially if they are all wound up? My experience is that the chances are slim.

That approach—the direct order—depends on the power of authority and the awe or fear the children have of the parent. Some parents can pull it off, but they often do so at the expense of the relationship. Most parents can't get children to obey a direct order.

Children are not in awe of their parents. Living with children day in and day out makes for a familiarity that reduces awe. (Have you ever heard a child call a parent "awesome"?) Awe comes with distance. If the parent's goal is closeness, awe won't be part of family life.

The Fear-Inducing Approach and Its Disadvantages

Fear is another story. If the parent has been punishing or angry in the past when her needs were trampled on, her children may have learned to fear her. After all, she is bigger and more powerful than they are, so she has the means to make them fear her. If she establishes that fear strongly enough, they will continue to fear her authority, her wrath, her ability to punish even after they grow to her size or larger.

Because of fear, her children may have learned to obey a direct order. If she were running an army during wartime this fear would be useful. However, she is living in a family, trying to build relationships, to meet needs (including her own), and to teach her children to meet their own needs. Her overall goal is to teach cooperation rather than compliance. Ruling by fear will defeat her purpose.

Issues around Obedience

Another problem arises when teaching children to obey direct orders from authority. Although it may make family living comfortable (if the parent is always a benign authority), parents have to consider whether they really want their children to obey someone else's orders all their lives. I don't. I want my children to think for themselves; I can't be sure that all the authorities they will encounter in their lives will be benevolent.

So let's go back to the parent on the couch with her headache and see what else she can do to solve the problem of her needs clashing with her children's needs.

Suffering Silently

She can suffer in silence and say nothing. Some parents have in them an overdeveloped martyr. Because parenting calls for a good deal of sacrifice just in the normal course of things, some parents learn to deny their own needs and keep their mouths shut. Their children never even know that the parent has needs.

Suffering Openly

The parent can suffer more openly. "Oh, you kids, I have such a headache and I feel so awful and you just keep on and on." (A big sigh goes with this statement.) The parent can try the guilt and blame approach, then go back to suffering in silence when that doesn't work. "You just don't care about anybody but yourselves. You're selfish and insensitive."

Yes, children *are* selfish and insensitive when it comes to getting their needs met, even at the expense of their parents. That is because young children are egocentric. They don't have the intellectual or emotional ability to put themselves into the place of another, look at the world through a perspective different from their

Children may respond to another's unhappiness by offering comfort.

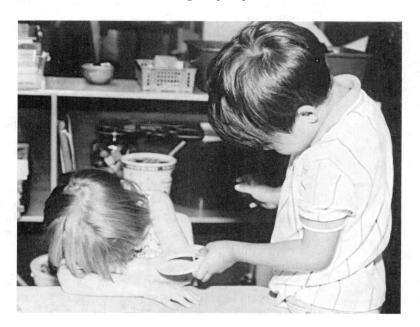

own, or feel what someone else is feeling. If a young child is happy, it can be hard for him to understand that someone else is unhappy. There are exceptions to this egocentrism, however. Children, even as young as toddlers, may respond to another's unhappiness by offering comfort with a pat or bringing a special blanket. It is quite possible for them to have sensitivity to the feelings of another. However, it's best not to count on it. In general, assume that young children don't understand another's feelings, unless they voluntarily show you that they do.

Instilling guilt and placing blame don't work right away—it takes years for the lessons to sink in enough to actually control the behavior. And when they do, they create side effects that harm self-esteem and get in the way of meeting needs.

PARENTING APPROACHES

The three parenting approaches described in the following sections are called the authoritarian approach, the permissive approach, and the authoritative approach.

The Authoritarian Approach

The authoritarian approach is the "do-as-I-say" way of relating to children. Authoritarians see their power as inherent in their position. In conflicts, they see win-lose solutions—and it's important that they win. That's the way they keep their authority.

The strict authoritarian parent demands uncompromising obedience. Rules are established and infractions punished. Parental needs and desires come before child needs and desires. Authoritarian parents may have a good deal of self-respect, but often lack respect for the child.

Children from strict authoritarian parents are sometimes withdrawn, discontented, and distrustful of others.

The Permissive Approach

By contrast, permissive parents seek to have little control over their children. These parents may take the role of guides and friends—being warm and involved with their children—or they may be less interested and involved and more lackadaisical. In an extreme permissive approach, parents just lay back and, if they so desire, their children walk all over them. Parental needs take a back seat to child needs. In a win-lose conflict, the children win because the adult doesn't take any power into his own hands. He grants all the power to the children. Since extremely permissive parents fail to display self-respect, their children win conflicts with them, but emerge dissatisfied. It's uncomfortable to be out of control and find few or no limits. It doesn't feel good to treat people like doormats, even when they invite you to do so.

Children of permissive parents sometimes put a lot of energy into controlling their parents and trying to get their parents to control them. As a result, they tend to be lacking in creativity, self-control, and self-reliance.

The Authoritative Approach

The "authoritative" approach [2] differs from the "authoritarian" approach. Authoritative parents listen to children's justifications and requests and make decisions that take into consideration the needs of the child. They provide limits and control when necessary. They believe in mutual respect.

Authoritative parents derive their authority from the fact of their experience, size, and ability. They know that they have lived in the world longer than their children and have expertise their children don't have. They see their role as using reason to guide, protect, and facilitate development.

Authoritative parents have firm standards, but a flexible approach. They are apt to use what's been called a "win-win" approach to parenting. They are concerned about their children's needs and also about their own needs. When the two clash, they don't sacrifice one for the other, but look for solutions in which both their needs and their children's are met. Resolution leaves both parties satisfied. Children of authoritative parents are likely to be self-reliant, independent, socially responsible, and explorative.

An important device for the win-win parenting used by authoritative parents is the problem-solving process.

The Problem-Solving Process

Let's go back again to the parent on the couch with her headache. She has a need—peace and quiet. Her children have a need—exercise and interaction. Here's how she uses a problem-solving process in this situation.

Putting the Problem into Words. She starts by stating her need and describing the situation as she sees it in as nonjudgmental a way as she can. She defines the problem related to but not the same as the people involved. [3] She says something like "We have a problem here. I need some peace and quiet and you two are making a lot of noise right now."

She doesn't expect this statement to change the behavior, though she may be surprised to find that words alone will do it. However, if her children don't go immediately to the backyard, she goes a step further and states their need. "It looks as if you need to run around and play loudly right now."

They may not be paying attention to her at this point, though it is possible that they will have heard her, since she is being sensitive to them, rather than insensitive. It's amazing how selective our hearing is. Most of us are more apt to pay attention to someone who understands us than to someone who does not.

Get Them to Focus on the Problem. If the problem continues, she'll have to gather up whatever energy she can, sit up, and find a way to get the children to focus on the problem of their needs conflicting. Just her full attention will probably get them to settle down a bit and talk to her. She'll draw them to her physically, hold them if necessary, and establish eye contact.

A Cultural Difference in Parenting Styles

The research on the three types of parenting styles was done on European-Americans and applies to European-Americans. However, Ruth Chao at U.C.L.A. questions the validity for Chinese parenting. Chao raises a paradox. Authoritarian styles of child rearing predict low achievement in school, yet Chinese children who are raised by authoritarian parents do well in school. Chao proposes that the concept of authority is ethnocentric and does not explain important facets of Chinese childrearing.

Authoritarian childrearing in the United States was handed down from Puritanical beginnings, which advocated harsh treatment of children. This view of authoritarianism in childrearing lasted two centuries. It wasn't until World War II that Americans became more permissive. The history of authority in China is very different. Authority in China is not harsh but gentle, coming as it does from a Confucian tradition related not to predestination but to social harmony.

Though authoritarian style childrearing is equated with distance and harshness in European-American tradition, in China it is equated with closeness, both physical and emotional. (The child sleeps with the mother, for example.) The mother is greatly involved in promoting success in the child and is the main caretaker. That situation contrasts with a European-American view of independence and individuality.

Training is another concept that differs culturally. To European-American parents, training involves something militaristic, rigid, and strict. The word has negative connotations. Chinese parents regard training as positive—an act of love. [4]

"We have a problem here," she'll say. "You want to play loudly and I want to rest quietly. What can we do about that?" she asks. This is not a rhetorical question, nor is it one she already knows the answer to. She is genuinely interested in finding a mutually satisfying solution rather than imposing one she's already decided on. Her tone of voice and facial expression reflect her attitude.

Brainstorming Solutions.   "You can go in your room," is one response to her. "You can go outside," is her first reaction. But then she thinks about it and decides that she should respond to the first suggestion rather than coming back with one of her own as a counter. "It's too hot in my room," she responds. That's true. (Otherwise she should consider moving.) "Why don't you go outside?" she asks.

"Too hot outside," comes the response.

"How about if we watch TV?" is another suggestion. The mother sees immediately that that would solve the problem. However, it isn't a satisfying solution in her mind because she perceives that the need her children have is for moving and interacting (active play), and TV is more like covering up the true need with a drug than it is responding to the physical and social urges the children have at the moment.

"Can we run through the sprinklers?" This suggestion makes sense to all of them. It's hot outside—too hot to roughhouse. But adding water changes the whole complexion of the situation.

"Good idea," she agrees. "Keep the hose on the lawn. The cement gets too slippery—and, besides, you'll be watering the grass so the water won't be wasted." She's setting some limits now and giving reasons for them.

Problem solved. She rolls over and closes her eyes as the children leave the room to change into their bathing suits.

Of course, parents don't always take a problem-solving approach and it doesn't always work out so well. Parents are human—less than perfect. Most parents, even those dedicated to a problem-solving approach, have certainly taken the authoritarian approach before. Some have made threats, even ones they never intended to carry out. ("Stop that right now or I'll really give you something to scream about!") Most parents have had their moments of permissiveness too, suffering in silence or whining, fussing, and blaming without doing anything about their own needs.

PROBELM SOLVING WHEN THE CHILD HAS A PROBLEM

Sometimes the child has the problem and it has nothing to do with the parent: "I hate my teacher," says Kyle, slamming his backpack down on the couch as he roars into the family room.

Opening Up Communication

The parent can respond with orders, admonitions, and/or criticisms, which may solve the parent's problem of feelings in response to the child's actions and statement. But those response won't solve the child's problem, which hasn't even been clearly stated yet. And those responses tend to close down communication instead of opening it up. It's better to listen carefully and reflect the feelings perceived.

Finding Out What the Problem Is

If the parent is willing to help the child with his problem, he or she has to find out what it is first. Here's how this parent, Kyle's father, did that.

> "You're really mad at your teacher," comes the response, reflecting the feeling behind the words and ignoring the vocabulary of the statement.
>   "I sure am. He's mean!"

Here is another chance for the parent to block the communication by pointing out how nice the teacher has been to the child in the past. However, instead of criticizing the child or sharing his own feelings about the lack of respect for the teacher, Kyle's father continues to listen. Without expecting a response, Kyle plunges on.

"He tells things that are none of his business!"

"You didn't like what he said."

"I sure didn't! What gives him the right to tell anybody I'm adopted?"

"You didn't want him to tell."

"That's my business and I'll tell whoever I want. But he better stick to his own business."

"I wonder how you could let him know that you feel that way. . . . " Kyle's father's voice has a speculative tone to it.

"I don't know." Apparently Kyle hasn't thought about that aspect of the situation. "It would be kind of hard to just come up to him and tell him."

"I see what you mean."

"Maybe I could talk to him when the other kids aren't around."

"That might work."

"Or you could talk to him."

"That's another idea."

"Ah, heck, I'll just forget it."

"You could do that too."

"I think he already knew I didn't like it because I saw him looking at me, and I bet I looked real mad."

"I wonder if he got the message."

"I bet he did! In fact, I'm almost sure that won't happen again. I did look real mad."

"You look like you feel better now."

"Yeh. Want to go play catch?"

"Sure. Go get the ball."

End of problem.

Reflecting Feelings and Exploring Solutions

Notice that the parent did nothing but restate what Kyle said and put the feelings into words. He didn't suggest a solution, but helped Kyle explore several of his own. When Kyle got the whole thing out of his system, he was ready to go on to something else, and his father was still available to help him do that.

PROBLEM SOLVING WHEN THE ADULT HAS THE PROBLEM

Sometimes the adult is the one with the problem. Say, for instance, Shawna, a childcare teacher, can't get a child, Jessica, to hang up her jacket.

The child has no problem at all. She arrives joyfully each morning, running through the door, throwing her jacket on the floor, and heads for the blocks.

Explaining Isn't Enough

On Jessica's first day, Shawna had explained the procedure of hanging up jackets, and Jessica had complied, with her mother's help. But the second day, Shawna was busy when Jessica arrived, and later she found Jessica's jacket on the floor.

She couldn't stand seeing it there, so she hung it up, and when Jessica came in from the other room she mentioned it to her. Jessica didn't seem to care.

From then on it was a losing battle. Jessica just wouldn't hang up her jacket, even with reminders, which eventually turned into nagging. Shawna hated hearing the tone of her voice when she nagged Jessica, and she got madder and madder. She even started threatening vague punishments, but Jessica still didn't care. Finally Shawna decided to try a problem-solving approach.

Taking a Problem-Solving Approach

"Look here, Jessica," she said, catching her arm as she arrived, jacket in hand, ready to fling it. "I have a problem. I get upset when I see you throw your jacket on the floor instead of hanging it up." Jessica was straining at the bit, anxious to get her hands in the finger paint that was enticing her, just out of her reach.

Shawna squatted down and turned her around so they were eye to eye and no finger paint was visible to Jessica. "What are we going to do?"

"Do?" Jessica squirmed.

"Yes, how can I get you to hang your jacket up?"

"There's no room," Jessica pointed out. And indeed when Shawna looked at the hooks, they were all full to overflowing.

"That's true," she admitted, easing Jessica over to the wall where the hooks were. "I'll make room for your jacket," she added, which she did, without letting go of Jessica. Jessica quickly stuck her jacket on a now empty hook and ran off to gooey up her hands in the finger paint.

Trying Solutions

The next time Jessica arrived, Shawna was waiting for her. "Look, Jessica," she said. "I put a new hook in and it has your name on it. Now you have a place for your jacket." Jessica hung up her jacket carelessly, without paying attention, and ran off to play. Shawna called after her, "Good job, Jessica."

The next day Shawna was busy when Jessica arrived; when she turned around, there was the jacket on the floor again! Shawna walked determinedly over to where Jessica was washing dolls in a plastic tub on a table. Touching her on the shoulder, she said, "This is a jacket reminder, Jessica."

"In a minute," said Jessica, turning to leave in the opposite direction from the waiting hook.

"Now," said Shawna firmly, taking by her by one soapy hand. "How can I get you to remember when you first come in? Think about it."

Later, when Jessica was painting, Shawna came up to her. "I have an idea," she said. "Make yourself a sign so you'll remember to hang up your jacket."

Jessica's face brightened at the suggestion. She took a clean paper and busily painted great orange blobs and blue swirls across the paper. "Here," she said when she finished. "Here's the sign. It says, 'Jessica, remember your jacket.' And that's me by the hook," she added.

When a Problem-Solving Approach Is Culturally Inappropriate

Cynthia Ballenger, in an article called "Because You Like Us: The Language of Control," points out some major differences in child-handling techniques between Haitian and North American preschool teachers. North American teachers focus on the individual child, the feelings, the situation, and the problem. They like to help the child look at consequences and make choices. The teacher remains rather emotionally unattached during the process of problem solving. Good or bad behavior is not usually mentioned during a problem-solving process conducted by a skilled North American teacher.

Haitian teachers, on the other hand, clearly distinguish bad behavior. They emphasize group values and the responsibility of the child to the group. Children's feelings are not a focus during this discussion; the discussion is about emotional ties and adult expectation. There's no feeling of detachment as there is when North American teachers are helping a child "problem solve" a situation. Haitian teachers don't talk about consequences but rather good and bad behaviors, which relate to respect and obedience. Haitian teachers do not use a detached and individualistic problem-solving technique, like North American teachers, but put emphasis on shared values in a moral community.

In spite of the fact that this chapter is about problem solving, it's important to realize there are other cultural perspectives on how to handle problems. You may feel more comfortable with the North American way that Ballenger describes. Or the Haitian way may resonate with you even if you aren't Haitian. Don't think of "right and wrong" when you compare these two approaches with managing young children's behavior; think of "different."

Shawna and Jessica went together to hang up the "sign" in a prominent place by the door so Jessica would see it the next day when she arrived.

When she arrived the next day, Shawna was standing by the sign. Jessica noticed both her and the sign, and she smiled and went to the hook to hang up her jacket. For several days, Shawna helped the sign work. Eventually jacket hanging became a habit with Jessica and she no longer needed either the sign or Shawna to remind her. Problem solved!

The Process

Shawna was clear about what the problem was and who owned it. She was the one with the feelings. She was the one who would benefit by finding a solution. It was her problem. She stated her feelings to Jessica. Sometimes stating feelings is enough and the child will change the behavior just to keep the adult happy. In this case, feelings weren't enough. Shawna had to figure out some solutions, and she did, with Jessica's help. Shawna was committed to solving this problem, so she continued to pursue it until a solution was discovered that worked.

A STRUCTURE FOR PROBLEM SOLVING

Here's an example of a RERUN sequence (explained in chapter 5), a way to give structure to a problem-solving approach. When you encounter a problem to solve, start by checking your own position. Are you clear about the problem? Do you know for sure what you want? Ambiguity on your part will change the whole situation.

I'll use an example from my own life of something I'm very clear about—young children running into the street. Since I have five children, I've been through this situation many times. I never take chances. I know there's a problem if my child is close to a street and can't be trusted to stay out of it. Let's say my three-year-old has been playing in the front yard with a toy truck. I have been watching him, because he is on the verge of understanding street safety. But just now he rolled the truck down the driveway and has started down after it. I'm not going to take a chance. I move fast and grab him before he goes into the street. Then I go through the RERUN sequence. Here's how it works:

> *Reflect.*   As my child squirms and protests, I let him know that his feelings are received and accepted. I reflect them back with such words as, "I see how unhappy you are about being stopped."

> *Explain.*   I help my child understand the situation. "I can't let you run in the street."

> *Reason.*   I give the reason for my prohibition. "You might get hurt."

> *Understand.*   I tune in to feelings—both mine and my child's. I try to understand the situation from both points of view. I don't have to say anything out loud at this point, I just need to be sure I have clarity. I may have to talk to myself to get it.

> *Negotiate.*   Since a three-year-old can talk, I can discuss the problem and together we can look for a mutually satisfying solution. If he had been two, I would have just given two alternatives. "You can stay up here on the porch, or you can play in the backyard." I might do that with a three-year-old too, if the talk turned into game playing and we weren't working toward a solution.

I try hard not to talk every situation to death. Notice the few words used in the RERUN sequence above. The negotiations are the only part that need more than a brief phrase.

With an older child and a less drastic problem, the negotiations can get quite lengthy, but I try to be aware of when I'm getting involved in a game. When negotiations are breaking down, I return to the beginning and go through the parts again. I may have to RERUN several times before the problem is solved.

This chapter so far has contrasted three general approaches to parenting and has examined at length one aspect of one approach, problem solving. This approach, the authoritative approach, is likely to lead to independence, respect, cooperation, and high self-esteem. However, everything said here is culturally bound and is based on white European, middle-class American values and may not work for everyone.

PROBLEM SOLVING AND COGNITIVE DEVELOPMENT

Let's look now at a different view of problem solving—one that is not tied to parenting, to needs, or to discipline. Instead this view of problem solving looks at cooperative problem solving in early-childhood classrooms as a way to enhance cognitive development. [5]

How do children encounter problems in the classroom (other than having needs, finding themselves in conflicts with teachers or other children, or misbehaving)? They come upon problems by accident, or they think up problems while they are playing, or the teachers think them up and present them to the children.

Child-Initiated Problems

For example, the children want to play in the boat in the play yard, but it's full of water from the last rain. That doesn't bother some children, naturally. They're happy to climb in anyway. But the rule is no water play outside when the weather is cold. So they go to the teacher.

A group of future engineers working on an earth-moving problem.

Stopping the Cycle of Emotional Abuse

Brian is a stepfather. He and Jennifer got married a year ago, and he made a vow to be the best father possible. But it's been a hard year! Amanda, who is four, and her two-year-old brother, Tyler, seem to hate Brian, no matter how hard he tries to love them. Brian's pictures of having a happy family life have slowly faded.

The worst part about this year for Brian has been his struggle with his own behavior. Whenever he gets mad at the children, he finds words rising to his lips that he never dreamed he would say to these sweet, innocent children. Take the other day, for example. The family was getting ready to go out to dinner to celebrate Brian and Jennifer's first anniversary. Tyler was all dressed up in a white sailor suit—he looked so sweet. Brian took him with him to get the car, but turned his back while he was opening the garage door. That was just enough time for Tyler to find a mud puddle. Brian grabbed him, but too late. Tyler stamped in the puddle and both of them were instantly splattered with mud.

The words that came to Brian's throat were choked back. He started to yell "You brat! You filthy pig!" at little Tyler when he realized that those were the very words his father had always used with him. He remembered the number of times he had been in this same situation—but on the other end. It seemed as though his father really wanted to convince him that he was a no-good-filthy pig, a real brat who wallowed in dirt just to make everyone unhappy. In fact, his father had convinced him of that; and it wasn't until he had gone into the Coast Guard as a young adult that he had discovered that down deep he loved neatness.

Brian shut his mouth tight, took Tyler by the hand, and led him back into the house to clean him up. Fifteen minutes later the family was assembled by the waiting car. Tyler was in a blue sailor suit this time, and Brian was in another pair of slacks.

Brian helped Amanda in, and was buckling her into her car seat when she announced in a loud voice, "I want pizza." Jennifer explained calmly that they were going to a nice restaurant on the lake because it was a special dinner, and that they would go out for pizza another time.

Amanda began kicking and screaming, making it impossible for Brian to buckle her into the belt. "I want pizza!" she repeated over and over.

Brian's inclination was to tell her exactly what he thought of her. The words that came to his mind were, "You selfish little brat. You always want your own way. You don't ever consider anyone else." Then, to add a little more sting, he thought about threatening to leave her home alone if she didn't shut up right away. That's what he thought; that's not what he said. What he said was "I'm really upset and I'm going to go back into the house for a few minutes until I calm down."

While he was in the house, he remembered the number of times his mother had used that same label—selfish brat—on him. He had never meant to repeat those words, and there they were trying to come out. She had always called him selfish whenever he wanted something different from what she wanted. When she got mad enough she even went so far as to remind him that he had been a "mistake." They hadn't wanted another child, but they got stuck with him. How that had hurt. It still hurt to think about it.

Brian left his self-imposed time-out much calmer. By the time he got to the car, he had thought of what to say, and was ready to say it: "I see how much you want pizza, but tonight we're going to a different restaurant." But as he slid into the seat beside Amanda, he saw that the storm had passed. She was busy telling her doll how pretty the restaurant by the lake would be. Jennifer winked at Brian, who gratefully squeezed her hand as he put the car in gear and backed out of the driveway.

Instead of solving the problem for them, the teacher says, "I wonder what you can do." Each child has a different idea, ranging from feasible to unfeasible.

"Turn the boat over," says Angie.

"Too heavy!" says Amber.

"Get a crane," says Charles.

A discussion ensues about how to get a crane or how to make one. The problem is still unresolved when three-year-old Steven arrives with margarine cartons, ready to bail. Then they discover no one can reach into the boat far enough to bail.

"We need string," says Amber. Off she goes to the teacher who usually provides what is needed when children think of projects.

She returns a short time later with a ball of string, scissors, and a hole punch. The children set to work cutting lengths of string and trying to tie them onto the margarine cartons.

Suddenly Angie has an idea. "This will work!" she says, running off toward the carpentry bench set up in another part of the play yard.

She comes back with a teacher in tow. In her hand is a drill. "Let's make holes and let the water out!"

And so they do. Problem solved.

Teacher-Initiated Problems

Perhaps the teacher sets up the problem. After talking about camping the day before, the teacher arrives at work with all kinds of materials for "building tents." [6] He presents the children with bedspreads, sheets, string, and rope, and suggests that they figure out how to make tents. They need no further invitation. The teacher acts as a facilitator instead of a director, and the children brainstorm solutions about how to support the cloth and keep it spread out. The teacher lets the children do the problem solving rather than doing it for them.

SUMMARY OF STEPS OF PROBLEM SOLVING

Here are four steps to problem solving: [7]

1. *Naming the problem.*   Defining the problem or putting it into words is the first step, as has been shown in each of the examples above.

2. *Generating solutions.*   It's important to bring forth multiple solutions. Too often children get stuck with just one idea and can't move beyond it. Brainstorming as a method implies that all solutions and ideas are encouraged even if they don't seem immediately workable. As the adult, it is important that you accept all ideas without criticism.

3. *Evaluating solutions.*   At this step you start looking at what might work and why. Usually this is an informal process, but it is also possible to write down on a piece of paper the pluses and minuses of each strategy.

4. *Choosing a solution to try and evaluating it.*   Sometimes the first choice works, sometimes it doesn't. It's important not to give up, but to go back through the problem-solving process when a solution fails.

How do children encounter problems to solve? They come upon problems by accident, think up problems while they are playing, or the teachers think them up and present them to the children.

SUMMARY

When people take a problem-solving attitude they are empowered. Empowerment makes a difference as adults and children alike gain in social, emotional, physical, and cognitive skills. Empowered people are more likely to see themselves as capable, to feel good about themselves, and to have high self-esteem.

The next chapter is also about empowerment. It deals with helping children grow to fulfill their potential by examining the messages we give them about their place in the world, about who they are, and about what they can do.

FOR DISCUSSION

1. Give an example of how using a direct order can get in the way of reaching a solution to a problem.
2. Give an example of what can happen to problem solving when a child comes to fear an adult.
3. What are your ideas, feelings, and experiences of demanding obedience from children?
4. Which of the three parenting approaches mentioned in the chapter do you prefer and why?
5. Give an example of a situation when a child has a problem and compare it with a situation where an adult has a problem. What is different about taking steps to solve the problems in the two different situations?
6. Make up a scene involving the "RERUN" process of problem solving.
7. Give an example of how a preschool teacher might use problem solving as a way of facilitating cognitive development.

PERSONAL REFLECTIONS

Thinking about your personal reactions and experiences will help you better understand and integrate the material in this chapter. Use these questions to interface between you and what you read. Use the pertinent ones to reflect on, write about, or discuss with others.

> How do you feel when someone tells you to do something (gives you a direct order)? Make up a scene when you might resist doing as you are told to do.
> When you were a child, was there a particular adult that you feared? How did that affect your relationship with that adult?
> Do you agree or disagree with the point of view the text took on teaching obedience instead of a problem-solving approach?

> Which of the three parenting approaches described in the chapter comes closest to the way you were raised? How would you raise a child of your own?

> What did you think of the explanation (taken from Ruth Chao's research) about the way the concept of authoritarianism is viewed by Chinese families?

> Discuss a situation in your past when you had a problem but someone else took over and acted as if the problem were his or hers instead of yours.

> How did you feel about the RERUN process as it was described?

> When did you ever experience a problem as an intellectual challenge?

NOTES

1. Ellen Galinsky says, "The five years I spent reading the research and conducting my own for my new book, *The Preschool Years*, . . . one finding continued to surface: the importance of the ability to solve problems. . . . In studies . . . those individuals, young and old alike, who could face problems and strategize how to solve them fared much better than others." Ellen Galinsky, "Problem Solving," *Young Children* (May 1989): 2.

2. D. Baumrind, "Current Patterns of Parental Authority," *Developmental Psychology Monographs* 4 (1971): 99–103.

3. If she stated the problem as inherent in the individuals, she would say something like "You're inconsiderate" or "You're being brats."

4. Ruth K. Chao, "Beyond Parental Control and Authoritarian Parenting Style: Understanding Chinese Parenting through the Cultural Notion of Training," *Child Development* 65 (1994): 1111–1119.

5. Jonathan Tudge and David Caruso, "Cooperative Problem Solving in the Classroom: Enhancing Young Children's Cognitive Development," *Young Children* (November 1988): 46–52.

6. This example is taken from Tudge and Caruso.

7. Steps adapted from Ellen Galinsky (1989).

REFERENCES

Ballenger, Cynthia. "Because You Like Us: The Language of Control. *Harvard Educational Review* 62(2) (Summer 1992): 199–208.

Baumrind, D. "Current Patterns of Parental Authority." *Developmental Psychology Monographs* 4 (1971): 99–103.

Baumrind, D. "Socialization and Instrumental Competence in Young Children." In *The Young Child: Reviews of Research*, vol. 2, ed. W. W. Hartup. Washington, DC: The National Association for the Education of Young Children, 202–224.

Bluestein, Jane, and Lynn Collins. *Parents in a Pressure Cooker: A Guide to Responsible and Loving Parent/Child Relationships*. Rosemont, NJ: Modern Learning Press, 1989.

Chao, Ruth K. "Beyond Parental Control and Authoritarian Parenting Style: Understanding Chinese Parenting through the Cultural Notion of Training" *Child Development* 65 (1994): 1111–1119.

Crary, E. *Kids Can Cooperate: A practical Guide to Teaching Problem Solving*. Seattle, Wa: Parenting Press, 1990.

Crockenberg, Susan, "How Children Learn to Resolve Conflicts in Families," *Zero to Three* (April 1992): 11–13.

Dreikurs, Rudolf, and Loren Grey. *Logical Consequences: A New Approach to Discipline*. New York: Dutton, 1990.

Galinsky, Ellen. "Problem Solving." *Young Children* (May 1989): 2–3.

Ginott, Haim. *Between Parent and Child.* New York: Macmillan, 1956.

Gonzalez-Mena, Janet, and Dianne Eyer. *Infants, Toddlers, and Caregivers.* Mountain View, CA: Mayfield Publishing Company, 1993.

Gordon, Thomas. *P.E.T., Parent Effectiveness Training.* New York: Peter H. Wyden, 1970.

Hart, Louise. *The Winning Family: Increasing Self-Esteem in Your Children and Yourself.* Oakland, CA: Lifeskills Press, 1987.

Miller, Cheri Sterman. "Building Self-Control: Discipline for Young Children." *Young Children* (November 1984).

Reynolds, Eleanor. *Guiding Young Children: A Child-Centered Approach.* Mountain View, CA: Mayfield Publishing Company, 1995.

Shure, M. *Raising a Thinking Child: Help your Young Child to Resolve Everyday Conflicts and Get Along with Others.* New York: Henry Holt, 1994.

Shure, Myrna B., and George Spivack. *Problem Solving Techniques in Childrearing.* San Francisco: Jossey-Bass, 1978.

Tudge, Jonathan, and David Caruso. "Cooperative Problem Solving in the Classroom: Enhancing Young Children's Cognitive Development." *Young Children* (November 1988): 46–52.

Strokes and Affirmations:
A Path to Self-Esteem

CHAPTER 10

In this chapter you'll discover:

> Why various means of recognition by one person of another are called "strokes"
> How adults can use strokes to change children's behavior
> How to use affirmations
> What can be wrong with calling a child "shy"
> How a "self-fulfilling prophecy" works
> Why a child who is loved might not feel loved
> Why a child might reject positive strokes
> The difficulties of trying to change the behavior and attitudes of a child who thinks he is "bad"
> Why a "difficult" child is a "needy" child
> How adult self-esteem relates to child self-esteem
> What can happen if you tell a child she is a good girl
> What "sexist" stroking is
> What is meant by "resilient children"

TEST YOURSELF

Look for the answers to these questions as you read the chapter:

1. What are strokes?
2. Some say that if babies are picked up when they cry, they get spoiled. What is another view?
3. How can positive strokes be used to change behavior?
4. What are affirmations?
5. Why did Irene avoid labeling a cautious child as "shy"?
6. What is a self-fulfilling prophecy and what does it have to do with affirmations?
7. Is it possible to "program" a child for high self-esteem? Why or why not?
8. How do the messages we carry around left over from our childhood affect the way we relate to children?
9. How can you change the negative messages in your head?
10. What is self stroking?
11. How can you encourage self stroking in children?
12. How can you be sexist when you stroke children?

WHAT ARE STROKES?

New babies need to be touched. The natural course of events right after birth is to stroke the newborn—just as a cat licks each of her kittens. This very human gesture is both physical and symbolic. Whether or not it is absolutely necessary at first, [1] it heralds a lifelong need each of us has—the need to be stroked.

Babies need physical stroking. Besides the loving touch that is given for no other reason than the desire of the adult, the handling and manipulating involved in washing, dressing, and changing convey an important message: "I care for you." Some cultures even go beyond the loving and caregiving touching and perform infant massage. [2]

But strokes aren't only physical. Parents and caregivers in mainstream American culture are told to talk to their babies when they touch them, and many adults do that naturally without being told. Thus *words* become linked with a pleasurable physical feeling. Although none of us ever outgrows the need to be physically stroked, we eventually learn to take words alone as strokes.

So strokes can be touch, words, or any other means of recognition. Eye contact and facial expressions count as strokes too.

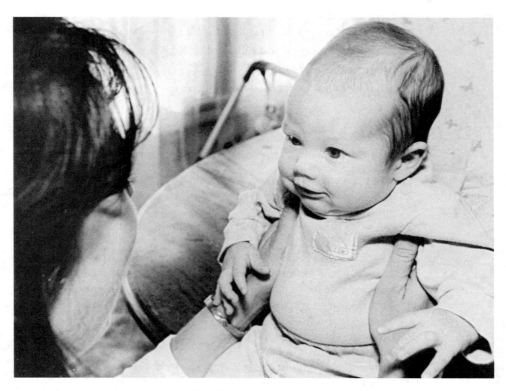

Words become linked with pleasureable feelings.

Babies Need Stroking

Susan and her mother, Mary, are having an argument. It started when Susan's new baby, Jake, was crying and Susan went into the other room and picked him up. She brought him out, holding him gently, saying to him, "What's wrong, Jakey? What do you need?"

"You're going to spoil that child!" complained Mary. "He just ate, so he can't be hungry. There's no reason to pick him up. You're just getting him used to being picked up every time he cries. He'll cry more and more if you keep doing that. You're *teaching* him to cry."

"No, I'm not!" responded Susan. "There is a reason to pick him up. He's crying—he needs something!"

"What does he need? He just needs to show you who's boss."

"You're wrong!" says Susan, turning to Jake. "What can I do for you, Sweetheart, you're so upset. How about a burp?"

She jiggles him on her shoulder, then pats his back and Jake rewards her with a loud belch.

"See," she turns to her mother. "He did need something. But even if he hadn't needed to be burped, he still needed some attention."

Susan is convinced of the importance of giving her son all the attention and affection he needs, starting right from the beginning. That doesn't mean she spends hours holding him, but she does try to be sensitive to when he really needs to be held and cuddled. Susan's mother grew up in a different era and doesn't see things the same way her daughter does. Mary thinks that if you reward crying in young babies by responding, the crying increases. Susan doesn't buy it.

The next time Susan arrived at her mother's house, she had some new information. "It's about spoiling, Mom," she started out. "Do you know that responding to crying in the early months actually reduces it?"

"That doesn't make sense to me!" answered Mary.

"It does to me," said Susan. "Crying is communication. In fact, it's the major way that babies communicate. Ignoring what they are trying to tell you doesn't make the crying go away; it just means that they have to keep trying. If they learn that you pick up their signals, they cry less, because they've been 'heard.'"

"Mmmmmm," said Mary, not yet convinced.

The conversation stopped when a wail from Jake filled the room. The two women looked at each other. Mary was silent as her daughter walked over to check her son. She stood for a moment looking down at him. His eyes were closed and his breathing steady.

"Well, aren't you going to pick him up?" asked Mary.

"I don't think he needs picking up right now. I don't know what the cry was about, but he's asleep. I think he needs to sleep more than he needs holding."

"Well, you do have some sense," said Mary. "I thought you were going to go overboard on this holding thing."

"Oh, Mom, I'm not the kind who goes overboard. You know that." Susan smiled affectionately at her mother. "I just want to make sure Jake knows I'm here to meet his needs, and that he can communicate them. I don't want his crying to go away. It's the way he talks to me."

"Well, I guess you know what you're doing." Mary smiled at her daughter, then gave her a big hug. "I guess I'm just not used to you being a mom too!"

Many adults were raised without receiving many positive strokes, verbal or nonverbal. Because it's not a part of their experience, they tend to not give positive strokes to children. Parent and caregiver educators emphasize the importance of strokes and teach how to give them. For example, when a child does something right, many adults ignore the event; attention comes only when the child misbehaves. However, when adults learn that paying attention to certain behaviors tends to make them reoccur, they see that it's worthwhile to change their approach.

USING POSITIVE STROKES TO CHANGE BEHAVIOR

Ana's two children have a good deal of trouble getting along with each other. Ugly squabbles constantly break out when they are together. Ana's usual method is to respond to them when they are arguing. She has taught them not to hit each other, but she can't seem to keep them from yelling at each other. She spends a good deal of her time settling their disputes. When Ana talks to her childcare provider, Irene, who is taking a class on managing children's behavior, she learns about the principle that when you pay attention to behavior it tends to continue; when you ignore the same behavior, it tends to disappear. "What you stroke is what you get," says Irene, quoting from the text [3] she is using in her class. She suggests that Ana start ignoring the arguing. She does. It gets worse.

Ana complains to Irene that the suggestion didn't work. "I ignored them and ignored them and they kept right on fighting."

"Maybe," says Irene, "you took away their strokes without replacing them."

"What do you mean?" asks Ana.

"You have to pay attention to them when they *aren't* arguing."

"Oh," says Ana.

She tries that approach. Whenever the two are playing nicely together she remarks about how well they are getting along. It isn't easy to do this, because she's used to doing her housework when there's peace in the family. But she makes a conscious effort. When a squabble breaks out, she leaves the room and starts washing dishes. Sometimes the squabble follows her, but she makes a point of ignoring the angry voices.

Ana doesn't feel entirely comfortable about this approach. It seems dishonest and unnatural to her. Her children ought to be good without her making this special effort. After all, cooperative behavior is what's expected. It shouldn't get special notice. It should be the norm.

But she realizes that it isn't. She also begins to realize that perhaps the squabbles weren't true disagreements anyway, but were bids for her attention. She continues to use the approach of stroking positive behavior and ignoring the rest.

It works! Of course her children still have their disagreements, but not so constantly anymore. Furthermore, Ana has grown closer to both of them since she's not so angry at the continual bickering. Ana has learned about the use of positive strokes.

WHAT ARE AFFIRMATIONS?

Ana also learned about affirmations from Irene. Related to strokes, affirmations give messages that validate the person as an individual who has needs and rights. Affirmations are positive messages about expectations. They encourage the child to be who he or she is.

Ana learned to use affirmations to help her children feel good about themselves so they wouldn't have such a need to squabble with each other. She had spontaneously been giving certain affirmations since they were born. For example, telling each child regularly "I love you" confirms the fact that she's glad they were born and that she has positive feelings about their existence. "I love you" is an affirmation.

Ana had a little trouble with the idea that with affirmations she was validating her children as *individuals*. Of course she recognized that each was a separate person, but what she wanted to emphasize in her family was their *connections* rather than their separateness. She wanted them to learn to put the family's needs before their own needs.

Ana brought up her concern to Irene one day when she picked her children up after work and the two had a discussion about this issue. "I don't want them to think about their own needs. That makes them selfish. They should put other people first," said Ana.

"But until your own needs are met, how can you think of other people?" asked Irene. "Think of this example," she went on. "When you fly, the flight attendant instructs you that in case of a loss of cabin pressure, you must put your own oxygen mask on before you help other people."

"I think that's an extreme example," Ana responded.

"Maybe, but I think it applies. And it points out that your own needs are important *in order for you to help other people.* Isn't that what your goal is—that your children not be selfish?"

"I see what you mean," said Ana.

The two didn't resolve this issue because Irene tended to *always focus on individuals* when she thought about young children and families, and Ana tended to

"Look how strong you are!" Affirmations can create self-fulfilling prophecies.

avoid focusing on the individual. Irene seemed to emphasize separateness. Ana liked to emphasize relatedness—embeddedness. But they understood that they disagreed on this issue and were friendly about it.

Affirmations can also be used to let children (or adults) know how they *can be* while accepting how they are at the present moment. Irene, who understood how this principle worked, avoided labeling a rather cautious child as "shy." She didn't use that word to explain his behavior to other people either. Instead, she helped him learn to determine when it was important to be cautious and when he could trust the situation. She also let him know that it was okay to feel his feelings. If he was slower to accept a new person or situation than other children were, she let him know that that was okay too. She affirmed his need to feel safe and the individuality of his pace of warming up. She also encouraged him to take a few risks, recognizing his potential as a person who can eventually come out of his protective shell and become more able to explore freely.

AFFIRMATIONS CAN CREATE SELF-FULFILLING PROPHECIES

The messages that adults give to children can have a great effect on them. What's at work here is something called self-fulfilling prophecy. [4] In other words, what adults believe about children and what they *expect* tends to come true as the children receive messages, both verbal and nonverbal, and are influenced by them. It's important to give children positive messages in *many* forms, including affirmations and strokes.

All these positive messages can lead to a feeling of self-worth—to self-esteem. [5] Parents and caregivers who understand what a strong influence early messages have on later behavior can learn to pay attention to what messages they're giving out. They can strive to give positive ones.

It is important to note that, although it's beginning to sound as though you can control whether or not a child has high self-esteem, the idea of actually *programming* a child for self-esteem is a simplistic one. A child is not a computer. You can control input to some extent, but you can't control output. You can send messages, but you have no guarantee as to how they will be received.

Take the simple act of telling a child you love her. You may love this child deeply, but what counts is not how much you love, but how much the child *feels* loved. There is no way to guarantee that even with many hugs and kisses and "I-love-yous" the child will perceive the messages in the way that they are intended.

It's easier to understand how to tear down self-esteem than it is to build it up. Children who live with constant criticism, who feel uncared for, and who have their needs neglected tend to have lower self-esteem. But that fact doesn't mean the converse—that if you meet a child's needs, guide him or her without constant criticism, and love this child a great deal, he or she will automatically have high self-esteem. It's more complicated than that. But even with the complications, it's easy to see that a preponderance of positive input is *more likely* to give positive results.

CHILDREN'S RESPONSE TO AFFIRMATIONS AND STROKES

How children respond to positive affirmations and strokes depends on their previous experience, which relates to their opinions of themselves and their reality about how the world is. Some children feel validated by affirmations; others don't. Some children accept the positive strokes they are given; others ignore or reject them.

Why would that be? These patterns have their roots in early experience. Imagine a baby who is ignored most of the time. He knows at some deep level that he needs strokes or he'll die. As an infant, he can't get them except by crying, and even then his cries are often ignored. He does get fed and changed often enough to keep him alive, but he doesn't receive his full quota of strokes. So when he gets old enough to create a ruckus, he does that. He soon learns that some behaviors bring adults to him. If the behavior is unacceptable enough, they even lavish attention on him. But it's not positive attention that he receives. He is yelled at, scolded, even punished. But because he is so desperate for strokes—so needing attention of any kind—he accepts these negative responses. He comes to expect them, and when he's old enough to think about such things, he even may regard negative strokes as his due— somehow convincing himself, consciously or unconsciously, that he deserves them.

That attitude, that concept of reality, is what makes it so hard to get through to a child who is used to getting negative strokes. Positive strokes are ignored. Positive affirmations go in one ear and out the other. They don't relate to the child's reality.

Imagine a child, Michael, who comes from this situation and who arrives in childcare at the age of four. The teachers are kind and loving to him; he spits in their faces. They tell him what a good job he is doing on his carpentry project; he throws it to the ground and stomps on it. He accepts the meals they serve him and he accepts their loving back rubs at nap time. But other than those two times, he refuses to accept positive strokes. He seems to *need* the negative ones. And he is an expert at getting them. He hurts other children. He destroys their things and laughs about it. He constantly butts heads with the teachers. He acts like a general all-round menace.

It is tempting to label this child for his behavior. He has a knack for making adults very angry. The staff begins to resent all the time they spend discussing him and his behavior at their regular meetings. No one feels like giving him positive strokes anymore. "That just doesn't work," they all agree.

Michael is a tough nut to crack. He is getting his strokes in the only way he knows how. His reality is that he is "bad," and therefore he believes deep down that he deserves the negative attention he gets. The positive strokes he gets from the staff are brushed off. They are not part of his reality. They don't belong to him.

Besides, the childcare program frustrates him because he can't get the same intense reaction his behavior gets at home. The teachers don't show their anger as passionately as the people he lives with. They don't hurt him the way he's used to being hurt. He doesn't understand this reality of the environment he spends his days in.

What to do about Michael? Of course the first thing to do is to report any suspected abuse. It is illegal to do otherwise. However, the abuse in Michael's case lies in the past. The authorities have already been involved, and the childcare staff has been told that the home situation is now under control. Their problem is Michael's behavior at school. Specifically, their problem is helping Michael control his unacceptable behavior, learn some prosocial behaviors, and come to feel better about himself.

Here's how they do it. In spite of the failure of their past efforts, they continue to focus on the positive aspects of Michael's personality. They search for tiny bits of acceptable behavior. Sometimes they joke that they need a microscope to do this searching, but they discover that when they look hard enough they can find positive behaviors—brief though they may be. Every scrap of positive behavior from Michael brings immediate teacher attention—hugs, smiles, words.

They also begin to see Michael in a new light. Instead of a difficult child, they see him as the *needy* child he is. They're not so tempted to use judgmental labels now. They also discuss how he could be if he overcame his problems and felt good about himself. Once they even took some time in a staff meeting to visualize this new Michael. They closed their eyes and "saw" the potential that lies beneath the difficult behavior.

When the teachers are with Michael, they control his behavior without rejecting him. It isn't easy. In fact, they really need an extra staff person to do this job properly. But after they realized how much time they were giving to Michael anyway, they agreed to do what was necessary in order to focus more fully on him.

Little by little they are managing to disconfirm Michael's reality of himself as a "bad person." They're changing his attitude by changing his behavior. They take a prevention approach—physically stopping him before he performs a malicious act.

When they first started this approach, they called in a substitute so they had plenty of staff, thus releasing a staff member to "track" Michael—to keep a constant eye on him. That meant even when the tracking teacher went on a break, he assigned someone else to take over, so that Michael was never unobserved during any part of the first few days of the new approach. His behavior began to improve—so much so that they were able to reduce the "tracking" to difficult parts of the day. This way they could dispense with the substitute and use the director's help for augmenting staffing. Eventually they needed to track only during transition periods, like after lunch and before nap, which was always a bad time for Michael.

Of course prevention doesn't always work. Sometimes the staff slips and accidentally lets Michael do something unacceptable. Like the other day while his teacher was tying another child's shoelace, Michael grabbed a shovel from a boy who was digging in the sandbox. When the child protested and tried to get the shovel back, Michael kicked him, and was continuing to kick when the teacher grabbed him.

The teacher's response was to separate Michael from the other children. He took him inside. The teacher stayed with him—not to scold him and tell him how badly he'd behaved (Michael already knew that), but to let him know that someone will provide the control that he still lacks and that he is supported and cared about.

The staff's idea is to not allow Michael to make others reject him, which is what used to happen regularly. He still hasn't made friends among the children, but he's beginning to form an attachment to his teacher—and that's helping build trust and give him a sense of the pleasures of closeness with another person. The "good Michael" who's been locked away inside the "bad one" is starting to emerge.

With Michael, remediation must be done. He must be "reprogrammed." (As already mentioned, it isn't as simple as reprogramming a computer, but the concept is useful here if you don't take it too far.)

Children usually don't need to be reprogrammed when parents and caregivers pay attention from the beginning to what messages they're giving and strive to emphasize positive ones. Messages, of course, don't come just from words. They come from actions as well—even little actions such as facial expressions and gestures of body language.

Not all children who come from an unfortunate background like Michael's have his same needs. Take Jeremy, for example, another four-year-old in the same center:

Jeremy is what's called a "resilient child." [6] He was shuffled from relative to relative after his mother left him in the arms of his grandmother the day he was born. His grandmother was able to keep him until he was fifteen months old, but then she had a stroke and Jeremy went to live with his aunt. He's only seen his mother twice in his young life, once last Christmas when she came to visit, and once when he was two and a half and he went to visit her—in prison.

When Jeremy arrived in this childcare center at the age of three, he had lived in four different homes and had been removed from the last one because of an abusive situation. You'd never know all this to look at Jeremy. He's a sunshiny kind of child who beams at anyone who notices him, and he's very good at getting people to notice him. There's something about Jeremy that attracts people to him, children as well as adults. His special friend in the center is the cook, and he can often be found hanging around the door of the kitchen, where she leans over the Dutch door and talks to him. His favorite time of day is when the cook brings the food into the classroom to get the children to help prepare the snack. There he sits, peeling carrots or cutting cheese into chunks with the other children, chatting happily with the cook.

In spite of his difficult home life, Jeremy seems to have managed to get enough positive strokes when he most needed them—during the first year or so of his life. That period with his grandmother seems to have helped him develop an attitude that he's a person worthy of positive attention. As a four-year-old, he seeks it—*and* he knows how to get it and use it. (See chapter 12 for more on the subject of resilient children.)

RELATION OF ADULT SELF-ESTEEM TO BUILDING SELF-ESTEEM IN CHILDREN

It has been said that you can't give something that you don't have. Self-esteem falls into that category. There is a direct relationship between the amount of self-esteem adults have and their ability to enhance the self-esteem of the children in their lives.

It's worth noting that the messages we give as adults are strongly influenced by the ones we've been given as children. Often we are unaware of the connection. We don't even know what messages we carry with us are left over from our childhood. One way to get in touch with those messages is to become aware of the voices floating around in your head—the ones that praise, criticize, and tell you how you should act. These voices create what's been called a "life script." [7] They have influenced you to be who you are. Once you understand the concept of the influence of early messages, you can use this concept to guide you in responding to children in positive ways rather than haphazardly giving out messages that may be negative.

Changing Negative Messages to Positive Ones

If you're walking around with mostly negative messages coming through the voices in your head, it will be hard for you to give out the number of positive ones that children need. So I have a suggestion: Get rid of those negative messages you're carrying around with you. One way to do that is to become aware of the voices and start writing down their messages—all of them, the negative ones and the positive ones. If you write each one on a separate slip of paper, eventually you'll have an array. Once you have collected at least ten, sit down and sort them out. Put the negative ones in one pile, the positive ones in another, and any that are a mixture in a third pile. Then take the mixture pile

There is a direct relationship between the amount of self-esteem adults have and their ability to enhance the self-esteem of the children in their lives.

and rewrite those messages so they have a positive effect in your life. Put them in the positive pile. Now take the negative messages and see if you can rewrite some of those as well. Perhaps you can't. Set aside those you can't rewrite and put the rewritten ones in the positive pile.

Now it's time to deal with the negative messages you're stuck with. Start by spreading them out in front of you. Take fresh slips of paper and write down some positive messages—ones you'd like to hear. Write one for each of the negative messages in front of you.

Once you have replaced those negative messages with some positive ones, pick up each negative piece of paper, tear it up, and throw it away! Make a big deal out of this act of discarding. As you tear up the paper, think about the conscious choice you have made not to listen to that message anymore. Although we can't program other people, we *can* reprogram ourselves!

Imagine yourself as you can be without those negative messages telling you how you are, directing your actions, and creating your personality. Put a picture in your mind of the *new you* acting in accordance with the stack of positive messages you have at your fingertips. Carry that picture with you. Accept it as true. Review the positive messages regularly. Take charge of your life! You can make choices about who you are and how you act. [8]

Children also make choices. They make choices about which messages to take in and listen to. (Just as you did as a child.) All the messages that are sent don't necessarily make the same impression. Some stick; others roll off children's backs like water off a duck.

But children don't have the same degree of choice that you have about from whom to get their messages. Children are pretty much stuck with the people who happen to be in their lives, at least for the first few years. They have very little control over where they get their strokes. You, on the other hand, can choose to get your strokes from people who really care about you—people who are good for you, who support you, who grant you your needs, and who don't tear you down.

Children may have limited access to stroking people; they usually aren't able to expand the numbers of people who stroke them. Sometimes they get all their strokes from just one person. You, on the other hand, can expand beyond just one person for your strokes. In fact, it is vital that you do so. Think of the total number of strokes you get as a pie. Divide up that pie in your mind (or you can do this on paper). Are your stroke sources evenly distributed or do you get most of your strokes from one person? If you get more than 25 percent from just one person, you are at risk for stroke deprivation when that person leaves even temporarily, or is for some reason unable to stroke you.

Self Stroking

By the way, be sure that your own name is on a piece of your stroke pie. You should be a source of your own strokes. If you don't know how to stroke yourself, learn! Start by noticing whenever you do something well. Congratulate yourself. Pay attention to your needs and when you meet them in a timely manner, praise yourself. Practice saying, "I did a good job on that!" and "Good for me, I took care of myself."

You should also teach children to be the source of strokes for themselves. You do this by examining your use of praise. Sometimes, in the name of being positive, we overdo praise or use it ineffectively. [9] We teach children to look to us for their rewards instead of looking inside themselves. It's easy to see when this has happened. Observe in a preschool or toddler program and watch children turn to adults for praise after every little accomplishment. "Look at me, teacher," they say, either verbally or nonverbally. For example, two-year-old Timmy stacks three blocks carefully, and then with great concentration adds a fourth to the stack; then he turns to look at his teacher.

There are several different responses the teacher might give. One response might be "Good boy, Timmy!" This is the kind of response someone just learning about behavior modification [10] might give. The idea is that a verbal reward (praise) will increase the behavior. Timmy will be encouraged to try something like this again.

But let's look more closely at that kind of reward. Calling a child a "good boy" when he performs can backfire. What if he tries and tries and doesn't accomplish the feat? Is he a bad boy? Or what if he doesn't try at all? Anyone who believes strongly in a positive approach wouldn't tell him that he's a bad boy, [11] but the absence of the label of "good" can easily be interpreted by a child as its opposite. It's best to avoid global judgments that reflect on the child's worth as a person when using praise to motivate.

The teacher might say "Good job!" making a nonspecific reference to the behavior (rather than a global judgment of the child). Even better, the teacher might say "Good stacking!" specifically labeling the skill and the outcome. Or the teacher might focus instead on the process—the effort put in. "You worked hard to get that block to stay on top."

Instead of words, the teacher might give a passing smile or a little pat (nonverbal stroke). All the things mentioned so far are examples of external stroking—they

We are not born knowing how to parent or teach children. We all must learn.

Sexism in Stroking

Jennifer is a single parent, mother of a four-year-old boy, Jason, and Julia, who is two and a half. She knows about the importance of strokes and affirmations and she gives them regularly. Here are some examples:

She regularly tells her daughter how nice she looks. She is pleased to note that her little girl is already beginning to take an interest in her own appearance. She notices when her daughter plays nicely with her baby doll, when she pets the cat gently. Lately she's been amazed to see that her daughter is trying to help her do things around the house. Small as she is, she works to make the bed, tries to unload the dish drainer, wants to fold clothes. Jennifer is very happy about these behaviors and, naturally, she wants them to continue, so she praises her daughter when she shows a willingness to help. Once when Jennifer was feeling very down about losing her job, Julia caught her with a tear rolling down her cheek. She left the room and came back dragging her own precious "blankey," which she tenderly gave her mother to help her feel better. Jennifer was really touched by this gesture and she told Julia that.

Jason is his mom's "big boy." He feels that he is the "man of the house" and that he needs to be responsible. Of course he slips now and then, but his mother still loves him greatly—accepting his need to play instead of being grown-up. She thinks his loud manner and his rough play are appropriate, even when they bother her a little. She's proud of the way he figures out things. "You have a good head on your shoulders!" she tells him regularly. She's pleased that he spends so much time playing with the construction toys she's bought him. He creates truly amazing structures and machines. She talks to him about what he'll be when he grows up and how happy she'll be if they can figure out a way to get him into a good college. She has great hopes and aspirations for her son.

When Julia does something well, Jennifer says, "You angel!" When Jason does something well, Jennifer points out what was so good about how he did it. She's more specific with Jason than with Julia.

Anything wrong with this picture? Jennifer is using strokes and affirmations effectively, but she is selective. She is stroking her daughter for some qualities and her son for others. Her children respond accordingly. Her daughter is becoming more and more interested in her appearance and in nurturing others, and her son is coming to see himself as a "doer" and as a capable problem solver who can use his head. Imagine the messages they are receiving about their futures. Will Julia come to see herself as someone beyond an angel who pleases others and makes them happy both by her appearance and by her nurturing actions? Will Jason learn to be a nurturer? How will Jason, the doer, relate to his family when he is grown? Will he go beyond providing the financial support that will come from the brilliant career he's being programmed for?

What Jennifer needs to do is to help her daughter also see herself as a "doer," not just a helper. She needs to catch Julia "thinking." Girls need to know that they are "smart" and capable just as much as boys do. It wouldn't hurt to talk to Julia about college too, even though the event is far in the future. She could also encourage her to play with a wide range of toys, not just those advertised for girls.

Jason needs to see himself as a nurturer as well as a problem solver. His heart should be as big and strong as his head and body. Jennifer can help him do this by finding nurturing men to expose him to, by making it clear that nurturing is appropriate for boys, and by stroking him for any nurturing he might do.

This little family provides a lead-in to the next chapter, which deals with the issues of sexism and sex roles.

come from someone else. However, children need to also learn internal stroking. They need to experience intrinsic rewards, to get a feeling of satisfaction.

One way to do that for Timmy, who stacked the four blocks, is to say, "You must feel good that you got that block to stay on top." This statement helps the child tune in on the good feelings of accomplishment. He learns eventually to stroke himself by bringing this good feeling to his conscious awareness. This approach takes the focus off the outside reward and puts it inside, where it does the most good of all.

Watch a group of children playing, with adults nearby supervising. Notice that some accomplish great feats and never look to an adult. Others must get attention for each little success, no matter how small. Adults are that way too, but it doesn't show the way it shows in children.

Learning New Skills

You may be saying to yourself that all of this sounds very artificial and highly manipulative. Why can't we just be natural around children?

The question is, What is natural? *Natural* means something different for each of us because of our individual backgrounds and experiences.

We aren't born knowing how to parent or teach children. We all must learn. What we learn from our own childhood experience seems natural to us, but nevertheless it is learned. Sometimes it is important to *relearn* because the skills we acquired from the way we were raised aren't in accordance with the goals we have for the children we live with or teach. Learning new skills isn't easy. Each new skill requires practice to perfect. Imagine expecting to play the violin beautifully the first time you pick up the bow. The same principle applies to parenting and teaching skills. Unless you are very good at picking up skills from models who were themselves practiced, you'll be less than perfect at first. You won't sound as bad as a beginning violinist; instead of being squeaky you'll sound fake. When you hear someone talking to a child in an artificial way, it's a sign that he or she is using a new skill. [12]

Other factors come into play when learning new skills in relating to young children. Cultural and individual differences may create discomfort as the new ways conflict with certain values or what have been called "stroke rules." [13]

Tips for Getting Yourself Nurtured

Here are some tips for setting yourself up to receive nurturing. One way to get it is to give it and then leave room for reciprocation. (I'll scratch your back if you scratch mine.) If reciprocation isn't forthcoming, one must then ask for nurturing. This is risky business, because when one asks, one might be turned down. However, asking is still a good approach.

Unless we tell others our needs, they'll never know about them. When my last son was born thirteen weeks early and was hovering between life and death in intensive care, friends said, "What can we do for you?" My first response was, "Oh, nothing." But then I thought about it and said, "Feed us." And they did. Every day when we came home from our lengthy and frustrating visits at the hospital, there was a cardboard box on our doorstep with a full meal inside it. What a blessing! Without our friends we would have lived on fast food and snacks. Not only the nourishment was important to us, but also the message that we were cared about—cared for. We needed that during that period!

We all need strokes and affirmations all the time, not just during crisis periods. Let's learn to get them so we give them and give them so we can get them. Think of it this way. The children we are raising and teaching now are the ones who will take care of us in our old age. The positive approaches we take now will pay off in the future!

SUMMARY

This chapter explored a particular type of nurturing (strokes and affirmations) that children need for their socialization process. It focused on adults as much as on children, because they are the ones who give children this kind of nurturing. However, adults can only give nurturing if they get it, and many adults learn early that you can't just sit back and wait for people to nurture you. You're as likely to be walked all over as nurtured if you're just sitting there waiting. Most people need to put some effort into discovering how to get nurturing for themselves.

Throughout this section so far, no distinction has been made between the socialization process for boys and for girls. The next chapter examines that subject at length, including why it is important to be aware of differentiation in stroking patterns.

FOR DISCUSSION

1. Give examples of three different kinds of strokes.
2. What did Grandma Mary find out from her daughter Susan about spoiling babies?
3. Give an example of how positive strokes can be used to change behavior.
4. Give three examples of affirmations.
5. What does labeling a child "shy" have to do with self-fulfilling prophecy?
6. How do affirmations relate to self-fulfilling prophecy?
7. What is an example of three messages you carry around left over from your childhood and how might those affect the way you relate to children?
8. Which of the negative messages in your head might you want to change?
9. Give an example showing how an adult might encourage a child to practice "self stroking."
10. Give an example of two sexist strokes.

PERSONAL REFLECTIONS

Thinking about your personal reactions and experiences will help you better understand and integrate the material in this chapter. Use these questions to interface between you and what you read. Use the pertinent ones to reflect on, write about, or discuss with others.

> What were the last three strokes you received?
> What is your belief about responding to babies when they cry?
> Do you have an example in your own life when positive strokes changed your behavior?
> What are three affirmations you would like people to say to you?
> Were you ever labeled as a child? How did that affect you?
> What is the message left from your childhood that affects you the most today?
> If you could erase one of the negative messages in your head, which one would it be?
> Draw your personal stroke pie and on each wedge write the name of a person who gives you strokes. The pie should represent 100 percent of the strokes you receive. How many pieces is your pie divided into? Is any one piece bigger than 25 percent of the pie? Did you include yourself on a wedge of your stroke pie?
> Did you ever experience sexist strokes?

NOTES

1. Klaus and Kennell discuss the importance of this early contact to the bonding process. M. H. Klaus and J. H. Kennell, *Parent-Infant Bonding*, 2nd ed. (St. Louis: C. V. Mosby, 1982).

2. I have been learning about infant massage. Some cultures have massage techniques in which each movement has a specific purpose. I also remember meeting Ellen White, an Indian medicine woman from Vancouver Island in British Columbia, who gave a workshop about infant massage at a conference at the University of Victoria in 1990.

3. Jean Illsley Clarke, *Self Esteem: A Family Affair* (Minneapolis: Winston Press, 1978).

4. Robert Rosenthal, "Pygmalion Effects: Existence, Magnitude, and Social Importance," *Educational Researcher* (1987): 37–41; Robert Rosenthal and L. Jacobson, *Pygmalion in the Classroom: Teacher Expectations and Pupils' Intellectual Development* (New York: Holt, Rinehart & Winston, 1968).

5. I am using the term *self-esteem* to mean the result of an ongoing process of self-evaluation. High self-esteem (or a feeling of self-worth) means that after an honest and *realistic* self-assessment of strengths and weaknesses, the individual concludes that he or she has more pluses than minuses.

6. Emmy E. Werner, "Resilient Children," *Young Children* (November 1984): 68–72. According to Werner, resilient children are those who tend to have the ability from infancy on to elicit positive responses from people; have established a close bond with at least one caregiver during the first year of life; have a perspective that allows them to use their experiences constructively; take an active approach toward solving problems; and have a view of life as meaningful.

7. Eric Berne, *Games People Play* (New York: Grove Press, 1964).

8. The exercise was inspired by Jean Illsley Clarke in her book, *Self Esteem: A Family Affair,* cited above.

9. Randy Hitz and Amy Driscoll, "Praise or Encouragement? New Insights into Praise: Implications for Early Childhood Teachers," *Young Children* (July 1988): 6–13.

10. Behavior modification is a particular approach for changing behavior based on behaviorist theory.

11. Some adults do use the terms *bad boy* or *bad girl* when a child misbehaves, but there's a real danger that children so called will label themselves. Calling a child "bad" can have disastrous consequences.

12. I remember when I was a beginner as a nursery-school teacher and my young son visited my class. His question to me afterwards was, "Mommy, why were you talking so funny to those kids?"

13. Jean Illsley Clarke, in *Self Esteem: A Family Affair* (cited above), gives examples of "stroke rules" that she collected. It's easy to see from the following examples how the rules can limit the strokes the person accepts: "Strokes must be earned"; "Strokes asked for are not as good as those not asked for"; "Negative strokes are more true than positive strokes are"; "A stroke has to be justified before I'll give or accept it"; and "People are supposed to know when you need strokes" (pp. 76–77).

REFERENCES

Barnard, K., and T. B. Brazelton, eds. *Touch: The Foundation of Experience.* New York: Bantam, 1990.

Berne, Eric. *Games People Play.* New York: Grove Press, 1964.

Clarke, Jean Illsley. *Self Esteem: A Family Affair.* Minneapolis: Winston Press, 1978.

Coopersmith, Stanley. *The Antecedents of Self-Esteem.* Princeton, NJ: Princeton University Press, 1967.

Dorn, Lois. *Peace in the Family.* New York: Pantheon Books, 1983.

Greenberg, Polly. *Character Development: Encouraging Self-Esteem and Self-Discipline in Infants, Toddlers, and Two-Year-Olds.* Washington, DC: National Association for the Education of Young Children, 1991.

Hitz, R., and A. Driscoll. "Praise or Encouragement? New Insights into Praise: Implications for Early Childhood Teachers." *Young Children* (July 1988): 6–13.

Klaus, M. H., and J. H. Kennell. *Parent-Infant Bonding,* 2nd ed. St. Louis: C. V. Mosby, 1982.

Kostelnik, M. J., L. C. Sein, and A. P. Whiren. "Children's Self-Esteem: The Verbal Environment." *Childhood Education* (Fall 1988): 29–32.

Kostelnik, M. J., L. C. Stein, A. P. Whiren, and A. K. Soderman. *Guiding Children's Social Development.* Cincinnati, OH: Southwestern, 1988.

Rosenthal, R. "Pygmalion Effects: Existence, Magnitude, and Social Importance." *Educational Researcher* (1987): 37–41.

Rosenthal R., and L. Jacobson. *Pygmalion in the Classroom: Teacher Expectations and Pupils' Intellectual Development.* New York: Holt, Rinehart & Winston, 1968.

Werner, Emmy E. "Resilient Children." *Young Children* (November 1984): 68–72.

Werner, Emmy E. "Resilience in Development," *Current Directions in Psychological Science* (June 1995): 81–85.

Werner, E. E., and R. S. Smith. *Overcoming the Odds: High Risk Children from Birth to Adulthood.* Ithaca and London: Cornell University Press, 1992.

Modeling and
Teaching Sex Roles

CHAPTER 11

In this chapter you'll discover:

> A brief history of women's position in the society of the United States
> How toys help define sex roles
> What girls may miss out on if they don't play with blocks in preschool
> How to make boys in preschool feel comfortable playing in the "dramatic play area"
> Another term for *fireman*
> The connection between language and power
> How children learn sex roles by imitating adults
> What's wrong with a lot of children's books
> How girls are taught to be dependent

TEST YOURSELF

Look for the answers to these questions as you read the chapter:

1. What rights did women lack before this century?
2. What role do toys have in defining sex roles?
3. Why should girls play with blocks and boys in the dramatic play area in a preschool?
4. How does language shape perception?
5. What are nongender specific names for *fireman, mailman, policeman,* and *chairman*?
6. How are language and power related?
7. What does "modeling is an important method of teaching sex roles" mean?
8. How do narrow sex roles limit a child's capabilities?
9. How do children's books influence sex roles?
10. What is "differential socialization"?
11. How are girls taught to be dependent?
12. How can you teach young children equality in sex roles?
13. What relationship does sexism have to culture?

WHY THINK ABOUT TEACHING SEX ROLES?

We live with many misconceptions concerning sex roles. [1] It may seem as though sex roles come automatically when children are born, and to some extent that is true. Shaping the sex role may even start prenatally now because many parents know the sex of their baby *before* birth. What many people don't think about when they accept traditional sex roles as a given is how narrow and confining they can be to children who grow into adults molded into a role they may not fit at all. Many don't consider how unfair, to both men and women, traditional sex roles can be. The unfairness shows up when we look backward at history to a time when women were clearly considered inferior to men and therefore had few rights as citizens of this country.

THE STRUGGLE FOR WOMEN'S EQUALITY

The Nineteenth Century

I once read the diary my great-grandmother kept on her honeymoon trip in 1876. The entry I remember best was her impression of women and machines at the Philadelphia Centennial Exposition. She marveled at the machines that could do so many things. But most of all, she was amazed that women could run them. My great-grandmother had a glimmer of women's potential on her honeymoon.

I don't know much about the life of my great-grandmother except that she gave birth to my grandmother and that she died young. I don't know about her personally, but I do know that in her day women were considered property—first of their fathers, and later of their husbands. They had few legal rights, and very little say in their own government. The Declaration of Independence, whose hundredth birthday celebration my great-grandmother attended, didn't include her. All men created equal meant *men*—not people (not women). [2]

My suspicion is that my great-grandmother didn't complain much, because people who are oppressed often internalize that oppression and are therefore convinced that the way things are is the way they are supposed to be. She may have suffered greatly—it's hard to know. Some people don't take good care of their property—they abuse it. I don't know if she was abused or not. If she was, it's quite likely that she went to her grave convinced that she deserved whatever it was that she got.

I didn't know my great-grandmother, but I knew my grandmother well enough to realize that the traditional role of women that was handed down to her didn't fit her very well. She grew up on her father's horse farm in rural Ohio and enjoyed a heady taste of freedom as a child. I have pictures in my mind of her riding bareback, long skirts hiked up, corset loosened, hair flying in the wind. She had settled down by the time I was born, but she still had the spice of her youth in her. She taught me to be "ladylike," but she didn't provide a strong role model for "lady" behavior.

Although my grandmother appreciated freedom, she seemed to have accepted the fact that both of her brothers were born with the right to vote, but she wasn't. She never joined the women's rights movement, which started in 1838 and was still going throughout her lifetime. Luckily for her, and for all of us, others were working to secure legal equality for women.

The Twentieth Century

Then came my mother's era. My mother wasn't born with the right to vote either, but the ratification of the Nineteenth Amendment gave her that right in 1920. Unfortunately, however, not *all* women were able to exercise their right. Women of color and poor women faced literacy and education tests, poll taxes, and intimidation and violence at the polls. These women were kept from voting for forty or fifty more years.

Women in my mother's era took off their corsets, cut their hair short, and cut their dresses even shorter. Although women could vote, and they looked "liberated" with cigarettes hanging out of their mouths just like men, there was still a long way to go to fulfillment. Their lives continued to be shaped by restrictive sex roles, myths about their capabilities, laws that worked against them, and institutions that kept them out. And for some women there was an even longer way to go because sexism didn't just deprive them of fulfillment; it was a basic survival issue! [3]

My generation of the 1950s still faced these problems, but the women's rights movement was temporarily forgotten. The women of the 50s faced sexist issues with little knowledge of their own history. A life goal for many college-bound women (who called themselves "girls" in those days) was to get their "MRS" degree and forget the B.A. All they wanted was a bunch of children. Perhaps they were reacting to having been born and raised in the post-depression period, which ended in World War II. In the 50s, middle-class people—both men and women—seemed to be trying to recreate their concept of a settled and secure life.

By the 1960s my generation of women was getting restless with all this security, which also meant confinement in traditional women's roles. We joined consciousness-raising groups when we saw some of our younger sisters throwing away their bras, growing their hair long, going to encounter groups, practicing free sex, and joining communes.

Many women of this period were rejecting the idea of an "MRS" degree and striving to go where traditionally only men had gone before. And some of them managed to break into some previously closed fields. A revitalized feminist movement grew out of women's second-class status and joined the civil rights and anti-war movements.

As both men and women began to see the oppression of women and the limited roles of men in a clear light, changes began to occur. Laws were enacted. Institutions began to open up. As a result of the liberation/women's rights movements, some things are different today. For women of color, the right to vote finally became a reality with the passage of the 1964 Voting Rights Act and its 1974 amendments.

The Women of Today

Every citizen can vote now, but life's still no bed of roses. Many African-American, Hispanic-American, Native American, Asian-American, and immigrant women are still undereducated and work in hard jobs for low wages while trying to care for their families (as do growing numbers of European-American women who are single parents).

Barriers still exist for women who are exploring nontraditional jobs and who are struggling to reach higher in the business world. Unfortunately, a "glass ceiling" keeps them at a lower level than men. [4]

Women now have a better chance to enter all professions because less recruiting and hiring is done in the private clubs of good-old-boy networks. The arrival of affirmative action, with recruiting plans and hiring committees, made things more fair for women and other protected groups.

However, there are still a number of problems for women in the work force. Women who do manage to work their way into jobs that have traditionally been men's have to be "superwomen." It's not easy for them to succeed with so many expectations put on them. It used to be that success came only if women acted like men when they competed in the traditional masculine arena. Now women are exploring new ways to do their jobs, using their feminine perspective, styles, systems, and skills. But sometimes they are punished for their femininity.

Yes, times have changed. The old riddle doesn't work any more—you know the one about the father and son who were in an accident and the father was killed. When they brought the injured boy in for surgery, the brain surgeon took one look, paled, and turned away, saying, "I can't operate on him—that's my son!" It used to be that people wondered how the father could be the brain surgeon if he was dead. [5]

Broader roles mean that mothers of young children are less likely to be criticized when they take jobs outside the home. Broader roles mean that some men feel freer to participate more fully in parenting their children; a few men even choose to be full-time, stay-at-home parents. Men can now enter more traditional women's fields such as nursing. However, when the average citizen meets a man and a woman dressed in green scrubs in a hospital corridor, the assumption still is that the man is the doctor and the woman the nurse.

Times haven't changed enough, and in fact there are indications that things are moving backward as a backlash hits the feminist movement. Women still struggle to enter some fields and are discouraged from exploring the whole range of occupations. They still make less money than men, often for equal or comparable work. They also do a "double shift," in many cases coming home to do more than their share of housework and childrearing if there is a man in the family [6], and all of the housework and childrearing if there is not.

Whether we will continue to move forward in eliminating institutionalized oppression of women, broadening sex roles, and creating an increasing range of opportunities for all individuals is an unanswered question. Whether women and men are fully able to be who they are and do what they choose depends on how the next generations of children are raised. We can't just sit back and assume that men and women already are or will one day be freed from confining sex roles. Sex roles are learned by every generation. There exists a danger of complacency as the younger generations accept as normal what feminists have fought so hard for. How easy it would be to lose the gains isn't clear, but it should be a worry.

SEX EQUITY AND CHILDREARING

Many forces work to confine children in narrow sex roles, prune back their potential, and limit their opportunities. Consider how television pounds out the message that some toys are for girls and others are for boys. This advertising works against what the nonsexist parents of the past worked for. Just a few years ago parents bought trucks for their girls and dolls for their boys. Maybe some still do, but as soon as the children are old enough to complain, they reject their parents' ideas. They know which toys are for whom from TV.

Toys and Sex Roles

Toys play an important part in defining sex roles. If you buy girls dolls, high-heeled shoes, makeup, and dollhouses, you give one set of messages. If you buy boys chemistry sets, tool kits, doctor's bags, building blocks, and wheel toys, you give another set of messages. Children learn roles and skills from playing; the toys they have to some extent determine which roles and skills they learn.

Visit a childcare program and examine the environment, specifically the block area and the dramatic play corner. [7] Notice if more girls are in the dramatic play

Help girls feel free to play in nonstereotypical ways.

corner. Do the boys tend to migrate to the blocks? If this is the case, examine the factors that might contribute to this situation. Sometimes the adults in the program subtly encourage this kind of sex differentiation. Notice the way the environment is set up. If the dramatic play area is a traditional "housekeeping" corner with frilly girls' clothes, shoes, and purses, most boys won't be attracted. If a variety of male or nongender-specific hats, shoes, ties, and accessories are added, that can help. What helps most of all is adding a little water to the play sink, and maybe some soap suds and sponges.

Because boys tend to dominate block play in most programs, some teachers have tried a variety of approaches to encourage girls to go into the area also. One technique is to arrange the environment so that the blocks are close to the dolls, or to put a dollhouse in with the blocks. Another idea is to put up "girls only" signs occasionally to give the message that this is valuable play for both sexes.

Why does it matter if boys never play house and girls never play blocks? It doesn't, if in other areas of their lives they are getting the skills they miss out on by avoiding these two activities. Dramatic play gives boys a chance to be nurturers, to experience domestic relations, to feel comfortable trying on a variety of emotions. Blocks give girls experience in spatial relations. They learn mathematical concepts as they manipulate "units." [8]

The Power of Language

Language has an influence on sex-role development. Language shapes perceptions. If you talk about firemen, policemen, and chairmen, you set an expectation that these jobs are filled by men and that it's an exception when there's a "woman policeman." Better to make these titles nongender specific. That can be accomplished by using the terms *fire fighter, police officer,* and *chair* or *chairperson.* [9] Children will get the message that either sex may fill these roles.

Some titles are already nongender specific, for example *teacher, doctor,* and *president.* However, children may consider them as gender specific because of their own experience. There's the story of the English girl who asked her mother, "What are they going to call the new prime minister now that Mrs. Thatcher's gone?"

"By his name, of course," answered the mother.

"But what's his *title?*" persisted the child.

"Prime minister," answered the mother.

"But that's a woman's title!" said the child.

Other Language Issues

Interruption as an indicator of power and importance.   Studies of "conversational politics" have found that people use language to show their power, as one person exerts control over another. For example, men tend to interrupt women more than the reverse. And although women introduced the topics of the conversation 62 percent of the time in one study, the conversations initiated by men were the ones that continued 96 percent of the time. (Topics initiated by women failed 64 percent of the time.) Men are skilled in "killing" conversations initiated by women. [10]

Interruption is an important indicator of relative power and importance. Children learn these interruption patterns early from their parents, who tend to interrupt girls more than they do boys. [11] Parents and teachers need to be aware of these patterns so when they see them occurring they can put a stop to them. That's not easy to do when you're an involved party, but it's possible. It's easier to look for the patterns when they occur between boys and girls and then intervene, insisting that the girls get their say. Empowerment of girls is important if there is to be sex equity.

Using language that is direct and informative.   Female parents and teachers can also help empower girls by teaching them to use assertive language. In order to do this, they need to model such language themselves. Women who live or work with girls can pay attention to how often they end a sentence with a question that dilutes the message. For example, "I want you to sit down in your car seat, okay?" or "It's time for lunch; will you come in now?"

Females can model assertive language by cutting down the number of times they hedge with phrases like *sort of* and *I guess*. They can also quit being ultra-polite. For example, "Your shoes are sort of muddy. It'd be really nice if you took them off before you walk on the rug. I'd sure appreciate it." That way of talking is very courteous, but depends on the goodwill of the listener to be effective. When being polite gives the message that the speaker is powerless, it's a good idea to find more assertive ways to speak. It's more powerful for a person to say what she means—to be direct and informative. That's what men do, and that's why they are more likely to be listened to than women. For example, a direct way to deal with the muddy shoes is this: "Please take off your muddy shoes. They'll dirty the rug." Or: "Muddy shoes belong on the mat by the door." Or if necessary: "If you walk on the rug with muddy shoes, you're going to have to clean it."

Using Modeling to Teach

Modeling is an important method of teaching sex roles. Children imitate the important people in their lives, so when girls see their female preschool teachers wait for a man to appear on the scene to unplug toilets or fix the broken handle on the cupboard, they pick up silent messages about women's capabilities. When a boy sees his father hand his mother a needle and thread and a shirt with a missing button, he gets a silent message about men's capabilities.

When children see their father reading the newspaper while their mother fixes dinner, then watching the news on TV while she cleans up after dinner, they get silent messages about sex roles. They come to see some activities as for women only and some for men only. They see a sexually determined power differential. In a household where tasks are shared, children get a broader idea of capabilities as well as appropriateness.

A good deal of modeling comes from television. *Power Rangers,* a children's television program widely criticized for its violence, at least has both boy and girl rangers. However, the "bad guy" is an evil old woman. Powerful elderly females as evil is a stereotype that has been with us for centuries. The witch hunts of the past show how such a negative stereotype can be used to oppress, even kill. Some older feminists facing the negative stereotype of being feminine and old have decided to redefine themselves as crones—the old woman as powerful, knowledgeable and wise, but not evil.

Books can leave strong stereotypical images. In early readers, Dick was always busy fixing something, while Mother, Jane, and Sally stood helplessly looking on. Dick and Father were active in a variety of ways. Mother, Jane, and Sally were passive except in the kitchen. It seems as though times should have changed by now, but as late as 1986, when books read to kindergartners were analyzed, the main character was male over 70 percent of the time. [12] And books for young children still show females being dependent more often than being independent. [13] The poor dear damsels constantly need help, and guess who they get it from? Males.

Differential Socialization

Adults socialize girls and boys differently, which results in females ending up in subservient roles. How does this happen? Besides modeling, how else do children learn sex roles and develop a gender identity? Why do many boys gain confidence, competence, mastery, and assertiveness and many girls come to see themselves as lacking those qualities? Why do many girls fail to identify themselves as strong, responsible, and powerful?

Differential treatment from parents.   Differential treatment starts at birth, when parents perceive their daughters to be more fragile than their sons. [14] From early on, parents encourage their sons to be active, assertive, and strong; and they protect their girls. They do more touching and talking to girls; they stress independence, self-reliance, and achievement-related skills to their boys. As children leave babyhood, the differential treatment continues into toddlerhood and beyond until eventually, lo and behold, the boys have a tendency to be active, clever, assertive, aggressive doers, and the girls often turn out to be sweet, dependent, verbal, and social. Whatever natural inclinations that fit the sex role the children might have been born with are greatly magnified by the socialization process. [15]

Differential treatment in preschool.   This same differential treatment continues when the children leave home for childcare or preschool. In the early 1970s, Lisa Serbin and her colleagues looked at how preschool teachers treated girls and boys. They found that teachers paid attention to boys' disruptive behavior, which reinforced it; the attention acted as a reward and encouraged the behavior to continue. Girls, on the other hand, received attention only when they stood or played near the teacher. [16] Direct reinforcement, even when it is unintended, is a powerful way to influence behavior.

Things haven't changed much from the early 1970s. Observe for yourself how adults in group care spend a lot of time looking over the heads of the girls who hang around them (being dependent and getting attention for it) to notice the boys, who are throwing blocks, hitting each other, or climbing the fence of the play yard.

Broaden all children's interests and skills.

The untrained adult will yell at the boys. The trained one will leave the cluster of girls and go over and handle the problem with the boys in some professional way—often touching them, getting down to their level, and making eye contact while he or she describes the unacceptable behavior and explains why it must stop. Both the yelling and the more professional intervention strategies are rewarding. They say to the boys, "I'm paying attention to you." The attention and the behavior that preceded it become solidly linked. Many boys never learn any other ways of getting the teacher to notice them. And many of the girls never break out of the "be-dependent-to-get-noticed" pattern.

While you are observing, notice how adults make conversation with young children. I'm sure you'll discover that girls are often noticed for their appearance. Childcare staff and visitors regularly make remarks like "Oh, you got your hair cut. It looks very pretty" and "I see you got new shoes!" and "What a nice design on your shirt." Those same adults are more likely to notice boys' abilities. They say things like "How strong you are to lift that heavy piece of wood" and "I saw you climb all the way up to the top of the jungle gym!" and "How clever you are. You figured out how to make that work!"

While all this is going on in preschool or childcare, at home parents tend to give help to their daughters more than to their sons (and the girls ask for help more often, which is not surprising, because they are rewarded for doing so). Girls are also more likely to be criticized for touching, handling, and manipulating

Sexism and Culture

Two parents meet outside the door of the childcare center where they have just arrived to pick up their children at the end of the day. They know each other slightly, and feel a connection because they are of the same culture, although one was born in the United States and the other in the "old country." Both speak English, but they are more comfortable talking to each other in their own language, which is what they are doing now:

"How did you like the last parent meeting?" inquires Parent A, making conversation.

"Well, to tell the truth, it upset me," answers Parent B.

"Oh?" responds Parent A.

"All that talk about letting boys act like girls and encouraging girls to be powerful bothered me a lot. I just don't think that's appropriate!"

"Hmm . . . ," says Parent A.

"I can't stand the thought of my son playing house and wearing dresses. That makes me sick to my stomach. And they let him do that if he wants to."

"Does he want to?"

"How do I know? I'm not there!"

"It does seem kind of strange to me too, but I don't think it hurts anything." Parent A leans casually against the stair rail.

Parent B stands, nervously rubbing her arms as if she is cold. She looks distressed.

"But the worst thing of all is that the teacher told me to send my daughter in pants and sneakers. She says that she's afraid to get dirty and that it's hard for her to run and climb with a dress and good shoes on. I guess she thinks I want her to look ugly, get dirty, and run around like a wild person!"

Parent A touches her friend's arm. "Does that really bother you?"

"Yes! That's not proper behavior for a girl! Do you think it is?"

"Well," says Parent A slowly, brushing her hair back from her face, while carefully considering her words, "I don't really like my daughter to get dirty, but I have to admit that what the teacher said is convincing."

"What's convincing? All that garbage about sexism and oppression?"

The two parents stop talking in their own language and switch to English as another parent arrives at the bottom of the steps. They greet her and move over to let her go up the steps and into the childcare center.

"Yes, sexism and oppression!" continues Parent A, as if there had been no interruption.

Parent B replies passionately, "I don't see that my daughter is restricted in her development. She's going to grow into a woman. She has to know how women act in our culture. She has to fit in. She'll never get a decent husband if she starts acting like the other girls in this country. I don't want her to be like them. I don't want her to lose her culture."

"I know what you mean," says Parent A slowly. "But I've been thinking about whether women's inferior status is something we should just accept because that's the way it's always been."

"Oh, you're as bad as they are!" snorts Parent B angrily, stepping backward on the stair. "I thought you would understand."

"I do understand," comes the answer, "but at the same time I'm confused. I just don't know what I think."

"Well, I do. And I warn you, if you listen to them, you'll end up like them. You'll be melted right into the melting pot! How would you like that?"

"I don't know," answers Parent A, looking doubtful as she slowly gets up, turns, and walks to the door of the center. "But I think," she says, pausing and turning around to watch Parent B climb up the rest of the steps, "that ensuring that my daughter grows up with a sense of her self-worth as a person is a good idea. I don't think oppression has to be part of our culture."

"I disagree that women who dress and act the way they are supposed to are oppressed. That's ridiculous. Look at me. Am I oppressed?" Parent B is at the door now too.

"I don't know," says Parent A, opening the door and stepping back to let her friend walk through first.

objects, and for active play. [17] In other words, girls are taught to be dependent and quiet, even passive, at home and at school, and boys are encouraged to figure things out for themselves and to be active in their play.

Not all sex-role behavior is learned. Physiology can contribute to male-female differences. We know that exposure to hormones during pregnancy, genetic influences, and other biological factors can influence the development of sexual identity and gender role. [18] However, *learning* has a good deal to do with how children see themselves and what skills they develop. [19]

We know that the adults in young children's lives have a great influence over their sex-role socialization. What are some ways that these adults can empower both boys and girls? How can they promote equality of development for both sexes? With stereotypes still such a part of all our lives, how can adults counteract their influence and help boys learn that they can express feelings and be nurturing, and help girls learn to be independent, assertive, and capable problem solvers? What can adults do to enable each child to fulfill his or her own potential rather than grow up bound by restrictive sex roles?

GUIDELINES FOR PARENTS AND TEACHERS

Here are some guidelines for teaching young children equality in sex roles:

> Help children develop awareness of sexist stereotypes. Point out such stereotypes in pictures, in books, and on TV. Look for stereotypes in commercials as well as in regular programs and movies.

> Create a nonsexist environment. Find books and pictures that show men and women doing similar activities and pictures of women and men in nontraditional occupations. Invite visitors who are in nontraditional jobs to the home, childcare, or preschool to talk about their work. (Or visit these workers at their workplaces.) Expand children's awareness beyond narrow stereotypical sex roles.

> Watch your own behavior. Do you treat girls differently from boys? What do you notice about them? What do you remark about? Do you give both sexes equal physical freedom? Do you allow both to express feelings? Do you encourage both to seek help at times and to be independent as well? Be observant of yourself and catch the ways you may be promoting narrow sex roles. When children ask about the difference between boys and girls, stick to anatomical differences and avoid mentioning dress, behavior, or personality traits.

> Teach an antibias attitude to young children and give them the skills they need to challenge sexism. [20] Teach them to recognize injustice and to speak out against it. When Brandon says to Lindsay, "You can't come in our fort. Only boys are allowed," help her speak up and say, "That's not fair!" (If he tries to exclude her on the basis of her behavior, the situation is different. For example, if he says, "You can't come in because last time you grabbed all the toys," she's getting feedback about something she can change. She can't, however, change the fact of being a girl, so for him to exclude her for that reason is unfair discrimination.) Children need to learn to speak up for their own rights. Teach them to do that.

> Help all children develop empathy. Notice when they are sensitive to the feelings of another. Pay attention to behaviors that show caring for another person.

> Help all children become problem solvers, in both the physical and the social worlds. Teach them to troubleshoot. Help them extend their perspective to include many possibilities. Help them learn to negotiate.

> Broaden children's views of themselves and their capabilities. Entice them to develop skills they've been avoiding. Find ways to get girls out in the yard in activities that increase their strength, courage, and dexterity. Figure out a way to get boys involved in activities that take eye-hand coordination and require careful manual skills. Some boys who avoid traditional preschool art projects will glue wood scrap sculptures or take apart an old radio.

> Notice how clothes get in the way and determine activities, especially girls' clothes. The crawling baby is hampered if she's in a dress. The slippery shoes of the preschooler keep her from running or climbing. Light-colored pants get stained knees if a girl crawls around on the grass or in the dirt. Will this situation cause problems for her, and serve to restrict her activities?

> Last, but definitely not least, check out your own attitudes. If you see the male of the species as more important, more deserving of power, worthy

Teach an antibias attitude to young children and give them the skills they need to challenge sexism.

of a higher status, you need an attitude adjustment. Until you get one, you'd better watch yourself carefully when you are around young children. You can't promote equality if down deep you don't believe in it! [21]

SUMMARY

This chapter examined the role socialization plays in creating differences between boys and girls. It came out strongly for equality of the sexes. In the next chapter the theme is continued as we look at stresses in families, and find that some of those stresses have to do with the feminization of poverty and the inferior status of women.

FOR DISCUSSION

1. Have women reached equality yet? How do you know?
2. How can you get children to broaden their range of toys?
3. What part does TV play in limiting children's concept of sex roles? Give specific examples.

4. Have you noticed the connection of power and language? Give some examples.
5. What are two examples of talking "assertively"?
6. Give two examples of modeling sex roles.
7. Give two examples of "differential socialization."
8. Give two examples of ways girls are taught to be dependent.
9. How can you empower both boys and girls?
10. Is sexism seen the same by all cultures? Explain.
11. How do clothes relate to equity issues?

PERSONAL REFLECTIONS

Thinking about your personal reactions and experiences will help you better understand and integrate the material in this chapter. Use these questions to interface between you and what you read. Use the pertinent ones to reflect on, write about, or discuss with others.

> What do you know about women's liberation in your own family history?
> How do you see your own sex role? Are you limited by it?
> How were you socialized? Do you remember how you came to understand what it means to be a male and what it means to be a female? Were you happy with what you learned? Are you now?
> Would you raise your children the way you were raised?
> Did you have a broad range of toys?
> How can you get children to broaden their range of toys?
> Are you guilty of remarking more about girl's appearances and boys abilities? How do you think that might affect both boys and girls?
> What are your ideas, thoughts, and experiences with sex roles and culture?
> If you could control TV, what would you do to promote sexual equality?
> What are some sexist stereotypes that show up on TV, in magazines, and in books?

NOTES

1. Sometimes a differentiation is made between *sex* and *gender*—*sex* meaning the biological fact of being male or female and *gender* referring to the person's identification as male or female through a socialization process. Usually sex and gender roles coincide, but in some cases a child of one sex may be socialized to be the opposite gender. John Money and Anke A. Ehrhardt, *Man and Woman and Boy and Girl* (Baltimore, MD: The Johns Hopkins University Press, 1972). I am using *sex roles* to mean gender roles, because that is common practice; however, strictly speaking, the proper term is *gender roles*.

2. The Declaration of Independence didn't include *all* men either.

3. Collins, Patricia Hill, *Black Feminist Thought: Knowledge, Consciousness, and the Politics of Empowerment* (Boston: Unwin Hyman, 1990).

4. U.S. Department of Labor, *A Report on the Glass Ceiling Initiative*, 1991.

5. You knew the answer is that the brain surgeon was the boy's *mother*, didn't you?

6. Arlie Hochschild, *The Second Shift* (New York: Viking, 1989).

7. Vivian Paley deals with this subject at length in her very informative, easy-to-read book, *Boys and Girls: Superheroes in the Doll Corner* (Chicago: University of Chicago Press, 1984).

8. Ordinary wooden "kindergarten" blocks, called "unit blocks," represent multiples of the basic square that is found in the set. Block play contributes a good deal to the concrete experience behind math knowledge, as well as giving the player experiences with principles of physics. Stuart Reifel, "Block Construction: Children's Developmental Landmarks in Representation of Space," *Young Children* (November 1984).

9. Other examples: *letter carrier* for *mailman*; *server* for *waitress*; and *angler* for *fisherman*.

10. Mary Brown Parlee, "Conversational Politics," *Psychology Today* (May 1979).

11. Lenore J. Weitzman, *Sex Role Socialization: A Focus on Women* (Mountain View, CA: Mayfield, 1979), 6.

12. N. J. Smith, M. J. Greenlaw, and C. J. Scott, "Making the Literate Environment Equitable," *The Reading Teacher* 40(4) (1987): 400–407.

13. H. White, "Damsels in Distress: Dependency Themes in Fiction for Children and Adolescents," *Adolescence* 21 (1986): 251–256.

14. Weitzman, *op. cit.*, pp. 1–2.

15. Weitzman, *op. cit.*, pp. 2–22.

16. Lisa A. Serbin, Daniel O'Leary, Ronald N. Kent, and Ilene J. Tolnick, "A Comparison of Teacher Response to the Preacademic and Problem Behavior of Boys and Girls," *Child Development* 44(4) (December 1973): 776–804.

17. B. I. Fagot, "The Influence of Sex of Child on Parental Reactions to Toddler Children," *Child Development* 49 (1978): 459–465.

18. A. C. Huston, "Sextyping," in *Handbook of Child Psychology*, ed. P. Musseu (New York: Wiley, 1983).

19. Money and Ehrhardt's research shows cases where external genitalia were ambiguous in newborns, so the babies were sometimes assigned the wrong sex. That meant that girls were raised as boys and the reverse. In spite of the fact that genetically and hormonally the child was a boy, for example, being socialized as a girl made him exhibit typically female behavior. This research gives a strong backing to the theory that sex roles are more learned than they are "natural." J. Money and A. A. Ehrhardt, *Man and Woman, Boy and Girl* (Baltimore: Johns Hopkins Press, 1973).

20. Louise Derman-Sparks and the ABC Task Force, *Antibias Curriculum: Tools for Empowering Young Children* (Washington, DC: National Association for the Education of Young Children, 1989).

21. That's a very strong statement, and one that may get me in trouble for including it in a book that claims to be sensitive to cultural differences. In some cultures sex roles are strictly defined, and the word *sexist* doesn't exist. That fact puts me in a double bind, because I feel it is important to accept and celebrate differences; *however*, I must also stand up against oppression of women.

REFERENCES

Booth-Butterfield, M. "The Cues We Don't Question: Unintentional Gender Socialization in the Day Care." *Day Care and Early Education* 8(4) (1981): 20–22.

Chow, E. N., D. Wilkinson, and Baca Zinn. *Common Bonds, Different Voices*. Newbury Park, CA: Sage, 1996.

Collins, Patricia Hill. *Black Feminist Thought: Knowledge, Consciousness, and the Politics of Empowerment*. Boston: Unwin Hyman, 1990.

Comer, J. P., and A. E. Poussaint. *Raising Black Children*. New York: Plume, 1992.

Derman-Sparks, Louise, and the ABC Task Force. *Antibias Curriculum: Tools for Empowering*

Young Children. Washington, DC: National Association for the Education of Young Children, 1989.

Fagot, B. I. "The Influence of Sex of Child on Parental Reactions to Toddler Children." *Child Development* 49 (1978): 459–465.

Faludi, Susan. *Backlash: The Undeclared War Against American Women.* New York: Crown Publishers, 1991.

French, Marilyn. *The War Against Women.* New York: Summit Books, 1992.

Hirsch, E. S., ed. *The Block Book.* Washington, DC: National Association for the Education of Young Children, 1974.

Hochschild, Arlie. *The Second Shift.* New York: Viking, 1989.

Honig, Alice Sterling. "Sex Role Socialization in Early Childhood." *Young Children* (September 1983): 57–69.

Huang, L. M., and Y. Ying. "Japanese Children and Adolescents. In *Children of Color,* eds. J. T. Gibbs and L. N. Huang. San Francisco: Jossey-Bass, 1989.

Huston, A. C. "Sextyping." In *Handbook of Child Psychology,* ed. P. Musseu. New York: Wiley, 1983.

Hymowitz, Carol, and Michaele Weissman. *A History of Women in America.* New York: Bantam Books, 1978.

LaFromboise, T. D., and D. G. Low. "American Indian Children and Adolescents." In *Children of Color,* eds. J. T. Gibbs and L. N. Huang. San Francisco, Jossey-Bass, 1989.

LaFromboise, T. D., and J. Trimble. "Multicultural Counseling Theory and American-Indian Populations." In *Theory of Multicultural Counseling and Therapy,* ed. D. W. Sue. Pacific Grove, CA: Brooks/Cole, 1996.

LaFromboise, T. D. "American Indian Mental Health Policy." In *Counseling American Minorities,* eds. D. R. Atkinson, G. Morten and D. W. Sue. Madison, WI: Brown and Benchmark, 1993.

Leong, F. "Multicultural Counseling Theory and Asian-American Populations. In *Theory of Multicultural Counseling and Therapy,* ed. D. W. Sue. Pacific Grove, CA: Brooks/Cole, 1996.

Levy, G. D., and D. B. Carter. "Gender Schema, Gender Constancy, and Gender Role Knowledge: The Roles of Cognitive Factors in Preschoolers'

Gender-role Stereotype Attributions." *Developmental Psychology* 21 (1989): 444–449.

Liss, M. *Social and Cognitive Skills: Sex Roles and Children's Play.* New York: Academic Press, 1983.

Maccoby, E. J., and C. N. Jacklin. "Gender Segregation in Childhood." In *Advances in Child Development and Behavior,* ed. H. Reese. New York: Academic Press, 1990.

Maccoby, E., and C. Jacklin. *The Psychology of Sex Differences.* Stanford, CA: Stanford University Press, 1974.

Money, J., and A. A. Ehrhardt. *Man and Woman, Boy and Girl.* Baltimore: Johns Hopkins Press, 1973.

Morrison, Ann M., Randall P. White, and Ellen Van Velsor. *Breaking the Glass Ceiling: Can Women Reach the Top of America's Largest Corporations?* Reading, MA: Addison-Wesley, 1987.

Neighbors, H. W., and J. S. Jackson, eds. *Mental Health in Black America.* Newbury Park, CA: Sage, 1996.

Paley, Vivian. *Boys and Girls: Superheroes in the Doll Corner.* Chicago: University of Chicago Press, 1984.

Parlee, M. B. "Conversational Politics." *Psychology Today* (May 1979).

Reifel, Stuart. "Block Construction: Children's Developmental Landmarks in Representation of Space." *Young Children* (November 1984).

Rheingold, H., and K. Cook. "The Content of Boys' and Girls' Rooms as an Index of Parents' Behavior." *Child Development* 46 (1975): 459–63.

Serbin, Lisa A., Daniel O'Leary, Ronald N. Kent, and Ilene J. Tolnick. "A Comparison of Teacher Response to the Preacademic and Problem Behavior of Boys and Girls." *Child Development* 44(4) (December 1973): 776–804.

Sheldon, Amy. "Kings Are Royaler Than Queens: Language and Socialization." *Young Children* (January 1990): 4–9.

Smith, N. J., M. J. Greenlaw, and C. J. Scott. "Making the Literate Environment Equitable." *The Reading Teacher* 40(4) (1987): 400–407.

Weitzman, L. J. *Sex Role Socialization: A Focus on Women.* Mountain View, CA: Mayfield Publishing Company, 1979.

White, H. "Damsels in Distress: Dependency Themes in Fiction for Children and Adolescents." *Adolescence* 21 (1986): 251–256.

Stress and Success
in Family Life

CHAPTER 12

In this chapter you'll discover:

> The characteristics of a successful family
> The stories of six families and the stresses they face
> Why stress is sometimes good for us
> Some factors that are common to resilient children
> How "protective factors" can counteract the effects of stress

TEST YOURSELF

Look for the answers to these questions as you read the chapter:

1. What are seven traits of successful families?
2. What are the kinds of stresses that Sara's family is coping with?
3. What are the kinds of stresses that Roberto's family is coping with?
4. What are the kinds of stresses that Hai's family is coping with?
5. What are the kinds of stresses that Michael's family is coping with?
6. What are the kinds of stresses that Courtney's family is coping with?
7. What are the kinds of stresses the Jackson family is coping with?
8. What do the six families have in common?
9. How are the six families different?
10. What are examples of stress being good?
11. What do resilient children have in common? Can you name five factors?
12. What does it mean to "balance stress with protective factors"?

All families experience stress and always have. Stress is nothing new to family life, though it seems now with the times changing so rapidly that we are under more stress than in the past. Certainly family structure is changing, and that alone creates stress. This chapter looks at the kinds of stresses that affect families today. It also looks at what makes for successful families. We'll start with success.

SUCCESSFUL FAMILIES

A successful family is one that functions in healthy ways; it supports and nurtures its members so that everyone's needs are met. Although happiness and satisfaction may come periodically to members of successful families, those aren't the only emotions they experience; they feel a wide range of emotions and are free and able to express them when appropriate. A successful family isn't a perennial sunshine family. It has its ups and downs, just as its individual members do.

There is much talk about dysfunctional families these days. Many people have begun to discover that some of the ways they were raised weren't good for them—they were abusive, created codependencies, and taught family members to ignore their own needs. The statistics vary, but it has been said that up to 98 percent of us grew up in dysfunctional families. If 98 percent of us are raised in a particular way, that way must be *normal*—a word often equated with *right* and *good.* So where does that leave us as far as dysfunctional families are concerned?

Because the family prepares its members for society, we'd better look beyond the family to see what this high rate of dysfunction is about. A quick look will show that the so-called dysfunctional family is not so out of tune with the present society, which nurtures a system in which some have power over others and not everyone gets needs met. Power, both in the society and in the family, is often wielded like a sword rather than radiated like light. Privilege and hierarchy, sanctioned by the societal system, often squelch our ability to be who we really are; they take our personal power from us. The dysfunctional family reflects the dysfunctional parts of society.

The theme of the strong dominating the weak is pervasive both in the family and in the society. If we take that theme to extreme, we see that world peace in the past has depended on the strongest nations stockpiling enough weapons to stop each other from making war. That's the ultimate in the power approach to getting along with others. No wonder families have been hard pressed to help their members grow in healthy, sane ways to become who they really are as unique people—each able to radiate the power inside.

We're beginning to change our approach, but change doesn't happen in an easy, linear way. It is often accompanied by periods of uncomfortable chaos, when things seem to get worse instead of better.

Many who desire this change are beginning to create their own scripts instead of living by the old myths of power in which the strong overcome the weak, one race dominates another, and men control the lives of women. They are altering the themes that have been handed down for generations.

Families are starting to raise their children for the emerging society—one in which it will be possible to raise children without abusing them and to be both connected and autonomous, one in which the dominator model gives way to a true equality model. Parents are learning how to use their power *for* or *with* their children instead of overpowering and dominating them. They are learning to *empower* their children. [1]

No matter how much things change, all family systems will continue to have some degree of dysfunction, or they wouldn't be of human origin. We'll never live in a perfect world, but we can improve it by focusing on what kinds of traits make for successful families—the traits that will allow each member to function effectively within the family and in the society beyond. What are these traits?

TRAITS OF SUCCESSFUL FAMILIES

Healthy involvement with each other is one trait of a successful family. Its members feel attachment to each other. They care. They don't just fulfill a social role; they have a deep sense of commitment. They give time and attention to the family. They don't get overinvolved in activities that exclude the family.

People in successful families recognize the signs of unhealthy codependence, in which one person encourages and enables another to lean too heavily on him or her, creating bonds that trap both of them. People in successful families understand the importance of independence and healthy interdependence. They know how to get their needs met in a relationship that allows the other person to get his or her needs met as well. They know how to take care of others without making them overly dependent on that care. They understand mutual nurturing.

Successful families tend to build and maintain self-esteem in their members instead of continually tearing it down. They know how to discipline children and to guide and control behavior in ways that leave self-esteem intact.

They know how to communicate effectively. They can both give and receive feedback. They have some skill at resolving conflicts in ways that do not neglect anyone's needs. They use problem-solving methods to deal with even small problems when they arise. They know how to cope with problems that can't be solved. They know how to express feelings in healthy ways. They know how to give and get strokes.

Successful families know how to protect their members, providing a secure environment within the home. Though a safe home is a haven from the outside world, it is also important that family members connect to the greater society. Therefore, two important family functions, protection and connection, seem to be opposites, but in reality balance one another.

Parents in successful families know how to pass on values to the next generation, through modeling, discussion, teaching, and problem solving. They also know how to accept differences when value conflicts arise.

So what does a successful family look like? Do they all have fulfilling jobs, live in nice houses, drive "newish" cars, and live stress-free lives? Of course not. Successful families come in all sizes, shapes, configurations, and financial conditions. Circumstances contribute to success, of course, but they aren't the sole determiners. If they were, rich people in good physical health would automatically be better at creating successful families than sick poor people, but that just isn't the way it works, is it?

No family is 100 percent successful, but some work at it. All families are in process. Think of success as a path—a path where no one gets to the final destination (just as no one reaches human perfection). Some start out on this path farther behind than others.

Compare these two families. One is comprised of a couple who both came from stable families where their needs were fairly well met. When they had children, they tended to create the kind of homelife they both experienced as children. They have their problems, of course, but they seem to take things in stride. They work at their marriage, at their individual development, and at their parenting. They had good models in their parents for this work. They are on the path of success.

The second family is comprised of a couple who came from less stable homes. They are also working at their marriage, at their individual development, and at their parenting, but they have to work harder because they haven't had the first-hand experience the first couple has had. They've had to come to the realization that their own upbringing was lacking, which means that they've had to learn healthy ways of dealing with their children. It didn't just come to them naturally. They are also on the path to success, but it's a rockier road for them, with numerous barricades to climb over and potholes to fall into.

What the two families have in common is that they have a vision of success. They are both on the path, moving toward their vision; and they are determined to make progress.

Let's take a look now at six families who, in spite of a number of pressures in their lives, are also struggling along the path to become successful families. Some are much farther than others. Stress is a theme in all of their lives. Let's see what kind of stresses they are coping with. (These six families are all enrolled in a government-subsidized childcare program that takes both low-income and full-cost families. The program runs a center and satellite family childcare homes.)

Sara's Family

Meet Sara. She was a teen parent when she had Ty four years ago; now she is twenty. Ty and his two-year-old brother, Kyle, are both in the center because Sara is in nursing school at the local community college.

Sara has had a hard time of it since she became a mother at sixteen. She lived with her mother for the first couple of years, but they argued over how she was raising Ty, and she left to join the homeless population of her city. She and Ty lived for a while in her car until the poor old thing quit running, sat in one place too long, and got towed. Then she lived under a bridge between the highway and the river. Pregnant again (as the result of being raped), hungry, and desperate, she finally found a social worker in an agency that hooked her up to some of the services available in her community (more about this in the next chapter).

Now Sara is in nursing school, and life is better, but it still isn't easy. She has financial aid and a place to live, but she's going crazy trying to go to school all day, study all night, and raise her boys at the same time. They reflect her stress and they have stresses of their own. Ty seems to have an attention-deficit problem; although the teachers in the center are working with him, he moves from one activity to another so fast that it's hard to keep track of him. He never seems to settle on any one thing and becomes frustrated very easily when he tries to do something. The result is that he throws regular tantrums.

Then there's Kyle. He appears to be a very sweet child, cuddling up to the teachers whenever he gets a chance. But his brother beats on him, which is starting to make him aggressive toward other children. He has to be watched all the time because he bites. The staff are thinking of putting him in one of the satellite family childcare homes available to the center because the stimulation of the center seems to be too much for him to handle.

Sara is learning about communication, discipline, and family relations from a parenting class and from her therapist. She doesn't feel very successful as a family head, but she is moving in the right direction. When she looks at her past she sees that she has come a long way. She has hopes for the future.

Roberto's Family

The second family is Roberto's. His four-year-old daughter, Lupe, is in the local Head Start program in the morning, and she comes to the center in the afternoon. Her father transports her from one program to the other when his old pickup is running and he's not working. Otherwise, his wife, Maria Elena, who takes English as a Second Language classes at the adult school, uses the bus to pick up Lupe and deliver her to the center. Maria Elena takes their baby, Paco, with her in the morning to class, where they have childcare, but she brings Paco to the center in the afternoon while she cleans houses to support the family. Roberto does odd jobs when he can get them and has been looking for steady work for some time.

Lupe has a hearing problem, and the teachers in the center keep telling Maria Elena and Roberto that they must take her to see a specialist. But they went once and there were so many papers to fill out, none of which they understood, and no one was there to translate for them; so they walked out and haven't gone back. The center staff is working to find them a translator so they can get the help that Lupe needs, but so far they haven't found one. Maria Elena is very worried about Lupe, and so is Roberto, but he is hesitant to put his name on any kind of papers that might bring him to the attention of the government. He just doesn't trust what might happen once the government becomes aware of him and his family. It was bad enough signing up for Head Start and for childcare, but at least those papers were in Spanish and he knew what he was signing. He didn't have to depend on someone with limited Spanish trying to explain them to him. His neighbor tells him he's being paranoid about this, but Roberto's family has had some bad experiences with government officials, and he doesn't want to repeat them. Roberto is wary!

Roberto has never even thought of whether his is a "successful family" or not. He's too involved in the daily struggle for survival.

He is anxious that his family live according to the traditions he grew up with, but he sees all of them being changed by rubbing up against other cultures. He resists that change, but at the same time he appreciates what he and Maria Elena are learning about childrearing from their involvement with Head Start and the childcare center. They are beginning to examine some of the "givens" of their own upbringing and thinking about whether they contribute to the goals they have for their children. They are most anxious to retain their culture and be the best parents they can be!

HAI'S FAMILY

The most vocal member of the third family is twelve-month-old Hai. He cries all the time. The staff tries hard to comfort him, but what works with other children doesn't work with Hai. The whole family, refugees from Southeast Asia, are obviously suffering from having had to leave their homeland, but the loudest sufferer is Hai. The center staff has never had a baby in the program who has been so unhappy for so long. He cries all day every day, except for the periods when he sleeps.

The staff doesn't know too much about the Nguyen family, except that they live with a number of relatives in a small house that they're pooling their money to buy. Although the house is crowded in the evenings and on weekends, there's no one home during the day to care for little Hai. Everyone's out working. Great-Grandma used to take care of him, but she's sick now and can barely care for herself. Perhaps he misses her, and that's why he cries so much.

Language must be a problem for Hai too. No one in the center knows more than a word or two of his language, and that must be very scary for him. And he doesn't stop crying long enough to listen to English.

The staff has tried to find out about Hai's diet, but his mother is very vague. She doesn't speak English too well, so she leaves things like food decisions up to them. The center provides the food for the children, but the staff is anxious to respond to any special cultural or family food preferences. They just can't find out from Hai's family what those might be.

They did find out, however, why Hai originally turned down everything they tried to feed him. It wasn't easy, but they managed to convey their concern and they found out that Hai was used to eating everything with rice. Since they started to mix the center's food with rice, Hai has become much more interested in eating—when he stops crying long enough.

Like Roberto's family, Hai's family is also rubbing up against other cultures, but they are so busy surviving in the new country, with its different cultures and different languages, that they are in culture shock. They are still reacting to what is new and strange to them, and they are not yet able to take in any benefits from the broadened experience.

MICHAEL'S FAMILY

The fourth family has one child enrolled in the center. Three-year-old Michael is a quiet boy with long dark eyelashes that sweep down on his cheeks when he lowers his eyes, which he does a good deal of the time. He is cautious and slow to warm up to people, but his slightly withdrawn manner has captured the hearts of the staff.

Michael's parents, Margaret and Beth, are a lesbian couple. Although the child comes every day, the staff has barely talked to his parents. They seem to move in and out of the center like shadows. Margaret usually brings Michael. She is friendly to staff, but always in a hurry. Because the staff members have mixed feelings about this couple, several are rather glad the two women are so unobtrusive and seemingly unwilling to engage in conversation. However, one staff member has strong feelings about the bias this family may be experiencing in the center. She wants to change the atmosphere and be sure that the parents and the child feel comfortable and accepted. She has begun to introduce the subject of antibias regularly at staff meetings, and this has brought forth some discomfort

Real Life Families: Some Statistics

According to the report of the Carnegie Task Force on Meeting the Needs of Young Children, 26 percent of babies are born to unmarried mothers, many of whom are adolescents; and almost 25 percent of all children in the United States spend part of their growing up years in a single-parent family.

Partly because of the above situations, one in four children under age three lives in a poverty-level family. Poverty makes meeting needs difficult, if not impossible. The number of children raised in poverty is growing rapidly. The overall number of children younger than six increased by 10 percent between 1971 and 1991, but the number of poor children increased by more than 60 percent!

Many children of poverty-stricken parents never grow up. Of every 1,000 infants, 9 die before age one, a mortality rate higher than that of 19 other nations. [2]

among the staff. At the last meeting she pointed out that although the program is committed to "celebrating diversity," there is no physical evidence in the center that lesbian and gay couples are considered normal families. Pictures abound (on the walls and in books) that show all kinds of family configurations, except same-sex parents. No books in the center show gay or lesbian families.

"What can we do to make school more comfortable for and accepting of Michael and his family?" was the teacher's question to the rest of the staff.

"Good question," responded one teacher. "This is something we should talk about. I'm concerned about Michael," she added emphatically.

"*I'm* concerned about his parents as well!" said the first teacher, equally emphatically. "What can we do to raise their comfort level?"

The staff is still working on this question, because they are in conflict with each other about what should be done. They can't even agree about the idea of bringing in books and pictures of families like Michael's. Some feel strongly that it's an equity issue they are discussing; others are taking a moral or religious stance. In the meantime, it's easy to see the discomfort level rise in Michael and his parents as they pick up unspoken messages from various staff members.

Although Michael's parents have many traits of the successful family, they are unable to benefit from what the staff might have to offer them to increase their knowledge of child development and family relations because of limited communication.

COURTNEY'S FAMILY

Family five commands a good deal of staff attention for all sorts of reasons. Courtney, the mother, has been married before, and two of her four children are in the program. Roland, her four-year-old, was abused by his father, and the family lives in fear that one day he'll arrive at school, claim his son, and take off with him. The staff has been warned of the situation and is aware of the restraining order that gives them the authority to refuse to let the father take Roland. Roland, after all his bad experiences, is fearful of men—and he doesn't get along with the other children either.

Courtney, Roland's mother, is married to Richard, who is a Native American. They have their own child, a two-and-a-half-year-old named Soleil. Roland's half sister looks more like her father than her mother, and her beauty is remarkable—literally. Adults passing through the center stop to discuss what a lovely child she is.

Soleil is remarkable in other ways too. She is intellectually mature way beyond her years, but socially she's still a baby. She confuses adults, who don't know what to think of her. They marvel at the way she is teaching herself to read, but become distressed by the fact that she kicks, screams, and even bites when a child refuses to give her a toy that she wants to play with.

Courtney is in a drug-recovery program and has just decided to continue her education. She wants to become a lawyer. Richard works in construction and he's going to college part time to become a history teacher. He has very strong feelings about his heritage, which the teachers found out about last Thanksgiving when they put up pictures of Pilgrims and Indians on the walls.

One of the teachers was just stapling the last picture up when Richard arrived with Roland and Soleil. He stopped, stared intensely at the picture, then turned abruptly to the teacher and said, "I'm sorry, but it's offensive to me that you're using caricatures of my people as decorations. It feels as if you're making fun of my culture."

The teacher stopped, stapler in hand, shocked by his words. "I don't understand. Thanksgiving stands for friendship and love. That's what these pictures are about—brotherhood—people helping people."

"Maybe that's the way you see it," explained Richard, "but what I see is that you're celebrating a day that marks the beginning of the genocide of my people. I don't want my children to have any part of such a celebration." He left the room abruptly, taking the children with him.

Later, during nap time, the other teachers were shocked to hear such a different version of the happy holiday they had always celebrated. But they took the pictures down and agreed to stress the harvest aspects of Thanksgiving rather than give it a historical slant.

Richard heard about this through Courtney, who brought the children back later in the day. When he arrived the next morning, children in hand, he remarked about the missing pictures to Roland's teacher and expressed his gratitude about the willingness of the staff to see his point of view and make some changes in their celebration. As a cross-cultural family, Courtney and Richard are exploring where their concepts of a successful family coincide and where they collide.

The Jackson Family

Holidays are a big issue for the sixth family—the Jacksons—as well. They have three children in the program and are pleased with everything but the celebration of what they consider Christian holidays. At a recent parent meeting, they got caught in the middle of an argument between two groups of parents. It started when Mrs. Jackson asked the staff to please downplay religious celebrations. "I don't want my children to learn someone else's religion," she remarked. "We'll teach our religion at home, so please leave religious observances out of the program."

One parent answered her by insisting that Christmas had nothing to do with religion. Two other parents rose to their feet, arguing loudly that it was a terrible shame that Christ had been removed from Christmas and that there ought to be more religion in the center rather than less.

When the director finally got the parents calmed down, Mrs. Jackson spoke up once again, this time about dietary differences. She was concerned that her children were being fed food that violated the dietary restrictions of her religion.

She spoke politely and with great concern. The director asked her to make an appointment for another time to discuss the problem.

Mrs. Jackson arrived the next day at the agreed-upon time and found the director in her office waiting for her. The two had met here earlier; before the family came into the program they had several discussions about whether or not the oldest Jackson child, who has spina bifida, could be accommodated in his wheelchair. Several modifications to the environment were required, which Mr. Jackson worked on with the help of Sara and Richard, who both have carpentry skills.

Mrs. Jackson and the director expected to have a good talk this time, because they had gotten along well in the past. Mrs. Jackson expressed her feelings that the teachers were not watching what her children ate, and the director promised to do all she could to make sure that the Jackson children were carefully monitored at meal and snack times. She also asked Mrs. Jackson if she would be willing to do a cooking activity with the four-year-old group and teach them how to make one of the special dishes of her culture. She agreed, and that was the beginning of her involvement in the program.

At present Mrs. Jackson is working night and day on a big fund-raiser for a climbing structure for the play yard. She's finding it very satisfying to use her talent, skills, and connections in the community to benefit the program and the children, some of whom, she realizes, are severely financially deprived. She has involved a number of other parents, and they are getting to know and appreciate each other in ways that only come from working together toward a common cause—something they could never have done by just attending parent meetings.

The Jacksons have a lot going for them as a successful family. But, like the rest of the families, they still have a way to go.

The six families have varying concepts, images, and dreams of what a successful family is. They all have many stresses in their lives. Their successes include varying degrees of the following:

> Commitment
> Attachment to each other
> Individual independence and group interdependence
> Ability to give and receive nurturing
> Ability to get needs met
> Coping skills
> Methods of building self-esteem
> Effective communication
> Ability to pass on culture, goals, and values

Their stresses include:

> Poverty
> Special needs of their children
> Problems with substance abuse
> Divorce and custody issues
> Stepfamilies and blended families
> Lack of support
> Communication difficulties
> Inaccessible resources
> Bias issues

WHAT DO THE SIX FAMILIES HAVE IN COMMON?

Besides being in the process of building toward success and experiencing stress, what do all of these families have in common? They're in the same childcare program. They love their children and want the best for them, although they have different ways of showing their love and different ideas about what "the best" is and how to achieve it.

How are they different? They represent different cultures and traditions, different family structures (with different degrees of outside acceptance of those family structures), and different degrees of match to the mainstream culture of the center. They also differ in their ability to handle the stress in their lives.

STRESS ISN'T NECESSARILY BAD

What can these families do to help their children? What can the center and family childcare staff do to help support the families and their children? They can start by recognizing that stress isn't necessarily bad. We all need some stress in our lives. Stress can be a growth factor. A physical example of how stress is useful can be seen in the way a baby's bones form to enable the child to walk. The leg bones that connect to the hip socket have a different shape in the newborn than in the child about to walk. What makes the shape change to accommodate walking? Stress—the stress of weight being put on them. A similar example relates to old age. The older woman at risk for osteoporosis babies her bones by never exercising and creates the very condition she's trying to avoid—her bones grow weak and brittle. Her bones need some stress to help keep them strong.

Of course, too much stress isn't any better than too little. Again an example from physiology. Look at the sports injuries of children who overuse their pitching arms, for example. Irreparable damage occurs from too much stress.

What is too much stress for one family, or for one person, may be optimum stress for another. Some people are knocked down by seemingly minor setbacks;

Stress isn't necessarily bad—we all need some stress in our lives. Stress can be a growth factor.

others manage much harder situations. Still others seem to take on adversity as a challenge and grow from it.

When I was first learning about child development, I took a trip to the high country above the California desert. There I observed a natural phenomenon that I have never forgotten: the bristlecone pine. I saw this gnarled, ancient tree, bowed by the wind and stunted by lack of water and the thin air and soil of its habitat, as the perfect symbol for the benefits of stress. Instead of weakening under adverse conditions, these trees grow stronger than other plant life in less stressful situations. Using their adversity to the maximum, they survive longer than any other living thing on earth. Somehow they take the hardships life has to offer and use them to their own advantage. Some children do that too.

We know that poverty, abuse, neglect, being shuffled around, lack of attachment, and not getting needs met can adversely affect children's lives. Obviously it is better for children to get what they need, be raised by people who care for them, have a stable home life, and meet loving acceptance inside and outside the home rather than having to live with abuse, neglect, bias, and discrimination. Yet we all know about "resilient children"—those children who, in spite of much hardship, manage to turn out with healthy personalities and find success and happiness in life.

WHAT WE CAN LEARN FROM STUDIES OF RESILIANT CHILDREN

Studies show that there are some protective and personality factors that are common to resilient children, who have the psychological strength to recover from misfortune or who emerge intact from a history of severe distress. [3] One vital factor that the children had in common was a sense of connectedness to someone in the early years. These children found attachment, usually in the first year (not necessarily to a parent). They received enough attention and nurturing early on to gain a sense of trust. Many of the children whose parents were not able to meet their needs found or created surrogate parents, inside or outside the home. Their lives may have been marked by abandonment, either physical or emotional or both, but they, at some period, found someone to believe in them and care about them. Even if they were shuffled from family to family, never belonging anywhere, they found sources of support. They made connections and those connections seem to have provided enough to keep them going in positive directions.

One reason these resilient children were able to make connections was that they had the ability to elicit positive responses from others. Even at a very young age, they were somehow able to gain other people's positive attention.

These children were problem solvers, taking an active approach toward negotiating, communicating, and grappling with the obstacles with which life presented them. They had not only the willingness but also the skills to take an active rather than a passive role.

Another important commonality these resilient children had was that at some point during their lives they found themselves needed by someone else. They had

Resilient children have experienced a sense of connectedness at some time in their lives.

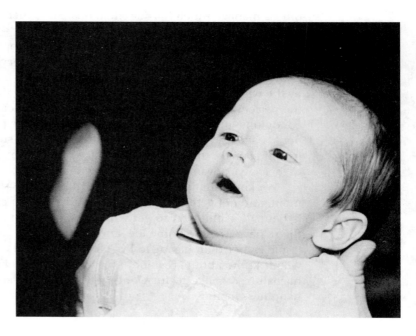

responsibility thrust upon them. They were required to help another person—a younger sibling, for example. Relating to someone else's helplessness gave them a sense of their own power.

Most important of all, perhaps, these children had a tendency to perceive their experiences constructively and each held a positive vision of a meaningful life. In spite of their hardships, life made sense. In other words, their attitude made all the difference in the world.

What can adults who live or work with children and have responsibility for their socialization learn from this research? How can children from families in stress be helped to be less vulnerable and, indeed, resilient? How can children grow up in stressful conditions such as poverty, family strife, instability, disabilities, bias, abuse, and neglect and not be harmed in their development? How can we help them grow in positive ways?

The key is to balance the stressful life events with protective factors. The stress must be decreased or the number of protective factors increased or, when possible, both. The protective factors are those just mentioned—a sense of connection, sources of support, skills for solving problems and for eliciting positive responses from others, and, above all, a positive attitude toward life and a feeling that it will all work out somehow.

HELPING ALL CHILDREN BECOME RESILIENT CHILDREN

How does that information translate into adult behavior? What are some tips for adults who work with children and families in stress?

1. Provide support for the child and for the family. Encourage connections; help build networks. Children and families need all the support they can get—both formal and informal.

2. Teach the skills necessary for making connections and gaining support. Teach children social skills. Teach them ways to initiate contact and maintain it. Reinforce contacts with peers and adults. They'll learn better if they start early (even in infancy) and have a chance to practice with small numbers of people. Encourage families to focus on positive discipline techniques (see chapter 7). Model prosocial behaviors, then pay attention to and reward such behaviors.

3. Teach problem solving (see chapter 9). Once children develop negotiating and communication skills, they'll be in a better position to take a more active role in grappling with their problems.

4. Give children responsibilities. Require them to help out. Hook them up to someone who is less capable than they are and needs them.

5. Most of all, provide role models. Children and families need to see people they can identify with doing all the tips just mentioned—finding support, demonstrating social skills and the ability to make connections, using problem-solving skills, and taking responsibility. Finally, they need role models who have faith that things will work out and that life has meaning.

Help all children become resilient by teaching them problem solving.

I don't mean to downplay the effect that stressful conditions have on children's socialization by painting too positive a picture. Neither do I mean to overemphasize resiliency. There are some obvious changes that could make a difference in some families' lives so that unnecessary stress would be eliminated and children wouldn't need to be super resilient.

To end on a cheery note, here's what Ellen Galinsky says: "Things can be hard, but they don't have to do us in. It isn't whether good or bad things happen to you; it's how you handle them that matters." She talks about how important it is to teach parents and their children to face problems, practice generating multiple solutions, figure out how to change what can be changed, and learn to cope with what can't. It's a matter of taking a can-do attitude and engaging in continuous problem solving. [4] It's also a matter of getting together as a society and facing the conditions that create ever growing poverty and changing them. [5] The time is now!

School Success Linked to What Goes on at Home

It's not social class, family structure, parent's marital status, ethnic background, or the amount of money a family has that makes a difference in how well children eventually will do in school. What counts most is what goes on at home.

Parents can be poor, unmarried, and uneducated, and still manage to groom their young children for a successful school career. It may be harder if one is poor, unmarried, and uneducated, but it is possible.

How do families manage to create early childhood experiences that result in future school success? They do it in a number of ways including by the way they relate to the children, the kind of home life they provide for them, what they teach them.

First of all, children must be protected. Families who groom their children for future success in school know how to protect them, keeping them from physical and psychological harm. They set limits. They monitor whereabouts and behavior.

These families see their children as capable and hold a vision of the future that includes the child as an able student. They encourage learning of all sorts by the ways they relate to their children, how they talk to them, and the activities they provide.

They teach their children social skills, defining appropriate behavior for them. They give them feedback to increase their sensitivity to others. They do this in a warm and nurturing way, creating an emotionally supportive environment that emphasizes decision making.

They help them learn to express themselves. They give them chances to develop a sense of responsibility and learn both leadership and follower skills. They encourage them to concentrate, focus, be attentive, and follow through. Most of all, they respect their children and themselves.

SUMMARY

This chapter started by examining traits of successful families and went on to look at a lot of problems. It may seem that the situations of some of the families portrayed are fairly bad. Yet, they are not hopeless; and each is working on acquiring more and more of the traits of successful families outlined at the beginning. Some arrived at the center already knowing about these traits; others are learning them from each other and from the center staff. In addition, each of the families is connected to some of the many community resources that address the variety of difficulties they are having. The next chapter looks at the community resources available to help families meet challenges, to alleviate some of their stress, and to support them in their coping.

FOR DISCUSSION

1. Give examples of three of the traits of successful families that are present in a family that you know.
2. Have you ever known a family like Sara's? How were they the same as Sara? How were they different?
3. Have you ever known a family like Roberto's? How were they the same as Roberto's? How were they different?
4. Have you ever known a family like Hai's? How were they the same as Hai's family? How were they different?
5. Have you ever known a family like Michael's? How were they the same as Michael's? How were they different?
6. Have you ever known a family like Courtney's? How were they the same as Courtney's? How were they different?
7. Have you ever known a family like the Jackson family? How were they the same as the Jacksons? How were they different?
8. What do resilient children have in common? Can you give examples of how the five factors work in a resilient child?
9. What are examples of protective factors that counteract stress?
10. Give an example of something you could do to help some child become a "resilient child."
11. What are five ways to help all children become resilient?
12. Think of an example of how the following sentence plays out in someone's life: "It's isn't whether good or bad things happen to you; it's how you handle them that matters."

PERSONAL REFLECTIONS

Thinking about your personal reactions and experiences will help you better understand and integrate the material in this chapter. Use these questions to interface between you and what you read. Use the pertinent ones to reflect on, write about, or discuss with others.

> How many of the seven factors of successful families did your family have while you were growing up?
> How was your family like Sara's?
> How was your family like Roberto's?
> How was your family like Hai's?
> How was your family like Michael's?
> How was your family like Courtney's?

> How was your family like the Jackson family?
> How was your family different from the six families in this chapter?
> What is an example from your own life of stress having benefits for you?
> Were you a resilient child? Which of the five factors in resilience fit your experience?
> What are protective factors in your life that help balance your stresses?
> "It isn't whether good or bad things happen to you; it's how you handle them that matters." Can you apply this statement to your own life?

NOTES

1. To empower is to allow people to experience their personal power, which gives them the feeling of being able to be themselves and of having some effect on the world or the people in it. People who are empowered don't need to overpower or manipulate others. They are free to experience being who they really are—to fulfill their unique potential; they will resist being cast into some preset mold.
2. From "Starting Points: Executive Summary of the Report of the Carnegie Corporation of New York Task Force on Meeting the Needs of Young Children," *Young Children* (July 1994): 58–60.
3. Emmy E. Werner, "Research in Review, Resilient Children," *Young Children* (November 1984): 68–72; Emmy E. Werner, "Resilience in Development," *Current Directions in Psychological Science* (June 1995): 81–85. E. E. Werner and R. S. Smith, *Overcoming the Odds: High Risk Children from Birth to Adulthood*. (Ithaca and London: Cornell University Press, 1992).
4. Ellen Galinsky, "Problem Solving," *Young Children* (May 1989): 2–3.
5. An example of a group of citizens who has set out to do something about unemployment in their states is the Human Development Corporation of California, Hawaii, Washington, and Oregon. This nonprofit community-based organization helps the unemployed to improve their lives and their communities by providing job training and placement so that they can become more self-sufficient through unsubsidized employment. Human Development Corporation of California, Hawaii, Washington, and Oregon, 1990 Annual Report.

REFERENCES

Beaglehole, R. "Validating All Families." *Interracial Books for Children Bulletin* 14(7, 8) (1983): 24–26.

Chow, E. N., D. Wilkinson, and Baca Zinn. *Common Bonds, Different Voices*. Newbury Park, CA: Sage, 1996.

Comer, J. P., and A. E. Poussaint. *Raising Black Children*. New York: Plume, 1992.

Clark, Reginald. *Family Life and School Achievement: Why Poor Black Children Succeed or Fail*. Chicago: University of Chicago Press, 1984.

Clay, J. W. "Working with Lesbian and Gay Parents and Their Children." *Young Children* 45(3) (1990): 31–35.

Coner-Edwards, Alice F., and Jeanne Spurlock, eds. *Black Families in Crisis: The Middle Class*. New York: Brunner/Mazel, Publishers, 1988.

Derman-Sparks, Louise. *Anti-Bias Curriculum*. Washington, DC: National Association for the Education of Young Children, 1989.

Dorris, M. "Why I'm NOT Thankful for Thanksgiving." *Interracial Books for Children Bulletin* 9(7) (1978): 6–9.

Dowrick, P. W. *Social Survival for Children: A Trainer's Resource Book.* New York: Brunner/Mazel, Publishers, 1986.

Dunst, Carl, Carol Trivette, and Angela Deal. *Enabling and Empowering Families.* Cambridge, MA: Brookline, 1988.

Fontana, Vincent J., and Valerie Moolman. *Save the Family, Save the Child: What We Can Do to Help Children at Risk.* New York: Dutton, 1991.

Galinsky, E. "Problem Solving." *Young Children* (May 1989).

Hewlett, Sylvia Ann. *When the Bough Breaks: The Cost of Neglecting Our Children.* New York: Basic Books, 1991.

Huang, L. M., and Y. Ying. "Japanese Children and Adolescents. In *Children of Color,* eds. J. T. Gibbs and L. N. Huang. San Francisco: Jossey-Bass, 1989.

Human Development Corporation of California, Hawaii, Washington and Oregon, 1990 Annual Report.

Kamerman, Sheila B., and Alfred J. Kahn. *Mothers Alone: Strategies for a Time of Change.* Dover, MA: Auburn House, 1988.

Kauffman, C., H. Grunebaum, B. Cohler, and E. Gamer. "Superkids: Competent Children of Psychotic Mothers." *American Journal of Psychiatry* 136(11) (1979): 1398–1402.

Kitano, Margie. "Early Education for Asian-American Children." *Young Children* 35(2) (January 1980).

LaFromboise, T. D., and D. G. Low. "American Indian Children and Adolescents." In *Children of Color,* eds. J. T. Gibbs and L. N. Huang. San Francisco, Jossey-Bass, 1989.

LaFromboise, T. D., and J. Trimble. "Multicultural Counseling Theory and American-Indian Populations." In *Theory of Multicultural Counseling and Therapy,* ed. D. W. Sue. Pacific Grove, CA: Brooks/Cole, 1996.

LaFromboise, T. D. "American Indian Mental Health Policy." In *Counseling American Minorities,* eds. D. R. Atkinson, G. Morten, and D. W. Sue. Madison, WI: Brown and Benchmark, 1993.

Leong, F. "Multicultural Counseling Theory and Asian-American Populations." In *Theory of Multicultural Counseling and Therapy,* ed. D. W. Sue. Pacific Grove, CA: Brooks/Cole, 1996.

Matheson, Lou. "If You Are Not an Indian, How Do You Treat an Indian?" In *Cross-Cultural Training for Mental Health Professionals,* eds. H. Lefley and P. Pedersen. Springfield, IL: Charles C. Thomas, Publisher, 1986.

Mayfield, L. P. "Parenthood Among Low-Income Adolescent Girls." In *The Black Family: Essays and Studies,* 4th ed., ed. Robert Staples. Belmont, CA: Wadsworth, 1991.

Moore, E. K., and M. K. McKinley. "Parent Involvement/Control in Child Development Programs." In *Early Childhood Development Programs and Services: Planning for Action,* ed. D. N. McFadden. Washington, DC: National Association for the Education of Young Children, 1972, 77–82.

Morrow, Robert D. "Cultural Differences—Be Aware!" *Academic Therapy* 23(2) (November 1987): 143–149.

Moskovitz, S. *Love Despite Hate: Child Survivors of the Holocaust and Their Adult Lives.* New York: Schocken Books, 1983.

Neighbors, H. W., and J. S. Jackson, eds. *Mental Health in Black America.* Newbury Park, CA: Sage, 1996.

Phillips, Carol Brunson. "Culture: A Process That Empowers." In *Infant Toddler Caregiving: A Guide to Culturally Sensitive Care,* eds. Jesus Cortez and Carol Lou Young-Hold. Sausalito, CA: Far West Laboratory for Educational Research and Development, 1992.

Pikcunas, Diane D. "Analysis of Asian-American Early Childhood Practices and Their Implication for Early Childhood Education." An EDRS document, 1986.

Powell, D. R. *Families and Early Childhood Programs.* Washington, DC: National Association for the Education of Young Children, 1989.

Powell, G. J., ed. *The Psychosocial Development of Minority Children.* New York: Brunner/Mazel, Publishers, 1983.

Skeen, P., B. E. Robinson, and C. Flake-Hobson. "Blended Families: Overcoming the Cinderella Myth." *Young Children* (January 1984): 64–74.

Soto, Lourdes Diaz. "Understanding Bilingual/Bicultural Young Children." *Young Children* (January 1991): 30–35.

Sue, Stanley, and Thom Moore, eds. *The Pluralistic Society.* New York: Human Sciences Press, Inc., 1984.

Washington, Valora, and Ura Jean Oyemade. "Changing Family Trends." *Young Children* (September 1985): 12–19.

Werner, Emmy E. "Research in Review, Resilient Children." *Young Children* (November 1984).

Werner, Emmy E. "Resilience in Development." *Current Directions in Psychological Science* (June 1995): 81–85.

Werner, E. E., and R. S. Smith. *Overcoming the Odds: High Risk Children from Birth to Adulthood.* Ithaca and London: Cornell University Press, 1992.

West, Betty E. "The New Arrivals from Southeast Asia: Getting to Know Them." *Childhood Education* 60(2) (November-December 1983).

PART 3

The Community: Socialization in the Community Context

P art 3 looks at the broader issues of socialization. We examined the child's developmental issues (Part 1) unfolding within a family context (Part 2). This section views the child's socialization in a community context. This socialization occurs in the family's immediate community—the group they identify with and/or the people who live in proximity to them—and also in the greater society and its institutions. We look at how television can influence the child and give messages that conflict with the goals and values of the family and the society. We examine how racism and classism enter into the socialization process.

We also look at some of the factors contributing to child abuse. What are those factors? What puts families at risk for damaging their children in the socialization process? Families in which abuse is present tend to be isolated from the community. That's an issue this part addresses—families and social networks. Many families don't know how to get the support they need. They are alone with their childrearing.

Parents who abuse their children often were themselves abused as children. The model they grew up with was that love hurts. Affection was coupled with pain. Because they are often isolated, they have no healthy models. They know no other ways to approach childrearing.

Isolation also creates the possibility that parents will hold unrealistic expectations of their children. They don't have basic child development information that spells out needs and capabilities at each stage. They expect far more from children than their developing abilities allow. For example, an abusive parent may expect her baby to understand her needs and take care of them. Perhaps she expects her baby to know that his crying is getting on her nerves. She tells him to stop, expecting that he can control himself. He can't. When the baby doesn't perform as expected, the parent may try to beat him into submission, seeing it as a matter of his will against hers. This child may learn early to read his mother's signals, stretching every capability he has to prevent himself from being abused. Abused children become very wary and many learn early to care for their parents in surprisingly mature ways. Those children are robbed of their childhoods.

Abuse occurs because the parent didn't get her own needs met in her family of origin and doesn't know how to get them met now. The needy little child in the parent competes with the needy little child the parent is raising. But there is no competition; the parent's needs win out because she is bigger and stronger. An abusive parent doesn't see that she's the one who should be parenting the child and not the reverse.

Child abuse is not just an individual concern; it is also a community concern. It needs the help of the community to stop. Many steps are being taken in that direction.

An important part of addressing the child abuse problem is mandated reporting. Many states require that those who work with children or their families report any suspected abuse to the authorities. The purpose of this legal and moral mandate is to save children and help families.

The focus now is on family support and prevention rather than just on detection and punishment. Isolated families must be drawn into the community, and that's just what is happening all over the country.

Though illegal in this country at present, child abuse as a way of socializing children worked toward a special societal need in the past. Cultures through history have used abusive childrearing approaches in the family to create the tough, warrior-type men and submissive women that the society valued and needed for protection and survival. It makes sense to teach children to withstand pain, to conquer feelings of fear, to armor themselves. In a society where war is a constant reality, those most able to fight (men) must be ready to kill and be killed to protect the group. Women, who, in general, are not as capable on the front lines, are needed to serve behind the lines to take care of the warrior men. It's easy to see where gender inequity arose when one acknowledges this model. Abusing children can prepare them for this kind of future, where basic needs and feelings must be put last and the survival of the group is what counts.

But it is time now for us, as a society, as a world community, to put aside the dominator model. We can no longer look to war as a means of group survival. A war that gets out of hand can easily kill us all—and the rest of life on earth. We must look beyond war to other means of solving problems. The survival of the planet depends on finding peaceful solutions. Outlawing child abuse and teaching healthy ways of raising children is a good start.

We must go further. We, as a society, must make some changes in the conditions that work against family health and functionality and the ability to socialize children in positive ways. We must take a good long look at the equality principle on which this country was founded and take further steps to eradicate racism, classism, and sexism, as well as educational, social, economic, and political inequalities.

Change takes individual effort. It also takes individuals working together. The book ends on this note—giving a view of how we can use advocacy to bring about the healthy changes that are needed for the future of America.

To become an advocate and make changes, it is necessary, unless we have do-gooder tendencies, for all of us to see that it is in our own best interests that America be made up of healthy families living in healthy communities. Those of us who live on the other side of town can't ignore the poverty that lies just across the tracks because it isn't part of our lives. Perhaps we don't see the connection right now, but we must become aware of the connection of America's present condition and how the future will unfold. The success of America lies in the success of her families and her communities. It's all related and it affects each and every one of us.

In spite of the notion of equality upon which America was founded, we've been handed a picture of society as a hierarchy—with some on the bottom, some in the middle, and some at the top. We unconsciously operate out of the model. I'd like to suggest that it is more realistic to imagine society as a net. Have you ever climbed on a cargo net—one of those rope affairs stretched on a wooden climbing structure in the park or playground? When you are on it alone, your every movement affects the entire net. Then, when you are sitting oh so still and someone else climbs on it, you are greatly affected. No matter how hard you try to stay still, the net moves this way and that.

Society is like that. What happens way over in another part may be out of the range of your senses, but it affects you—it affects us all. We need to acknowledge our interconnectedness. We aren't just individuals in families, we are all part of the community of America and of the world beyond!

Community Resources

CHAPTER **13**

In this chapter you'll discover:

> What isolation can do to a family
> Social networks and community resources
> Why families need more support than ever before
> How six families use and contribute to community resources
> How to go about looking for a community resource

TEST YOURSELF

Look for the answers to these questions as you read the chapter:

1. What are some of the negative effects isolation can have on families?
2. What does a "stroke pie" show?
3. What forms may social networks take?
4. What are the four current trends that illustrate the changing needs for formal and informal support for families?
5. How does Sara's family both use and contribute to community resources?
6. How does Roberto's family both use and contribute to community resources?
7. How does Hai's family both use and contribute to community resources?
8. How does Michael's family both use and contribute to community resources?
9. How does Courtney's family both use and contribute to community resources?
10. How does the Jackson family both use and contribute to community resources?
11. What are some ways to find the community resources a family might need?
12. What limits some community resources so that they aren't open to everybody?
13. How might an agency's values and goals affect the service they offer?

he last chapter examined what makes a successful family—the traits that allow the system and its members to function effectively. It also looked at six families under stress who are struggling along the path to becoming successful. This chapter looks at the community's contribution to helping families in their struggles. We'll examine how the community and the institutions and people in it support the family and help it function.

SOCIAL NETWORKS

Some families see themselves as part of a larger social network and they know how to both contribute to and make use of this network. They do not isolate themselves from the outside community if they can help it. They have a broad perspective that includes the world beyond the family and they use feedback from that world. They are able to both give and receive help from the outside social network.

Some families don't seek help or support from the larger community. They wish to see themselves as self-sufficient and they regard outside support as a sign of weakness. Others see themselves as part of family or kinship networks, but hesitate to use the formal institutions that have been set up to help them. They may also regard needing "outside" help as a sign of weakness, or perhaps they have just never considered it. Many families have no idea what is available in their communities. Some of these families get along fine; others experience a feeling of isolation.

Isolation has a number of negative effects on families. It limits role models for children. It can lead to a sense of hopelessness. And it can even lead to child abuse.

Developing a Broad Base of Support

In healthy families each member has a broad base of support and knows how to get strokes from people outside the immediate family. Without such a broad base of support, undue pressure falls on those within the family; if those who usually give strokes are unable to do so, the individual is left depleted.

How does one know that his or her support base is broad enough? Here's a little exercise called "stroke pie" to help you examine your own stroke sources. (Stroke pie was discussed briefly in chapter 10.)

Draw a circle representing the total number of strokes you receive at this point in your life. Cut the circle into pie wedges to represent the people who give you those strokes. Assign an appropriate-sized slice to each person. Then evaluate your slices. Do you have a number of slices or just a few? Are some slices much bigger than others? Are you overly dependent on a single person for your strokes?

Here are sample stroke pies of two people, Kim and Jennifer:

Kim assigned three quarters of the pie to her boyfriend and the remaining quarter slice to her mother. Then came the day that her mother discovered she had cancer, which was about the time the boyfriend found someone else. Kim's strokes disappeared all at once, and she had no one to turn to for support.

Jennifer used to be in that position too; she was dependent on her husband for most of her strokes, with a few coming from her sister. But when she became a parent and discovered that she needed to give out more strokes than she got back, she knew that she'd better broaden her base of support. She purposely developed a close relationship with two mothers she had met in her Lamaze class and another mother she met in the park. She not only started swapping childcare with these women but also used them for information, and for nurturing too.

Four years after Jennifer's son was born, her stroke pie looked very different from the way it had looked when she first became a mother. Her pie was now divided into nineteen pieces, with friends, relatives, neighbors, son, office mates, parenting support group, and two jogging buddies all represented by slices. Her husband's huge slice was cut down to less than a quarter of the pie and their relationship was blossoming since she had quit depending on him and her sister so heavily to meet all her emotional needs.

Jennifer created a social network for herself. Each individual and each family has a stroke pie that comprises their social network. Each looks slightly different.

Forms Social Networks May Take

In some families, individual members have their own social networks. In others, the family shares a network that consists of individuals and groups that comprise what can be thought of as a greater family, or an extended family. Some families are attached to a number of people beyond their own relatives in formal and informal ways. In a Mexican family, for example, this attachment may include, besides relatives, *compadres*—the children's godparents. Compadres are more than friends; they have a special kind of family relationship even though they may not have blood ties. Other families have special friends who are "aunts and uncles" to the younger generation. They are like family, but are not blood relatives.

For some families, the neighborhood where they live may be the most important part of the social network. Neighbors can become a close-knit group that serves as a mutual aid society—sharing resources, providing guidance for children, and contributing to the social life of its members through periodic gatherings and celebrations of all sorts. These kinds of neighborhoods are becoming more scarce as the American population increases in mobility and at the same time isolates itself from those who live nearby; but they still exist in some places.

For some families, a religious institution serves the same functions as the close-knit neighborhood described above. It provides friendship, a social life, mutual aid, social services, support, counseling, and education, along with worship services, celebrations, and spiritual guidance.

Community Institutions That Serve Families

Other formal and informal groups and institutions with specialized functions make up a part of the social network of the community. Some of them have been around since the country began, like police and fire departments; others are just now in the process of developing in response to changing needs.

Four ongoing trends illustrate needs for formal and informal support for families. Those trends are increasing numbers of mothers of infants and young children in the workforce; the growing challenge for low-income families to attain economic self-sufficiency; the feminization of poverty; and teenage parenting. [1]

Employed mothers.   More mothers than ever before are working. Mothers of children under six are a fast growing group in the labor force. Many of these women are single heads of families who are the only source of financial support of their families. Others—mothers in two-parent households—are working to make ends meet because one salary isn't enough. [2] The response to this current trend by the greater society has been to provide outside childcare in a number of forms. Government, schools, employers, churches, corporations, and individuals are getting involved in the childcare scene.

Economic challenges.   Growing numbers of families today find themselves in acute economic distress. Because parents are unable to work for a variety of reasons, or are working for wages that keep the family mired down in the bog of poverty, children are greatly influenced by lack of money, food, and even shelter. The community response to this problem is lagging far behind the need, as witnessed by growing numbers of homeless in every community.

The feminization of poverty.   Someone once said that most women are just one husband away from poverty. Look around you. Who is most needing financial help? Women. One in three families headed by women is in poverty, compared with only one in ten headed by men, and only one in nineteen headed by two parents. [3] A generation ago most poor people were old. That has changed now as a result of a local, state, and national response to conditions and problems of the elderly. The composition of the new poverty group is different, and community response has been slow, unfortunately.

Teenage parenting.   Teen parents are often undereducated and have trouble finding employment. They may also be undersupported and struggle greatly through the early years of their children's lives. The number of teen parents contributes to the feminization of poverty. The children of teen parents often grow up themselves to be teen parents. A mother of a daughter who is now four says, "My mother had her first baby at fifteen; so did I. Now my daughter is four, and I have about ten years to figure out how to keep this pattern from continuing."

Programs exist across the country to address the needs of teen parents, including infant programs on high school campuses that provide parent education for young mothers and contribute to their skills and self-esteem by allowing them to finish school while their babies are cared for.

FAMILIES USING COMMUNITY RESOURCES

Let's take a look now at how the families introduced in the preceding chapter reflect these trends and how they connect with the social networks outside themselves. Notice how they both use and contribute to the community resources available.

SARA'S FAMILY

Remember Sara? She's the twenty-year-old with two sons—Ty and Kyle—who is in nursing school at a community college. She went through a very difficult period, being homeless for a while. But by now she's an expert in the resources her community has to offer. She's tied into the financial aid program at her college, which gives her support. She also receives childcare in an on-campus subsidized program for low-income students, which is funded by the state. She gives back to these two community resources by serving on the advisory committee of the financial aid program and by contributing volunteer time to the childcare center. She was asked to help with fund-raising for the center, but made a decision to take care of herself and her sons by declining. She knows that fund-raising can be very time consuming, and with her studies and her family, time is at a premium right now.

When Sara was pregnant the first time, she received assistance from WIC (Women, Infants, and Children), a federally funded nutrition program designed to help ensure that children get the nourishment they need through the prenatal period and into the first year of life.

Ty was born prematurely, which made life even harder for a time. Going to a support group for preemie parents for a while helped Sara get through this period. The group, which was hosted by her local hospital, was led by a social worker and funded by a special foundation grant.

By the time of her second pregnancy (which resulted from being raped while she was homeless), the WIC funding had been cut in half, and she could no longer get into the program, which was unfortunate because she and Ty often didn't have food. She worried about her unborn baby a lot during that period. Kyle too was born prematurely, and by then the funding for the preemie support group had also been cut, so she was on her own. But she did finally get into a teen parent program that enabled her to finish high school. Now she has moved on to college with a plan and hope for her future through the vocational program she is in.

When Sara first went on AFDC, she lived in terror that someone would decide that she was neglecting her children and take them away from her. She had seen this happen to several women during her homeless period. She couldn't bear the thought of losing Ty and Kyle, so she was very cautious whenever she discussed anything with her social worker. She felt she had to protect herself. It took her a long time to decide that the worker understood her situation, saw her as a good mother, and wasn't about to report her for neglect to Child Protective Services, which is the government agency in her county that handles child abuse cases.

Recently Sara discovered a food co-op where, by paying a small amount to join and volunteering a few hours, she can get a good deal of food at very reasonable rates. She's also discovered that she can get family counseling services, which the childcare center recommended because of Ty's attention-deficit problem and Kyle's aggressive behavior (you may remember that he bites). The director of the childcare program is also talking about referring both boys to a special education preschool program run by the county office of education. Sara is hesitant about taking the next steps for this service because she hates the thought of changing programs. Besides, the hours of the special ed program don't fit her school schedule very well and she'd still need childcare. Transportation would be a problem and she doesn't want her boys shuffled back and forth from one program to another, so she's dragging her feet on following up her investigation of what could be done further for her children.

Because of her low-income status, Sara is entitled to health benefits from the government, but she sometimes has a hard time finding a doctor who will see her and the boys.

Sara has been in a lot worse shape in the past than she is now. She remembers eating once a week at a community dinner for the homeless, served in a church by a local women's service group. Sara had very mixed feelings about being there. She couldn't help but be grateful, of course, but she felt strangely alienated from everyone there; not only from the other homeless people but also from the good-hearted women who donated their time, energy, and casseroles. She hates being on the receiving end of charity!

Christmas always brought up the same awful feelings; it still does, even now. It's great that the community rallies once a year to provide gifts for her boys and a turkey for her table, but every year she has those same mixed feelings of gratitude, shame, and anger. She'll be glad when she gets through school and can support herself. Then she'll be the one doing the giving for a change. She can hardly wait.

ROBERTO'S FAMILY

Roberto's family, if you remember, is composed of his wife, Maria Elena, his four-year-old daughter, Lupe, and baby Paco. Roberto at first resisted signing up for any community resources because he was too proud; besides, he was suspicious of anything connected to any government. But one day he found himself persuaded to send his daughter to Head Start, a federally funded preschool program for low-income children. He discovered early on that with Head Start comes a community aide, who helps the family get connected to other services that they need, many of which are provided right at school for the children, like vision and hearing screening. The hearing screening proved to be a problem because they discovered that Lupe has a hearing deficit and now the family is expected to do something about it. Roberto is convinced that it would have gone away on its own if it hadn't been discovered. Roberto and Maria Elena went to the place the school told them to go, but there were many papers to fill out and no one spoke their language, so they left. Now Roberto feels very uncomfortable every time he gets a notice from school urging him to follow up on the referral they gave him.

While he was still getting used to all the changes in his life that came as the result of enrolling Lupe in Head Start, Maria Elena announced that she wanted to take English as a Second Language classes at the adult school. "I won't have time to drive you," Roberto told her firmly, convinced that that would end the matter.

"I can take the bus," said Maria Elena.

"And who will take care of Paco?" asked Roberto.

"They have childcare at the school," Maria Elena shot back.

Roberto was stunned. This had all been worked out without him. What would happen to him if his family didn't need him any more? He felt shaken.

He needed to talk to somebody, so he went first to his compadre, Juan, godfather of Lupe, and told him how he felt. Just talking about it made him feel better. Then he went to his priest and talked some more. The priest suggested counseling, but Roberto thought that would show the world that something was wrong with him, and that was exactly the problem he wished to avoid. He felt that enough was wrong with him because of what was happening in his family; he certainly didn't want to announce to the world that he was weak and needed help. The priest made another suggestion, however, that Roberto followed up on. He told him about a clinic that might help with Lupe's problem. It was a community effort run by bilingual volunteers, so he would at least be able to talk to someone in his own language—someone who knew something about medicine. Roberto felt much better when he came home from talking to the priest. Maria Elena noticed the difference and gave him a big hug when he came in the door.

HAI'S FAMILY

The Nguyen family is so busy working that they haven't had time to find out about any resources in their community except for childcare; and that isn't working out too well, because Hai cries all the time he's there. The family, refugees from Southeast Asia, have been relocated several times, and Hai seems to be expressing the suffering all of them feel. Being crowded is nothing new to this family; they've always lived in close quarters with the extended family in one residence. Their house is packed most of the time. They have to eat in shifts, but they work in shifts too, so that comes out all right.

One thing they're glad of is that Hai doesn't cry at home the way he does at the center. It's not that crying babies haven't always been part of their lives, but now Great-Grandma is sick, and they worry about disturbing her. Oh, yes, they do use a community resource—a home health nurse who comes in to look after Great-Grandma. Although they were suspicious at first of medical care that they didn't understand, they decided it wouldn't be such a bad idea to learn about how things work in this country. The only problem is that language creates terrible barriers, and they don't understand as much as they want to. They often wonder what the nurse is doing and what the various medications are for, but they have to wait until the oldest cousin, who understands English, gets home to find out. Even then things don't always make sense because the approach to health care is so different.

There have been some scary misunderstandings about health matters—like the time Great-Grandma had a reaction to some medication and they had to take her to the hospital emergency room. That was a horrible experience because they had no idea what was going on. And when they put her in the hospital for two days, it was very frustrating because the medical staff wouldn't let the family take care of her. In fact, they were asked to leave. They didn't understand this at all!

The family is very lonely at times when they think of home, but they are learning to make this country home. They know how to support each other, pooling resources and knowledge, which helps a lot. They aren't used to getting outside help, so that's something new to them. They are learning English rapidly and soon will have an expanded view of the community they live in and what is available to them.

MICHAEL'S FAMILY

Michael, a three-year-old, is the son of a lesbian couple. Michael and his parents are isolated from many of the social networks that support other families. They don't want to be, but they have had bad experiences in the past when they reached out and found themselves rejected. They have their own group of friends, and they find closeness and community there. In some ways they are like the Nguyen family, who necessarily looks close to home for support.

In other ways they are not like the Nguyen family, because the institutions that they deal with don't recognize them as a family. This became clear and evident the day that Michael fell and needed stitches. Margaret, his biological mother, was at work in another town and couldn't get to the hospital right away. Beth, his other mother, had to hold the crying Michael in the emergency room—no treatment could be started until Margaret arrived to sign permission papers. Beth had no recognized legal connection to Michael.

Having their relationship disregarded as valid and legal by community agencies was nothing new to them—but this hurt the most because it involved Michael. They had had previous difficulties not experienced by heterosexual married couples—like not being able to get a loan to buy a house and being refused job-related medical benefits. That doesn't even count the difficulties of living in a neighborhood where some neighbors didn't like them even though they had never gotten to know them.

Beth and Margaret aren't without friends. They both have jobs and each has found personal friends and support systems at work. But these systems don't help the family much, because except for a few, the work friends don't know about the rest of the family.

Margaret especially feels isolated at work, because of the secret she keeps from her friends and associates there. But in her last job she was more open, and she ended up feeling a lot more isolated than she does now. She finally left that job because she couldn't stand it anymore.

Both Margaret and Beth worry about their son and what will happen when he is old enough to understand what outsiders say about the family. They feel very protective of him and of each other, and sometimes feel as though they live in a little cocoon separate from the rest of the world. They don't really want to live that way, but they wish they could keep the cocoon for Michael. They know, however, that soon he's going to grow beyond their protection and will be on his own in what feels to them like a cold and cruel outside world.

Margaret is secure about her relationship to Beth, but she suffers from the reaction she gets from so many who find out. She felt angry a lot of the time, and she knew she needed help in coping with the anger. She finally found a therapist to talk to. It took a long time, because she looked for someone who really understood her and could help without judging her family composition. She is surprised that being open and honest with a professional therapist can be so helpful. She's urging Beth, who has the same angry feelings about the way she's treated, to talk with someone too. However, Beth hesitates, feeling that going into therapy means she's admitting that something is wrong with her.

Things are a little better now, because Beth has found a teacher at Michael's center who is accepting and friendly. She feels relieved that at least one outsider isn't cold and cruel.

COURTNEY'S FAMILY

Courtney's family consists of her second husband, Richard; four-year-old Roland from Courtney's first marriage; and two-and-a-half-year-old Soleil, Courtney and Richard's daughter. Roland's two older brothers are also part of this family, but they live with Courtney's parents.

This family has been involved with the legal system for some time, starting with drug abuse, and then with child abuse during Courtney's first marriage. Now the family lives in fear of the boys' father returning to heap more abuse on previously abused little Roland. There's a restraining order to keep the father from coming near the boys, but Courtney still worries.

Courtney is just about to graduate from a drug rehabilitation program and is very proud of herself for being clean. She has turned her life around and is enrolled in college, the first step toward becoming a lawyer. She has strong feelings about making the legal system work better for everybody.

Richard too has strong feelings about the system. He is a Native American who, though born outside the reservation, has spent periods of his life going back to connect with his roots. He finds the tribal system and the religion of his people appealing, in contrast to impersonal institutions. He knows what real community is—people linked in emotional, social, and spiritual ways that provide mutual help and support. His dream is to become a history teacher and help the next generation see that change is necessary if this country (and, indeed, the planet) is to survive.

Courtney, like Sara, went through a difficult time in the past, which resulted in her being connected with a number of social service institutions. Some of them seemed to be supportive of her; some she regarded as "the enemy."

She remembers a very difficult period when she was told that if she didn't leave her boys' father because of the abuse he poured on them, she would lose her children. She felt extremely helpless at this point, and if it hadn't been for a local women's shelter, she never would have been able to take such a big step. When she finally left the shelter and struck out on her own, she was still threatened with the loss of her children because she couldn't provide decent housing for them. The only place she could afford that would rent to her was very run down. Luckily, there was a new program in her community that was designed to help families overcome obstacles like that. A social worker from this program, instead of removing her children to foster care, came out with tools to show her how to fix the broken windows, replace the screens, and repair the plumbing, so that she and her children would have a safe place to live. This same social worker gave her some skills for guiding her children's behavior, and got her into the rehabilitation program that turned her life around. Courtney is very grateful for the community resources that she sees as saving her life and helping her keep her children.

THE JACKSON FAMILY

The Jackson family is different from some of the other families because they haven't been through a hard time. They're a stable family, clear about their identity, their values, and their lifestyle. They're not looking for changes as much as trying to keep things the way they are. Like Margaret and Beth, Michael's parents, the Jacksons' problems arise from being different from and therefore misunderstood by the greater community.

They are not in crisis and so are not looking for the same kind of support as some of the other families examined so far. The community resources they use and enjoy are both those of their own group—the religious and cultural groups they belong to—and those of the greater community, resources such as the library, recreation programs and facilities, museums, and other institutions that enhance the quality of their lives. They appreciate music and plays and support the local groups that provide them. This family at present has no need for the kinds of programs that are helping the other families already discussed—general assistance and welfare programs, food programs, housing assistance, social services, child abuse programs, or legal agencies.

It's not that this is a perfect family; they have their problems too. Mrs. Jackson is feeling isolated, and she's thinking of looking for friends outside her religious community. She had hoped to find a friendly group when she moved into the neighborhood she lives in. In her old neighborhood the women got together regularly and talked over coffee. In this one, however, the neighbors don't seem to want to get to know each other. The women are gone during the day and seem to be busy evenings and weekends. Mrs. Jackson invited both next-door neighbors over when she first moved in, but although they were polite and pleasant, they never reciprocated, and now they just talk once in a while across the driveway.

Now, however, Mrs. Jackson has gotten involved with fund-raising at the childcare program, and she's beginning to feel connected to a group. She likes the women who are working with her, and she hopes to continue enjoying their company after the fund-raiser is over.

Mrs. Jackson is also involved in a new project. Her father, who has lived by himself since his wife died, is growing more and more feeble, and the Jacksons recently decided that he should move in with them. She is busy investigating what kinds of services are available to help them out. She has discovered the senior center near the library, where her father can enjoy company, take part in various classes and activities, and have a hot lunch on the days she works. She's feeling good about how this move will work out. It will be nice to have her father with her—and good for the children to know their grandfather better.

CONNECTIONS TO THE COMMUNITY

Each of these families has connections to the community beyond their own doors, yet each perceives that community in a slightly different way. Each uses the services of agencies and informal groups. Some give back as much as they receive; others either aren't in a position to reciprocate or don't yet understand the give-and-take aspects of community living. Many of the families we've examined live with multiple stresses in their lives. Some find the support and services they need; others feel the need for more. Some are denied access to available resources.

Let's look at a summary of the kinds of institutions and programs available in varying degrees to most of these families.

A SUMMARY OF COMMUNITY RESOURCES

Though none of these families have needed police or fire protection lately, they all know that they are two community services that are available at the touch of the telephone push buttons. They also know about the community resources that are available to enhance the quality of their lives—the parks and recreation department, the library, the local museum, and the two-year community college, all of which have regular programs for adults and children.

Childcare programs, Head Start and other early-education programs, and schools, both public and private, provide education to all members of the family. Local hospitals and the county health department provide preventative care and

Finding Community Resources

How do you find out what resources are available in your community? A simple way is to start with the phone book; some have a special section right in front. Or the library may have a listing. In some communities, a local organization such as Head Start or a childcare resource and referral agency puts together and updates lists of resources that are available to families.

By word of mouth is the way many families find out about the individuals and institutions that can serve them. If a family is connected to a childcare center, the chances are someone on staff knows what's available for specific problems.

Some families enter "the system" because of a crisis or a problem. That's the way they get introduced to the world of accessible resources in their community. In some cities and towns a crisis center is available twenty-four hours a day to serve those who are in serious trauma for whatever reason. Some communities also have women's shelters where the abused and their children can find refuge. Public health and mental health systems are usually also able to respond to crisis situations.

If your child seems to have a special need, a place to start asking about it is your doctor's office. If you're not connected to a medical system, public schools often have the resources to assess special needs or may be able to refer you to another source.

Clergy often serve as counselors and advisors to individuals and families. They can guide their clients to appropriate community resources for their particular problem.

It's not always easy to find just what you need; in fact, it is sometimes downright difficult. However, with persistence, you'll usually locate whatever there might be. Unfortunately, most communities lack the full range of resources that they need, and many families are left with solving their own problems or looking for help or support from relatives, friends, and neighbors.

health maintenance to varying degrees, including some perinatal services and a variety of health-education programs. They also, of course, provide services for the sick.

The Personal Responsibility and Work Opportunity Reconciliation Act (PRWOR) signed into law in 1996, has changed welfare by eliminating the guarantee of cash assistance to needy families with children. Aid to Families with Dependent Children (AFDC) is now called Temporary Assistance for Needy Families and is funded through block grants. The requirements are stricter and the time limit is two years. Times are changing and the challenges are growing for people unable to work to support themselves or their families. How these changes and challenges will affect children is a big question mark, but the risk factor has obviously grown much larger.

Some community resources are designed to support families in times of emergency and stress, such as child abuse prevention programs, which offer telephone

Early childhood programs provide education and support to families.

hot lines, parent education services, and respite childcare. Mental health programs that offer therapeutic services and counseling programs are designed as short-term crisis intervention, and some provide long-term help to individuals and families as well. These programs also have experienced reduced funding, which makes them less effective than they used to be. Families who can afford to pay for services continue, of course, to find them available. Substance abuse programs run by both professionals and volunteers also help people get on their feet and live satisfying and productive lives.

Most communities have any number of support groups. Support groups can be both formal and informal and can respond to any number of needs: general parenting groups, women's and men's support groups, substance abuse, codependency, overeaters anonymous—you name it, there's a support group somewhere for it. Mrs. Jackson has even found a spina bifida support group that is attended by parents whose children were born with this condition.

AVAILABILITY OF COMMUNITY RESOURCES

Although the list of community resources may be lengthy, not all are available in all communities. Even those communities that have a variety may not make them available to all families. What are some of the factors that determine availability of community resources?

Funding is one factor—often there's not enough to go around, or it's stretched so thin that no one can do a good job of helping and supporting families. Lack of funding results in declining services and increased competition for limited resources.

Some programs serve a specific population and families must qualify to be eligible to receive services. Further, some families qualify for services but have no access to them because of lack of transportation or language barriers. (Or perhaps they don't even realize that such services exist.)

When families do connect with services available to them, they may find the services inappropriate to their need—sometimes because of cultural insensitivity on the part of the providers of the service. Lack of respect may be a factor when there's a mismatch between services and the families they are designed to serve. When clients are looked down on by the people who serve them, it's often because the agency is using a deficit model to define the people who come to them for help. This model may be quite out of tune with the reality of cultural or class differences.

Each of the community resources that families deal with have a spoken or unspoken set of goals and values. When these goals and values are in tune with those of the family, a match is made, and the chances are better that the support or intervention will be effective. Some goals and values are conscious, written into the agency, some are misinterpreted by outsiders, and some are unintended.

For example, in one medium-sized town there are two agencies serving pregnant women. One is Planned Parenthood, whose purpose is to offer a variety of services as well as counseling that allows women to make decisions that are right for them about family planning. Planned Parenthood is not just for pregnant women; it has a variety of services for both men and women. It offers abortion as one of several options for pregnant women to consider.

On the other side of town is a group called Birthright, whose goal is to help pregnant women opt against abortion. They provide counseling and support to women who might otherwise find it difficult to have their babies, doing what they can to make it more attractive to continue the pregnancy than to end it. These two agencies, which serve the same population, have contrasting goals and values and are clear about their differences.

Usually an agency's goals are not so clear, and often families don't look beyond the offer of services to understand the agency's goals or value system anyway. Of course, they can find them by examining incorporation papers, mission statements, or patterns of board policies. However, families do not usually set out to investigate the goals and value systems of the agency where they seek help or support. They may become aware of a lack of communication, a mismatch, or a lack of respect, which signals a goal or value conflict, but most of us don't even clarify our own goals or values very often, let alone compare them with those of an agency. However, goals and values do make a difference if we are to serve our community and be served by it. Goals and values are themes in the two chapters that follow.

SUMMARY

This chapter looked at how the community supports families and provides resources through informal and formal social networks, institutions, and agencies. Examples of how several families use the resources made up a good portion of the chapter. It ended with a look at goals and values, which are themes in the two chapters that follow.

FOR DISCUSSION

1. What do you know about the negative effects isolation can have on families?
2. Name some "social networks" that you are acquainted with.
3. Why do families need formal and informal support more now than ever before?
4. Give examples of how Sara's family might both use and contribute to community resources?
5. Give examples of how Roberto's family might both use and contribute to community resources?
6. Give examples of how Hai's family might both use and contribute to community resources?
7. Give examples of how Michael's family might both use and contribute to community resources?
8. Give examples of how Courtney's family might both use and contribute to community resources?
9. Give examples of how the Jackson family might both use and contribute to community resources?
10. What would you tell a family about how to find the community resources they might need?
11. Do you know someone who needed a community resources but it wasn't available to that person? Why wasn't it available?
12. Do you know someone who used an agency that didn't fit their culture or their needs?

PERSONAL REFLECTIONS

Thinking about your personal reactions and experiences will help you better understand and integrate the material in this chapter. Use these questions to interface between you and what you read. Use the pertinent ones to reflect on, write about, or discuss with others.

> What are some of the negative effects isolation has had or might have on you?
> If you made a "stroke pie," what would it show about you?

> What social networks are you a part of, if any?

> Have any of the four trends mentioned in the chapter affected you personally?

> Imagine you had to find a community resource for yourself. How would you start looking?

> Have you ever been turned away from a community resource that had something to offer you? Why were you turned away?

> Have you ever had a negative experience with an agency in your community? What happened? Why did it happen?

NOTES

1. Valora Washington and Ura Jean Oyemade, "Changing Family Trends," *Young Children* (September 1985): 12–19.
2. According to the Bureau of Labor Statistics, it takes 1.3 wage earners per 4-person family to achieve a lower-level standard of living, 1.7 for the moderate level, and 2.0 wage earners for the higher level. Blanche Bernstein, "Since the Moynihan Report," in *The Black Family: Essays and Studies*, 4th ed., ed. Robert Staples (Belmont, CA: Wadsworth, 1991), 24.
3. Washington and Oyemade, *op. cit.*, 13.

REFERENCES

Bernstein, Blanche. "Since the Moynihan Report." In *The Black Family: Essays and Studies*, 4th ed., ed. Robert Staples. Belmont, CA: Wadsworth, 1991, 24.

Dunst, Carl, Carol Trivette, and Angela Deal. *Enabling and Empowering Families.* Cambridge, MA: Brookline, 1988.

Edwards, Patricia A. and Lauren S. Jones Young. "Beyond Parents: Family, Community, and School Involvement," *Phi Delta Kappan*, (May 1992): 72–80.

Fernea, Elizabeth Warnock. *Children in the Muslim Middle East.* Austin: University of Texas Press, 1995.

Hale-Benson, Janice E. *Black Children: Their Roots, Culture, and Learning Styles.* Baltimore, MD: The Johns Hopkins University Press, 1986.

Hale, Janice E. "An African-American Early Childhood Education Program: Visions for Children." In *Reconceptualizing the Early Childhood Curriculum: Beginning the Dialogue*, eds. Shirley A. Kessler and Beth Blue Swadener. NY: Teachers College Press, 1992, pp. 205–224.

Heath, S. B. *Ways with Words: Language, Life, and Work in Communities and Classrooms.* Cambridge: Cambridge University Press, 1983.

Huang, L. M., and Y. Ying. "Japanese Children and Adolescents. In *Children of Color*, eds. J. T. Gibbs and L. N. Huang. San Francisco: Jossey-Bass, 1989.

Kochman, T. *Black and White: Styles in Conflict.* Chicago: University of Chicago Press, 1981.

LaFromboise, T. D. "American Indian Mental Health Policy. In *Counseling American Minorities*, eds. D. R. Atkinson, G. Morten, and D. W. Sue. Madison, WI: Brown and Benchmark, 1993.

LaFromboise, T. D., and D. G. Low. "American Indian Children and Adolescents," In *Children of Color*, eds. J. T. Gibbs and L. N. Huang. San Francisco, Jossey-Bass, 1989.

LaFromboise, T. D., and J. Trimble. "Multicultural Counseling Theory and American-Indian Populations." In *Theory of Multicultural Counseling and Therapy*, ed. D. W. Sue. Pacific Grove, CA: Brooks/Cole, 1996.

Lee, Joann. *Asian Americans*. New York: New Press, 1992.

Lefley, H., and P. Pedersen, eds. *Cross-Cultural Training for Mental Health Professionals*. Springfield, IL: Charles C. Thomas, Publisher, 1986.

Leong, F. "Multicultural Counseling Theory and Asian-American Populations. In *Theory of Multicultural Counseling and Therapy*, ed. D. W. Sue. Pacific Grove, CA: Brooks/Cole, 1996.

Neighbors, H. W., and J. S. Jackson, eds. *Mental Health in Black America*. Newbury Park, CA: Sage, 1996.

Phillips, Carol Brunson. "Culture: A Process that Empowers." In *Infant/Toddler Caregiving: A Guide to Culturally Sensitive Care*, ed. Peter Mangione. Sacramento, CA: Far West Laboratory and California Department of Education, 1995.

Ross, Allen. C. (Ehanamani). *Mitakuye Oyasin: We Are All Related*. Denver: Wichoni Waste, 1989.

Sue, Stanley, and Thom Moore, eds. *The Pluralistic Society*. New York: Human Sciences Press, Inc., 1984, 188.

Tedla, Elleni. *Sankofa: African Thought and Education*. New York: Peter Lang, 1995.

Wardle, Francis. "Are You Sensitive to Interracial Children's Special Identity Needs?" *Young Children* 42(2) (1987): 53–59.

Washington, Valora, and Ura Jean Oyemade. "Changing Family Trends." *Young Children* (September 1985): 12–19.

Werner, Emmy E. "Resilience in Development," *Current Directions in Psychological Science* (June 1995): 81–85.

Werner, E. E., and R. S. Smith. *Overcoming the Odds: High Risk Children from Birth to Adulthood*. Ithaca and London: Cornell University Press, 1992.

Socializing Agents

CHAPTER 14

In this chapter you'll discover:

> Four "socializing agents"
> How bias affects young children
> That social class isn't as invisible as it seems
> The effect of "school tracking"
> Some things about "kindergarten readiness" that you probably never thought of
> How to decide by looking at a classroom whether the teacher "celebrates diversity"
> That everyone doesn't get an equal education in spite of our American ideal
> The influences of a four-year-old peer group
> Some problems with expecting television to socialize children

TEST YOURSELF

Look for the answers to these questions as you read the chapter:

1. What are the four "socializing agents" discussed in the chapter?
2. What is the meaning of this statement: "Many families have a primary focus of attention"?
3. How can the status of the family affect the child's socialization?
4. How does being the target of bias affect socialization?
5. How does being raised in a biased family affect socialization?
6. How does classism affect socialization?
7. How does racism affect socialization?
8. How do schools "track" children and what are the effects of such a practice?
9. What are some of the issues that relate to "kindergarten readiness"?
10. What are the characteristics of a kindergarten-aged child who doesn't behave according to the school's expectations?
11. If you walked into a kindergarten classroom and looked around at the environment, what clues could you find that would tell you the teacher's attitude toward diversity?
12. What does a full antibias curriculum include?
13. What is the meaning of this statement: "We have great discrepancies in our public school system in America today"?
14. What are the characteristics of a peer group of four-year-olds?
15. What are the functions of the peer group?
16. What is included under the label, "mass media"?
17. Why is television a poor socializer?
18. What do young children learn from watching television?
19. How do TV commercials affect young children?

The family is the first and major socializing agent, and as such has responsibility for early socialization patterns. As the child grows from infancy and moves outside his or her home, other agents in the community come into play. In the past, outside agents were fewer; relatives, neighbors, and informal community networks shared a good deal of responsibility for socialization. Today, television is usually the first socializing agent outside the family, with childcare a close second. Later, school comes into the picture, with after-school activities and perhaps eventually clubs such as scouts. The socialization process becomes more and more shared. Other institutions such as hospitals, government agencies, and service industries may also come into the picture. These organizations have taken over many of the activities that were once the function of the family, the extended family or kinship network, and neighbors, all of whom used to make up the informal community.

This chapter looks at four major socializing agents: the family, the school, the peer group, and television.

SOCIALIZATION AND THE FAMILY

Each family belongs to subcultures and networks that reflect their social-class position, ethnic-group membership, and, possibly, their kinship. These subcultures and networks influence the ways in which families socialize their children. Families and socialization featured prominently in Part 2. This section deals with information in addition to that already given.

The language the parents use, and sometimes insist that their children use, influences to some extent their ties to one group or another. "Speak Spanish," demands a mother who sees her children drifting away from their roots to dissolve into mainstream America. "Speak English," demands another, who sees language as a way to carry out her upward-bound goals. "Don't say *ain't*," admonishes another because she feels that's what "uneducated" people say, knowing that language helps people fit into the right group. "Gettin' kinda uppity, ain't ya?" asks another mother, who feels alienated by her son's new way of speaking when he comes back from college for the first visit home. She sees language as a divider.

In addition to social class and ethnic group, families are sometimes tied to other families through occupations or interests, which also affect children's socialization. The family that surfs together, for example, if any of the members get good enough, may find themselves traveling the world to compete. The experiences their children get in socialization may be quite different from the children of workaholic parents who are tied to their corporate "family."

Many families have a primary focus of attention; it may be religious activities, or school achievement, or even making money. Some actively mold their children to their own interests by constantly involving them. They also do it by evaluating other people, so the children come to see whom the family prefers them to associate with and who should be avoided. The outdoorsy family whose members devote themselves to nature and to ecology issues may be quite critical of the family next door—a nightclub comedian and his singer wife who spend most of their work and leisure time in smoke-filled rooms, or the family on the hill that owns the manufacturing plant in town that has been suspected of polluting the environment.

Status, that is, the family's position in society, affects socialization, and can in turn affect where the child finds herself when she grows up. Children of wealthy families have a different set of experiences and expectations than, for example, children of poverty-level families. Consider the difference between a child born into a Beverly Hills family with two parents, four cars, and a pile of money compared with a child who was born in jail and who is sent to live with her grandmother in a run-down trailer park near the railroad tracks while her mother finishes serving a term for dealing drugs. Which child is most likely to grow up defining her choices as the "sky's the limit"?

The family not only gives the child status but also makes him or her aware of the status of others. Family members teach, whether consciously or not, whom to copy and whom not to copy. The message about the status of outsiders is clear in some families—just who is above and who is below.

The "goodies" the society has to offer are more available to some children than to others. For some, privilege is a major socializing force; for others, privilege's counterparts—bias and discrimination—play that role.

THE ISSUE OF BIAS

Bias is everywhere, and we've all felt its effects, though some of us are targeted more than others. We feel bias because of our gender, social class, skin color, ethnic background, the way we talk, body type or condition, mental capabilities, age, sexual orientation, the amount of money or education our family has, or our family configuration, to name a few of the factors that make us the targets of bias.

Bias hurts everybody—and especially children. It hurts those who are its targets because they must put energy into struggling against the negative messages that they receive—energy that could be used for development. In addition, it hurts them because they find their opportunities limited; doors are shut to them.

Bias also hurts those who are not targets when they participate in the belief that they and others like them are superior. This belief not only dehumanizes them but also distorts their reality. Bias is bad for everybody!

We need to become aware of our areas of privilege and how bias works. We need to become sensitized in order to help ourselves and others think critically and to speak up in the face of bias.

The key is empowerment. Target groups must be empowered to develop a strong self- and group-identity so they can stand up in the face of attack. Nontarget groups must also develop a strong self-identity, but without a feeling of superiority. Each individual must be free to, and indeed encouraged to, develop to his or her full and unique potential.

Classism

Let's look more closely at one area of bias—social class—by examining a child who is a target for classism:

> Peter, who is four, was born into a middle-class family. However, soon after Peter's birth, his father left his mother. Daddy came back just long enough to make a baby brother before departing for good, leaving Peter's mother with two little boys to raise. The family slipped into poverty practically overnight.
>
> Although Peter's mother was raised with the values, expectations, and behaviors of the middle class, she began to change as the effects of poverty molded her. She couldn't keep up her same connections. When she was single and after she was first married, she used to enjoy lunch out with her friends; now her lunch hour was full of errands and appointments, and, anyway, she didn't have the money to squander on a nice lunch. She struggled hard to remain on her former level, but try as she would, she was pulled down. She began to feel strange around people who had so much more money than she did. She also felt strange around the other mothers she met whose children were in Peter's Head Start class. She didn't seem to belong anywhere anymore.
>
> She remembered how she and her friends used to criticize poor people who didn't keep their kids clean. "It doesn't cost anything to keep clean," she used to say. But she discovered that it did. She had to go to the laundromat to wash; that cost plenty—in money, time, and energy. And since her water heater broke, even bathing the boys was harder. She had called the landlord three times already to get it fixed, but she was still without hot water after four days.
>
> The last straw came when she popped back into the childcare center to leave the diaper bag she'd forgotten to drop off and found Peter's little brother being scrubbed down in the sink. She knew then that she'd crossed the line and had become one of the people she used to frown on. She remembered a conversation with a teacher friend about how some kids arrive at school so dirty and smelly that you just want to give them a good scrubbing. Now her own child had become one of them. She was embarrassed to tears—and angry as well. How dare they bathe her baby without her permission? He wasn't *that* dirty. She'd heated water on the stove and given him a sponge bath that very morning!

We don't know if this mother was really experiencing a biased attitude or not. We don't know why the teacher was washing the child or how she felt about it. She perhaps thought she was doing the mother and the child a favor, but the mother perceived the action as an insult, maybe because she had once been on the other side of classism.

Not all families are newly poor like Peter's mother, and many people have not experienced both sides of the poverty line. Some families come from a long tradition of poverty and have never known anything else. They are used to people "looking down on them" and perhaps even blaming them for their poverty.

For some Americans, social class is hard to see, because we, as a society, deny the existence of such a thing. For a long period the middle and upper classes were even able to pretend that social class didn't exist because they didn't see poor people before their very eyes. All that is rapidly changing; poverty shows everywhere. Poor people aren't tucked away on the other side of town anymore. They're apt to be downtown and even in the parking lots of shopping malls, holding up signs that say "Will work for food."

Social classes exist even though they aren't the permanent, set-in-stone phenomena we see in other countries. We still don't commonly call them *social classes*, though. Sociologists speak of "socioeconomic levels." Whatever you call them, there are differences in the experience of the children who are raised at each level. [1]

Social class is one factor in socialization and race is another; however, they are often lumped together. Social class may be ignored entirely, for example, when comparing cultural differences of African-Americans and European-Americans. Often poverty-level African-Americans are compared with middle-class European-Americans without acknowledging that there are class differences. It's important to be aware that there are poverty-level people in all cultural groups—and also middle-class people—and you can't just be blind to social class differences.

Let's turn now to racism, which is another important factor in socialization of children.

Racism

Those who have experienced racism don't have to read about it to understand it. If you haven't experienced it, it's hard to understand to what extent it exists and what it feels like. It's easier for those who aren't a target for racism to understand it in terms of its counterpart, *privilege.*

Privilege can be thought of as an "invisible package of unearned assets," which it's possible to cash in on whenever it pleases the person carrying the privilege. Most of those who have it are quite unaware of their privilege; they regard it as the way things are. Those who don't have privilege are very aware of its lack. Privilege shows more in its absence than in its presence. [2]

Let's look at the privileges that a four-year-old white, middle-class child, Lindsay, enjoys because of her skin color:

Lindsay doesn't have to represent "her people," who, in fact, are seldom lumped into one skin-color category. If she arrives at preschool dirty, it's an individual family matter, or perhaps attributed to her social class, but it doesn't reflect on white people in general. She can wear secondhand clothes. She can pick her nose or even use bad words and it's her family that's reflected, not the white race. If her family gets her to school late, no one attributes it to either their genes or their culture. If she arrives at school tired, the teachers may blame the parent, but not anyone else. Lindsay's family has the privilege of representing only themselves, not reflecting or living in the reflection of stereotypes of a group of other people with their same skin color.

Lindsay lives in the best neighborhood her family can afford; though money is, of course, a factor, it is not the major factor. They have the privilege of choosing where they want to live within their price range and they made that choice assuming that their neighbors would display good or at least neutral feelings toward them. If they have alienated their neighbors, it's more likely because of something they've done rather than because of who they are.

Lindsay will come to see herself and her family as "normal," if she hasn't already. She sees herself and her people represented on television and in books, magazines, and newspapers. She easily finds the food her family eats in the local supermarket. Lindsay's mother can take her anyplace she likes to get her hair cut and feel reassured that someone there will know how to cut it. When Lindsay is older and learns about history, she'll be shown that her people (or at least the males) made this country what it is.

Lindsay's mother doesn't worry about educating her children to detect racism. She doesn't even consider teaching them how to operate when racism is present or how to protect themselves from it.

Angelica and her twin brother, Mario, who go to Lindsay's preschool, have a different experience:

Angelica and Mario's mother is well aware of the possibility of racist attitudes toward her children. One of the antiracist strategies her mother uses is to send them to school fashionably dressed. The teachers sent Angelica home with a parent handbook the first day, with the sentence, "Please send your child in old play clothes" highlighted. After a week, one teacher stopped the three of them as they were leaving and complained that it was hard for the children to participate in all the many and varied messy activities because of their clothing. She asked that they come in old clothes that didn't matter. The mother listened, but the next day Angelica arrived dressed in a new fancy dress and her brother in a starched shirt and a pair of slacks. The teachers never understood why their message didn't get through. If they had been able to have a heart-to-heart talk with Angelica's mother they would have discovered that she see's her children's appearances as reflecting on their family. She wants her children to look well cared for. She doesn't want her children to fit into any stereotypes racists may have of her people. Although racists are everywhere, if Angelica and Mario are well dressed and look well cared for, it will be harder for some people to see them as inferior to other children. She is also well aware that clothes and grooming won't matter to a real racist who will only see skin color.

For Janice, the issue is hair:

Janice is the parent education coordinator at a fairly large childcare center. One of the parents she has concerns about is Betsy who is the adoptive mother of Lacy, an African-American five-year-old. Betsy doesn't know how to take care of her daughter's hair and it bothers Janice a lot. She sends her in the morning looking uncombed. After nap time she wakes up looking even worse. Janice has taken to combing Lacy's hair twice a day, on arrival and after nap. Lacy loves it! Janice keeps meaning to ask Betsy for a conference to explain to her some of the things she doesn't know about her daughter's hair. She also wants her to understand that an African-American child can't afford to look as if nobody cares about her, even if it's not true. People will judge her, and her people!

These three stories show some of the factors that affect socialization. The child's race, family income level, and circumstances influence how others respond to him or her on a personal level. These same factors often determine the kind of formal education that child is likely to receive. We've already examined childcare and early education in other chapters. The focus of the next section is on the public school system.

SCHOOLS AS SOCIALIZING AGENTS

Some children arrive in kindergarten already less ready to grapple with the kindergarten curriculum than other children. Sometimes this is merely a matter of developmental differences. However, some children enjoy a variety of early experiences that fit nicely into what they need for kindergarten. Other children's early experiences are different; kindergarten presents an alien world to them. As a result, children are sometimes labeled and separated into groups by their "abilities" (this is called tracking). If children are tracked and labeled early, their educational course is set, sometimes for life. That means some are given the message that they're learners—winners in the race called school. They tend to take the ball and run with it; they're successful. Others learn early that they're "slow," which they translate to mean "stupid"; they're losers. Once tracking begins, the educational opportunities become limited for some and expanded for others.

Getting into Kindergarten

Even getting into kindergarten may be an issue facing families who send their five-year-olds off to public school. Public school administrators and teachers are under a great deal of pressure to provide accountability to government funding sources. Those who pay the bills want to be sure they're getting their money's worth. The way they determine accountability is through test scores, so testing has finally reached clear down to the beginning—to kindergarten. [3]

The effect of linking accountability to achievement as proved by testing is to make teachers anxious to have only the most teachable children in their classrooms. Say a child enters in September who isn't ready to buckle down and do whatever the teacher, the school, the district, or the state considers kindergarten work (which more and more reflects the test items that will appear during the spring testing period). This child wants to play, and his motivation is so strong that it takes all the teacher's behavioral management techniques and more to get him to settle down to "seat work" for even a few minutes a day. It's easy to say this child isn't ready for kindergarten. And it's even easier to decide to determine readiness *before* the child enters and settles into the class. Therefore, some schools now have screening tests to decide who can come into kindergarten and who can't.

On the surface, that approach may make sense, but dig down just a little. Think about the child who has been at home with an overburdened parent for five years—a parent who doesn't have the time or the resources to contribute to his

Ready to Learn

Kindergarten readiness is always a hot topic among parents of preschoolers, but getting children ready starts way back in infancy. There's even a campaign to get children "ready to learn" before they enter kindergarten. Here are some general indicators that children are prepared to enter kindergarten:

1. Children who are ready to learn are those who feel good about themselves. The problem is that much of the discipline used makes children feel bad about themselves. Children don't feel good about themselves by being made to feel bad. Discipline should not only leave self-esteem intact but also actually raise it when adults use modeling, guidance, and feedback. Communication is an important part of discipline when adults discuss feelings and behavior instead of criticizing the child. Adults who understand such things separate the child from the behavior, saying things like "I won't let you hit your sister. It hurts her" instead of "Stop that, you bad boy!"

2. Children who are ready to learn are those who gain knowledge from mistakes. Some of the best lessons come from things that don't work. It's easy to take the lesson out of a mistake by rescuing children so they don't learn about consequences of their actions. Or the opposite situation occurs when the adult reacts to a mistake with harsh punishment. When children become fearful of mistakes, they quit risking. Reasonable risks are good learning devices. The child who avoids them, misses out on a lot of important lessons.

3. Children who are ready to learn can communicate. They have lots of experience in talking and listening. They know how to carry on a conversation. A conversation means not just talking, but listening and responding appropriately. Adults should start emphasizing communication young. Even infants enjoy conversations and taking turns "talking." They also play with language. As they grow older, keeping a playful attitude toward language helps encourage it.

4. Children who are ready to learn can weigh alternatives and make sound choices. Visualizing alternatives and their consequences is an important life skill. Children who arrive in kindergarten with plenty of opportunities to practice this skill come better prepared. When the "prepared child" gets hit by another child, she asks herself, "What are some ways I can react and what are the consequences of each?" The child without the ability to visualize alternatives just lashes back without thinking. Aggression in the face of aggression is a poor choice. Some children never learn that, unfortunately. Some children have no ability to imagine any other response than hitting.

5. Children who are ready to learn can concentrate and focus. If they can't do that, the problem may be too much television. It seems as though children develop a long attention span from watching television, because they are willing to sit and stare at it for hours. But turn it off and what happens? They don't know how to entertain themselves. We add to the problem by overscheduling their time. Children don't develop long attention spans when they are never allowed to just play for long periods, never free to follow their inclinations to get involved in something of their own choice, never encouraged to work at length on some project they are interested in. Adults tend to interrupt them, hurry them up, get them going on the next event. Preschool programs can contribute to the problem if they keep children on a tight schedule, move them rapidly from one activity to another, and never give them a chance to work at length or in depth on anything.

informal education. Is he better off spending another year in the same environment? Not that home can't be a rich and wonderful learning environment; it can, but by age five many children are ready to move out from home a little. In another case, the school may kindly advise the parent that the child needs preschool, but there is no money for a private one, and no access to any other kind. Why can't he go to the free public kindergarten that's offered conveniently close to home? Why can't the kindergarten *provide what he needs* rather than requiring him to fit a predetermined curriculum?

Think about the child who has been in preschool and has outgrown it. For three years he's done the wonderful activities his school offered and taken part in a variety of field trips and many cognitive and socialization experiences. He's done it all and now he's ready to move on. But he didn't "pass the kindergarten test," as his parents put it, so now they are trying to talk the preschool into enrolling him for a fourth year.

Think about the upwardly mobile family who considers education the key to their child's success and is absolutely devastated to learn, as they put it, "He flunked kindergarten before he even got in." Their expectations are shattered as they see the child they once considered "bright" defined, in their own minds, as "dull."

Kindergarten readiness is one issue, closely linked to another—that of classroom behavior. Most public school classroom teachers depend on parents to send their children with an ingrained set of behaviors that allows them to perform according to the rules and enables them to learn in the style the school sees as appropriate to the group size and the ratio of children to teachers. Some parents manage to comply with this expectation. And some children, even in spite of their parents or their homelife, are willing and able to conform to what school requires. But other children aren't or can't. Expected school behavior may be quite alien to what's needed by some children at home and in the neighborhood where they live. Social skills taught at home may not work in school.

Consider the streetwise inner-city child who has learned, even by the age of five, to survive by interpersonal skills that allow him to manipulate people and situations. He gets little chance to use those skills in school—except out of the teacher's sight during recess. Interaction during class time is strictly controlled and certain expectations are enforced according to a set of rules. He comes to school self-reliant and independent, but his manner borders on defiance and that attitude gets him in trouble. He's also aggressive. He knows he can solve problems through physical action, but at school he finds he's expected to use words alone. "Fight back and don't tattle" is the rule at home. School rules are different: Don't ever touch anybody; tell the teacher if you have a problem. The child who has incorporated the home rule is going to have problems in school, starting right away in kindergarten.

It may seem reasonable to try to give this family a new set of childrearing practices to help their child do well in school and eventually rise out of the circumstances the family is in, if not immediately, at least by the next generation. But the truth is that it's not easy to change childrearing practices. And an outsider taking on such a task is taking on a good deal of responsibility unless he or she clearly understands how the childrearing practices serve the culture, the family, and the child. In addition, it is quite difficult to teach people how to raise their children unless they have a special reason for wanting to change. Changes in childrearing practices tend to come *after* social and economic changes have been effected.

In the meantime, this little streetwise child has a problem. If he conforms to classroom expectations, learns the rules, and takes them home to apply them, they won't work in the same way they do at school. Some children are flexible enough to learn a new set of skills and apply them where they work while keeping the old set for the times when the new set doesn't work. However, other children never adjust to the school environment.

Not all children who don't fit valued classroom behavior are physical and aggressive. Take the little girl who finds herself in a classroom where self-direction, initiative, independence, and competitiveness are the skills stressed. These skills are the ones seen as functional to the higher-level, higher-paying, middle-class occupations and social positions. But the little girl doesn't see the connection and perhaps has no expectations of growing up to a high-level job anyway. She only knows that while the teacher is urging her to be special, to do well, to stand alone, to stick out, and to be a winner, all she wants is to fit in and be loved. She doesn't want more stars on her star chart than anyone else. She doesn't want to sit isolated and do her own seat work without talking or looking at someone else's paper. She wants hugs and attention from the teacher. She wants to sit on her lap at story time. She wants to socialize with her classmates. She wants the same warm group feelings she gets at home. She wants to be a part of things, not separate and individual and alone.

This little girl won't get in trouble like the little boy in the first example. She'll be thought of as sweet, but probably not too bright (though she may, in fact, be quite intelligent). Eventually she will fade into the background and become invisible like the other children who don't give the teacher problems. Feeling that she doesn't fit in, she may give up on education early and find something else to do with her life. Or, less likely, she'll figure out how to learn even under the alien conditions of the classroom and end up going all the way through college as an invisible person, doing very well, but not drawing attention to herself. [4]

Responding to Diversity

When children arrive at school, they may or may not find a cultural environment that reflects themselves or the diversity of the American population. The environment reflects the attitudes of the people who create it. If the teacher sees only dominant culture as valuable and therefore worth recognizing, the classroom will show only white faces in the pictures on the walls, will acknowledge only dominant culture heroes and holidays, and will contain only books written for, by, and about dominant culture people. Sometimes teachers who have this attitude don't realize the limitations of what they offer to children. If they are European-Americans, they might not understand any culture but their own, which they naturally see as normal and right—the only way. Such culture-blind teachers may claim to be color blind. In their attempt to not be bigoted, they ignore differences, thinking that noticing them shows prejudices.

Other teachers regard differences as important, and take an ethnic-studies approach toward acknowledging them. They accept and promote differences in a attempt to increase understanding and acceptance of them. Taking a multicultural-tourist approach, these teachers may emphasize ethnic holidays, serve ethnic foods, and teach about customs, history, art, or artifacts of assorted cultures. This approach can make some children feel accepted who wouldn't otherwise feel that way, as well as broaden the view and experience of all the children in the classroom. A difficulty is that studying cultures in bits and pieces tends to trivialize or exoticize them. A multicultural-tourist approach may also focus more on foreign cultures than on how those cultures have evolved when transplanted to the United States. This approach represents an add-on to the curriculum, rather than a change in it. The classroom reflects the multicultural-tourist curriculum by having pictures displayed and books available that show, for example, African tribespeople, Balinese dancers, and Chinese New Year's celebrations. A typical theme for December in a multicultural-tourist curriculum is "Christmas Around the World" or the broader "December Holidays," showing celebrations of Hanukkah, Christmas, the Festival of the Lights, and Kwanza.

Some teachers approach diversity in the classroom by looking at commonalities in the everyday world rather than just celebrations. "We're all ethnic and cultural beings—same and different at the same time" is the message. This approach may take the theme that we all have needs, but how we meet those needs varies. Teachers may have their children study, for example, ways of carrying babies or kinds of grains eaten by various cultures. Studying breads from around the world as a theme is an example of approaching diversity from the we're-the-same-but-different angle.

Other teachers, more and more since Louise Derman-Sparks's book, *The Antibias Curriculum*, [5] came out in 1989, see the importance of changing their whole curriculum to reflect an attitude of respect and dignity toward differences.

An antibias approach aims at true integration and equity, regarding empowerment as an issue. Teachers who use this approach teach their children to be sensitive to realities different from their own as well as to think critically about injustice. Antibias is not just a cognitive approach; it includes feelings and actions too. A full antibias curriculum includes promoting equity for all aspects of human diversity—culture, race, ethnicity, gender, sexual orientation, ability, and age.

Inequity and Schools

How well children are educated and how good their school experience is for them depends on many factors, not the least of which is how many resources are available to the school they attend. Jonathan Kozol has written an eye-opening book about the discrepancies between the funding of inner-city schools in poor districts and schools in richer districts. In a nutshell, his message is that many children are being cheated out of a decent education—they don't have a chance.

Inner-city children tend to arrive in kindergarten to find an overburdened teacher trying to handle too many children in a decaying classroom that is badly in need of repair. Equipment, if there is any, is run-down; materials and books are minimal. Children who live in the suburbs have a different experience. They arrive in kindergarten to find much better conditions, even though now, in these hard times, few schools enjoy an abundance of economic resources. Even so, some of the wealthier districts have twice the funding per child of poorer districts in the same geographical region. In addition, parents in those wealthier schools get heavily involved in serious fund-raising to augment the tax-based income. Parents who know how to fund-raise and have connections to wealth have moved far beyond little bake sales. We have great discrepancies in our public school system in America today. It's quite likely that the child of wealthy or even middle-class parents will get a much better education than the child of poor parents. [6]

THE PEER GROUP AS AN AGENT OF SOCIALIZATION

Although the peer group is not as important for younger children as for older ones, it is nevertheless an influence. Who makes up the peer group for young children? Kids in the apartment complex, on the block, and in school or childcare become friends and playmates. Sometimes the composition of the peer group is controlled by parents as they arrange to get their children together with other children. The formal or informal play group is an example of this kind of peer group. Other times children form their own peer group.

Children don't play in groups at first, though they may interact a good deal with whoever is around. If you watch toddlers in a group situation, such as an early-education program, you find that they often play side by side—aware of each other, but not interacting very often. One might influence the content and actions of the other's play, but each remains headed in his or her own direction, carrying on a private conversation and individually involved with toys or materials. Then you see that more and more often these pairs of children begin to interact. Soon the pairs become threesomes and the peer group begins to form, eventually becoming a solid group with activities, norms, interests, rules, traditions, expressions, and gestures of its own. The peer group becomes a subculture.

To see the peer group influence, watch how something called "behavior contagion" works in a preschool classroom. One child starts screaming excitedly over something. In a few minutes the whole room is screaming and racing around after the leader who started it. Or one child starts swinging belly down on the swings, and soon all the swinging children have flipped over to prone positions.

Communication among peers can involve a very sophisticated set of signals. Watch a couple of four-year-olds playing with action figures in a sandbox. Each knows what's pretend and what's not. Adults may not be so sure. When angry noises are heard from a distance, the protective adult may rush over to see what's

Peers are a socializing force.

happening and discover that the children are only pretending. Both children know it's pretend, but the adult isn't sure—it sounded so real!

Usually adults don't teach children how to play pretend. They learn informally from each other how to choose up and sort out roles and characters, how to determine the direction the action will take, and how to signal when something is pretend and not real. They agree upon all this as they go along, usually in a manner that's so smooth it's hard to notice, as an observer, how it's coming about.

Functions of the Peer Group

The peer group functions so that children learn to give and take as equals. That's a different lesson from relating to parents or teachers. The peer group has its own system of modifying behavior through rewards and punishments, which mostly come in the form of acceptance and rejection. "If you don't play nice I won't invite you to my birthday party!"

Learning to get along with others who are your age and status is important. Developing relationships of one's own choosing is also important and different from learning to get along with the people who just happen to be in your life because of the family you were born into.

The peer group also teaches a set of lessons that children don't get from adults; some of these lessons lie in areas that are sensitive and taboo. Much sex education comes from peers—whether parents and teachers like it or not.

Learning to get along with others who are your age and status is important.

The peer group serves as a step in developing independence, as children move out from their parents and family into a new set of circumstances. The group is centered around its own concerns and not necessarily bound by adult norms. It has its own hierarchy.

Another function of the peer group is to place the child in history. We don't recognize ourselves as members of a particular generation until we grow up and look at the generation coming up behind us. It is through the contrast that we identify ourselves as a generation of peers.

THE MEDIA AS AN INFLUENCE ON SOCIALIZATION

Mass media—newspapers, magazines, comic books, radio, movies, and, especially, television—present a very different form of socialization than any other, because they offer no opportunity for interaction.

Television is the medium with the greatest socialization effect, surpassing all the other media by far in its influence on the young child. The very fact that television is not an interactive agent is greatly significant to the development of young children. While watching, children have the feeling that they're interacting, but they're not. That's one of the disadvantages of television as a socializer—it satisfies social needs to some extent, but doesn't give children the social skills (or the real-life practice in those skills) that allow them to function effectively with people. Since the average child watches three to four hours of television a day, the time left for playing with others and learning social skills is drastically reduced.

Of course, parents can control the time their children spend watching television, but many don't. They can monitor the selection of programs, but some allow their children to watch whatever happens to be on. Some parents don't consider how they could use television to teach decision making. They don't make children aware that when one program ends they can either weigh the various merits of next offerings or turn the set off. Some children, especially those with a remote control in hand, flick through the channels periodically, randomly stopping at whatever catches their interest at the moment. That's very different from critically examining options and consciously deciding on one.

Children learn through watching television. Some of the things they learn are beneficial, others are not. They learn about the world and the ways of the society. They learn something about occupations, for example, getting an idea about what a nurse does, what a doctor does, and how the two relate to each other. They learn about the institutions of the society—what goes on in court, for example. They learn the language to go with these roles and settings—and they learn some language you'd rather they didn't know!

Children also learn about current themes and issues, both from newscasts and dramas—issues such as kidnapping, the homeless, and the spread of AIDS. Most of these issues and themes are not happy ones, and many are very frightening, especially when children watch programs that are intended for adults.

Children learn more than facts from television; they also get a good daily dose of stereotypes and a lot of misleading information about their world. Most of all, they get a big helping of violence and another of commercial advertising.

Commercial Advertising

What's wrong with commercials? They're compelling, eye-catching, and even more interesting than a lot of programming. What's wrong is that they create artificial needs in children (and, indeed, in all of us). They are as manipulative as they can be, coaxing us, practically forcing us, in subtle ways, to go out and buy, buy, buy. They teach consumerism very effectively.

If you want to see how effective television commercials are, stand in the cereal aisle of a grocery store for just ten minutes and watch the interactions between parents and children. None of the child's biological signals related to nutritional needs are in play in the cereal aisle. In fact, even if the shelves were rearranged so the most nutritious cereals with the least additives were at children's eye level, little hands would be reaching and pointing at the familiar sugar-filled cereal boxes they know so well from television.

Violence

Turn on the television set during prime time, and, unless you select your programs carefully, you're likely to see an act of violence within five minutes and several more not too long afterward. Saturday morning is even worse. [7] Violence is interesting and interest sells products, so we get exposed to a good deal of violence. The question is, What does violence do to children?

For one thing, it eventually desensitizes them. If it didn't, how could people sit and eat a meal while watching people in living color be tortured, mutilated, shot, and even blown sky-high before their very eyes? That's enough to turn one's stomach, yet we get used to it by watching television.

Years of studies show that television watching and aggression go together. Children who watch more television are more aggressive. However, it's hard to tell whether television *causes* the aggression or whether children who are more aggressive just tend to watch more television. However, some experimental studies show that children who are exposed to a violent televised episode are more aggressive when they are put immediately into a real-life anger-provoking situation. These children show more physical aggression than children who watch something nonviolent before being put into the same situation. [8]

Television viewing of violence and real-life violence are connected. A long-term study followed three hundred boys for thirty years. The boys who watched more TV violence at age 8 turned out to do more spousal violence and more criminal violence by age 32. [9]

One way to discover the effects of television on children is to study a group of children who have not been exposed to television and then observe them after television comes into their lives. Such a study was done in Northern Canada in a

Television and Young Children

The following list of television guidelines may seem drastic and unrealistic, but television has a powerful impact on children, so drastic measures to counteract it are called for.

1. Don't expose infants to television. Don't use it as entertainment, and don't get in the habit of using it as a baby-sitter, no matter how tempting it is to do so. Infants are distracted by the disconnected noise and movement of television. They don't need distractions; they need personal interactions with people and objects in the real world.
2. Examine your own television habits. If you are addicted to the tube, the chances are any children in your care will also become addicted. Deal with your own addiction and take precautions so that children don't become TV addicts.
3. One way to avoid the risk of addiction in children is to avoid exposing them to television altogether. Children grow up just fine with no TV. If you decide you want children exposed, do it with caution and awareness. Never turn the TV on and flip channels. Using a TV guide, make a conscious decision about what program to watch, turn the set on to watch it, and then turn it off when it is over.
4. Sit with children while they watch television. Then you are there to handle feelings, explain what needs explaining, clarify any confusion, and clear up misconceptions. You are also there to turn off the set when the program is over.
5. Whatever you do, don't let children fill their time with television. Active play should be the major pastime of the early years, not uninvolved visual entertainment.

These guidelines have been used by adults with good success. If you grew up with TV in your life and have never been without it, consider trying two weeks without TV; you'll find it makes a positive difference in your life, once you get over your withdrawal symptoms. Getting loose from the clutches of the tube will also make a positive difference in young children's lives.

remote place where television hadn't yet penetrated. Then, when television was introduced, researchers were able to make comparisons. They found that violent behavior increased in both boys and girls. [10]

If we want to confront violence in our society, we must pay attention to these kinds of studies. We must regard television as the dangerous device it is and bring it under conscious control. We must not let it continue to influence children in negative ways. The children slouched in front of sets today are the ones that grow up to be tomorrow's citizens. What kinds of citizens will they be?

To summarize, television influences the socialization of children in a number of ways. It replaces active involvement with the world and the people in it, giving children little chance to learn and practice a variety of social skills. The average child who watches four hours of television a day misses out on his or her full share of early *active* learning. Television also replaces real needs with artificial ones that are created by product manufacturers and distributors to get children to want, want, want. And it affects children's behavior through the sheer quantity of violence that is portrayed.

Television has benefits too, especially when adults concern themselves with what children are watching and for how long. It can be a teaching tool when adults watch with children, explaining what they don't understand and putting it into a moral context.

Whether you're focusing on the negative or the positive effects, or both, it's easy to see that television viewing influences the knowledge, behavior, and attitudes of children.

SUMMARY

This chapter looked at four major socializing agents: the family, the school, the peer group, and television. Throughout this chapter and the preceding ones, a number of societal issues concerning the socialization of the young child were mentioned. This chapter wrapped up the book by exploring how public policy relates to these issues.

FOR DISCUSSION

1. What other socializing agents can you think of besides the four discussed in the chapter?
2. Give an example of how the status of the family affects the child's socialization.
3. Give an example of how being the target of bias can affect socialization.
4. Discuss how being raised in a biased family could affect socialization.
5. Give an example of how a family's income level could affect the way their children are socialized.
6. Give an example of how racism affects socialization.
7. Do you know someone who was "tracked" in school? How did that experience affect that person?
8. What are your thoughts, ideas, and experiences with "kindergarten readiness"?
9. How are children expected to behave in kindergarten? Do you know a child who doesn't behave that way? Why doesn't he or she?
10. How might that behavior affect that child's kindergarten performance?
11. What would you expect to find on the walls of a kindergarten room where the teacher had an antibias curriculum?
12. Have you had experience with the "great discrepancies in our public school system in America today"?
13. Describe how a four-year-old peer group operates.
14. What are your feelings, ideas, and experiences in relation to television and young children? How do they relate to what the chapter said about television?

15. What do young children learn from watching television?

16. What is your experience with TV and its effect on children?

PERSONAL REFLECTIONS

Thinking about your personal reactions and experiences will help you better understand and integrate the material in this chapter. Use these questions to interface between you and what you read. Use the pertinent ones to reflect on, write about, or discuss with others.

> What was an important socializing agent in your life?

> Was the status of your family a factor in your socialization?

> Were you ever a target of bias? How did that affect you?

> Were you raised in a biased family? How did that affect you?

> How did your family's income level affect the way you were raised?

> What part did racism play in your socialization?

> Were you "tracked" in school? How did that experience affect you?

> What do you remember about starting kindergarten?

> Did you know of a better school than the one you went to? A worse one?

> What do you remember about having friends when you were kindergarten age or younger?

> How do you think television affected your life when you were a child?

> Do you remember learning something from watching television?

NOTES

1. As a borderline middle-class person, I have a lot of personal issues concerning social class and the denial that it exists in this country. I was raised in a single-parent family back in the days when such a family was considered "broken"; I was considered disadvantaged. My family was like many we see nowadays. In one generation it went back a class or two: My grandparents had come from farms, but had gone to college (even the women) and had worked themselves into comfortable middle-class positions in the society. But my mother skipped college and got married; so when my father left, her lack of job skills and her single-parent status made her an instant low-income person. We went to live with my grandparents and to share my grandfather's meager pension. My grandparents felt very strongly that we mustn't be regarded as poor people (even though we were), and much emphasis was given to a middle-class upbringing. Manners were stressed and contrasted with those of "real" poor people. A good deal was done to mold our image of ourselves and give us middle-class expectations, values, and ways. But, being poor, we never quite made it, and that's why I consider myself a borderline middle-class person. I can fake it enough to enjoy the privileges, but I'm insecure about my social status. Scratch my surface and you'll find I don't really know how to behave properly. I'm missing the background and knowledge of the true middle-class person.

2. Peggy Mcintosh, "White Privilege and Male Privilege: A Personal Account of Coming to See Correspondences Through Work in Women's Studies," Working Paper No. 189, Wellesley College, Center for Research on Women, 1988. Mcintosh first introduced me to this idea, and the description of Lindsay is inspired by her paper.

3. As a parent volunteer in my son's elementary school, I have seen the effects of testing on five-year-olds. The day I helped with the standardized achievement tests in kindergarten stands out in my memory. The children were told not to be nervous and that this was nothing to worry about—a double message because everything about the atmosphere that day said: "This is *very important*." In addition, the parents had been sent a notice to be sure that the children got a good night's sleep and a hearty breakfast every day during the week of the testing. So in some cases, the atmosphere both at home and in the classroom conveyed the message that tension existed around these events—that they were different from what the children usually experienced in kindergarten. Even though the children were told not to be nervous (which in itself makes one suspicious enough to be nervous), two cried, one threw up, and one had to go home with a headache. These events alone were enough to influence the test scores, not only of the afflicted group but also of the group not showing any symptoms as well.

4. Teresa McKenna and Flora Ida Ortiz, eds., *The Broken Web: The Educational Experience of Hispanic American Women* (Encino, CA: Floricanto Press, 1988).

5. Louise Derman-Sparks, *Antibias Curriculum* (Washington, DC: National Association for the Education of Young Children, 1989).

6. Jonathan Kozol, *Savage Inequalities: Children in America's Schools* (New York: Crown Publishers, 1991).

7. Eight of ten programs contain violence, with prime-time programs averaging five violent acts per hour and Saturday-morning cartoons averaging about twenty per hour. G. Gerbner, L. Gross, and N. Signorielli, "Living with Television: The Dynamics of the Cultivation Process," in *Perspectives on Media Effects*, eds. J. Bryant and D. Zillman (Hillsdale, NJ: Erlbaum, 1986).

8. Bandura and Walters did the classic study of children modeling after seeing films of adults punching an inflated "knock-down" figure. Many other studies since have shown similar results. A. Bandura and R. H. Walters, *Social Learning and Personality Development* (New York: Holt, Rinehart & Winston, 1963).

9. L. R. Huesmann and L. S. Miller, "Long-term Effects of Repeated Exposure to Media Violence in Childhood," in *Aggressive Behavior: Current Perspectives*, ed. L. R. Huesmann (New York: Plenum Press, 1994): 153–186.

10. Kenneth William Hirsch, "Media Violence," in *Mass Media and Society*, 5th ed., eds. Alan Wells and Ernest Hananen (In Press).

REFERENCES

Abbott, M. W. "Television Violence: A Proactive Prevention Campaign." In *Improving Children's Lives*, eds. G. W. Albee, L. A. Bond, and T. V. Cook Monsey. Newbury Park, CA: Sage Publications, 1992, 263–278.

Bandura, A., and R. H. Walters. *Social Learning and Personality Development.* New York: Holt, Rinehart & Winston, 1963.

Boutte, G. S. "Frustrations of an African-American Parent: A Personal and Professional Account." *Phi Delta Kappan* 73(10) (1992): 786–788.

Boutte, Gloria S., Sally LaPoint, and Barbara Davis. "Racial Issues in Education: Real or Imagined?" *Young Children* (November 1993): 19–23.

Bowser, B. P., and R. G. Hunt, eds. *Impact of Racism on White Americans.* Beverly Hills, CA: Sage Publications, 1981.

Brandt, G. L. *The Realization of Anti-Racist Teaching.* London: The Falmer Press, 1986.

Brislin, R. *Culture's Influence on Behavior.* Fort Worth, TX: Harcourt Brace Jovanovich, 1993.

Clark, L., S. DeWolf, and C. Clark. "Teaching Teachers to Avoid Having Culturally Assaultive Classrooms." *Young Children* 47(5) (1992): 4–9.

Comer, James P. and Alvin F. Poussaint. *Raising Black Children*. New York: Plume, 1992.

Coner-Edwards, Alice F., and Jeanne Spurlock, eds. *Black Families in Crisis: The Middle Class*. New York: Brunner/Mazel, Publishers, 1988.

Corsaro, W. A. *Friendship and Peer Culture in the Early Years*. Norwood, NJ: Ablex, 1985.

Derman-Sparks, Louise, and the ABC Task Force. *Antibias Curriculum: Tools for Empowering Young Children*. Washington, DC: National Association for the Education of Young Children, 1989.

Derman-Sparks, Louise and Elizabeth Jones. "Meeting the Challenge of Diversity." *Young Children* 47(2) (January 1992): 12-17.

Edwards, Patricia A. and Lauren S. Jones Young. "Beyond Parents: Family, Community, and School Involvement." *Phi Delta Kappan* (May 1992): 72–80.

Gerbner, G., L. Gross, and N. Signorielli. "Living with Television: The Dynamics of the Cultivation Process." In *Perspectives on Media Effects*, ed. J. Bryant and D. Zillman. Hillsdale, NJ: Erlbaum, 1986.

Hirsch, Kenneth William. "Media Violence." In *Mass Media and Society*, 5th ed., eds. Alan Wells and Ernest Hananen (In Press).

Hopson, Darlene, and Derek Hopson. *Different and Wonderful: Raising Black Children in a Race-Conscious Society*. Upper Saddle River, NJ: Merrill/Prentice Hall, 1990.

Huesmann, L. R., and L. S. Miller. "Long-term Effects of Repeated Exposure to Media Violence in Childhood." In *Aggressive Behavior: Current Perspectives*, ed. L. R. Huesmann. New York: Plenum Press, 1994, 153–186.

Katz, J. *White Awareness: A Handbook for Anti-Racism Training*. Norman, OK: University of Oklahoma Press, 1979.

Kozol, Jonathan. *Savage Inequalities: Children in America's Schools*. New York: Crown Publishers, 1991.

Mcintosh, Peggy. "White Privilege and Male Privilege: A Personal Account of Coming to See Correspondences Through Work in Women's Studies." Working Paper No. 189, Wellesley College, Center for Research on Women, 1988.

McKenna, Teresa, and Flora Ida Ortiz, eds. *The Broken Web: The Educational Experience of His-panic American Women*. Encino, CA: Floricanto Press, 1988.

Medicine, Beatrice. "Child Socialization Among Native Americans." *Wicazo Sa Review* 1(2) (Fall 1985): 23–28.

National Center for Clinical Infant Programs. *Head Start: The Emotional Foundations of School Readiness*. Washington, DC: Author, 1992.

National Task Force on School Readiness. *Caring Communities: Supporting Young Children and Families*. Washington, DC: Association of State Boards of Education, 1991.

Paley, Vivian G. *White Teacher*. Cambridge, MA: Harvard University Press, 1979.

Peck, J. T., G. McCaig, and M. E. Sapp. *Kindergarten Policies: What Is Best for Children?* Washington, DC: National Association for the Education of Young Children, 1988.

Phillips, C. B. "Nurturing Diversity for Today's Children and Tomorrow's Leaders." *Young Children* 43(2) (1988): 22–27.

Powell, Gloria J., ed. *The Psychosocial Development of Minority Children*. New York: Brunner/Mazel, Publishers, 1983.

Shepard, L. A., and M. E. Smith. "Synthesis of Research on School Readiness and Kindergarten Retention." *Educational Leadership* 444 (1986): 78–86.

Spencer, Margaret Beale, Geraldine Kearse Brookins, and Walter Recharde Allen, eds. *Beginnings: The Social and Affective Development of Black Children*. Hillsdale, NJ: Lawrence Erlbaum Associates, Publishers, 1985.

Steele, C. M., "Race and the Schooling of Black Americans." *The Atlantic Monthly* 269(4) (1992): 69–78.

Valsiner, Jaan, ed. *Child Development Within Culturally Structured Environments*. Norwood, NJ: Ablex, 1988.

Washington, Valora. *Black Children and American Institutions*. New York: Garland Publishing, 1988.

Washington, Valora, and Ura Jean Oyemade. "Changing Family Trends." *Young Children* (September 1985): 12–19.

Zillmann, D., J. Bryant, and A. C. Huston, eds. *Media, Children, and the Family: Social Scientific Psychodynamic, and Clinical Perspectives*. Hillsdale, New Jersey: Lawrence Erlbaum Associates, 1994.

Social Policy Issues

CHAPTER **15**

TEST YOURSELF

Look for the answers to these questions as you read the chapter:

1. Who is responsible for America's children?
2. Are children born with equal opportunity?
3. What does "ready-to-learn" mean?
4. How could the media help the national ready-to-learn goal?
5. How does our health care system work against the national ready-to-learn goal?
6. What part does Head Start play in the national ready-to-learn goal?
7. What would a "children's movement" entail and why do we need one?
8. What are the recommendations from the National Panel on Child Care Policy?
9. What is the Parent Services Project an example of?
10. How can you show that preventing problems in early childhood is more cost effective than solving them later?
11. What are three broad recommendations from the Children's Defense Fund Group?
12. What are some ways to be an advocate for children?

This book looked at ways families socialize children for high self-esteem as well as how the community contributes to the socialization process. Along the way we examined obstacles in the way of a healthy socialization process, not the least of which are poverty, lack of access to quality education and childcare, and the media.

What can we do, as a society, to address these issues? What can the community do to ensure that all children get an equal chance to develop high self-esteem and fulfill themselves in this society? How can we help all children "make it"? This chapter examines social policy issues that relate to these questions.

WHO IS RESPONSIBLE FOR AMERICA'S CHILDREN?

An underlying social policy upon which this nation was founded is that families are responsible for their own children. However, it is becoming clearer and clearer that, although families must still take primary responsibility for their children, many fami-

What's keeping us from putting forth a giant effort to meet the needs of our children?

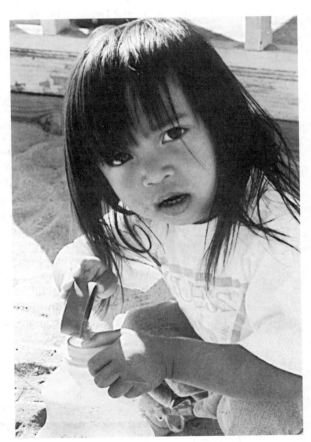

lies are not, at present, able to be completely self-sufficient. It's not that these families care any less about their children than more self-sufficient families do, it's just that they find themselves in circumstances that prevent them from being able to meet all their children's needs. The question is, If families can't meet their own children's needs, how much will the society take over the responsibility for those unmet needs?

The future of America depends on *somebody* providing for the needs of America's children—all of them. If we've reached a place in our economic, political, social, and moral history where masses of children are neglected, it's time for us, as individuals and as a society, to change that situation.

What's keeping us from putting forth a giant effort to meet the needs of America's children—of *our* children? One often unspoken theory behind the society's reluctance as a whole to put forth monumental effort to improve the lives of all its citizens is the idea that we each get what we deserve. This perspective justifies leaving things as they are. Those who make it are given credit for their ability to work hard and be rewarded; the people who don't make it are seen as not having tried hard enough. The view is that the people who live on the crumbs at the bottom of the barrel were born with the same chances of getting the whole contents of the barrel as everyone else. On the surface that may seem to be true. After all, this is America, land of opportunity, home of the free.

Children and Equal Opportunity

But let's look a little closer at who makes it and who doesn't and see if they were indeed born with the same opportunities. Take three pregnant women who live twenty miles apart from each other: the first, a sixteen-year-old who lives with her mother and five brothers and sisters in a run-down two-room apartment in a gang-ridden neighborhood at the edge of a decaying industrial section of a large city; the second, a twenty-five-year-old who lives with her jobless husband in a small duplex in the older part of a suburban area; and the third, a twenty-eight-year-old who lives with her executive husband in a single-family home, surrounded by grass and flowers on a pleasant tree-lined street in a newer development in the sprawling part of the outer suburbs.

The sixteen-year-old's baby starts out already behind because of her mother's age, physical condition, and situation, which includes lack of prenatal care, poor diet, and the industrial pollution of the neighborhood. The second woman's baby also starts out behind because when her husband lost his job, they lost their insurance and medical benefits, so she's getting not getting prenatal care either. [2] In addition, she supports the family by working in a childcare center for minimum wage, which barely pays the rent, let alone utilities and food. This family is sometimes hungry. The wife receives no benefits from her job, except for sick leave, which she has used up because of frequent illness from being exposed to the children she works with. She worries constantly about the family's financial condition, about her husband, who is deeply depressed, and most of all about her baby. The third woman's unborn baby gets all she needs before she is born, including good food, plenty of prenatal monitoring, and a relatively healthy and peaceful environment.

Does Every Child Get an Equal Start?

The Carnegie Report of the Task Force on Meeting the Needs of Young Children indicates that many children under three are affected by one or more risk factors that make healthy development difficult. Of the children born in this country, 26 percent are to unmarried mothers. Many of these mothers are teenagers, because, according to the report, about one million adolescents become pregnant each year.

Poverty is a factor in the lives of one in four children under age 3 in this country, and that number is increasing. Although in a recent twenty-year span the number of children younger than six increased by 10 percent (between 1971 and 1991), the number of *poor children* in that age range increased by more than 60 percent!

More than five million children younger than three are in childcare. Much of that childcare is of substandard quality.

Nine of every 1,000 infants die in this country before age one, a mortality rate higher than that of nineteen other nations. Furthermore, African-American babies are twice as likely to die within the first year as are white babies.

Immunization among two-year-olds was less than 60 percent in most states and less than 30 percent in some. [1]

Which of these babies will even be alive at the end of the first year? The chances are excellent that one will, but the other two face the risk of dying before their first birthday. [3]

What about when these three babies reach kindergarten? What are their relative chances of entering public school ready to learn? According to a national survey of kindergarten teachers, in California 38 percent of children enter kindergarten not ready to participate successfully. In Hawaii, it's 47 percent, in Arkansas and Delaware 42 percent, in New Mexico 40 percent, and in New York 36 percent. [4] Which of the babies of the three pregnant women is most likely to arrive at kindergarten prepared? Any guesses?

READY TO LEARN: A GOAL FOR ALL OF AMERICA'S CHILDREN

Ready to learn—what does that mean anyway? Is it as simple as teaching four-year-olds across the nation their ABC's? No! It means that children must get their basic needs met—food, shelter, health care, security, and peace in the family. They need a variety of early experiences that enrich their minds, tickle their curiosity, and enliven their spirit. They need adults in their lives who understand developmentally appropriate practices and encourage children to embrace learning joyfully.

Let's look closer at this issue of "ready to learn," which is a goal put forth by President Bush and agreed upon by the governors of all fifty states. The goal was stated: By the year 2000, every child in America should start school ready to learn.

What are the means to reaching this goal? We already have policies and programs in effect that contribute toward the "ready-to-learn" goal. Unfortunately, not one of them is adequately funded at this point; and not one of the services reaches all of the families that need aid. In addition, we have one policy that actually works against the ready-to-learn goal: the deregulation of television.

MEDIA

As pointed out in the last chapter, television is teaching powerful beneficial lessons every day in virtually every home across the nation. But it also teaches stereotypes, aggression, and violence; it does this while it commercially exploits young children.

To be an effective early teacher, television must increase developmentally appropriate and growth-enhancing options for children among its offerings. In addition, parents must become aware of its potential—both good and harmful. A strong campaign of parent education is needed.

Imagine the good that could come of a national conference on children's television that could provide opportunities for media representatives to talk with children's advocates, educators, parents, and sponsors about television strategies to work *for* the school-readiness goal instead of against it. [5]

At this point, social policy is working against such a goal because of deregulation by the Federal Communications Commission (FCC). Regulations that started in the 1930s and increased in the 1960s and 1970s gave children protection by allowing intervention in cases where they were exposed to commercial exploitation or other forms of abuse by the media. The idea was to ensure that television provided for social good, rather than increasing social ills. It's time now to reinstate those regulations. We allow other regulating bodies to protect our children from unhealthy influences. It's time to allow the FCC to continue to do the good work they started. Television is a strong social force. It needs to be used in growth-enhancing ways. [6]

ADEQUATE HEALTH SERVICES AND NUTRITION FOR ALL

Good health and nutrition are vitally linked to readiness to learn. To enter kindergarten ready to learn, every child must have a healthy birth, adequate pre- and postnatal nutrition, and medical protection and care in the early years.

Adequate nutrition starting before birth is a must for healthy development. WIC (Women, Infants, and Children), a federal nutrition program already in place, can accomplish this goal through augmented funding. WIC only serves a fraction of the eligible population.

Good health and nutrition are vitally linked to readiness to learn. To enter kindergarten ready to learn, every child must have a healthy birth, adequate nutrition, and medical protection and care in the early years.

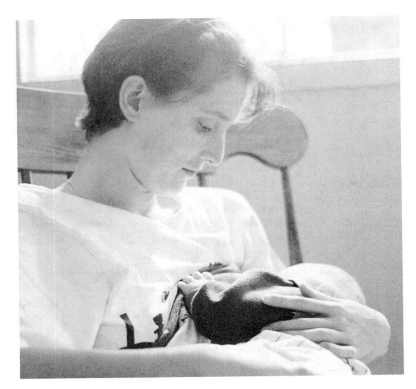

Health care delivery has been a patchwork system involving federal, state, and private sectors. Unfortunately, this system does not meet the need. For health care to be available to all, each sector of the society must commit to finding ways to make health care accessible and affordable to everyone who needs it.

Public health insurance should be expanded to all poor families. Additional community and migrant health centers should be established to serve the medically underserved. The National Health Service Corps, which provides scholarships and loan repayments to health professionals, should be adequately funded. The childhood vaccine program should be augmented to serve all infants and preschoolers who now go unprotected. Community health centers should receive adequate financial support for maternal and child health programs. Employers should offer subsidized health insurance with dependent coverage to all employees regardless of pay level. Plans should fully cover cost-effective services such as prenatal care and preventive care for children. In addition, employer wellness policies should support families by providing adequate sick and family leave. Employers can also provide increased on-site health education. [7]

But just providing services is not enough. Families must take responsibility to seek out and use the services that are available. Some may need to be educated about how to use medical care services.

Head Start

One national program has made some progress in its goal of addressing the problems of low-income families for over twenty-five years—Head Start. It was originally conceived as a quick catch-up summer-school program that would teach children in a few weeks what they needed to know to start kindergarten. But once it was determined that you can't make up for five years of poverty with a six-week preschool program, Head Start expanded far beyond its original beginnings.

Head Start has been successful in its efforts to meet many of the needs of the population it serves. It makes a difference in the lives of young children and their families. What policies would enable Head Start to do more than it already does?

1. Expand to serve all eligible children. (Head Start serves only a fraction of eligible children.)
2. Become an even more comprehensive program with services that address a wide variety of family needs.
3. Consider changes in program models to respond to teen parents' and working parents' needs.
4. Implement new economic self-sufficiency projects.
5. Broaden the parent-involvement component. [8]

Head Start has proved that its approach to changing lives works, and the national program is now in the process of moving downward to serve families of younger-aged children. Traditionally a program designed to serve families of preschool-aged children, Early Head Start grants are now being used to provide services to infants and toddlers, pregnant women, expectant fathers, parents, and guardians. The goal is to help families fulfill parental roles and move forward toward economic independence while providing for their children's physical, social, emotional, and intellectual development.

It's time for this society to put young children as a national priority.

Head Start's purpose has always been to involve low-income families in the solutions to their own problems by empowering them politically and economically, instead of just offering them services; but it is sometimes thought of as just a preschool program and is always in danger of being cut back to that narrow focus. It is imperative that Head Start retain its family focus because the strength of the family directly relates to their children's future. To make a difference, a program like Head Start can't just deal with children, it has to include the whole family.

Head Start is a national effort, aimed to be locally responsive and locally controlled. If the federal government doesn't provide full Head Start services, as outlined here, to each community, the model could be adopted by communities who want to start their own Head Start programs.

Childcare

It is time for this society to consider young children as a national priority. We have a civil rights movement, a women's movement, and an ecology movement. We need a children's movement. [9] The Federal Child Care bill, which was passed at the beginning of the 1990s, is a step in the right direction. A demonstration at the nation's capital on June 1, 1996, was another step. The "I Stand for Children" demonstration drew people from across the country to merely stand in the Capital Mall and show by their presence their concern for the nation's children.

 Culturally Responsive Care

Changing demographics present a challenge to childcare programs: They must now more than ever before discover how to deliver *culturally responsive care*. A report recently released from California Tomorrow proposes five core principles for care in a diverse society:

1. Principle one involves adults' understanding how racism impacts the development of children's self-identity and their attitudes toward others.
2. Principle two advocates building on the culture of the families and promoting cross-cultural understanding among children in childcare.
3. Principle three relates to preserving children's home language and encouraging all children in childcare to learn a second language.
4. Principle four has to do with childcare staff working with families to nurture the well-being of children.
5. Principle five involves childcare staff engaging in ongoing dialogue with families as well as self-reflection about diversity.

In addition to the five principles, professional development, recruitment and retention of a diverse workforce, ongoing research, and dissemination of research results to parents are all essential to the kind of care that promotes children's healthy development in a diverse society. [10]

In the future, we, as a society, must offer enough choices so that parents can find childcare and early education in tune with what they want and need for their children. Head Start isn't the only answer. The choices must include ways parents can care for their own children and systems that provide for care by others.

We already have models in place: center care, family childcare, and in-home care. Creative alternatives in the workplace that allow working parents a greater role in caring for their own children include flextime, which allows parents to stagger work schedules; part-time work; job sharing; parent subsidies, which allow parents to be at home more with their children; flexible benefits plans; and flexible leave policies.

We can't just have *more* childcare; we need to have *better* childcare. We have to upgrade the training, status, and salaries of childcare teachers, who are grossly underpaid, putting them in the ranks of the poor. Children suffer from burned-out teachers and high turnover rates. [11] Quality childcare makes a difference. We can't promote economic independence for families without also promoting good childcare. Childcare is a means to family preservation and a key component in school readiness. Indeed childcare is often seen as the answer to problems of the economy, a means of addressing the miseries of poverty, and a strong tool for eradicating bias in the next generation, besides providing general early education for young children.

The problem is that poorly funded childcare doesn't live up to all the dreams we have for it. Quality is a major issue. Without quality, childcare doesn't do its job. It is hard to have quality when no one wants to pay the cost. Quality doesn't come cheap. Instead of recognizing and acknowledging that fact, consumers and funding sources continue to allow childcare policy that keeps childcare workers at poverty-level wages.

 Recommendations from the National Childcare Staffing Study Revisited

The quality of services many American children receive is directly affected by high staff-turnover rate due to the lack of status, pay, and training. To correct these problems The National Center for the Early Childhood Workforce recommends that:

1. Childcare teaching staff salaries be raised to be more consistent with the demands and responsibilities of the job
2. The health of childcare providers and children be assured by means of comprehensive, affordable health coverage, which does not reduce current wage rates
3. Access to higher education opportunities be increased for those employed and considering employment
4. Current and future social policies be clarified
5. Support for research be increased, research that identifies factors promoting long-term stability and productivity in the childcare workforce
6. Comprehensive high-quality child care be provided to families of all incomes without relying on the subsidies provided by the childcare workforce through their low wages [12]

ECONOMIC DEVELOPMENT

You can't just take the child out of the family and provide education and childcare without looking at the factors that influence what the child goes home to. Poverty is a big influence on family life, and therefore on children's readiness to learn when they reach kindergarten age.

Early-childhood programs, such as Head Start, and quality childcare can help break the cycle of poverty and disadvantage by helping the parents and by preparing the next generation to take full advantage of educational and training opportunities. Not all such programs, however, are equally effective. The most effective programs are small, flexible, and interdisciplinary. Like the Head Start model, effective programs do far more than merely deliver early-childhood education and care for children. In order to meet children's needs, they provide comprehensive services to the whole family. They connect the family to the greater community.

An example of such a program is the Parent Services Project, started by Ethel Seiderman in Fairfax, California, which has spread to a number of state-funded childcare programs throughout northern California. This project serves as a model of how childcare can go far beyond just providing care for children, by also supporting families.

A key to alleviating poverty is jobs—jobs that pay enough to live on. Increased employment can be enhanced by community involvement in identifying available jobs, improving access and reducing barriers (such as discrimination), improving training, and developing job search and interview skills in underemployed people.

Who is going to do all that? We all must. No single approach will eliminate poverty in America. It will take a massive effort on the part of government at all levels, educational institutions, corporations, foundations, communities, and individuals.

An example of a group of citizens who has set out to do something about unemployment in four western states is the Human Development Corporation of California, Hawaii, Washington, and Oregon. The Human Development Corporation (HDC), a nonprofit community-based organization, provides job training and placement to help people become more self-sufficient through unsubsidized employment. HDC uses funds from a variety of sources, including federal, state, and county government, private industry councils, the United Way, and private donations. It also runs businesses to generate income that supports the corporation in its work of helping low-income people. The mission is to help low-income, unemployed, and underemployed women and men live lives of greater human dignity through access to education, training, better job opportunities, and improved social conditions. [13]

TAKING A PREVENTIVE APPROACH

It sounds as if there is much being done at this point with all these examples. However, what is being done is a drop in the bucket compared with the need. Unfortunately, a good many of the services mentioned respond to emergency situations rather than preventing them in the first place. Here's a little parable to illustrate the point:

Once there was a kindly man walking by a river. He looked out into the strong current and saw a young child struggling in the swirling waters. He threw off his shoes and plunged into the swiftly moving water. It took all the strength he had, but he finally managed to pull the child from the grip of the river, drag him up on the bank, and give him CPR. The child was saved! But lo and behold, the man looked up from the child he had just rescued and saw another child in the water. Again he raced into the river, fought hard, and managed to save this child too. But the same thing happened. He looked up in time to see yet another child struggling in the swift current. Dead tired, he dragged himself once more to the river and plunged in. He continued in this manner until he collapsed from exhaustion and was no longer able to save any more children. That was the end of his rescue mission. Sadly enough, he had been so busy saving children that he was never able to leave long enough to walk upstream to stop whoever was throwing the children into the river in the first place!

This parable shows how our society operates in regard to children at this point. Instead of taking prevention measures, we allow children to founder in dangerous waters, then we try to rescue them. It would be much more economical and energy-effective to walk upstream and stop them from being thrown in! It's cheaper to prevent damage than to repair it.

BROAD RECOMMENDATIONS FROM THE CHILDREN'S DEFENSE FUND GROUP

A common problem of the rescue approach is that children are often rescued from their own parents because they don't get adequate care. That kind of rescuing can be disastrous. Children placed in foster care must deal with the emotional effects of separation and are often left with lifelong scars. Many children could remain at home if there were more programs that focused on strengthening families rather than on removing children. The costs of taking children from their families are enormous. Besides the emotional costs, there are financial burdens that taxpayers must shoulder. It costs much more to provide foster care than it would to give families what they need to keep their children home. Happily, there has been a recent trend for keeping families together. This trend is reflected in the proposals of the Children's Defense Fund group, which is making recommendations for systemic reforms aimed at keeping families intact: [14]

1. Create in every community a network of comprehensive services to strengthen families and give them the tools they need to support and nurture their children.

2. Make family preservation services and other specialized community-based treatment available to all families in crisis.

3. Improve the quality of out-of-home placements so special needs are met and children are returned to families or adopted as appropriate.

Speak out for children. They can't speak out for themselves.

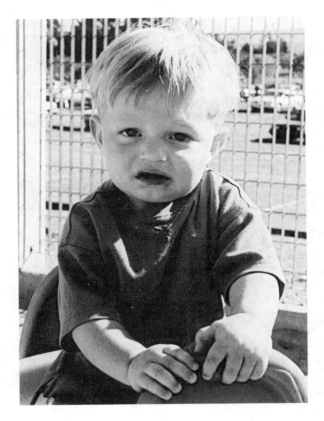

ADVOCACY

Marian Wright Edelman's advice to her children is: "If you see a need, don't ask, 'Why doesn't somebody do something?' Ask, 'Why don't I do something?'" [15] That's good advice for all of us.

Anyone who cares about America's future must become an advocate for making the world a better place for children and families. Here are some ways to do that:

1. Get involved! Start by informing yourself about the status of children and families in your neighborhood, community, state, and nation. Use your own eyes. Visit local programs that serve low-income children and see the effects of poverty. Read. Get a copy of *The State of America's Children*, published by the Children's Defense Fund, 122 C Street N.W., Washington, DC 20001, (202) 628-8787.

2. Speak out for children! Inform others through speaking to religious groups, at candidate forums, and community groups. Write a letter to the editor of your local newspaper.

3. Do something this week to help children. If you're not already involved, volunteer at a Head Start program, a childcare program, or a school. If you are

already busy during the day, or don't want to work directly with children, offer your services as a fund-raiser. Every program needs more money than it has and most are involved in varying degrees of fund-raising efforts. If you want to feel good, take a look at a director's face when you arrive in his or her office and offer to help with fund-raising.

4. Be a role model for your community. Don't wait around for someone else to take the reins. If you show you care, others are likely to follow your example.

5. Register and vote. Elect candidates who keep children and families a priority.

6. Understand how public policies make a difference. Public policies, though they may be conceived of on a national level, influence our lives and those of our children. Policies are decisions about goals and objectives, which become plans of action, translating eventually into programs.

The part of the advocate in helping create policy involves the following steps: [16]

1. Identify a problem that requires action.

2. Convince someone to accept responsibility for helping to solve the problem. This someone may be the government.

3. Develop and propose acceptable solutions to the problem.

It is your responsibility to understand how public policy makes a difference in the lives of children.

4. Monitor the implementation of the solution.

5. Evaluate the program.

It's important to hold your leaders accountable. One way to do this is to keep track of how lawmakers vote on issues of importance to children.

SUMMARY

This chapter examined how we, as a society, can use the social policy we have, as well as instituting new policies, to upgrade the lives of the children of this nation. It examined the issue of who is responsible for American's children, and concluded that we all are.

We, as a society, need to make our children a top priority. We need a children's movement in order to ensure that all children have their needs met. We could easily make a rallying point around a single goal, one already espoused by President Bush and all fifty governors: We could try, all of us, at every level of the society, to *ensure that by the year 2000, every child in America will start kindergarten ready to learn*. We could put an enormous effort into upgrading the quality of children's lives by strengthening their families, providing for their needs, and making available rich early experiences that engage their minds and bring joy, spirit, and curiosity to their lives.

We, as an American community, can work toward making a greater contribution to the socialization processes of our children. We can look for ways to give all children the opportunities necessary to build a healthy sense of self. We can keep the view that all children deserve an equal chance to fulfill themselves in this society. It won't be easy, but what better way to use our energy to prepare for the future of America than through caring for its children?

FOR DISCUSSION

1. What does the question "Who is responsible for America's children?" refer to?

2. What are your ideas, feelings, and experiences related to equality opportunity for children?

3. What are your ideas about getting the nation's children "ready-to-learn"?

4. What are your ideas about how the media help the national ready-to-learn-goal?

5. What are your experiences with the health care system and how do you think it affects young children?

6. What do you know about Head Start?

7. Do you think we need a "children's movement"?

8. If you were to make recommendations to create or improve on our national childcare system, what would those recommendations be?

9. What could childcare programs do to support parents that they aren't doing now?
10. What are your ideas about providing the nation's children with what they need, if their parents aren't able to?
11. What are your ideas and feelings related child abuse?
12. What are your ideas and feelings related to foster care?
13. Have you ever been involved in advocating for children?

PERSONAL REFLECTIONS

Thinking about your personal reactions and experiences will help you better understand and integrate the material in this chapter. Use these questions to interface between you and what you read. Use the pertinent ones to reflect on, write about, or discuss with others.

> How do you feel about the society taking responsibility for the nation's children?

> Do you feel that at your birth you had an equal start with other children in this nation? Did your parents? Did your grandparents? If not, why not?

> Did you enter school "ready-to-learn"? If not, why not?

> What are your experiences with the health care system and how has it affected you?

> Have you ever had any involvement with Head Start?

> If there were a national "children's movement," would you join it?

> What have been your own experiences with childcare? Does our system need improvement?

> How could the society support parents more than it does now?

> What experiences have you had with child abuse?

> What experiences have you had with foster care?

> Do you think children need adults to advocate for them? Why or why not?

NOTES

1. Statistics taken from "Starting Points: Executive Summary of the Report of the Carnegie Corporation of New York Task Force on Meeting the Needs of Young Children," *Young Children* (July 1994): 58–60.
2. Seventy nations of the world provide medical care to all pregnant women. America is not one of those nations.
3. The United States ranks nineteenth in the world at keeping its infants alive and forty-ninth (behind Albania and Botswana) in immunizing its nonwhite infants against polio, mostly because of our high level of poverty. Stephen Shames, Jonathan Kozol, and Marian Wright Edelman, *Outside the Dream: Child Poverty in America* (New York: Aperture, 1991).

4. Ernest L. Boyer, *Ready to Learn: A Mandate for the Nation* (Princeton, NJ: The Carnegie Foundation for the Advancement of Teaching, 1991), 149.

5. Boyer, *op. cit.*, p. 140.

6. Nancy Carlsson-Paige and Diane E. Levin, *Who's Calling the Shots: How to Respond Effectively to Children's Fascination with War Play and War Toys* (Philadelphia: New Society Publishers, 1990), 127–128.

7. *The State of America's Children* (Washington, DC: Children's Defense Fund, 1991), 68–73.

8. Recommendations loosely adapted from Valora Washington and Ura Jean Oyemade, "Changing Family Trends: Head Start Must Respond," *Young Children* (September 1985): 15.

9. James Steyer, in a speech at Sonoma State University, Rohnert Park, California, May 2, 1992.

10. H. N. L. Chang, A. Muckelroy, and D. Pulido-Tobiassen, *Looking In, Looking Out: Redefining Child and Early Education in a Diverse Society* (San Francisco: California Tomorrow, 1996.) This report by California Tomorrow relates directly to the National Association for the Education of Young Children's Position Statement, which is part of that organization's goal to build support for equal access to high-quality educational programs that recognize and promote all aspects of children's development and learning, enabling all children to become competent, successful, and socially responsible adults. NAEYC Position Statement, "Responding to Linguistic and Cultural Diversity: Recommendations for Effective Early Childhood Education," *Young Children* (January 1996).

11. According to the Child Care Employee Project, every year 40 to 60 percent of childcare teachers leave their jobs. Child Care Employee Project, *Child Care Employee News* 7(3) (1988).

12. Marcy Whitebook, Deborah Phillips, and Carollee Howes, *National Child Care Staffing Study Revisited: Four Years in the Life of Center-Based Child Care* (Oakland, CA: Child Care Employee Project, 1993).

13. Human Development Corporation of California, Hawaii, Washington, and Oregon, 1990 Annual Report.

14. *The State of America's Children*, p. 121.

15. *The State of America's Children*, p. 15.

16. Adapted from Stacie G. Goffin and Joan Lombardi, *Speaking Out: Early Childhood Advocacy* (Washington, DC: National Association for the Education of Young Children, 1989), 10–11. This book gives lots more information and specifics about how to be an advocate for children and families.

REFERENCES

Boyer, Ernest L. *Ready to Learn: A Mandate for the Nation*. Princeton, NJ: The Carnegie Foundation for the Advancement of Teaching, 1991.

Bridges, Child Development Division, California Department of Education, Sacramento, Vol. 2, No. 1 (Spring, 1996).

Carlsson-Paige, Nancy, and Diane E. Levin. *Who's Calling the Shots: How to Respond Effectively to Children's Fascination with War Play and War Toys*. Philadelphia: New Society Publishers, 1990.

CDF (Children's Defense Fund). *The State of America's Children*, Washington, DC: CDF, 1994.

Chang, H. N. L., A. Muckelroy, and D. Pulido-Tobiassen. *Looking In, Looking Out: Redefining Child and Early Education in a Diverse Society*. San Francisco: California Tomorrow, 1996.

Child Care Employee Project. *Child Care Employee News* 7(3) (1988).

Fontana, Vincent J., and Valerie Moolman. *Save the Family, Save the Child: What We Can Do to Help Children at Risk*. New York: Dutton, 1991.

Galinsky, E. "Family Life and Corporate Policies." In *In Support of Families*, eds. M. W. Yogman and T. B. Brazelton. Cambridge, MA: Harvard University Press, 1986, 109–145.

Gardner, M. "Poverty's Legacy—Fragile Families, Vulnerable Babies." *The Christian Science Monitor* (December 18, 1989): 10–11.

Goffin, Stacie G., and Joan Lombardi. *Speaking Out: Early Childhood Advocacy*. Washington, DC: National Association for the Education of Young Children, 1989.

Halpern, R. "Major Social and Demographic Trends Affecting Young Families: Implications for Early Childhood Care and Development." *Young Children* 42(6) (1987): 34–40.

Hayes, Cheryl D., John L. Palmer, and Martha J. Zaslow, eds. *Who Cares for America's Children?: Child Care Policy for the 1990's.* Washington, DC: National Academy Press, 1990.

Hewlett, Sylvia Ann. *When the Bough Breaks: The Cost of Neglecting Our Children.* New York: Basic Books, 1991.

Kagan, S. L., D. R. Powell, B. Weissbourd, and E. Zigler, eds. *America's Family Support Programs: Perspectives and Prospects.* New Haven, CT: Yale University Press, 1987.

Kagan, S. L., and E. F. Zigler. *Early Schooling: The National Debate.* New Haven, CT: Yale University Press, 1987.

Kamerman, Sheila B., and Alfred J. Kahn. *Mothers Alone: Strategies for a Time of Change.* Dover, MA: Auburn House, 1988.

Lynch, E. W., and M. J. Hanson. *Developing Cross-cultural Competence: A Guide for Working With Young Children and Their Families.* Baltimore: Paul H. Brookes, 1993.

Louv, R. *Childhood's Future.* Boston: Houghton Mifflin, 1990.

Moore, E. K., and M. K. McKinley. "Parent Involvement/Control in Child Development Programs." In *Early Childhood Development Programs and Services: Planning for Action,* ed. D. N. McFadden. Washington, DC: National Association for the Education of Young Children, 1972, 77–82.

National Association for the Education of Young Children Position Statement. "Responding to Linguistic and Cultural Diversity: Recommendations for Effective Early Childhood Education." *Young Children* (January 1996).

National Center for Clinical Infant Programs. "Head Start: The Emotional Foundations of School Readiness." Washington, DC: Author, 1992.

National Task Force on School Readiness. *Caring Communities: Supporting Young Children and Families.* Washington, DC: Association of State Boards of Education, 1991.

Peck, J. T., G. McCaig, and M. E. Sapp. *Kindergarten Policies: What Is Best for Children?* Washington, DC: National Association for the Education of Young Children, 1988.

Powell, D. R. *Families and Early Childhood Programs.* Washington, DC: National Association for the Education of Young Children, 1989.

Shames, Stephen, Jonathan Kozol, and Marian Wright Edelman. *Outside the Dream: Child Poverty in America.* New York: Aperture, 1991.

Shepard, L. A., and M. E. Smith. "Synthesis of Research on School Readiness and Kindergarten Retention." *Educational Leadership* 444 (1986): 78–86.

Starting Points: Executive Summary of the Report of the Carnegie Corporation of New York Task Force on Meeting the Needs of Young Children. *Young Children* (July 1994): 58–60.

Strong Families, Strong Schools: Building Community Partnerships for Learning. U. S. Department of Education, September, 1994.

"Ten Quick Ways to Analyze Children's Books for Racism and Sexism." New York: Council on Interracial Books for Children, 1986.

The State of America's Children. Washington, DC: Children's Defense Fund, 1991.

Washington, Valora, and Ura Jean Oyemade. "Changing Family Trends: Head Start Must Respond." *Young Children* (September 1985).

Weissbourd, B. "The Family Support Movement: Greater than the Sum of Its Parts." *Zero to Three* 4(1) (1983): 8–10.

Whitebook, Marcy, Deborah Phillips, and Carollee Howes. *National Child Care Staffing Study Revisited: Four Years in the Life of Center-Based Child Care,* Oakland, CA: Child Care Employee Project, 1993.

Zigler, E., and W. Berman. "Discerning the Future of Early Childhood Intervention." *American Psychologist* 38 (1983): 894–906.

Zigler, E. F., and J. Freedman. "Head Start: A Pioneer of Family Support." In *America's Family Support Programs: Perspectives and Prospects,* ed. S. L. Kagan, D. R. Powell, B. Weissbourd, and E. F. Zigler. New Haven, CT: Yale University Press, 1987, 57–76.

Index